ONE LORD, ONE FAITH

A
BRIDGEPOINT
BOOK

BridgePoint,
the academic
imprint of
Victor Books, is
your connection
for the best in
serious reading
that integrates
the passion of
the heart with
the scholarship
of the mind.

ONE LORD, ONE FAITH

REX A. KOIVSTO

A
BRIDGEPOINT
BOOK

Copyediting: Robert N. Hosack
Cover Design: Joe DeLeon
Cover Painting: *AMAZEing Grace* by Kathie Reynolds, courtesy of the Billy Graham Center, Wheaton, Illinois.

Library of Congress Cataloging-in-Publication Data

Koivisto, Rex A.
   One Lord, one faith: a theology for cross-denominational renewal
   Rex Koivisto.
      p.   cm.
   Includes bibliographical references.
   ISBN 1-56476-076-6
   1. Church—Catholicity.   2. Church—Unity.   3. Church renewal.
   4. Christian sects.   5. Interdenominational cooperation.   I. Title.
BV601.3.K625   1993
   262'.72—dc20   92-42715
                                                                      CIP

BridgePoint is the academic imprint of Victor Books.

© 1993 by Victor Books/SP Publications, Inc. All rights reserved. Printed in the United States of America.

1   2   3   4   5   6   7   8   9   10   Printing / Year   97   96   95   94   93

CONTENTS

FOREWORD

 One of the most arresting and promising develop-
ments of modern evangelicals is the desire among
many to return to catholicity. This is not only a
phenomenon among evangelicals, but one that is
happening among mainline denominations and
among Holiness, Pentecostal, and Charismatic
bodies as well. The return to catholicity is a surprising development given the sectarian outlook that has dominated evangelical
Christianity during the twentieth century.

But no one should be surprised that evangelicals are returning
to catholicity because evangelicalism in its main tenets has always
been truly catholic. That is, evangelicalism at its best is committed to the Gospel, to the Apostolic interpretation of the faith,
and to the core of Orthodox teaching that was developed in the
first six centuries of the church.

What *One Lord, One Faith* accomplishes is a clear and insightful recovery of the ancient evangelical and catholic outlook. Consequently this book will address the sectarians among us who
have led us astray by teaching and practicing an exclusive ecclesiology and a limited theology; it will lead us into an understanding
of the catholic fullness of the faith; and it will help us recover a
sense of belonging to the whole church.

Rex Koivisto's brilliant analysis of Protestant sectarianism and
his lucid call to a fullness of catholicity charts a future direction
for American evangelical Christianity. We will all be spiritually
healthier and considerably more effective in ministry if we allow
the teachings of the early church to set our agenda for the future.
For this reason I hail the publication of this work and trust it will
receive the wide attention it deserves.

Robert Webber
Wheaton College

DEDICATION

For my family:
Joanie, my companion and support of fifteen years,
and the Triple K Klub—
Kristin
Kristopher (Kris!)
Karrson

P R E F A C E

This book is about catholicity. It is not about Roman Catholicism, but about catholicity. Catholicity refers to the great universality of the church as the body of Christ—not just in some mystical sense, but in all the fullness of its "real-time" diversity on planet earth. And catholicity presupposes a large-hearted attitude on the part of Christians to perceive the church this way, because by definition it encompasses real believers who do not quite act or talk, or think, or even believe all the same things that I do on areas outside of the central tenets of the Christian faith. I am convinced that this precious quality has been significantly tarnished midst our sad assigning of each other into different Christian cubbyholes—a process that allows for little dialogue or mutual communication, and which tends only to decrease our ability to enjoy all we have in common with each other, "across boundaries," in Christ.

Perhaps you've noticed: there is a great deal of diversity today in what passes under the term Christianity, especially in North America. For example, some 85 major Christian denominational families exist in the United States alone, discounting the subdivisions of major groups included within those 85.[1] If these are included, then there are some 224 distinct denominational groupings in the United States.[2] The large majority of these groups are Protestant subgroups, although even Eastern Orthodoxy and Roman Catholicism offer certain subcategories as well.

So what is the problem with such diversity? One may say that diversity among Christians does not really matter. Well, it does. For one, it impacts the perception others have about claims we have to follow after Christian unity. We often sing, for example, Samuel John Stone's 1865 hymn, *The Church's One Foundation:*

> Though, with a scornful wonder,
> > Men see her sore oppressed,
> By schisms rent asunder,
> > By heresies distressed. . . .

13

Somehow that seems to be an honest enough depiction of the problem around us. But have you ever sung that famous hymn written by Sabine Baring-Gould in the same year, *Onward Christian Soldiers,* and missed the little line tucked away toward the end that seems to be out of tune with reality?

> We are not divided,
>> All one body we,
> One in hope, in doctrine,
>> One in charity.

Are we *not* divided? Are we all *one* body? Somehow this does not square with today's level of Christian experience. A more honest version, as Robert McAfee Brown pointed out, would go,

> We are all divided,
>> Not one body we,
> One lacks faith, another hope,
>> And all lack charity.[3]

And this "dividedness" *does* have an impact on our mission as Christians. Brown gave one sad account of some of the implications of what I would call a lack of Christian catholicity some years back on the mission field:

> ... the leader of the "untouchables" in India renounced the caste system. He likewise urged his sixty million fellow untouchables to renounce the Hinduism that had been responsible for the caste system. But Christianity had no appeal to the untouchables as a possible alternative to Hinduism. "We are united in Hinduism," they said, "and we shall become divided in Christianity." The argument was unanswerable.[4]

But it is all too easy to blame *denominationalism* as the disease to cure in our lack of unity. I disagree; I will argue that the problem is not the presence of this kind of diversity. Denominationalism, I will try to show, has value when understood as catholic diversity. The problem is the *mutual exclusivity* that often subsists within, or even spawns this diversity—what may more appropriately be labeled *sectarianism.* Sectarianism is the posture of believing my own particular group of Christians has a superior

14

claim to represent the body of Christ, to the exclusion or minimization of other genuinely Christian groups.

The church must have a degree of diversity along with its unity. But sectarianism provokes a *diversity* without the requisite New Testament relational *unity*. This kind of mutual exclusivity runs counter to the nature of the church itself, if the New Testament has anything at all to say in the matter. Such exclusiveness is a sectarianism of the worst sort. The Christian community envisioned in the New Testament is one church, a church catholic. And although I will argue that this does not require an organizational unity, it requires a *relational* unity. That is mandated. And that requires an end to sectarian attitudes.

My point is that the attitude of sectarianism is far more at the root of the problem of Christian disunity than is the presence of denominational diversity. The "dividedness" of Christianity is related, not so much in the fact that there are varieties of Christian communities (denominations), but that those communities often make mutually exclusive claims to be the only (or best) representative of the Christian faith (sectarian tendencies). Sectarians who claim to be genuine Christians view others making the same claim (but who are in a different Christian group) as spiritually suspect, at best. In this way the ancient catholicity, the historic "unity in diversity" is lost. Sectarianism reigns supreme and genuine fellowship and cooperation within the entire body of Christ is lost. So, with this book, I am out to "do in" sectarian attitudes as the true enemy of catholicity.

This book needs somewhat of an explanation. Although I have taught Bible and theology for over twelve years at a Christian theological school, I have never taught a course specifically on ecclesiology or church history (although I recognize the incredible value of reflecting on and integrating each). Nevertheless, this area of study concerns me greatly. And I have spent my entire adult life actively involved in the give and take, the joys and pain, of being a part of Christian community.

As you will observe in the text, I have been a part, in youth work, single adult work, Sunday School, camp counseling and speaking, preaching, teaching, and pastoring as an elder of the group known as the Christian (or Plymouth) Brethren.[5] And although this Brethren Movement began in large part with a large dose of catholicity (to be explained later), I know of too many

Brethren who maintain a sadly sectarian posture toward other Christians. They have therefore at times displayed a significantly less than catholic attitude.

But my exposure over the past twenty-four years to the church catholic, the body of Christ, has been far broader than to just my own Brethren Movement. I have had the privilege of speaking at numerous denominational and nondenominational fellowships outside of my typical circles of relationship. I have had the privilege of worshiping with brothers and sisters in historic and free churches; liturgical and non-liturgical; whether congregational, presbyterian, or episcopalian in structure. And in each instance I have found genuine faith and a vibrant Gospel testimony. I have observed in "real time" that the body of Christ is far broader than my own denominational context.

Part of this broadening process is the privilege I have had to work alongside men and women of genuine faith in a non-denominationally affiliated Christian college. It is hard to make a sectarian comment with patient and firm brothers and sisters from other traditions around—who also know the Word of God. Would that more of us had that kind of regular interaction.

So, a word about the design of this volume. The book is intended to take you from a discovery of what catholicity is in the New Testament, through a review of the ebb and flow of its experience in the history of the church, until it finds its current expression in (historic) denominationalism (chaps. 1–3). I then argue (in chap. 4) that the key problem contributing to the development of sectarian attitudes in denominations today is a failure to understand the nature of tradition, especially among Protestants.

Chapter 5 suggests that an application of healthy biblical hermeneutics in a community context is the key for detecting the presence of tradition, which allows one to be able to distinguish it from the core of orthodoxy which unites all true Christians. My next chapter is an attempt to define this core of orthodoxy around which catholicity must hover. At this point (chaps. 7 and 8), I try to make this all real by introducing you to my own Brethren tradition and applying the principles developed in the earlier chapters to it by way of illustration. You may find this helpful in recognizing what it takes to detect and manage the presence of tradition within your own denominational context. If you do not wish to delve into this particular application of the material, please feel free to "fast forward" to chapter 9, where I try to give some practical suggestions for developing a catholic spirit in Christians today.

A C K N O W L E D G M E N T S

There are many people who helped make this book a reality and who deserve my thanks. First, thanks belong to Dr. Garry Friesen, my academic dean, whose flexibility on a time crunch enabled me to be the first to try out a new extended sabbatical program at Multnomah School of the Bible and who gave valuable criticism of the entire manuscript during his own much-needed vacation time, so I could keep a deadline. Thanks also to Malcolm Miura, my graduate assistant, for his research help. To those who reviewed various parts or chapters of the manuscript and offered helpful suggestions, I tip my hat. That group includes Dr. Albert Baylis, Dr. Dan Scalberg, Prof. Ray Lubeck, and Prof. Ron Frost, all of Multnomah, and Mr. Greg Hicks of Mission Portland.

Thanks must also go to librarian Jim Scott and the staff of Multnomah's John and Mary Mitchell Library, for their incredible flexibility and helpfulness—and especially to Donna Rodman for her efficient help and cheerfulness on interlibrary loans. And, thanks must also go to Mike Hamel and Bill Conard of Interest Ministries for their helpful critique of an early draft. Of course, any mistakes that remain are my sole responsibility.

In the encouragement sector, thanks must go to Mr. David Sanford of the Luis Palau Evangelistic Association and to all those who prayed for this project from my home assembly in Portland.

I cannot overlook my editor, Robert Hosack, for his championing the cause of this book for me—a rookie writer, who even cheers for the Portland Trailblazers rather than the Chicago Bulls!

Thanks must also go to Bob and MaryLou Matthews, whose generosity granted me two separate, entire weeks at "Eventide," their delightful cabin on the beautiful Oregon coast, so I could be free from distraction while working on this book.

Special thanks also go to my in-laws, Bob and Ruth McNicol, whose lives have been a constant example to me of a genuine

18

spirit of catholicity toward all who love the Lord.

And, most of all, thanks to my wife, Joanie, and to our "triple K Klub" (Kristin, Kristopher, and Karrson) for their long-suffering to endure a year of *far less* than a full husband and daddy during this project.

May our Lord grant that this effort will be of benefit to His church—the entire church catholic.

One

THE CHURCH AT THE START: ROOTS IN GENUINE CATHOLICITY

"I therefore know no distinction, but am ready to break the bread and drink the cup of holy joy with all who love the Lord and will not lightly speak evil of His name."

—Anthony Norris Groves

 It was 1969. I was an undergraduate student at a university in California during the height of the counterculture movement. Myself: I was a new Christian, come to personal faith just before entering college. The mood on campus was common for the era: anti-anything-that-was-viewed-as-establishment. And it seemed that everyone was at least a touch on the radical edge, from philosophy professors who canceled classes to join in the anti-war demonstrations, to those "Jesus Freak" types who strode onto campus and preached loudly in the Agora adjoining the cafeteria. And any of us who claimed to really believe in Christ came in for a fair share of scholarly and social ridicule. So I prepared myself for challenges every day as I walked on campus.

One day as I arrived for classes, I recall seeing bright iridescent orange signs posted all over the campus. Approaching the nearest one, I wasn't very close at all when the message shouted out to me:

> **TO HELL WITH CHURCH!**
> LECTURE IN HALL 1003
> FRIDAY, 3:30 P.M.
> BE THERE

21

My first thoughts were: "Oh great! Another blast at Christianity." But I made a mental note to be there and offer my two bits' worth of apologetics.

I arrived early that Friday. The lecture hall was already packed with people. I was certain the crowd mostly consisted of opponents to the Christian message, who were simply looking for more evidence to chortle at Christianity.

The lecturer was an off-campus unknown. "Probably an antiwar, antiestablishment political activist who came over from Berkeley," I thought. He began (as I expected) by lambasting the institutional church as just one more example of "establishment" oppression. I gritted my teeth. "Right On!" punctuated the lecture hall from time-to-time. But before long he did an unexpected transition: "But check this out: don't confuse the 'establishment' churches with Christianity. The essence of Christianity has always been Christ. Don't reject Christ because of the folly of the church." He then developed a fair Gospel message and apologetic on his own before a bewildered and increasingly hostile audience.

The audience left angry. They felt cheated. Based on the signs that had lured them in, they came expecting a lecture sympathetic with their anti-Christian preferences—and here they got a dose of "fundamentalist" Christianity. But the point for all to see was that, to the lecturer, Christianity had little to do with the "establishment" church. The church was the "bad guy." And Christ was not to be confused with the institutional church.

Before long, and not to be outdone, the local Roman Catholic Coalition sponsored a series of lectures on campus in response. Their signs, posted on similarly eye-catching material, retorted:

> **IT'S A HELL OF A CHURCH!**
> LECTURE IN HALL 1205
> THURSDAY, 3:30 P.M.
> BE THERE

Few people came to this lecture, however. It was not as if they felt they couldn't trust these kinds of signs anymore. It was simply a fact known by the earlier lecturer: nobody wanted to hear anyone speaking favorably about any "institutional" organization. The church was too "establishment" for 1969. The first lecturer at least had that right. The mood of the era was certainly "to hell with church!" But his antithesis was a problem. Was it really Christ *or* the church? Or had he got the notion of the church a bit confused?

Two primary indictments of the church on the part of the budding intellectuals there led to a justification of this frustration:

✚ A disgust over the authoritarian history of the church prior to the Reformation (the rather arrogant and petty papal forcing of a schism into Eastern and Western church, religio-political corruption in Europe, the Crusades, the Spanish Inquisition).

✚ Frustration over the church subsequent to the Reformation (the proliferation of denominations and sects with competing and mutually exclusive claims, yielding much in the way of hypocritical strife).

So, the church as an "institution" was *bad*.

·But suspicion of organizational institutions claiming the name church is not just found among antiestablishment types who survived the sixties. The same is apparent among Protestants, particularly evangelical Protestants, and especially those of the free church tradition,[1] who are fairly quick to look with disdain on the more historic institutional churches claiming some sort of apostolic succession,[2] such as the Roman Catholic, Eastern Orthodox, or Anglican/Episcopalian churches. Marsden, for example, observes the following:

> One of the striking features of much of evangelicalism is its general disregard for the institutional church. Except at the congregational level, the organized church plays a relatively minor role in the movement. Even the local congregation, while extremely important for fellowship purposes, is often regarded as a convenience to the individual. Ultimately, individuals are sovereign and can join or leave churches as they please.[3]

The alternative to these large institutional structures woven around episcopal succession is, in fact, the highly proliferate patchwork of hundreds and thousands of independent Protestant groups. Although the anti-institutional mode left over from the sixties can support a stance against institutionalization in the church, what of the other criticism, that Protestant Christians are incredibly divided? Do these divisions destroy the unity of the church? That is the problem that must be squarely faced in to-day's church, for denominational and sectarian lines continue to exist and have an impact on popular perceptions of the church.

As confusion over the nature of the church persists, just how *are* we to understand it? Is the church to be conceived of as an external and visible organization, a purely invisible or spiritual organism of some sort, or both? If it is external in any way, is it to be exclusively identified with any of the existing external structures? And how are we to conceive of any notion of *one* church in view of the multiplicity of external and mutually exclusive claims of the existing Christian organizations? The historic organizational structures of the church argue toward a unity around an historic episcopate. The multiple Protestant subgroups more frequently argue toward a doctrinal and moral purity in the church and that organizational unity must play a second position to that. With all that, where really *is* the church?

This chapter will begin our examination by looking at the church in the New Testament (I hope, with some fresh questions), and will review our look at the New Testament from the standpoint of the early subapostolic church of the second century. We should find that the church understood itself to be one great community gathered around a core of apostolic teaching and that outside that apostolic core there was, even then, a diversity. The second century term for this was that the church was a *catholic* church. Let me explain.

THE CHURCH IN THE FIRST CENTURY: A COMMUNITY OF BELIEVERS IN THE SON OF GOD

We often use the term church today in reference to a structure or building. We say, "Meet me in the parking lot of the Baptist church on Third and Oak." We mean, of course, that there is a building there used by a group of Christians who identify with Baptist distinctives. At other times, we use the term church as a specific subset of the church at large: a denomination or association of like-minded Christians. We have this meaning when we say, "I belong to the Lutheran church." It's another way of saying, "I'm a Lutheran." But both of these uses are derivative rather than foundational, and may mislead us in terms of capturing the flavor of what the church is really about.

As we turn to the New Testament (the first place the term is used in its typical sense of Christians), we find several dimensions regarding the nature of the church. The earliest allusion to the use of the term is in fact connected to people: Jesus responds to Peter's confession and says *"you* are Peter and on this rock [alluding to Peter] I will build my church [=community of people]" (Matt. 16:18). Jesus was establishing for Himself one great messianic community. The emphasis is primarily on Peter as a prototype of the personal confessor of faith in Jesus and His messianic claims. As such, the idea is that the church is *primarily a people*, not a structure or organization.[4]

The church is not a building, although it typically needs one in which to meet. It is not an institution, although it requires (especially as it grows) institutional elements of leadership and organization. It is, instead, fundamentally a people who have come to faith in Christ and therefore gather together on the basis of that shared faith.[5]

With this in mind, as we look at the New Testament, the people of Jesus Christ are seen in three dimensions: as a *locally gathering community in a geographical area* (typically a city); as a *locally gathering community in a home;* and as the *entire community of believing persons, which may never gather in any way in this life*. Let's look at each of these successively. Each element will help us to understand more effectively the manifestations of the church as it exists in denominational variety today.

The church as believers gathered locally. The "church"[6] in the majority of its occurrences in the New Testament is conceived of as a concrete phenomenon: a community of persons within the same geographical area who believe in Christ, regularly gathering together to fulfill mutual functions as believers.[7] Luke, for example, refers to the church in Jerusalem (Acts 8:1, 3; 11:22; 14:27), the church at Antioch (Acts 13:1), the churches in Iconium, Lystra, and Pisidian Antioch (Acts 14:21-23), and the church at Ephesus (Acts 20:17). Each of these is visible, actual, and visitable: a community of believers in Christ who gather together in a specific geographical location. Paul, similarly, writes to the "church of God in Corinth" (1 Cor. 1:2; 2 Cor. 1:1), to "the churches in Galatia" (Gal. 1:2), "to the church of the Thessalonians in God the Father and the Lord Jesus Christ" (1 Thes. 1:1; 2 Thes. 1:1), and refers to a church at Cenchrea (Rom. 16:1).

The church in these instances can be nothing other than the visible, interrelating, localized communities of Christian believers. From early on they are portrayed as possessing identifiable leadership structures (local "elders" [NIV, NASB] or "bishops" [KJV, NRSV] and "deacons")[8] and practicing the cultivation of mutually supportive spiritual gifts (1 Cor. 12–14). Even our Lord Jesus Himself used the term church in reference to such a localized group of His followers when He referred to taking an unresolved discipline problem, in the last resort, to "the church" for judgment (Matt. 18:17). In theological discussions of the church, it is common to describe this aspect of the church as the "local church."[9] This use of the term church (or churches) may be illustrated as shown in figure 1.1.

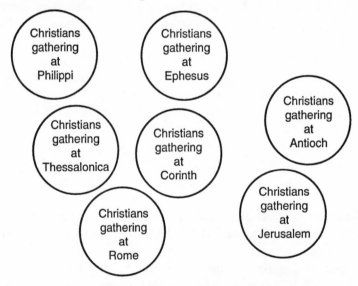

Figure 1.1.
The Church as a Local Gathering of Christian Believers

But it is not entirely appropriate to understand this first use of the term church as the strict equivalent of today's "local church" (that is, considering that in one city, *Filmore Street Baptist Church* is one "local" church, while *Metro Presbyterian* is another "local" church). For there is a more fundamental use of the term church that has often been overlooked in the discussions of this local, visible church. That use is for the "house" churches that made up the "local" church.

The church as a household gathering of believers. In Jerusalem, where some 5,000 believers were known to reside, the church really had nowhere to consistently meet "as a whole." They could not maintain free access to the increasingly hostile precincts of the temple. They could not rent a stadium or coliseum. Therefore, it is most probable that the regular functions of the church were in fact accomplished in "house gatherings" (cf. Acts 2:46-47).[10] Within larger, citywide congregations, the gatherings in given homes are also referred to by Paul as "the church." When they were living at Rome, for example, a "church" gathered in Aquila and Priscilla's house (Rom. 16:3-5), and it appears Roman house churches were found in other homes clustered around Asyncritus (Rom. 16:14) and Philologus (Rom. 16:15).[11] Priscilla and Aquila had done this same thing earlier when they lived in Ephesus: they had a "church" in their home (1 Cor. 16:19). Philemon, as a part of the greater church at Colossae, had a "church" in his home (Phile. 1-2), as did Nympha, who was apparently in that region but nearer the geographical church at Laodicea (Col. 4:15).

It becomes very apparent, then, that there were at root at least two "levels" of the "local church" in the New Testament era: the general area, or "city-church" (which gathered infrequently) as well as the particular, or "house church" (which gathered frequently). Abraham Malherbe appropriately notes the following in this regard:

> Although they may have formed separate communities, such [house] groups were not viewed as being separate churches. Luke's description of the church in Jerusalem is not clear on this point, but it does convey the impression that he thought of it as one church despite the smaller groups that composed it. This is supported by his (and the Pastoral Epistles') relating presbyters, or bishops, to cities rather than to individual groups (Acts 14:23; 20:17; Titus 1:5). By that time, however, more than one house church would presumably have existed in most localities with which the literature is concerned. More significant is that Paul and his followers, although they knew of separate groups in an

area, wrote one letter to the church in that immediate area, apparently on the assumption that it would suffice for all the groups (e.g., Romans). On this understanding, the individual house churches would together have represented the church in any one area.[12]

Due most likely to a lack of adequate physical space to regularly support the entire citywide church (a similar situation would exist today in large cities), congregations met in homes to fulfill other functions of the church.[13] Only on special occasions did the entire church in a city gather together, and only then when a larger home was available to them.[14] This use of the New Testament term church may be illustrated as shown in figure 1.2.

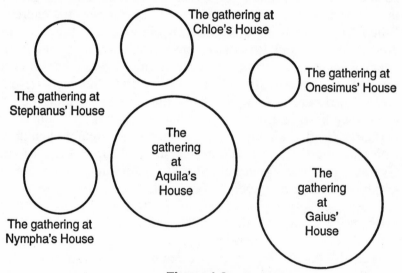

The gathering at Chloe's House

The gathering at Onesimus' House

The gathering at Stephanus' House

The gathering at Aquila's House

The gathering at Nympha's House

The gathering at Gaius' House

Figure 1.2.
A Close up of a Local City-Church: Numerous House Churches

The "local congregation" of today, when viewed in this light, is not the same as, say, the "local congregation" of Corinth.[15] The local congregation of today is simply a larger version of a first-century house church in a given city and likely developed as owners gave over their homes to the use of the church by moving out.[16] The developed house church of the first century is thus to be understood as the equivalent of what is called the local church today. *Filmore Street Baptist* is one house church in a city; *Metro*

Presbyterian is another; *Our Savior Lutheran* would be a third. The "local church" in the city, on this understanding, would include them all, as well as all other gatherings of believers in the apostolic Gospel of Christ at various locations in the city.[17]

The church as all believers everywhere. This leads to a third consideration of the use of the term church in the New Testament. The term is used in the singular to refer collectively to all of the individuals found in all the local and house congregations, throughout the world.[18] This is a natural extension of the notion that all the house churches in the homes in Corinth, for example, are the "church" (singular) at Corinth. For, although the city groups did not meet together as often as did house churches, believers knew they were a part of something bigger than the few dozen people they met with weekly in their house churches.[19] And yet the church was not understood to have any sort of regional or provincial identity beyond the local city-church.[20]

Luke shows how this extended idea of the church was used in his statement in Acts 9:31, "Meanwhile the church [note the singular] throughout Judea, Galilee, and Samaria had peace and was built up" (NRSV).[21] This notion that there is one church, and only one church, is found in certain foundational texts in the New Testament itself, dating from the teaching of our Lord:

> Simon Peter answered, "You are the Christ, the Son of the living God." Jesus replied, "Blessed are you, Simon son of Jonah, for this was not revealed to you by man, but by my Father in heaven. And I tell you that you are Peter, and on this rock *I will build my church,* [note the singular] *and the gates of Hades will not overcome it.* I will give you the keys of the kingdom of heaven; whatever you bind on earth will be bound in heaven, and whatever you loose on earth will be loosed in heaven." (Matt. 16:16-19)

The focus of the term church within this passage is the "church at large" or the "church as a whole." The term sometimes used to express this broad meaning of the term is the "universal" church to distinguish it from the "local" church discussed above.[22]

This notion of one inclusive community is found in two other key passages in the teaching of Jesus, His teaching on the Good Shepherd, and His high priestly prayer. In the former, Jesus indicates the basic idea that there is in fact one church, by His use of the shepherding metaphor to describe His relationship to His followers. In the latter, the unity of all those who would believe in Jesus with one another indicates the notion of one collective body of disciples:

> I am the Good Shepherd; I know my sheep and my sheep know me—just as the Father knows me and I know the Father—and I lay down my life for the sheep. I have other sheep that are not of this sheep pen. I must bring them also. They too will listen to my voice, and *there shall be one flock and one shepherd.*
> (John 10:14-16)

> My prayer is not for them alone. I pray also for those who will believe in me through their message, *that all of them may be one,* Father, just as you are in me and I am in you. May they also be in us so that the world may believe that you have sent me. I have given them the glory that you gave me, *that they may be one as we are one: I in them and you in me. May they be brought to complete unity to let the world know that you sent me and have loved them even as you have loved me.* (John 17:20-23)

There is little question about the fact that Jesus had one community of His followers in mind here. Moreover, the expression of "love" is to be a key characteristic of this "one" community.[23] The highlight is on relational unity and mutual support within that great community, with structural or organizational unity necessarily in the background. The fundamental idea still is that Jesus conceived of all of His disciples as "one people."

In Paul's writings, this notion of a general or universal church comprising all believers is found in a number of places. In Galatians 1:13, for example, when Paul was recounting for his readers his past life, he notes "how intensely I persecuted the *church of God* and tried to destroy it." Already in this early epistle, Paul had in mind the entire company of believing communities rather than one localized house or city-church.[24] In 1 Corinthians, both the localized use of church as well as this universalized use are found. Examples of the trend toward the latter include the following:

> Do not cause anyone to stumble, whether Jews, Greeks, or the *church of God.* (10:32)[25]

And in *the church* God has appointed first of all apostles, second prophets, third teachers, then workers of miracles, also those having gifts of healing, those able to help others, those with gifts of administration, and those speaking in different kinds of tongues. (12:28)[26]

But even more telling passages are found among what are known as Paul's "prison epistles," particularly Ephesians and Colossians. Note here the clear reference to the one, universal church by Paul's use of the singular to refer to *the entire collective body of believers* at all places:

And God placed all things under his feet and appointed him to be head over everything for *the church.* (Eph. 1:22; cf. Col. 1:18)[27]

His intent was that now, through *the church,* the manifold wisdom of God should be made known to the rulers and authorities in the heavenly realms. (Eph. 3:10)

To him be glory in *the church* and in Christ Jesus throughout all generations, for ever and ever! Amen. (Eph. 3:21)

Make every effort to keep the unity of the Spirit through the bond of peace. There is *one body and one Spirit* – just as you were called to one hope when you were called – *one Lord, one faith, one baptism; one God and Father of all, who is over all and through all and in all.* (Eph. 4:3-6)[28]

For the husband is the head of the wife as Christ is the head of *the church,* his body, of which he is the Savior. Now as *the church* submits to Christ, so also wives should submit to their husbands in everything. Husbands, love your wives, just as Christ loved *the church* and gave himself up for her. . . . and to present her to himself as a radiant church, without stain or wrinkle or any other blemish, but holy and blameless. . . . After all, no one ever hated his own body, but he feeds and cares for it, just as Christ does *the church* . . . This is a profound mystery – but I am talking about Christ and *the church.* (Eph. 5:23-32)

Now I rejoice in what was suffered for you, and I fill up in my flesh what is still lacking in regard to Christ's afflictions, for the sake of his body, which is *the church.* (Col. 1:24)

In these passages, Paul is clearly depicting an understanding of the church that extends beyond the local church to include *the entire company of the redeemed:* the church, to Paul, was far broader than the particular house church or city congregation of which one was a part. In participating in the local congregation, one was a part of something big. The saints in Corinth, for example, were saints "together with all those who *in every place* call on the name of our Lord Jesus Christ, both *their Lord and ours*" (1 Cor. 1:2, NRSV).[29] The one singular term "church" came to draw a circle of commonality around *all* those who believed in Christ. There is therefore an underlying unity of faith connecting all Christians everywhere.[30] This broad use of the term church may be illustrated by the diagram in figure 1.3.

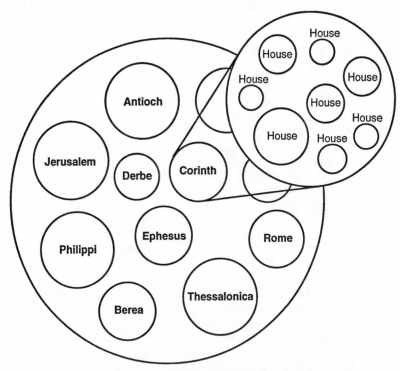

Figure 1.3.
The Universal Church: All the Gatherings
Who Call on Christ

Some thinking on unity. We have seen the centrality of the "oneness" or the unity of the church. But a key question here is this: how did the apostolic church understand its own unity? If these believers were somehow a part of something bigger than their house church or local church, how did they understand themselves to be "one church"? Did they understand themselves to be primarily a part of some overarching organizational unity under the leadership of the apostles, so that to leave the organizational unity of the apostolic church was to depart from the true church? Or did they understand their unity to be something different? It would seem that, although the apostles certainly served as a sort of loose organizational focus, the notion of organizational unity really was a secondary consideration rather than a primary consideration in terms of the church's self-definition in the apostolic era. The primary focus was in fact on *relational* unity around a core of shared beliefs. Let's explore these together for a bit.

The first focus of New Testament teaching on church unity is the teaching that genuine unity among Christians is primarily a *relational* unity (love and harmony) rather than a focus on *organizational* unity (external connectedness) within the church. Several passages bring this into sharp relief for us. Foundational, of course, is the teaching of Jesus Christ on the topic. As mentioned earlier, several passages in the teaching of Jesus indicate His teaching that there is but one church. The necessity of unity of that one church universal comes into the forefront most directly in His high priestly prayer recorded in John 17. There, in praying for His disciples, the Lord Jesus prayed beyond them for others to come:

> My prayer is not for them alone. I pray also for those who will believe in me through their message, *that all of them may be one,* Father, just as you are in me and I am in you. May they also be in us so that the world may believe that you have sent me. I have given them the glory that you gave me, *that they may be one as we are one:* I in them and you in me. *May they be brought to complete unity to let the world know that you sent me and have loved them even as you have loved me.* (John 17:20-23)

The question here, of course, is whether or not Jesus had in mind a broad organizational unity among His followers. But such an idea seems alien to the spirit of the passage. There is a more basic unity that Jesus had in mind, a unity of love. J.H. Bernard well observed:

There is no suggestion of a unity of organization . . . Jesus had said already that His sheep would ultimately be One Flock, even as they had One Shepherd (10:16). But the mystical phrases used in this passage transcend even that thought. For He prays that the unity of His disciples may be realized in the spiritual life, after the pattern of that highest form of unity, in which the Father is "in" the Son and the Son is "in" the Father.[31]

Hendrickson, in like manner, notes at this point the following:

The unity for which Jesus is praying is not merely outward. He guards against this very common misinterpretation. He asks that the oneness of all believers resemble that which exists eternally between the Father and Son. In both cases the unity is of a definitely *spiritual* nature. To be sure, Father, Son, and Holy Spirit are one *in essence;* believers, on the other hand, are one in mind, effort, and purpose.[32]

Similarly, C.K. Barrett contends:

It is . . . clear that John has little interest in the church as an institution . . . and, unlike Ignatius, he does not appeal for unity in institutional terms. The church's unity is not merely a matter of unanimity, nor does it mean that the members severally lose their identity. The unity of the church is strictly analogous to the unity of the Father and the Son; the Father is active in the Son—it is the Father who does his works (14:10)—and apart from the Father the deeds of the Son are meaningless, and indeed would be impossible; the Son again is in the Father, eternally with him in the unity of the Godhead, active alone in creation and redemption. The Father and the Son are one and yet remain distinct. The believers are to be, and are to be one, in the Father and the Son, distinct from God, yet abiding in God, and themselves the sphere of God's activity (14:12).[33]

The consistent emphasis within the Gospel according to John is, in fact, this relational kind of unity that is summarized by the "mark" of the Christian (to use Francis Schaeffer's term),[34] love:

A new command I give you: Love one another. As I have loved you, so you must love one another. By this all men will know that you are my disciples, if you love one another. (13:34-35)

My command is this: Love each other as I have loved you. Greater love has no one than this, that he lay down his life for his friends. . . . This is my command: Love each other. (15:12-13, 17)[35]

The language is almost identical to the "unity" language of John 17. The unity of the one church is at root a relational unity of love. That is where the internal unity of spirit manifests itself in *visible* unity: external actions of love that demonstrate an internal commitment to love.[36]

This same kind of thinking is found in the unity statements of the Apostle Paul when he says, "Make every effort to maintain the unity of the spirit in the bond of peace" (Eph. 4:3). The NRSV, by retaining the participle, catches the connection of this verse to the preceding verses a bit more clearly than the NIV does:

> I therefore, the prisoner in the Lord, beg you to *lead a life worthy of the calling to which you have been called,* with all humility and gentleness, with patience, *bearing with one another in love, making every effort to maintain the unity* of the Spirit in the bond of peace. (4:1-3)

Loving forbearance, you see, is the means by which *real unity* in the church is accomplished between real Christians.[37] Again, church unity at root has its concern in *relational* unity among believers rather than external organizational unity. Claims of unity of the church based on an external, organizational unity no more demonstrates the call by our Lord and the apostle for loving relational unity than does claiming that a marriage is healthy and loving simply because it stays together. Maintaining an external unity may force problems of disunity to be addressed, but it does not prove that genuine relational unity exists. And it is relational unity that marriage, and the church, are to exemplify.

Now this does not mean that where the relational unity of love exists that there is not the need for a visible unity such as organizational unity exhibits. It sometimes does. If I cannot unite organizationally with my brother or sister simply because relationally I cannot stand the thought of trying to live together in community with them, then the organizational unity question brings to the front issues of more fundamental relational disunity.

A second dimension regarding church unity in the New Testament is its focus on a unity grounded on foundational Christian truth. This certainly makes sense, since it is in fact *believers in Christ* who gather together on the basis of a common faith.

Granted this, one must suspect that there is agreement on that common faith. They came to believe something to be true about God, themselves, and the work of Christ. And that faith is what unites them. It is a *shared* faith.

This is precisely what we find in Paul's teaching in Ephesians 4. Directly following his plea toward loving forbearance, and to maintain the "unity of the Spirit in the bond of peace" he gives the doctrinal grounds for that relational plea:

> There is one body and one Spirit—just as you were called to one hope when you were called—one Lord, one faith, one baptism; one God and Father of all, who is over all and through all and in all. (4:4-6)[38]

As Andrew Lincoln points out, this doctrinal statement connects readily in the writer's mind with the relational unity that he calls for:

> For the writer of Ephesians also there is a clear link between the unity of the Church and various acclamations of oneness in vv. 4-6. The behavior for which he has called, the maintenance of the unity of the Spirit, can now be seen to be the only consistent practical expression of the foundational unities he enumerates here. At the same time, by reminding his readers of these distinctive realities to which they are committed, he reinforces both the sense of cohesion he wants them to have as members of the Church and the sense of their distinctive identity vis-à-vis the surrounding society.[39]

Now this particular doctrinal statement by Paul is not necessarily intended as a comprehensive summary of doctrinal orthodoxy.[40] Rather, his point is simply that Christian unity, the unity of the church, is a relational unity of a particular people who have come to share a common faith in some doctrinal realities. Without those doctrines, there would be no particular need to call for relational unity among this particular people. They are called to relational unity since they share a common faith. If they did not share a common faith, there would not need to be any special call for their relational unity.

Some thinking on unity in diversity. There is one church. Its unity is two-pronged: a unity of loving relationships grounded in a unity of apostolic faith-content. But this notion of unity means something even more. It includes within it an implicit and important idea of unity in the face of the realities of diversity and threats to unity. There was only one church, despite the reality of conflict, alienation, and cultural differences.[41] This idea of unity in diversity is not a fresh one, but one that is approached from many angles in the New Testament, and to this fundamental notion of unity and diversity we turn next.[42]

There are several factors in the New Testament that show the need for understanding a unity in plurality within the church itself: the doctrine of spiritual gifts, the doctrine of the Christian conscience ("gray areas"), and the cultural diversity implicit within the very notion of multiple congregations.

Spiritual gifts are described in the New Testament primarily, but not exclusively, within the context of their functioning within a local house church/congregation. The most important passages are 1 Corinthians 12–14, Romans 12, and Ephesians 4. But without going into detail about the nature and function of gifts at this point, it is important to realize what they teach us regarding the nature of church unity and diversity.

Paul states that "There are different kinds of gifts [diversity], but the same Spirit [unity]. There are different kinds of service [diversity], but the same Lord [unity]. There are different kinds of working [diversity], but the same God works all of them in all men [unity]" (1 Cor. 12:4-6). Later, after describing the need in a body to have a diversity of parts (foot, hand, ear, eye), he warns against uniformity in the place of diversity: "If they were all one part [uniformity], where would the body be? As it is, there are many parts [diversity], but one body [unity]" (12:19-20). And, finally, so as to emphasize the folly of expecting unity to arise from uniformity, he asks "Are all apostles? Are all prophets? Are all teachers? Do all work miracles? Do all have gifts of healing? Do all speak in tongues? Do all interpret?" (12:29-30). Paul is asking quite plainly whether there is a uniformity of spiritual gifts. The plain answer to these rhetorical questions is "No!" There is not a uniformity of spiritual gifts, but there is one body. God promotes the common good through diversity, not uniformity. Unity is found within diversity, not within uniformity.

The teaching on spiritual gifts here indicates that; within a congregation interrelational unity and functioning is based on the acceptance and need for diversity of spiritual giftedness. The New Testament doctrine of spiritual gifts teaches a congregational unity in and through diversity. A second area of New Testament witness to this notion is in matters of individual conscience.

The New Testament teaching on the Christian conscience gives an important place to diversity among believers. There are "gray areas" of diversity in the Christian community in addition to the blacks and whites of uniformity. These are issues in which genuine Christians may legitimately hold differing opinions, since they are matters of implicit rather than explicit biblical teaching. The primary New Testament passages are Romans 14–15 and 1 Corinthians 8–10. Again, without detailing Paul's teaching on this issue, suffice it to say that he taught that genuine believers can differ on their interpretation on some matters of the Christian life and that it is the duty of Christians to accept this diversity without expecting uniformity of practice. The exception is deferring to the weaker brother lest he "stumble" by going against his own conscience.

In Romans, Paul notes the diversity in Christian practice: "Some believe in eating anything, while the weak eat only vegetables" (14:2, NRSV). But (people being people) the temptation is to expect uniformity in practice on these matters, since on matters of moral substance God does expect uniformity of practice. So Paul warns against expecting and demanding uniformity: "Those who eat must not despise those who abstain, and those who abstain must not pass judgment on those who eat; for God has welcomed them" (14:3, NRSV). The "despising" of some, and the "passing judgment" of others is based on the expectation of conformity to certain views on diet. It is expecting uniformity rather than allowing for diversity.

In 14:5-6, Paul applies this principle to the matter of celebrating or not celebrating sacred days. He again argues for an allowable diversity: "Let all be fully convinced in their own minds" (14:5, NRSV). His point is this: think through your position on these matters and come to conclusions; but allow others the courtesy of having come to differing conclusions and so honor their conscience. Allow for diversity by honoring your brother/ sister's diversity from you, even though you are convinced of your position. Do not expect uniformity in all areas of Christian conviction.

So, like Paul's teaching on the spiritual gifts, his teaching on the Christian conscience also emphasizes that within the local congregation there must be a unity between believers that allows for diversity. Again, while this notion mostly has a focus on the local congregation, this idea would also have important implications for cross-congregational diversity as well. Recalling Paul's teaching of the two dimensions of the local congregation at Rome, it is easy to see how house churches there may well have gathered around cultural themes and thus tended to pit one house church in a city against another on these matters (the same may have been true in Corinth, where one house church may have favored Paul, another Apollos, another Peter, etc.). House churches in Rome which had a decidedly Jewish-Christian cast may have been reflected in the dietary and sacred day restrictions, and attracted those who felt better with those kinds of restrictions. Those house churches which had a more Gentile cast may have felt greater freedom in these areas.

Thus even in a local area like Rome, we may be seeing a house church to house church rivalry expressed in these words of Romans 14–15. Paul's teaching then is certainly appropriate for cross-congregational unity in diversity.

This naturally leads to the third area: looking at the church as a whole aggregate of all believers everywhere. Are we to understand then the need for diversity as a grounds for unity well beyond the local congregation?

We have looked at unity and diversity in the doctrine of spiritual gifts, and we have mentioned the cultural differences implicit in Paul's teaching on the Christian conscience, especially as it relates to interpersonal or even house church to house church tensions. Is this unity and diversity needed beyond the local collection of house churches in Rome or in Corinth or in Jerusalem? Was there a diversity on secondary issues between Jerusalem and the other city-churches? Yes, quite so.

A key example is the relationship of the city-church of Jerusalem (the aggregate of house churches there) and the city-church at Antioch on the Orontes (the first "missionary church"). It is clear that we must understand the church at Jerusalem to be predominately Jewish in flavor: those who believed in Jesus as their Messiah in Jerusalem came by and large (if not exclusively) from the religious and cultural milieu of first century Judaism.

On the other hand, the church begun in Antioch on the Orontes had a large infusion of Gentiles within it. Luke records those early days:

> Now those who had been scattered by the persecution in connection with Stephen traveled as far as Phoenicia, Cyprus and Antioch, telling the message only to Jews. Some of them, however, men from Cyprus and Cyrene, went to Antioch and *began to speak to Greeks also*, telling them the good news about the Lord Jesus. The Lord's hand was with them, and *a great number of people believed and turned to the Lord.* (Acts 11:19-21)[43]

The cultural situation in Antioch meant that a *new* experiment in Christian faith was beginning there: Gentiles, lacking the strict instruction in Torah that the Jews in Jerusalem had, side-by-side with less strict Jews of a more Hellenistic bent, were coming to faith in Christ and were fellowshiping together. A question soon arose: what degree of conformity to the expectations of the Torah-trained Jewish church in Jersualem should be required of them?

But what we find in the interrelationship between these two city-churches is a combination of unity and diversity. The unity required a fundamental core of doctrinal uniformity (or else one was not really a part of the *Christian* community). This was supplied by affirmation of Paul's Gospel message by the leaders in Jerusalem when he went to "set before them the gospel that I preach among the Gentiles" (Gal. 2:2). The pillars of the church at Jerusalem "gave me and Barnabas the right hand of fellowship when they recognized the grace given to me" (Gal. 2:9). But outside of that core of doctrinal uniformity there was room for diversity with sensitivity to the cultural needs and preferences of each group.

The need for doctrinal conformity to core issues may be further illustrated by Paul's conflict with Peter when he visited Antioch (Gal. 2:11-21). The issue was the Jewish propensity to separate from the Gentiles on matters pertaining to Jewish dietary restriction. The Jewish Christians, long taught these dietary restrictions from their Scriptures, believed that those teachings of Scripture should carry over into the new community of Christ.

Because of these inherited teachings, Peter, who exercised his freedom in the Gospel to eat with Gentiles when the members from his Jerusalem "home church" were absent, felt the pressure to withdraw when they were present and reminded him of these matters. Paul publicly rebuked him on this. Peter was thus communicating that the Gentiles lacked something in terms of full acceptance with God on the basis of Christ alone. It damaged the truth of the Gospel. Hence, uniformity must be pressed. Paul challenged: "You are a Jew, yet you live like a Gentile and not like a Jew. How is it, then, that you force Gentiles to follow Jewish customs?" (Gal. 2:14) Jerusalem cultural/religious customs must not be tolerated if they contaminate the core issues of the Gospel. But, as long as the issues are matters of personal preference and flexibility rather than an "expected uniformity," they can be allowed their diversity.[44]

Similarly, we note the problem of the teachers who came down to Antioch from Jerusalem and argued, "Unless you are circumcised, according to the custom taught by Moses, you cannot be saved" (Acts 15:1). This was again imposing a Jewish culturally/religiously conditioned element upon the Gospel message. But it should be noted: this was an interpretation of the Scriptures. Teachers from the church of Jerusalem were attempting to apply their Scriptures (our Old Testament), which taught circumcision, to Gentile Christians. This sparked a trip to Jerusalem by Paul, Barnabas, and others to resolve this dispute. The Jerusalem Council of Acts 15 was the result.

Did the Jerusalem Council impose Jewish religio-cultural practices, which even had biblical support, such as circumcision, on the Gentiles? No. That would water down the free grace of the Gospel. God was doing something new in the church. In some way the message of circumcision was not universally binding any longer for the people of God. But what is interesting is the opposite as well: they did not require of the Jews to *stop* such practices. The letter which ensued from this (Acts 15:24-29) merely asks the Gentiles to exhibit cultural and religious sensitivity to these matters and concludes: "You will do well to avoid these things."

The church came to realize that the vastly different cultural backgrounds between Gentiles who came to Christ and Jews who came to Christ would require congregations that predominately reflected one of these diverse backgrounds to be sensitive to congregations who reflected the alternative. There *will be* diversity. But unity must be displayed in the midst of that diversity rather than expecting a uniformity.

The conclusion is this: the church of the first century understood itself as the corporate body of Christ, made up of all who believed in Jesus for salvation regardless of background or geographical locality. As such, they were one people. But their oneness included both uniformity and diversity. The uniformity was on core issues pertaining to the Gospel. Their diversity was in secondary issues arising from cultural diversity or the interpretation of the Scripture as it applied to secondary issues.

THE CHURCH IN THE SECOND CENTURY: ONE CHURCH UNITED IN DIVERSITY IS THE CHURCH CATHOLIC

Catholicity and its definition. As we move into the second century, we find ourselves just one step removed from the biblical material. In one sense, we have left the authoritative source of normative ecclesiastical practice. But, on the other hand, we find here the earliest interpretive expressions of the concepts of unity in diversity found in the New Testament. And we are still looking at a community of Christians in close continuity with the apostolic faith. That community is also interpreting itself in apostolic terms (without yet possessing our New Testament in its complete sense). Once we turn to the second century, we immediately become aware of a broad concept of the church that includes all believers in all of the Christian communities worldwide, with all their diversity.

The Christians in the second century developed a term for understanding the church as the one general church spread abroad, and including all of the local and culturally diverse churches: the term they chose for this biblical concept was the adjective "catholic" from which we derive the concept of "catholicity."[45] Though not particularly a biblical term (any more than "trinity" would be later), it certainly captured well the broad New Testament notion of the general, universal church, with its unity and diversity. The church of Jesus Christ was understood to be a *catholic* church. It included not only those, for example, who met regularly in Nympha's home in Cenchrea, and those in the entire area who met together periodically at Corinth. It also included "all those who in every place call on the name of our

Lord Jesus Christ" (1 Cor. 1:2, NRSV). That was the entire church that Christ was building. That was the one church that Christ was building. That was the *catholic* church.

The unity of the church indicates that Jesus is building only one church. Catholicity indicates that that one church is universal and includes a multitude of individual congregations, and it therefore possesses diversity within its oneness. It includes what Dulles refers to as a "plentitude" and "pluralism," a fullness and a differentiated unity.[46] The notion of this broader church may be seen in the earliest known Christian usage of the term "catholic church." In Ignatius' *Letter to the Smyrnaeans* 8.2 (ca. A.D. 112) we find these words: "Wherever the bishop appears let the congregation be present; just as wherever Jesus Christ is, *there is the catholic church.*"[47] It is clear here that "catholic" is the equivalent of "universal" as opposed to "local" church. The bishop (overseer) is related to the local congregation; while Jesus Christ is related to the *whole* church.[48] Thus, the *catholic* church extends to every place that Jesus Christ is present by faith.

Similarly, in the introduction to the *Martyrdom of Polycarp* (ca. A.D. 156), the second century subapostolic writer began as follows: "The church of God which sojourns in Smyrna, to the church of God which sojourns in Philomelium, and *to all the sojournings of the Holy Catholic Church in every place.* Mercy, peace and love of God the Father, and our Lord Jesus Christ be multiplied."[49] Once again, it looks rather clear that catholic is the equivalent of "universal" or "entire" rather than "local," since the church of God at Smyrna and the church of God at Philomelium were local congregations, while the "Holy Catholic Church" was to be found "in every place."[50]

As noted, this broad notion of the universal church implies a diversity in unity.[51] The churches in Judea were culturally and organizationally diverse from the Gentile churches, the church at Rome was diverse from the one at Corinth or Philippi or Ephesus or those in Galatia, but they constituted one church of Christ through a common bond of faith in Him. Catholicity is the acknowledgment of sharing a common faith with those who are not "walking with us" in all our particular characteristics, but who nonetheless belong to Jesus Christ.[52] This high view of catholicity was summed up centuries later in the breadth-statement of the seventeenth-century German Protestant theologian, Rupert

Meldenius: "Unity in essentials, liberty in incidentals, and in all things charity."[53]

Although the primary idea was that of unity in diversity, the notion of catholicity expected (as was mentioned earlier) a certain core of uniformity, that is, there was a basic doctrinal orthodoxy inherent within it. After all, the unity was a unity in *something*. It needed to be a unity in the apostolic faith.[54] If it were not, then it was not a unity of "all those who in every place *call on the name of our Lord Jesus Christ.*" They called on the same Lord because they responded to the same apostolic message.

But how was one to find the genuine apostolic message midst the competing claims? The Gnostics and the Marcionites early on presented alternatives to the apostolic message and claimed authoritative grounds for doing so. Catholicity, in view of such heretical developments, came to be used to provide a means to deduce the *content* of the apostolic faith.[55]

Vincent of Lérins in the first half of the fifth century issued a famous maxim in this regard. As far as genuine apostolic faith among Christians is concerned, he said it is to be found in "what all men have at all times and everywhere believed."[56] Therein a high view of catholicity was used to guard against doctrinal hyper-specificity, so as to find core orthodoxy in a common, apostolic faith shared with all who believe in the same Lord.

So important was catholicity to the early centuries of the church, that it became part of the earliest confessional statements of Christians. The third-century Apostle's Creed, for example, reads: I believe in the holy *catholic* church.[57] The Nicene Creed of the fourth century, amplified on this earlier statement: I believe in one holy, *catholic,* apostolic church.[58] Christians in the earliest centuries understood themselves to be part of something big and inclusive when they thought of themselves as a part of the church catholic. The faith they shared was spread abroad throughout the earth and included a diversity around a core of orthodox faith that went with that simple fact.

Catholicity and sectarianism. Another way to look at catholicity is to contrast it more thoroughly with its opposite: sectarianism. Sectarianism may be defined as a *narrowing of the ground of acceptable Christian fellowship and cooperation due to a broadening of what is considered orthodox doctrine.*[59] It is therefore my (or my

44

group's) refusing to allow for diversity in others and demanding conformity with all my views, as if my view (in full detail) alone had divine sanction. It is the notion that I, or my own specific group, alone has a market on the truth, to the exclusion of others.

All particular doctrines are equally important in this understanding. It is seeking unity in uniformity rather than unity in diversity and expecting other Christians to comply fully with my views before I can have genuine fellowship with them—as well as holding them doctrinally suspicious until they do. Sectarianism can plague any group of Christians, or any individual Christian. Ironically, some sectors (praise God, not all!) of my own denominational connection, the Christian Brethren, have suffered from trends toward this kind of sectarian thinking even though as a movement, the Brethren began with a strong push toward catholicity. Nathan Smith, in his *Roots, Renewal, and the Brethren,* interviewed a number of former Brethren individuals who had left the movement and discovered that they had experienced sectarian attitudes in the specific churches of which they were a part. I will here cite some of these comments, because they illustrate what sectarianism is really about most clearly (and remember: the Brethren are not unique in having examples of this problem). An ex-Brethren academician from the East Coast commented:

> I was no longer under the understanding that the Brethren way of meeting was the one true way of meeting. This was the way I was brought up. The Brethren way was the Christ-intended way for the church to meet.[60]

A Brethren worker on the West Coast said similarly:

> I grew up in a small assembly in the Midwest. There were no more than fifty people in the assembly. This fellowship was all one knew. Other Christians were commonly referred to as people who did not have the truth. They were gathered to denominational organizations as opposed to us who were gathered to the name of the Lord Jesus. They were not separated Christians as we were.[61]

A third-generation Brethren woman said:

> The impression I gained in the Brethren was that we were a notch above all other Christians. We had the right truth. Others had the truth, but we had the *right* truth.[62]

These kinds of expressions illustrate a sectarian attitude. But the Brethren are not alone in their susceptibility to this. One time I was visiting a well-known Christian conference center on the Oregon Coast with some relatives. A popular speaker was about to enter the pulpit so we decided to drop in and listen. His message was interesting and enlightening, but I was somewhat shocked at a statement he made to the mixed denominational audience. He grabbed his Bible and shouted, "I'm a Baptist! A Baptist! And I'm proud to be a Baptist!" I think he forgot that this was not his typical audience, for he only had a few muffled "amens" to his outburst. The rest of us non-Baptists simply sat there in shock. Visibly shaken, he tried to regain his composure and lamely completed his message.

I wish I could say that I've never been guilty of similar things. But, sadly, I cannot. Insular ministry has all too often had a similar sectarianism-building effect on me.

Sectarianism is this attitude of one-upmanship toward the rest of the body of Christ. It is a cancer that develops in some surprising places. The sectarian attitude is roundly rebuked in the teaching of our Lord when the disciples reported that they had tried to stop someone who was casting out demons in Jesus' name, but did not follow with the disciples: "Do not stop him . . . for whoever is not against you is for you" (Luke 9:50).

The sectarian attitude can even be seen in the Pauline literature, within segments (competing house churches?) of one local congregation. At Corinth, Paul decried the mutually exclusive claims breaking down the unity of Christ and its catholic diversity of teachers:

> I appeal to you, brothers, in the name of our Lord Jesus Christ, that all of you agree with one another so that there may be no divisions among you and that you may be perfectly united in mind and thought. My brothers, some from Chloe's household have informed me that there are quarrels among you. What I mean is this: One of you says, "I follow Paul"; another, "I follow Apollos"; another, "I follow Cephas"; still another, "I follow Christ." Is Christ divided? Was Paul crucified for you? Were you baptized into the name of Paul? (1 Cor. 1:10-13)

Sectarianism is a subtle thing, moreover. Even the notion of *catholicity* itself has been used as a rallying point for sectarian thinking: If one group does not practice catholicity the way that is expected, or does not unite with the "only truly catholic group," then they are considered "out" of the church. In this sense, one is forced to question the sufficient catholicity of classical Roman Catholic or Eastern Orthodox theology when they reserve the term for themselves and any who would unite with them, due to exclusive claims of direct succession from the apostles.[63] As Flew and Davies put it several decades ago, "there is no communion [church or denomination] on earth which is fully catholic, for no communion possesses, in the full and absolute sense, the 'wholeness' of the Gospel."[64]

Genuine catholicity has a far broader scope than this. It sees genuine faith in the Gospel as basic, wherever it may be found. It bridges across diversities of form and finds commonality in that which is fundamental. This is important even to the most elementary definition of the church in the first place: "The church can be defined as the *whole body* of those who through Christ's death have been savingly reconciled to God and have received new life."[65] To understand it as only your group alone is the antithesis of catholicity, sectarianism.

CONCLUSIONS AND IMPLICATIONS

1. In the New Testament, there are three fundamental dimensions of the church: the believers who frequently gather as a house church; the believers who periodically gather as a local (city) church; and the entire community of believers in Christ who do not have opportunity to gather all at one time, but of which each believer is a part. Only occasionally has the first dimension been emphasized today, and, at that, not often in balance with the other two. Nor has this emphasis adequately perceived the equation of today's local church with the house church. More frequently, the local church has been confused with the city-church of the New Testament. This too easily leads to isolationism and sectarianism, especially when banded with an inadequate doctrine of the church universal. Too strong an emphasis on the local congregation at the expense of the entire church catholic can lead to isolationism and sectarianism. Too strong an emphasis on a collection of similar-minded congregations (denominations) similarly can lead to isolationism and sectarianism. Too strong an emphasis on the church universal at the

expense of the local communities can lose sight of the fact that the church is foundationally people meeting in community. All three levels of the church must be kept in balance for account-ability, support, and catholicity to develop in healthy ways.

2. The emphasis on one church in the New Testament focuses on the necessity of having an appropriate perception of each believer's unity with all believers in the local (city) church and wherever there are gatherings of believers in this world. Every believer is brother/sister to every other believer, regardless of the house church or broader local/city-church with which one may meet regularly. A refocusing on the local congregation as a grown-up house church and simply a part of the city-church, made up of all the genuine believers in their own local house-churches can recapture the breadth-dimension of the entire church by realizing the diversity that the genuine church has in a realistic local geographical community. When I can recognize that the *Downtown Methodist,* or *Open Bible*, or *Metro Presbyterian,* or the *Gospel Hall,* or any other churches sharing in the historic apostolic Gospel in my town are house churches of the church of my city (Portland, or Houston, or Denver, or Winne-mucca, for that matter), then I am on my way to appreciating the New Testament teaching on the church catholic: unity in diversity.

3. The broad extent of inclusion within the believing church of every locality demonstrated in the New Testament shows a diver-sity of cultural and even doctrinal/practical emphasis. Although by definition each actual community is formed of those who have overtly responded to the Gospel message, and hence acknowl-edged a certain core of Christian orthodoxy thereby, diversity on certain secondary elements is evident even within the pages of the New Testament.

4. An appropriate doctrine of the church will include an un-derstanding of the unity of all believers in Christ, and this entails a tolerance of diversity on secondary matters. This unity/diversity tolerance is summed up in the very early and biblical notion of "catholicity." Uniformity is expected on the apostolic faith; diver-sity is allowed on other areas.

"To Hell With Church?" Hardly, if one understands the na-ture of the church in its most fundamental terms. The intent in the late 1960s was "To Hell with Institutionalism," and the

48

church was perceived as just one more example of that. Certainly that is at times true. And it is at all times tragic. But that simply points up that the notion of catholicity considered in this chapter did undergo some transformation in the subsequent history of the church. As a result, the basic notion of allowable diversity referred to here began to be lost, particularly in the process of institutional uniformity. And it is to that we must turn if we are to recover a broad, biblical breath of catholicity once again. And to that, we will devote the next chapter.

Two

THE CHURCH IN HISTORY:
THE EBB AND FLOW OF CATHOLICITY

*"I believe in the Holy Catholic Church and sincerely regret that it
does not at present exist."*

—William Temple

 I recall some years back entertaining a visitor
from England who had arrived in Oregon after
traveling across country from the East Coast. As a
resident of the great Northwest, I was sure that he
would have been impressed with the magnificent
ring of Cascade volcanoes such as Mt. Hood or
(then, whole) Mt. Saint Helens surrounding us, or the mighty
Pacific Ocean viewed from the rugged Oregon Coast, or the awe-
inspiring Columbia River Gorge. Barely stifling my pride, I ven-
tured a question: "What impresses you most about America?" I
was taken aback by his comment: "Very little." Not a little curious, I asked for an explanation. He responded, "America, I've
discovered, is a country with no history to speak of." Ignoring the
physical beauties he had seen, this foreigner was struck by the
brevity of America's lifetime. The most "historic" thing Americans had to offer him was some Old-West site of a mere century's passing. Accustomed as he was to a history expanding over
multiple centuries, the United States seemed like a mere babe
with an easily measurable lifetime.

But the story goes far to explain our American attitudes toward history as a whole. Pragmatists that we are, we often don't
really care about history or what it teaches us, or even how it has
influenced us. And this is sad, particularly when it comes to
American Christians. For as Christians our corporate history
goes back many centuries before the events of 1776. Yet we are

51

stuck with a shortsighted, narrow vision of the past and have lost sight of the nearly twenty centuries of Christian theological thinking and spirituality.

I am reminded of a "Peanuts" comic strip that illustrates our problem. Charlie Brown's younger sister, Sally, is writing a paper for her school homework under the title "Church History." Charlie, curious, observes her first few lines: "When writing about church history, we have to go back to the very beginning. Our pastor was born in 1930." Charlie simply rolls his eyes.

We may laugh at Charlie's sister, but we American Christians have a similar, narrow historical vision, do we not? We give appropriate attention to the *Bible,* but how much attention do we give to the history of the church's *handling* of the Bible? And there is much in that history which has formed *who we are* and *how we perceive ourselves* as Christians, and *how we look at the church catholic,* if we will but look.

There are some initial considerations to be addressed at this point. To some who venture into this reflective process of observing church history, we are not really looking at the history of the *church* at all, but rather to the history of Roman Catholic organizational structures and its political struggles. The *real* church, they would say, is to be found instead in the persecuted minorities who truly believed in Christ throughout church history, and who often protested against the errors of an institutionalized church. And this genuine *believing* church can all too often be missed, since it left little record of itself. Most of what remains are the disdainful critiques of those "nonconformist" groups found in the official records of the institutional church.[1]

Unfortunately, this approach to church history fails to grapple with the fact that the genuine apostolic faith is not *opposed* to institutional structure, organization, and leadership, but that it can live with little or with much of it. Genuine believers can therefore be found both within and without the organizational structures of a hierarchical church. To disallow the organizational church in discussions of church history is just as serious an omission as is the limitation of genuine church history *to* organizational structures. But since the core issue in identifying the church is genuine faith, one must conclude that at times the teaching position of the organizationally-structured church obscured both this core Gospel message and the historic tilt in favor of the priority of Scripture as the focus of apostolicity. Hence, the inevitable development of protest movements, of which the Protestant Reformation is but one (albeit a major one).

Nevertheless, it is a rather bleak experience to review, even briefly, the history of the church at large. The current diversity of the church did not result, in the main, from amiable diversification. Rather, it was often the result of quarrels and squabbles. The allowance of diversity in all too many instances overtook and squelched the unity, as relational disputes pitted group against group. However, it is not correct to say that such human foibles failed to accomplish the divine plan to advance the church into a diversity that it could have had on more amiable grounds.

God began the mission advance of the church despite what appears to be the reticence of the original Twelve to evangelize the Gentiles (Acts 8:1). The fallout between Paul and Barnabas resulted in the advancement of the Gospel on two fronts rather than one (Acts 15:36-41). This does not justify human failure. It simply indicates that God often uses human failure to advance the kingdom. And the diversification frequently develops a cultural and social focus to the kingdom message that would otherwise be lost. But we are getting ahead of the story. Let's take a look at the structural development of the church and the implications this had for genuine catholicity.

PHASE I. THE DEVELOPMENT OF THE ANCIENT CATHOLIC CHURCH: ONE VISIBLE CHURCH IN ONE FORM

In the earliest centuries of the church, there was an inevitable, ongoing organizational development. This is the same sociological phenomenon that takes place with any expanding group of people. The church moved, as it grew, toward strong organizational structures which allowed it to care for and propagate itself in a balanced fashion. In addition, it developed two ideas which would force a shift in the understanding of the church in subsequent generations, and require a Reformation to address: the notion of *apostolic succession* (bishops linked by an understood direct connection to the apostles) and *sacramentalism* (the church dispenses the sacraments which are the channels of grace necessary for salvation). These twin ideas served as the foci of this organizational unity and were definitive in subsequent years in shaping the church's self-identity.

With these twin ideas the notion of catholicity began to undergo a transformation. Rather than a relational unity around a core of shared faith that allowed for diversity on secondary matters, catholicity began to be understood as a characteristic owned exclusively by the visible organization that claimed direct link to the apostles through the bishops, and which supplied for all people the elements necessary for salvation. And with this organizational claim to catholicity, genuine catholicity began to be obscured. The term "catholic" itself began to be understood as meaning "orthodox" as opposed to "heretical." The "catholic church" then meant "the Christian church that was not heretical."[2]

Now that is not to say that organizational development is an unbiblical notion. Within the New Testament we see that the church is already undergoing a degree of development organizationally. In the earliest periods described, especially in the Book of Acts, organization is rather informal and leadership somewhat unstructured.[3] The church is primarily a "movement" that has a "lay leadership" of the apostles.[4] Leaders in the churches are selected from within by the apostles or their associates on the basis of maturity rather than on any type of formal theological training.[5] By the time of the later epistles, the pastorals, a more formal leadership recognition process is identified, and leadership has focused itself on the offices of "elder/overseer" and "deacon." The leadership of the local church as a whole is a plurality of elders/overseers, which are perhaps the community of individual house church leaders. But again, the church is at root people who have believed the Gospel message about Jesus.[6]

Between the completion of the final books of the New Testament and the earliest subapostolic writings, it is uncertain what changes occurred. But by the late first century and the early second, things had continued to grow organizationally, and things looked a bit different. The epistle commonly known as *1 Clement* (an epistle from the church at Rome to the church at Corinth, written about A.D. 96) suggests a situation similar to the observable structure of the New Testament local city-church: there is a plurality of presbyters (elders) functioning in Corinth at that time.[7] The writer also appears to go somewhat beyond this by suggesting a threefold order of leadership for the church that paralleled the Old Testament offices of high priest, priest, and Levite.[8] One of the plural elders/presbyters may therefore possibly be in view as the leader.

Polycarp, bishop of Smyrna in the early second century, seems to indicate that it is still the practice of the congregation at Philippi (to which he wrote some time between 110–117) to be led by a group of elders, although he seems to distinguish himself as a bishop (overseer) among a group of elders.[9] At roughly the same time (ca. 113) Ignatius, bishop of Antioch, places the focus of local ministry in three distinct offices: one bishop (overseer), a group of elders, and a group of deacons.[10] The single bishop was perceived by him as the guarantor of the church's unity, and the protector of orthodoxy against the heresies of the Gnostics. Nevertheless, even in Ignatius, the bishop is still an overseer within the context of a local congregation rather than in a supervisory role over several congregations.[11]

A further development later in the second century was the notion that the monarchical bishop gained his authority via what was understood to be direct "apostolic" succession. Irenaeus, bishop of Lyon (A.D. 130–200) wrote his extensive work *Against Heresies* sometime between 182 and 188, in the face of the Gnostic threat. He argued that the certain succession of bishops, particularly those in Rome, guaranteed the passing on of orthodox apostolic doctrine.[12]

By the third century, the continued focus on the bishop as the protector of orthodox doctrine due to his apostolic succession led to the notion that the unity of the church was somehow connected with this collection of bishops. The key leader who promoted this next step was Cyprian, bishop of Carthage (A.D. 200–258):

> This unity we ought to hold and preserve, especially we who preside in the Church as bishops, that we may prove the episcopate itself to be one and undivided. Let no one deceive the brotherhood with falsehood; no one corrupt our faith in the truth by faithless transgression. The episcopate is one; the individual members have each a part, and the parts make up the whole. The Church is a unity; yet by her fruitful increase she is extended far and wide to form a plurality . . .[13]

And again, in an oft-repeated phrase: "He cannot have God for his father who has not the Church for his mother."[14] But the Cyprianic phrase that stuck (and galls Protestants) most was "there is no salvation outside of the Church."[15] This meant, to Cyprian, that there was no salvation apart from the legitimate

55

sacraments available only through the apostolically succeeded bishops of the external, visible, catholic church.[16] The visible church is now the necessary anteroom of salvation, rather than the community living room one enters via the anteroom of the Gospel message.[17]

Thus, Cyprian's notion of the church was entirely a visible one. And Cyprian's view became the predominant one. Yet, one must beware of saying that the genuine church of Jesus Christ, the saved and elect of God, must therefore be looked for in other quarters than in the visible structures of the third century church and its successive developments. In Cyprian's age of external imperial persecution (prior to the reprieve of the Constantinian era) as well as the earlier challenges of heretical Gnosticism and Montanism, genuine faith was in fact likely found predominantly *within* the threatened visible structures of the church. And its leadership provided many examples of genuine faith as well.

The focus on the visible, institutional structures transmitted in the episcopate led to an external emphasis which could all too easily divert the primary focus away from the presence of genuine faith and relational unity, and hence produce a loss of genuine catholicity among all true believers. The church as a community of genuine believers tended to give way to the church as identified by the correct episcopal structure and sacramental treatment. The church is now identified most clearly in terms of its possession of a priesthood and sacramental system, and the ancient catholicity of a shared faith becomes subsidiary to the presence of a legitimate episcopate.[18] The shift to a clerical definition of the church impacted catholicity to an enormous degree.[19] As long as broad-minded and godly persons were in church leadership positions, abuses could be kept in check. But the structures were in place for potential abuse. And the damage to catholicity was not long in coming, for the outcome of the Cyprianite understanding of the church would be to classify as unchristian any who were outside these external structures of the institution. Two pivotal examples from this period will suffice to show how this worked out in practice: The Novatian schism and the Donatist schism.

The Novatian schism was one in which a more "puritan" element within the church developed as a result of the imperial persecutions under the Roman Emperor Decian (which took place in A.D. 249–250). Novatian, who became the leader of the group, was the chief orthodox theologian in Rome, and had been passed over in favor of the relatively unknown presbyter Cornelius as the next bishop of Rome in 251. Due to the laxity in allowing the "lapsed" to return (the lapsed being former members who denied Christ and sacrificed to the pagan gods to avoid martyrdom), Novatian split with the church and set up another, "purer" group, which was to last until the seventh century.

But the central issue is this: the Novatianists were entirely orthodox in their theology. Novatian, in fact, had written a standard theological treatment in Rome on *The Trinity* between 240–250. Where Novatianists diverged was in their rejection of the laxness of the institutional catholic church. Nonetheless, due to the prevalent notion of the church in external institutional terms, the Novatianists were considered schismatic and were therefore considered "outside" the pale of salvation. With this institutional, visible model of the church showing its colors with Novatianism, Rome demonstrated therefore how their model of the church had diverged from a truly *catholic* understanding of the faith.

Similarly, within half a century, this scene was repeated with the Donatist controversy. In 303, yet another great persecution broke against the church, sponsored this time by the Emperor Diocletian. This persecution did not ease up until a decade later when Constantine's "Edict of Milan" permitted freedom of worship for Christians. But in North Africa, a Christian revolt took place soon after peace was restored. The revolt was primarily due to two things: the laxness of the institutional Catholic church in readmitting the lapsed after this terrible period of persecution and with the appointment of a new "impure" bishop of Carthage named Caecilian.[20]

A counter-bishop named Majorinus was therefore quickly appointed by the dissenters in Carthage, who was succeeded by Donatus in 313. Orthodox in every way, and even stricter in their expectations of the community, the Donatists multiplied rapidly, and were even persecuted by the "official" church (with State help) for a period of time. Like the Novatians, the Donatist church did not die out until the seventh century, when the Muslim conquests of North Africa put them under. But, like the "official" Catholic church, the Donatists considered themselves the only true church, since they had the only clergy free from "deadly sins," and therefore possessed the only valid sacraments.

But the Donatists, like the Novatianists, were not accepted as "catholic" in their faith because they were not connected organizationally with, and opposed the policies of, the structural church which claimed the title "Catholic." This was certainly a point at which the broader church catholic would include believers within *both* structures, but their emphasis on the *structures* as definitional of church catholicity led to a denial of the very thing they claimed.

Once external threats (political or theological) were removed, and the church was first protected and then sanctioned by the state under Constantine and his successors, participation in the external structures alone *did not* guarantee genuine faith. In fact, the structures tended to work against such faith. Once membership in the church was expected, predominant purity of the church in terms of a faith-entrance requirement could not be guaranteed. The church continued to view itself as the door of salvation through its uniform structures and sacraments.

An important passage for understanding the meaning of the word "catholic" as it was developed in the first three centuries is found in Cyril of Jerusalem (A.D. 348), written not long after persecution quieted down during the Constantinian era:

> The Church is called Catholic because it exists *throughout all* the inhabited world, from one end of the earth to the other; and because it teaches, *universally and completely, all* doctrines which ought to come to the knowledge of men concerning things both visible and invisible, both in heaven and on earth; and because it brings into subjection to godliness the *whole* race of men, both of rulers and of ruled, both of learned and of ignorant; and because it *universally* treats and heals *every* kind of sins which are committed by soul and body, and possesses in itself *every* form of virtue that is named, both in deeds and words and in spiritual gifts of every kind.[21]

In Cyril, the notion of *universality* is clearly present. There is little to critique in the idea as expressed by him. The difficulty was not in the definition, but in its application to the organizational structure of the church, which alone was able to dispense the grace needed for salvation through the episcopally ordained clergy—handling sacraments which it alone possessed.

As mentioned, with the conversion of emperor Constantine to Christianity and the issuing of the Edict of Milan (A.D. 313), Christian persecution let up.[22] By 381, Theodosius had made Christianity the official state religion. And with that, the inevitable took place: the church and state began to merge so that the church was viewed as a sort of "department of State," a position it held until the demise of the Eastern empire with the Islamic invasion of Constantinople in 1453.

In the West, the church-state liaison worked similarly. There, the church as Institution did not have political structures with which to align itself, particularly after the fall of Rome in the fifth century. Instead, the church itself (as an Institution) took on the functions of the state. Although persecution ceased in this context as well, the externalized notion of the church, and its function in terms of economics and political stability, led to the minimization of the focus on *faith* as the grounds for participation in the community of Christ. The church became an organization with which one aligned oneself, rather than a fellowship of those who had responded to Christ in faith. And it was an organization that was important to align oneself with for political and social reasons. The necessity of genuine faith as the crucial inaugural requirement began to recede into the background.[23]

This period may be summarized by noting that the term "catholic" came to be understood as an "orthodoxy" that was to be guarded by the structures of the church, and later the state, from generation to generation via the notion of structural or apostolic succession. Outside the structures of the one, institutional church, catholicity was understood to be non-existent.[24] From one perspective, in this period the term catholic became a mark or badge of identifying the true church.[25] It became *exclusive* in its outlook rather than *inclusive*. Catholicity, as a term, ironically took on sectarian dimensions. The ancient notion of catholicity as relational unity within diversity became lost as structural unity excluded more and more kinds of diversity and especially organizational diversity that was otherwise very orthodox.

PHASE II. THE GREAT SCHISM:
TWO COMPETING CLAIMS TO BEING THE ONE CATHOLIC CHURCH
Novatianism and Donatism were relatively small organizational splits. In 1054, the greatest split to date ravaged the church. The

cleavage of East and West, ostensibly over doctrinal issues in that Great Schism, led to the independent development of cultural and doctrinal foci. The East (now known commonly as Eastern Orthodox) deplored the increasingly high-handed treatment afforded them by the Bishop of Rome who claimed a greater primacy among the bishops than they believed was his due.

But even after the terrible split, in which each group anathematized the other and "unchurched" them, each party continued to understand the church primarily as a visible, historical entity in continuity with the apostles. They simply restricted the term "catholic" (now = "true") to their own exclusive group. Each one made mutually exclusive claims to be the one truly catholic church.[26] The claim was made, for example, by Pope Boniface VIII in 1302 that only those Christians who acknowledged the jurisdiction of the Bishop of Rome could be saved.[27]

Western Protestants, of course, are used to the exclusive claims of Rome, especially prior to Vatican II (of which too many Protestants are still ignorant). As recently as the First Vatican Council (1870),[28] such strong words as these were issued by the Roman Catholic Church:

Hence we teach and declare that by the appointment of our Lord the Roman Church possesses a superiority of ordinary power over all the other churches, and that this power of jurisdiction of the Roman Pontiff, which is truly episcopal, is immediate; to which all, of whatever rite and dignity, both pastors and faithful, both individually and collectively, are bound, by their duty of hierarchical subordination and true obedience, to submit not only in matters which belong to faith and morals, but also in those that appertain to the discipline and government of the Church throughout the world, so that the Church of Christ may be one flock under one supreme pastor through the preservation of unity both of communion and of profession of the same faith with the Roman Pontiff. This is the teaching of Catholic truth, from which not one can deviate without loss of faith and of salvation.[29]

But what is not so frequently heard by Protestants is the similar, mutually exclusive, claim of the Orthodox. Orthodox scholar Timothy Ware capsulizes these rarely heard words:

Orthodoxy, believing that the Church on earth has remained and must remain visibly one, *naturally also believes itself to be that one visible* Church. This is a bold claim, and to many it will seem an arrogant one; but this is to misunderstand the spirit in which it is made. Orthodox believe that they are the true Church, not on account of any personal merit, but by the grace of God.[30]

The original spirit of catholicity (where the church is found wherever Christ is known), of course, is lost in the competing claims and disallowance of organizational diversity. And, of course, this disruption of 1054 left the Eastern Orthodox basically untouched (or uncontaminated, depending on one's perspective) by the Protestant Reformation, since the Reformation occurred in the West as a reaction to perceived corruption within the Roman church in the sixteenth century.

Again, catholicity is understood by *both* Roman Catholicism and Eastern Orthodoxy as exclusive rather than inclusive. As such, each has been consistently able to define the other out of legitimacy. Each group perceives itself as alone properly "catholic" and as such may exclude the other. And underlying both is the continuing notion of the church as entirely visible, based on the succession of a priesthood which alone has the divine authority to administer the sacraments and thus to dispense salvation. Both claim an authentic Tradition which reaches back to the apostles. In the West, the authority tends to focus on one man, the Bishop (pope) of Rome. In the East, the authority is not so vested, but rather rests on the authority of the ecumenical councils where the Bishop of Rome is viewed as a first among equal bishops.

The structural understanding of catholicity as orthodoxy, seen in the Novatian, Donatist, and Great Schisms, may be illustrated as shown in figure 2.1 on page 62. The key issue is exclusivity rather than inclusivity, despite commonality of matters pertaining to faith.

In the West, at least, this understanding of the church catholic as focused in the institutional structures of the visible church began to receive serious challenges in the Middle Ages (the precursor to the Protestant Reformation). During the Middle Ages, a number of voices began to express concern over the implications of this perception of the church.[31] John Hus (1372–1415), as one key example, concluded in his work *The Church* (1413), that the church is something broader than simply the Roman Catholic Church:

The unity of the Catholic Church consists in the bond of predestination, since her individual members are united by predestination, and the goal of blessedness, since all her sons are ultimately united in blessedness. For the present time her unity consists also in the unity of faith and virtue and in the unity of love. . .[32]

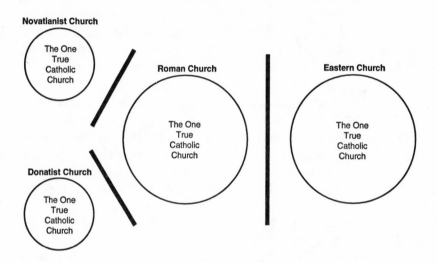

Figure 2.1.
Organizational Definitions of Catholicity[33]

This, of course, is to recapture some of the basic essentials of catholicity so long obscured. Shockingly, for his era, Hus asserts that the church of Rome is only a *part* of the body of Christ:

> However it should be noted that the Roman Church properly speaking is the congregation of those faithful to Christ, who live in obedience to the Roman bishop, just as the Antiochian Church is said to be the congregation of those faithful to Christ who are subject to the Bishop of Antioch; and the same holds true for Alexandria and Constantinople. . . .[34]

And again, as Hus concludes:

Thus the pope is not the head nor are the cardinals the entire body of the holy, Catholic, and universal Church. For Christ alone is the head of that Church and all predestined together form the body, and each alone is a member of that body, because the bride of Christ is united with Him.[35]

For his efforts, John Hus was charged with heresy in Rome and was summoned before the Council of Constance where he was ultimately condemned for his views on July 6, 1415. He was burned at the stake and a copy of his work was symbolically destroyed by fire.[36] Indeed, a number of the Reformational concepts had early echoes in questions raised during the Medieval period.[37] The late Medieval period, in this sense, paved the way for some renewed thinking on the very nature of the church and its catholicity.

PHASE III. THE REFORMATION AND ITS DEVELOPMENTS

To the Reformers of the sixteenth century, a renewed vision of the church was needed from the start. The church was understood as catholic, but it was not to be identified with the external structures of the Roman Catholic Church alone (in principle, this would apply to the Orthodox Church alone as well). The Reformers argued that the church was to be identified with God's *elect*, that is, those who genuinely believed. Wherever the Gospel was preached and faith was present, *there* was the church — regardless of the external structure.[38]

The Lutheran *Augsburg Confession* of 1530, put well this new notion of the church:

Also they [the Lutheran churches] teach that one holy Church is to continue forever. But the *Church is the congregation of saints, in which the Gospel is rightly taught and the Sacraments rightly administered.* And unto the true unity of the Church, it is sufficient to agree concerning the doctrine of the Gospel and the administration of the Sacraments. Nor is it necessary that human traditions, rites, or ceremonies instituted by men should be alike every where, as St. Paul saith: "There is one faith, one baptism, one God and Father of all."[39]

Similarly, the *Belgic Confession* of 1561:

The marks by which the true Church is known are these: *If the pure doctrine of the gospel is preached therein; if she maintains the*

*pure administration of the sacraments as instituted by Christ; if
church discipline is exercised in punishing of sin;* in short, if all
things are managed according to the pure Word of God, all things
contrary thereto rejected, and Jesus Christ acknowledged as the
only Head of the Church.[40]

Again, the *Thirty-nine Articles* of the Church of England (1563):

The visible Church of Christ is a *congregation of faithful men, in
which the pure Word of God is preached, and the Sacraments be duly
ministered according to Christ's ordinance,* in all those things that of
necessity are requisite to the same.[41]

And, most thoroughly, the *Westminster Confession of Faith* (1647):

I. The catholic or universal Church, which is invisible, *consists of
the whole number of the elect,* that have been, are, or shall be
gathered into one, under Christ the head thereof; and is the
spouse, the body, the fullness of him that filleth all in all.

II. The visible Church, *which is also catholic or universal under the
gospel* (not confined to one nation as before under the law) *consists of all those who, throughout the world, that profess the true
religion,* and of their children; and is the kingdom of the Lord
Jesus Christ, the house and family of God, out of which there is
no ordinary possibility of salvation.

III. Unto this catholic visible Church Christ hath given the ministry, oracles, and ordinances of God, for the gathering and perfect-
ing of the saints, in this life, to the end of the world: and doth by
his own presence and Spirit, according to his promise, make them
effectual thereunto.

IV. This catholic Church hath been sometimes more, sometimes
less visible. *And particular churches, which are members thereof, are
more or less pure, according as the doctrine of the gospel is taught
and embraced, ordinances administered, and public worship per-
formed more or less purely in them.*

V. *The purest churches under heaven are subject both to mixture and
error;* and some have so degenerated as to become no churches of
Christ, but synagogues of Satan. Nevertheless, there shall be
always a Church on earth to worship God according to his will.[42]

The original notion of catholicity has certainly returned here.
Unity is no longer understood in terms of organizational unity,

nor is it connected with a purely visible organizational structure. Unity is found around a core orthodoxy (to the Reformers, the Gospel and sacraments), allowing for diversity (traditions). Avis put well this new notion of the church:

> The concept of the Church which was fundamental to the thought of the Reformers (including of course the Anglicans)—namely, that only the gospel was of the *esse*—had profound implications for the doctrine of succession and with it the key concept of catholicity, one of the four creedal attributes of the church. Here a radical reinterpretation was effected. . . . By making the gospel alone the power at work in the Church through the Holy Spirit, the Reformers did away with the necessity of a doctrine of apostolic succession, replacing it with the notion of a succession of truth. *Correspondingly, the gospel of truth was held to be sufficient to secure the catholicity of the Church.* The Reformers believed with all of Christendom that the Church was one, holy, catholic and apostolic, but this was understood in a radically new sense in which the *gospel itself became the decisive and dominant criterion.*[43]

The church was thus to be found wherever the genuine Gospel was preached and hence saving faith was found, whether inside or outside external structures provided by the sacerdotal system.[44] Luther himself held that "not external organization or ties but continuity in doctrine and practice with the ancient church constituted true catholicity."[45] Donald Bloesch, similarly identifies the key distinction which arose in Protestant thought:

> [To the Reformers] a church that is truly catholic is a church based on the apostolic doctrine contained in the New Testament, not a church supervised by bishops who supposedly stand in an unbroken succession to the original apostles. It is the doctrine that validates the ministry and not vice versa."[46]

The later Puritan writer Richard Sibbes certainly caught the spirit of the Reformational model of the church catholic when he said, "Beloved, that that makes a church to be a catholic church . . . is the catholic *faith.*"[47]

The new conception of the church catholic was not structural at all. It was, in fact, related more to the presence of the proclamation of the Gospel. The church as a structure was no longer the door through which one entered into salvation; the Gospel was the door through which one entered the church. The true church was really made up of the elect, known fully only to God. Further, the visible church was not made up of those who visibly associate with the structure. Instead, the visible structure of the church was made up both of the elect (who truly believed and belonged to Christ), and the nonelect who did not genuinely have (but merely professed) faith. The newer conception may be illustrated as shown in figure 2.2.

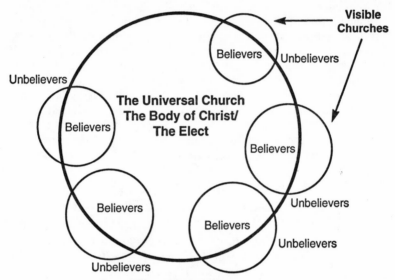

Figure 2.2.
The Reformational Concept of the Believing Church over Structural Church

But Protestantism was not at all uniform, nor was it particularly united. Protestantism was, in effect, the opportunity for Christian nonconformity to develop itself according to conscience, free from the control of the centralized organization. Nonconformity was not new,[48] of course, but with the Reformation, its ability to develop freely was.[49] Protestant nonconformity rallied around its material principle, the Gospel of justification by faith and its formal principle, *sola Scriptura.* But as distinct Protestant groups followed their own principles, new groups were formed as older ones became more established—often because of the purported failure of earlier groups to be completely consistent with the Reformation principles.

And, although conceptually there were grounds for a healthy

return to catholicity with the Reformers, in practice this did not quite occur. Despite an attempt by the Reformers to form a coordinated movement at the Marburg Colloquy in 1529, theological and personal differences caused things to break down, and such an alliance never took place.[50] As a result, tensions developed between the diverse Protestant groups. Caspar Schwenckfeld acutely observed the problem during the Reformation itself, writing in 1530: "The Papists damn the Lutherans; the Lutherans damn the Zwinglians, the Zwinglians damn the Anabaptists and the Anabaptists damn all others."[51] Certainly this is not the expression of the spirit of catholicity even though the newer doctrinal perception was there.

Luther had his loyalists, who organized ultimately as Lutherans, with the *Augsburg Confession* as their mutual creed. Calvin and his followers, the Reformed, rallied around his *Institutes of the Christian Religion,* and ultimately found their distinctive emphases reflected in the *Westminster Confession of Faith* a century later in 1647. The radical reformers (the Anabaptists), emphasized a state-free church and believer's baptism and were harassed by the more state-liaison-minded Lutherans and Calvinists.[52] Influential Anabaptist thinkers were the Reformer Ulrich Zwingli (1484-1531) in Switzerland (who stopped short of some of the implications of his thinking and whose group merged with the Calvinists after his death), and Menno Simons (1496-1561) in Holland (where the Anabaptists came to be known as the *Mennonites).*

In England, Henry VIII by his Act of Supremacy in 1534, split with the Pope to form the Church of England, or Anglican Communion. The Church of England wavered in its alignment for a time and finally aligned itself with Protestant theology under Thomas Cranmer's *Book of Common Prayer* (1549/52), and the *Thirty-nine Articles* (1553/71).

The later sixteenth- and seventeenth-century Anglicans saw the rise of a *Puritan* party in their midst, concerned with reforming the church beyond the minimal changes brought about as a result of Henry VIII's actions. The Puritans, for one thing, did not favor the inherited episcopacy of the church, but they disagreed among themselves as to what form of church government was most biblical: the *Presbyterian* Puritans favored an interconnected rule by elders, a presbytery; while the *Congregational* Puritans favored independent local congregations. When it became clear to some that each of the Puritan branches still maintained a strong connection with civil rulers, the Separatist movement began, emphasizing complete religious liberty from state interference. The result: the *Baptist* movement.

But there were some serious interrelational problems with the Reformational notion of catholicity at its outset. The fresh Reformational notion of the church developed closely alongside a rising nationalistic spirit in Europe to produce the idea that the each territorial ruler (king or prince) possessed the divine right of regulating his country's religious affairs and of punishing those who disturbed that church's peace. Thus, each territory allowed only one state-sanctioned church.[53] Although the specific church (Lutheran, Reformed) of a given territory did not view itself as the sole church of God on earth, but simply an aspect of the overall church catholic, a given territory yielded but one *sanctioned* church for which state taxes went in support, and for which state-sanctioned education was allowed.[54]

This, in turn, tended to discourage the populace from recognizing the need to make a personal faith response to Christ (since the state church is that into which one is *born)* and to equate loyalty to a given church with allegiance to the state.[55] Although the territorial notion of the church was in many ways necessary for the ultimate success of the Reformation,[56] it directed Protestantism all too easily toward an external, institutionalized model sanctioned by the state, and therefore susceptible to the minimization of a genuine faith requirement. And, at least within each territory, diversity was discouraged but grudgingly allowed. Catholicity therefore, in practice, lost ground once again. The territorial model may be diagrammed as follows in figure 2.3 on page 69.

The seventeenth century: Protestant catholicity defaced and redefined. In the seventeenth century, doctrinal division in Europe, together with the tendency to establish a "state" church (the notion of "territorialism"), contributed to the terrible *Thirty-Years' War* (1618-1648). The original notion of a broad catholicity among Protestants was supplanted by mutually exclusive claims, with each denomination seeking to prove its sole legitimacy as the true church in a given territory.[57] When war broke out be-

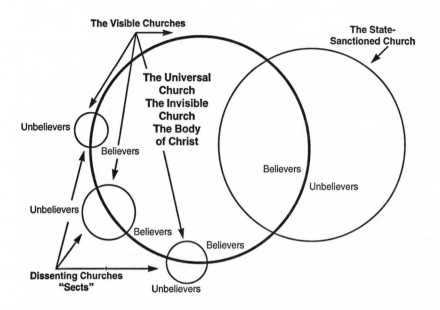

Figure 2.3.
Territorialism: The State-Sanctioned Visible Church

tween the princes in Europe, each had a Christian denomination as an ally. Each denomination believed the alliance with the prince was legitimate, so that his conquests would likewise extend the reach of that denomination. Pannenberg, writing as a modern European, cites the devastating effect this has had on modern European attitudes toward the church:

> The ruthless conduct of the religious wars discredited the churches, but even the fact that each belligerent party believed it had an exclusive claim to absolute truth and communion with God was enough to discredit them all. The largely indecisive outcome of the wars of religion produced a permanent situation in which the churches held a questionable position, and skepticism concerning their militant exclusivism was by no means necessarily based on a total rejection of Christianity. Clearly the denominational quarrels did severe damage to the credibility of Christianity in modern times.[58]

During the *Thirty-Years' War,* Fredrich von Logau wrote several satirical poems regarding the implications of such religious wars:

> If Christ's way to change the world
>   Had been to persecute and kill,
> Why, then *he* would have crucified
>   Those Jews who sought to do him ill.

Again,

> Lutheran, Popish, Calvinist —
>   These three creeds their views propound
> But our doubts must still remain —
>   Where can Christendom be found?[59]

Another of the results of this period was development of alternative Christian societies such as the *Quakers,* or the Society of Friends. Developed in England in the 1650s and 1660s, they focused on an "inner light" theology that stressed experience, avoided external religious trappings, and stayed aloof from the state and political involvement. The key leaders of the Quakers were George Fox (1624–91), and, in America, William Penn of Pennsylvania.

In England, near the end of the *Thirty-Years' War* on the continent, a critical event emerged which would define a new religious toleration there by producing a fresh understanding of the church—built on the Reformers' model. That event was the *Westminster Assembly* of 1643–49. During a civil war in England which pitted their Parliament against their king, Charles I, Parliament convened this Assembly of 121 religious leaders to establish a form of church government more consistent with the principles of the Reformation. Among the many key elements which this Assembly produced (including the *Westminster Confession* and the *Larger* and *Shorter Catechisms*), a fresh view of the church began to emerge among some of the participants.

This fresh view was particularly promoted by the "Dissenting Brethren" among the participants: Puritans who had returned from exile abroad and had tasted of toleration on the Continent. These Puritan dissenters resisted the will of the majority of the Assembly to establish a presbyterian form of polity, in the place of the episcopal, and have it enforced by the state. Instead, these dissenters urged allowance of diversity by *disestablishment*. In a key discussion on this issue, Hudson identifies the extension of ideas of the church implicit in the Reformation that were extended by these dissenting Puritan divines:

> The new element which was to be introduced into this type of thinking [by the seventeenth century Puritan divines] was the application of the basic convictions of the Reformers to a situation in which religious diversity existed within a particular geographical area rather than between different geographical areas. Formerly it had been a question as to whether or not a church in England could be and was in communion with a church in Holland. The answer of Protestantism in general had been that they both could be and were in communion with one another. In seventeenth century England, it was to be suggested that this was equally true of Anglican, Presbyterian, Congregational, and Baptist churches when they were located on opposite corners in the same city. Each could be and should be regarded as constituting a different "mode" of expressing in piety, thought, and organization that larger life of the church in which they all shared.[60]

Certainly this notion of allowing for diversity so as to follow the individual conscience is a significant change of understanding in the age of territorialism that had produced the *Thirty-Years' War*. And, although the Dissenters did not win the day in the Westminster Assembly, and the Parliament which sponsored the Assembly itself was defeated by the supporters of Charles, the ideas of these Independents were so persuasive that they ultimately led in England to the *Act of Toleration* of 1689. There, the "established" Church of England itself had its status reduced to only the greatest of many "denominations." This, in turn, led to the spread and acceptance of this denominational model of catholicity in preparation for the revivals of the next century.

The eighteenth century: revivals of catholicity. The eighteenth century brought the great Anglican revivalist preachers of George Whitefield (1714–1770), and John (1703–1791) and Charles (1707–1788) Wesley. The followers of the latter two organized themselves into distinct groups of Anglicans known as Wesleyans, or *Methodists*. These men, in the midst of their revivalistic preaching, capsulized this spirit of catholicity. John Wesley, for example, said:

71

I . . . refuse to be distinguished from other men by any but the common principles of Christianity. . . . I renounce and detest all other marks of distinction. But from real Christians, of whatever denomination, I earnestly desire not to be distinguished at all. . . . Doest thou love and fear God? It is enough! I give thee the right hand of fellowship.[61]

Again, Wesley spoke with a richly catholic heart as follows:

I dare not, therefore presume to impose my mode of worship on any other. I believe it is truly primitive and apostolical. But my belief is no rule for another. I ask not, therefore, of him with whom I would unite in love, 'Are you of my church, of my congregation? Do you receive the same form of church government and allow the same church officers with me? Do you join the same form of prayer wherein I worship God?' I inquire not, 'Do you receive the Supper of the Lord in the same posture and manner that I do, nor whether, in the administration of baptism, you agree with me in admitting sureties for the baptized, in the manner of administering it, or the age of those to whom it should be administered?' Nay, I ask not of you (as clear as I am in my own mind) whether you allow baptism and the Lord's Supper at all. Let all those things stand by—we will talk of them, if need be, at a more convenient season. My only question at present is this, 'Is thine heart right, as my heart is with thy heart?'[62]

Whitefield, while preaching from a balcony in Philadelphia, looked up to heaven and cried out these words:

Father Abraham, whom have you in heaven? Any Episcopalians? No! Any Presbyterians? No! Any Independents or Methodists? No, no no! Whom have you there? We don't know those names here. All who are here are Christians. . . . Oh, is this the case? Then God help us to forget party names and to become Christians in deed and truth.[63]

In America, with the influence of Jonathan Edwards and George Whitefield, the Great Awakenings brought revival among the Protestant groups which had begun to die of deism. Gilbert Tennant, a prime mover in the *First Great Awakening,* similarly caught this broad catholic spirit associated with an appropriate denominational view of the church:

All societies who profess Christianity and retain the foundational principles thereof, notwithstanding their different denominations and diversity of sentiments in smaller things, are in reality but one church of Christ, but several branches (more or less pure in minuter points) of one visible kingdom of the Messiah.[64]

Many were converted, but by the nineteenth century the sense of catholicity, strong in Whitefield and the Wesleys, became lost in the proliferation of nonconformist groups competing with one another and suspicious of each other. In part, the subsequent sectarian attitude led to the parallel developments of the (Plymouth) Brethren Movement in England and Ireland, and the Campbellite Movement in America, where unity in Christ alone was the focus, and the denominational divisiveness disallowed. But before long, each group had introverted into believing that it alone practiced genuine catholicity and that unity was found in gathering only in their particular way. And in so doing, lost it.[65]

PHASE IV. AMERICAN DENOMINATIONALISM[66]

As noted, one of the consistent patterns of European Protestantism was the ongoing claim that there could be something known as an "established" or "state" church in a given country, which enjoyed special support of the governmental institutions.[67] As America was colonized by the Europeans, each colony followed suit and set up one or other Protestant denomination as the "established" church of that colony.[68] This is simply the ongoing attempt to relate church to state in a meaningful way, but it did have serious ramifications for any persons in a given colony who did not belong to the specific "established" church of that colony. Settlers who did not belong to that particular denomination were subjected to state-sponsored restrictions, or, at least, taxation used to support the sponsored "established church" of the colony.

But with the success of the American Revolution and the framing of the Constitution, America began a new experiment. The new nation declared itself in its 1791 Bill of Rights to be opposed to the "establishment" of any given denomination. To allow for the "Free Exercise" of all denominations, church was to be henceforth and forever in the United States of America *separated* from the state. All established churches would need to support themselves without the use of public funds, support, or coercion.[69]

Cut from the competitive bonds of seeking state support, American Protestant denominationalism developed a sort of pluralistic acceptance of other denominations as a part of "Christian America."[70] As Loetscher points out:

> Rejection of church establishment [in America] molded former established churches and former dissenting sects into a new type—'denominations,' which showed mutual toleration and often mutual recognition and reciprocity.[71]

Protestant groups turned their energies from attempting to gain state support toward convincing people of the Christian message. This, together with a strong, common postmillennial vision of a Christian America drove people forward in their social and evangelistic efforts.

There is a sense in which one may understand the nature of modern denominationalism, especially in America, as really an expression of a return to the catholicity that has been lost both in the two sides of the Great Schism as well as the sectarian developments of the Protestant Reformation. In fact, the catholic spirit which grew up in the Great Awakening lent its legitimating power to denominationalism so that the two are closely interpenetrated. As Richey notes:

> Catholic Christianity played a distinct role in legitimizing denominationalism. The tradition of toleration or voluntarism witnessed most strongly to the inviolability of conscience and will and thus to dissent. It made separate congregations and denominations viable as the effective responses to the Christian gospel. Its conception of affectionate unity was servicable to the cause of revival, as when Jonathan Edwards pled for a concert of prayer and a union of wills consenting to being in general. . . . Catholicity served to state the meaning of denominationalism as a form of the church. It conceived the quite real and existing distinctions of doctrine, practice, and government as already overcome in a unity of fundamentals and practically overcome when Christians would unite in charity.[72]

Although some perceive that denominationalism is an essential evil, a degradation of Christianity into categories of social and class status,[73] there is an understanding developing out of the nineteenth century "Christian America" notion that denomina-

tionalism is in fact a positive, nonsectarian approach to understanding the church catholic. Hudson summarizes this idea well,
when he writes the following:

> The whole structure of American Protestantism rests upon a par-
> ticular understanding of the nature of the church—the denomina-
> tional theory of the church. . . . The word denomination was
> adopted by the leaders of the Evangelical Revival, both in En-
> gland and America, because it carried with it no implication of a
> negative value judgment.[74]

The bottom line is that it is the notion of denominationalism in
the American church-state separation which most easily can allow a proper notion of a broader notion of catholicity to flourish.[75] Let me explain.

In the first place, the notion of denominationalism actually had
its impetus, as mentioned earlier, in the seventeenth century
Congregational Puritan longing for freedom of conscience that
was itself linked to a broader idea of the church catholic. These
ideas found fertile fields later when not just the independent
Congregationalists but all Protestant groups in the new United
States were denied state union options. There was a sense in
which this new voluntarism among the churches in America produced a competitive element (when converts or adherents were
sought competitively against other Protestant groups), but more
often than not a broader understanding of the nature of the
church developed. And with that, the perception of denominationalism as a "healthy thing" occurred: understanding that denominationalism itself implied that each Protestant group was
only a *part* of a larger *whole* and therefore had no basis to conceive of itself as the "church of God on earth" in contrast to all
the others. The latter approach is sectarianism, not denominationalism. Hudson admirably puts it this way:

> Denominationalism is the opposite of sectarianism. The word "de-
> nomination" implies that the group referred to is but one member
> of a larger group, called or denominated by a particular name.
> The basic contention of the denominational theory of the church
> is that the true church is not to be identified in any exclusive sense
> with any particular ecclesiastical institution. The outward forms of
> worship and organization are at best but differing attempts to give
> visible expression to the life of the church in the life of the world.

No denomination claims to represent the whole church of Christ. No denomination claims that all other churches are false churches. No denomination claims that all members of society should be incorporated within its own membership. No denomination claims that the whole society and the state should submit to its ecclesiastical regulations. Yet all denominations recognize their responsibility for the whole of society and they expect to cooperate in freedom and mutual respect with other denominations in discharging that responsibility.[76]

I think we can conclude that denominationalism as it developed in the United States actually has produced a climate for a broader understanding of the church catholic than ever before. Certainly denominational groups at times were spawned on sectarian lines and sometimes maintained them for some time, but the more closed a group became, the farther it moved itself from a biblical conception of the church, and the greater potential it had for defining itself outside of the bounds of orthodoxy altogether.[77]

The denominational model of the church keeps any one denomination from becoming the dominant model of the visible church by keeping state enforcement out of the picture. In this way, mutual toleration must be forced to the foreground, and any competition among denominations must become friendly competition. The denominational model may be diagrammed as in figure 2.4 on page 77.

The nineteenth century. In the nineteenth century, at least up until the American Civil War, the denominational situation was quite different from what it is today. Without an Establishment clause, a number of the colonially established denominations lost members, while those most ready to adapt to the great potential of the Western Frontier (especially after 1803 when the Louisiana Purchase doubled the size of the country) multiplied rapidly. The largest three Protestant denominations by 1850 were the following: Methodists (1,324,000 members), Baptists (815,000 members), and Presbyterians (487,000 members). These were followed by the Congregationalists, Lutherans, Disciples of Christ, and Episcopalians. Quakers, Reformed, and other groups made up smaller numbers.[78]

Of more importance in the nineteenth century is the movement toward cooperative unity among all of the evangelical de-

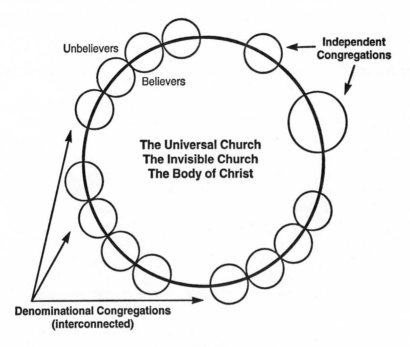

Figure 2.4.

The Denominational Model of the Church Catholic

nominations. Although several models of Christian unity were offered during the period,[79] the one that won out was that of voluntary societies of cooperation (the rough equivalent of modern "parachurch" organizations). Loetscher notes:

> Might it not be assumed that all who accepted the minimal doctrines essential to pietism were true Christians, already one in Christ's invisible church, and therefore quite competent, without further ecclesiastical definitions or restrictions, to cooperate in the much-needed Christian activities? Clearly this suggested a new and larger—and much looser—conception of what the Christian community really is. The challenge of such a program was that it made concrete in actual working organizations at least the shadow of Christian catholicity, which had been lost as a visible reality since the fragmentation of Anglo-Saxon Protestantism [following the Reformation].[80]

This certainly "fleshed out" a practical catholicity among Christians loyal to their individual denominations. But, unfortunately, this evangelical spirit connected itself with a rising nationalistic spirit in America and therefore sought to build an American Christian civilization. And, combined with the sectional and social conflicts leading up to the Civil War, many denominations underwent tragic divisions and separations.[81]

The twentieth century. The predominant changes of the twentieth century came with the influx of liberal theology in the mainstream denominational schools, seminaries, and pulpits. After the Civil War massive changes transformed American culture: rapid industrialization, increased immigration, and growing urbanization. With this transformation came overwhelming social problems. The rapid acceptance and proliferation of Darwin's theory of evolution within the scientific community, as well as the importation of German higher criticism of the Bible, brought deep changes within the historic evangelical empire and its representative denominational structures. Traditional categories of faith were emptied of their historic meaning, or redefined to fit in with a new "Modernist" Christianity.[82] To meet the needs of increased immigration, urbanization and the ensuing poverty, a "social gospel" of action began to supplant a more personal and doctrinal gospel of individual justification by faith.[83]

This rapid theological transformation was simply too much to bear for many who held to the historic evangelical faith. The result was what came to be known as the *fundamentalist* reaction. Citing the denial of a number of key elements of apostolic faith and the authority of Scripture, and seeing the irreformability of the denominations that espoused these modernistic ideas, the fundamentalist departure took place. Numerous new denominations and schools were spawned to train their own pastors to counter the great enemy of liberalism.[84]

The advent of fundamentalism was in some ways a reaffirmation of the great evangelical consensus of the nineteenth century. But, in other significant ways, it was different. The fundamentalist movement was, after all, a reactionary movement. It affirmed as fundamental many of the things that were denied or altered by the liberal Modernists. In reaction to the social gospel, it tended to avoid most forms of social involvement. But fundamentalism has had as its hallmark *separatism*, separatism from liberalism and from anyone tainted with the disease. But with separatism has come an increased tendency toward denominational and local church sectarianism in many ways. The trend toward catholicity is itself viewed with great suspicion, since it may mean that I must consider fellowship with others who do not have as complete a doctrinal purity as I have.

Thus, as a result, the twentieth century has seen the development of an alternative to fundamentalism: *neo-evangelicalism*.[85] Neo-evangelicalism is distinct from fundamentalism not in doctrine (there is a high degree of compatibility here), but in issues pertaining to separation. Neo-evangelicals tend to have a broader view of catholicity and Christian social involvement, one more in keeping with the denominational theory of the church practiced during the nineteenth century.[86]

This can be seen in the pivotal New York crusade of the Billy Graham Evangelistic Association in 1957, which divided the fundamentalist camp into two groups. Many fundamentalists bolted from supporting the crusade when Graham refused to require a doctrinal statement of the participating churches other than support of his Gospel preaching and even allowed liberals to cooperate. His consistent policy of toleration of differences in deference to the free proclamation of the Gospel has continued to alienate fundamentalists from Graham.[87] Indeed, to some, the difference between an evangelical and a fundamentalist is their attitude toward Billy Graham.[88]

Perhaps the most recent trend toward catholicity in the twentieth century evangelicalism has been the trend of evangelicals toward an appreciation of the more liturgical, historic churches. One result of this trend is the pivotal *Chicago Call*.[89] The Chicago Call was produced in May of 1977 by a group of forty-five evangelical leaders, summoning evangelicals (many of whom found their faith in connection with the free churches) to more historic forms of Christian life and practice. This is certainly one of the more far-reaching trends in American evangelicalism toward a broader understanding of the church catholic.

Another twentieth century development relating to church catholicity has occurred in connection with what is known as the ecumenical movement.[90] The ecumenical movement is typically dated from the Edinburgh Missionary Conference of 1910, which was the first multidenominational missionary conference that had a truly international makeup. The denominational structures

involved sensed the potential of greater unity—not only cooperative unity, but also the potential of organizational mergers. Several organizations sprung from this, which ultimately merged into
the *World Council of Churches* in 1948, which met at Amsterdam
with delegates representing 147 churches from 44 countries.[91] Another expression of cooperation (and occasional structural mergers) between denominations in the twentieth century includes, in
the United States, the formation of the *National Council of
Churches* (NCC) on November 29, 1950.[92] A third expression is
found in the *Consultation on Church Union* (COCU), which developed out of a proposal for a structurally united church "truly
catholic, truly evangelical, and truly reformed" and was inspired
by a sermon preached by Eugene Carson Blake at Grace Cathe-
dral in San Francisco on December 4, 1960. In 1962, representatives from four denominations gathered in Washington, D.C. The
movement has grown to nine denominations to date.[93] The focus
has been to represent African-American and Anglo-American
churches seeking to overcome racism, sexism, and nationalism
and to express a truly inclusive church.[94]

Accentuating the movement toward Ecumenical cooperation is
the momentous event of the Roman Catholic Council, *Vatican II*
in the early 1960s. In the documents produced by this Vatican
Council, a significant redefinition of the church was conceded by
Rome.[95] As a result, for the first time, Roman Catholics can
freely participate in ecumenical dialogue in head-to-head discussion, without demanding or expecting the organizational return
of other Christian groups to the fold of structural Roman Catholicism. Vatican II has become in many ways a fresh understanding
of the church for Rome. The sectarian appropriation of the title
Catholic has in many ways undergone a fresh modification that
calls for interaction.[96]

Among fundamentalists, similar trends toward ecumenical cooperation have occurred, although the focus on merger and/or
structural unity has been strongly avoided in favor of either a
federational model or more commonly a simple cooperative model, and with more specific, evangelical doctrinal statements. Par-
alleling these more inclusive groups, the fundamentalists formed
cooperative groups with similar goals and functions, but with
evangelical doctrines that included assertions on separation in
their doctrinal statements. So, on September 17, 1941, the *Ameri-*

can Council of Christian Churches (ACCC) was organized in New York City under the leadership of Carl McIntire. And, internationally, the *International Council of Christian Churches* (ICCC) was formed in Amsterdam, The Netherlands, in August of 1948.[97] This latter body split in 1970, and a new group is being formed to compete with it among fundamentalists, the *World Council of Biblical Churches.*

With similar goals, but with a greater emphasis on cooperation rather than separation, evangelicals have also formed their own cooperative groups. In May of 1943, the *National Association of Evangelicals* (NAE) was formed in Chicago, as a direct descendant of the Evangelical Alliance of 1867. In August, 1951, the *World Evangelical Fellowship* (WEF) came into existence in Woudschoten, Netherlands. This group was established by members of the former British-based *World's Evangelical Alliance* (founded 1846).[98]

In January of 1965, the editors of *Christianity Today* magazine summarized, in an issue devoted to assessing the strengths and weaknesses of the ecumenical movement, seven points that force evangelicals to consider issues of ecumenicity if they affirm in any way the catholicity of the church. These points are as follows:

1. The Church of Jesus Christ is both an actual reality in history and an invisible number of believers known only to God.

2. The existence of the one Church as churches, extended over time and space, is not per se a contradiction of the church's essential unity.

3. The Church is one in Jesus Christ, having one Lord, one faith, one baptism, and one hope. Deeply held differences have given rise to denominationalism. These differences have not destroyed the inner unity of Christians in Jesus Christ but have impaired the reflection of that unity in the visible churches.

4. By the fragmentary denominational reflection of their unity in Jesus Christ, by their rivalry on mission fields at home and abroad, by sometimes denying to others the liberty of conviction they claim for themselves, churches give imperfect witness to the Gospel and create obstacles to the fulfillment of the mission of the Church.

5. Churches whose existence derives only from sociological, racial, or cultural differences ought not to remain separate and divided. They should seek, wherever possible, union with other churches of like convictions.

6. Churches whose separate existence is grounded in basic theological differences of faith and order should not ignore these differences, but should seek to resolve them by looking toward a visible manifestation of true unity in Jesus Christ and by recognizing that certain of these differences of faith and order may be as much a part of Christian truth as is the truth concerning the unity of the church.

7. In the endeavor to achieve external, visible unity, any ecumenical effort that evades or ignores essential matters of faith and order will lead only to greater confusion and ultimate failure. Any unity not based upon the common theological affirmation of the faith once for all delivered will be an expression in history of something other than what the Church in Jesus Christ is divinely appointed to be.[99]

This evangelical expression outlines the crucial concerns well. The issue is not primarily unity, but unity in diversity that does not sacrifice a core of orthodoxy, and one that respects denominational diversity.

Certainly, the issues of the ecumenical movement among mainline denominations and among evangelicals have brought the issue of the catholicity of the church clearly to the forefront once again in the waning decade of the twentieth century. Ecumenical discussions force the issue of a core orthodoxy common to all Christians. And wherever the core orthodoxy of genuine faith exists, there is the church catholic. Visible organizational unity does not and cannot confirm or establish genuine catholicity. That comes only from embracing those of a genuinely orthodox faith despite their secondary diversities as brothers and sisters in Christ.

SUMMARY AND CONCLUSIONS
In the late second and early third centuries, the idea of catholicity as an all-inclusive faith, embracing a unity of all who believe everywhere despite their cultural and secondary diversities, came to shift into a notion of "truth" or "orthodoxy." The catholic church, instead of meaning the "complete" church thus came to

mean the "true" church as opposed to the heretics. This shift, tied in with the tendency to identify the church as a visible organization headed by leaders whose leadership is certified by direct succession to the apostles, resulted in a subtle sectarian shift in the idea of catholicity. Genuine believers who were otherwise orthodox were thus considered outside the church since they were separated from the visible "catholic" church, apart from which salvation was unavailable. The Novatianists and Donatists, who were stricter in church discipline but otherwise orthodox in doctrine, were considered "out" and lived a separate existence for many centuries. Because of their separate existence, they were considered "outside" the visible catholic church, although by sharing the same faith, they were actually *in* the church catholic, the body of Christ.

The shift away from genuine catholicity toward a "true church" concept connected with the visible, organizational understanding of the church is no more apparent than in the Great Schism of 1054, where Rome and the Eastern churches broke from each other, each claiming to be the only catholic church and labeling the other outside the catholic church.

The return to a more catholic understanding of the faith began to take shape in the West during the Medieval period, but actually came to full fruition during the Reformation. The church, for the Reformers, existed wherever the Gospel was preached, church discipline was exercised, and the sacraments administered. Institutional structures were secondary. Although this fresh idea was in fact a return to first and early second century usage, it unfortunately quickly fell prey to the territorial notion of the church and the growing nationalism within Europe. The result: the terrible wound on Protestantism inflicted by the Thirty-Years' War during the seventeenth century. A major step forward in understanding, however, was provided by the Puritan dissenters of the Westminster Assembly in England, who argued for a denominational understanding of the church which allowed for freedom of conscience in others as well as themselves. The church was made up of *all* who believed, but they must be allowed to follow conscience as they sought to obey Scripture.

The eighteenth century revivals in England and America enhanced the denominational theory of the church. And, with the political disestablishment of the church and state in America as a

result of the War of Independence, denominational independence and voluntarism enabled the church to flourish.

The nineteenth century carried this fresh vision of the evangelical empire in America forward. Denominations were understood as cooperative arms of the church catholic that enabled the
kingdom of God to move forward for social and spiritual progress
in America. It was only the social conflict of the Civil War that
brought sectional strife and denominational breakdown.

The twentieth century saw the collapse of the evangelical empire and a major rift in the denominations. Theological liberalism
and the social gospel had infiltrated the mainline denominations
in massive doses. These combined to form a more "modernistic"
approach to the faith in order to face new problems of immigration, industrialization, and poverty. But, with the denial of the
core orthodoxy of apostolic faith in the process, many of evangelical faith bolted to form new fundamentalist denominations
and structures. This sad, but necessary, reaction led to an impov-
erishment of evangelicalism of its nineteenth century social concern and led to a fearful, sectarian separation that lingers to this
day in many fundamentalist circles.

The ecumenical movement, as another twentieth century phenomenon, has produced a fresh desire for denominational cooperation, whether on an organizational model, a federational model, or a cooperational model. And, despite trends toward
reductionistic approaches to the core of orthodoxy, the idea of a
broader catholicity of the church has pushed many denominations to consider greater attempts toward visible unity. Those
ecumenical trends have tended, in the larger groups, to minimize
the doctrinal expectations of members and have been rather fluid
in their allowance of the very theological liberalism that led to
the fundamentalist split. Yet evangelicals and fundamentalists
have both developed parallel organizations with a stronger
ground in doctrinal unity.

But evangelicalism has, in the last half of the twentieth century, emerged again as a vital, genuine expression of the catholic
faith. With the Chicago Call, and with its desire for a more
carefully defined, genuine ecumenism, evangelicalism has shown
a fresh concern for the church as a whole once again. The denominational understanding of the church catholic, coupled with
a renewed evangelical faith, and a healthy ecumenism, can once

again capture the broad strokes of ancient catholic thinking about the church. Evangelical trends toward cooperation, in the face of modern ecumenicalism, signals again the broader view of the church as all those who believe rather than as primarily a structural organization.

Church history is important, because, for all Christians, it is *our* history. Despite the errors and follies throughout the centuries, it is *our* church. But it is one thing to think historically and conceptually about catholicity. It is another to begin to see what grounds there are for diversity in the church today. It has been argued that the spirit of catholicity is inclusive rather than exclusive, that it is rooted in those who share a common faith. The denominational theory of the church has been suggested as the most viable model from which to experience such catholicity (not as an opponent of appropriately grounded ecumenism, but as a preserver of matters of conscience) — through a necessary diversity in the church. So, a closer look at the denominational model of catholicity is required. And for that, we must turn to the next chapter.

Three

DENOMINATIONALISM AND CATHOLICITY

Denominationalism is the opposite of sectarianism.
—Winthrop Hudson

 A few years back an enterprising student in our graduate program developed a fascinating T-shirt to sell his fellow students. On the front of the shirt, beneath a small emblem of the school logo, he presented a long list of theological distinctions with check-mark boxes for the wearer to select to the left of each one:

☐ Dispensationalist
☐ Ultradispensationalist
☐ Calvinist
☐ 5 point
☐ 4 point
☐ 3 point

☐ Covenant Theologian
☐ Wesleyan Perfectionist
☐ Arminian
☐ Pentecostal (First Wave)
☐ Charismatic (Second Wave)
☐ Neo-charismatic (Third Wave)

On and on it went down the list. At the bottom of the list of some forty (overwhelming) options was the last, lonely item with a box to the left of it:

☐ Plain Ol' Christian.

I like that option. And perhaps you are like me. Sometimes we grow weary of the kinds of choices that we are forced to make theologically. Or worse, the kinds of pigeonholes people put us in when we make those choices. We just want to be a "plain ol' Christian" and be done with it. And sometimes our perceptions of denominationalism are that way: simply ways to pigeonhole ordinary Christians.

We are all guilty of the same tendency. When we see an extreme Pentecostal playing loose and free with the text of the Bible as she extols her experience, we tend to class all Pentecostals we meet with that stereotype. When we meet a dogmatic hyper-Calvinist who can speak of nothing but election, we tend to classify all Calvinists that way. When you meet and react to an exclusive, reclusive Plymouth Brethren and find out later I am from among the Brethren, you will tend to have suspicions about me. And that is one of the problems we must face with denominationalism. Denominationalism, as we have said, is historically a theory of the church catholic. But while it includes all genuine believers despite their doctrinal distinctions in secondary areas (all genuine "plain ol' Christians" will have differences on all forty choices on my T-shirt!), we must come to terms with this diversity and some of its practical implications. Yes, I am a "plain ol' Christian," but I tend to read my Bible at certain points differently (and with conviction!) from other "plain ol' Christians." And because of that, a fuller assessment of denominationalism is needed as a way of expressing the underlying unity I share with my brothers and sisters who read their Bibles a bit differently, and whose convictions I am unable to change. This approach to denominationalism is a fundamental attempt at expressing the unity and diversity necessary for the church to retrieve its spirit of catholicity.

DEFINING DENOMINATIONALISM

I would define a denomination as *a formal or informal association of Christian churches*[1] *that are related to each other by a heritage of commonly consented doctrinal distinctives.*[2] A denomination may be distinguished from the entire body of Christ in that a denomination does not presume to include all genuine believers, but only a segment of them (only a sect presumes to make up the entire body of Christ). Further, a denomination is distinguished from the local congregation in that it is a fellowship (as noted, formal or informal) between like-minded congregations that collectively adhere to what (to them) is a more faithful understanding of what it means to be a Christian community. As Donald Tinder points out in his fine discussion on the subject:

Although a true denomination never claims to be the only legitimate institutional expression of the church universal, it frequently
thinks itself to be the best expression, the most faithful to the
Scriptures and to the present activity of the Holy Spirit. Had it not
thought so, at least when beginning, why else would it have gone
through the trauma of separating from (or not joining with) an
older denomination? A true denomination does not, however,
make exclusive claims upon its members. It frees them to cooperate with Christians from other denominations in various specialized ministries.[3]

The key factor in terms of practically identifying denominational relationships is the easy reciprocal reception of persons
from other congregations on the basis of shared principles. This
yields a defining circle of denominational relationship.

Baptists serve as an example. All Baptists share common principles such as the autonomy of the local congregation, separation
of church and state, adult baptism by immersion, the sole authority of the Bible, and the need for individual conversion. But not
all Baptist groups have free flowing interchange of fellowship.
Some Baptists are strongly Arminian in their theology (such as
the *Free-Will Baptists); others* are strongly Calvinistic (such as the
Reformed Baptists). In terms of salvation and divine sovereignty,
these two groups are far away from each other. There may exist
among the Baptists even closer affinities, but matters of denominational polity and the place of the local church may keep them
in distinct circles, such as the *Conservative Baptist Association of
America* and the *Southern Baptist Convention*. Therefore, these
four separate Baptistic groups are separate denominations because they do not fellowship with one another automatically and
are sometimes, in fact, suspicious of one another. Although they
are united on some doctrine, other matters keep the separate
groups from being able to have open fellowship from congregation to congregation. They would therefore more appropriately
be referred to as a "denominational family," because the grouping is logical (they are all Baptist), and not social (they do not
have fellowship links).[4] So, as stated, a denomination is a formal
or informal association of churches that are related to each other
by a heritage of commonly consented doctrinal distinctives.

Denominationalism may be defined as that theory of the church
which acknowledges the validity of multiple denominations as
dimensions of a truly *catholic* church. As Goen well puts it:

At its best, denominationalism represents a family theory of the church; recognizing that no one group in its finite historical situation can be the whole church, they pursue their own best insights while remaining more or less in communion with other groups pursuing somewhat different understandings, all with as much honesty and humility as sinners can muster.[5]

A denominational theory of the church expects diversity and does not demand or expect (or even necessarily desire) organizational unity between the denominational expressions of the church. A denominational ecumenist, therefore, would never argue for anything more than a loose federation of congregations around a core of orthodoxy as a means of expressing cross-denominational unity. A denominational ecumenist would never argue for complete organizational uniformity under one structure, which would destroy or hinder diversity. And just as a spirit of catholicity spawned the denominational theory of the church, so denominationalism preserves for us today the spirit of catholicity. Robert Webber writes, in this regard:

The fact is that the differences between churches do matter. The question is not, "How can we overlook these differences?" but "How can we achieve a church which includes the many facets of truth?" In other words, how can we have unity without conformity, recognizing the manifold and diverse nature of the church, affirming it whole, both in its many expressions throughout history and its many expressions in culture now? This is true catholicity; it is not obtained by overlooking differences but by accepting them and understanding them as a vital part of the nature of the church.[6]

CRITIQUES OF DENOMINATIONALISM

Criticism of denominationalism is not uncommon. And there are some dangers inherent in denominationalism that we must be alert to. But there are primarily three groups who tend to criticize denominationalism most strongly: Ecumenists, Independents, and Restorationists. We must listen carefully to their concerns and respond at this point.

From ecumenists. Ecumenists are those who argue that the goal of the churches and denominations should be one visible, organizationally connected church.[7] They understand that when our Lord and Paul spoke of one church, they meant a visible organizational unity.[8] Therefore, to support denominationalism is to support division and schism in the church. Denominations are believed to be the greatest barrier to the goal of genuine ecumenical organization, and therefore they must ultimately be dismantled and realigned. Many American Protestants who support ecumenism are from theologically liberal camps,[9] although an increasing number of evangelicals are conceding the point and arguing for some modified form of ecumenism. Ecumenism essentially adopts the old argument of Roman Catholicism that the church's oneness must be visible and organizational and that denominationalism destroys that needed visible and organizational unity.[10]

One of the more recent critiques of denominationalism comes from the hand of an evangelical; one with whom I find myself in deep sympathy, at least in terms of his main purposes. A former minister of the *Orthodox Presbyterian Church* (OPC) who of late aligned himself with the *Presbyterian Church in America* (PCA), John Frame is associate professor of apologetics and systematic theology at Westminster Theological Seminary-West in Escondido, California. Frame's most helpful book is entitled *Evangelical Reunion: Denominations and the One Body of Christ.*[11]

Frame is a sympathetic and involved churchman who nonetheless believes that there is a " 'curse of denominationalism' that . . . defames our Lord and so often enfeebles our witness."[12] He lists three major biblical/theological problems with denominationalism, and then, in a chapter entitled "What's Really So Bad About Denominationalism?", he assembles fifteen practical problems he sees with it. Due to the importance of his criticisms to my argument in favor of the historic denominational theory of the church as a means for recapturing catholicity, I will list and respond to his central arguments here.[13]

The primary arguments, from a theological/biblical base, are these: (1) Christ founded one church and commanded us to preserve its unity. Denominations have no role to play in biblical church government, but are instead destructive to that government. (2) The denominational division of the church has always been the result of sin.[14] The people involved should have solved their problem by biblical reconciliation, not by denominational division. And (3) denominationalism has imposed on us the bur-

den of subjecting ourselves and our congregations to human organizations that cannot claim in full the promises and the gifts of
God.[15]

Before interacting with these arguments in detail, I want to
acknowledge my sympathy with the same desires as Frame, that
is, an expression of faith that is not marred or inhibited by denominational barriers. I would simply differ from him in seeing
denominationalism per se, as the core problem.

Frame's first core issue is his claim that our Lord established
one church and commanded us to preserve its unity. Further,
that denominations have no role to play in biblical church governments, but are destructive to that government. As we observed in chapter 1, yes, Jesus did establish one church. And yes,
He did command us to preserve its unity (at least He commanded so through Paul). But as was pointed out, the unity is not
necessarily to be understood as an organizational unity but rather
a *relational* unity of love. The unity is a unity in diversity which
requires the constant understanding of tolerance and acceptance.

The church is understood in the New Testament as a gathered
community (whether in the context of home or locality), but the
universal church, the entire body of Christ did not *gather*. The
only linkage between the churches were the apostolic missionaries, with a slight priority given to the mother church at Jerusalem. But failing an episcopal succession of some sort (which
Frame, like me, finds hard to support on biblical grounds), we
cannot posit the divine *intention* of an *ongoing* sort of government
over the *whole church*. [16] The need for that, based on a desire for
structural unity, yielded a uniform government in the subsequent
few centuries; but to argue that Jesus requires of us some sort of
structural unity I find clearly wanting in the New Testament.

In addition, Frame asserts that denominational structures find
no parallel in the New Testament, with only local, regional, and
universal applications for the word church. But I would demur
once again. First, this is an argument from silence at best. It is to
argue that one is restricted to church forms and structures which
are only ambiguously described in the New Testament and may
well have occurred in a multiplicity of forms before standardiza-
tion in the second and third centuries.[17] Since denominational
structures are not found in the New Testament understanding of
the church, they are wrong. I would argue that the universal

church cannot be captured by any sort of organizational structures,[18] but that does not mean that larger organizational structures are wrong. Frame himself wants there to be some sort of transdenominational structures, but does he really have biblical warrant for that?

On the contrary, I would see the denominational structure as a microcosm of the universal church just as the house church (what we call the "local" church) is the microcosm of the city congregation. It is an association of local (house) churches sharing an interpretive tradition. That, after all, is what the united church of the first few centuries was. It was only after the interpretive and non-interpretive traditions began to diverge so significantly from apostolic warrant in Scripture that structural diversity (denominationalism) broke loose at various points, even prior to the Reformation.

Frame's second core issue is that denominational division of the church has always been the result of sin in one or both sides of a division. Therefore, the formation of a new denomination is, ipso facto, wrong. God does not condone sin; therefore, anything that is the result of sin (like denominationalism) is wrong. I must disagree here. Certainly God does not condone sin. Nobody contests that. But all human endeavor, even the most noble, is tainted by human sin. Does that not make all human endeavor wrong? Certainly Oscar Cullmann is correct at this point:

> In all salvation history, a distinction is to be made between human contingency and continuity with the economy of salvation revealed in the Bible. Salvation history thus includes non-salvation history, which, as a result of human sin, always resists the flow of the divine plan, but is still not able to destroy the continuity of the divine activity. Thus human jealousy, greed for power, and contentiousness are a constant threat to the divinely willed unity in diversity. A false ecumenism which seeks merger confuses these two streams. It considers the historical origin of the different confessions [denominations] and the resulting variety as such to be resistance to God, as merely an example of human bungling.[19]

Paul and Barnabas had a falling out after the Jerusalem Council in Acts 15, before the second missionary journey, at which Paul took the hard line against John Mark. Does that nullify the divine blessing of that second journey? Or of the rest of Paul's ministry? Or does it mean a loss of blessing only on Barnabas' journey to Crete with John Mark? Such thinking is wrong. Certainly it does not condone sin and minimize human responsibility to get reconciliation with those with whom one is in conflict. But God does further His purposes in the face of human errors and gross sins. And just as God used persecution in Acts 8 to get the church on about the business of the Great Commission (a sin on the part of the persecutors), so God can use human conflict and sin to diversify and spread abroad His church. I am not saying here, again, that this is the ideal. However, the presence of sin in the history of certain aspects of the church (and some forms of denominationalism fit that description) does not mean that element is necessarily wrong.

Further, I would have to suggest that to say that sin is at the root of *all* denominationalism is a rather strong overstatement. It does not take adequately into account the need for godly humans to follow their consciences before God when they differ from one another (the central argument of the Westminster dissenters). A denomination can easily be formed as a result of an autonomous independent Bible church, for example, beginning a new church plant. If the two follow similar patterns and share similar values and doctrinal distinctives, and retain receptive relations, a new denomination has begun. But in what sense do we have sin (or at least sin to blame)? The group was begun on the grounds of any number of things: geographical convenience for some members, evangelistic potential for others. But is this sin? I think not.[20]

From independents. Further, beyond those with ecumenical concerns, some who speak for a strong independent local church argue against denominations as well, but for different reasons. To these spokesmen, denominations hinder the free establishment of independent, autonomous megachurches. Elmer Towns, for example, in his work *Is the Day of the Denomination Dead?*, argues for the primacy of the local church and the illegitimacy of denominational structures.[21] He states, for example, that

> we conclude denominations are not the perfect will of God. He could never plan a church to express false teaching [which denominationalism must tolerate]. Therefore, denominations exist within the permissive will of God. He condescends to use the frail creations of religious organizations.[22]

And again:

> But the nagging question remains unanswered: Did God originally
> plan a splintered gospel outreach? This manuscript maintains that
> the local church sits at the center of God's purpose and plan. God
> has a perfect will. But He also has a permissive will, which is the
> source of God's blessing upon denominations. . . . The denomina-
> tions have splintered the work of God, have allowed the liberals to
> rape local churches, have introduced insipid bureaucracy into the
> cause of Christ and have estranged the love of Christians for Jesus
> Christ.[23]

This position argues that for the local church to reach its maxi-
mum potential, denominationalism must be abandoned, since it
serves no purpose but to hinder such aims. Denominations do
nothing but attempt to control the work of God from the outside.

But again, I would see here a confusion of denominationalism
as a theory of the church, and *sectarianism* that can appear in the
context of denominationalism. Further, the danger with Towns'
strong emphasis on the local congregation and the megachurch is
that the breadth of the church catholic may be lost completely
and sectarianism may reappear under the guise of "my church is
better (bigger, more effective, more fundamental) than your
church," rather than "my denomination is better than your denomination." These are twin expressions of the same problem.
But denominationalism is not the culprit. Sectarianism is the
culprit.

Furthermore, the difficulties served by denominationalism
pointed out by Towns in his book are often the result of bureaucratic interference by strong denominational structures into the
work of the local pastor. But that is not a problem of denominationalism per se, but only the problem of certain "tight" organizational structures of some denominations. It also could be the
expression of "Lone-Ranger" types of independent pastors who
do not wish to respond to any form of authority, be it legitimate
or not.

From restorationists. Restorationist type movements follow
the more theological model of the ecumenists on the defacing of
the one church through denominationalism, but they offer a different solution: abandoning the denominations and gathering

simply on original biblical bases, as "Christians" or "disciples" or "brethren" on strict biblical terms. The church is to be understood as those who gather to Christ alone and avoid traditional entrapments.

In England and Ireland, the strong sectarian nature of denominationalism during the early nineteenth century spawned my own (Plymouth) Brethren Movement, which "received all whom Christ received" around the Lord's Table, gathering there simply "to the name of the Lord Jesus Christ." True unity was to be found in abandoning, or "coming out" of the denominations and meeting simply as "Christians" or "Brethren" in the name of the Lord. Claiming no creed but the Bible, and desiring to perpetuate nothing but what they found there, they attracted hundreds and thousands of believers away from denominational labels to their form of Christian simplicity and unity.[24]

Similarly, in America, a parallel American Restoration Movement began with Barton Stone and Thomas and Alexander Campbell. Strong in their desire for Christian unity and critical of denominational pride and separatism, they abandoned denominational connections and united their two separate (Baptistic and Presbyterian) groups around the name Christians or Disciples. Like the Brethren in England, the Stone-Campbellite Movement claimed no creed but the Bible, remembered the Lord weekly, and attracted great numbers of believers away from denominationalism to their form of Christian simplicity.

Certainly the greatest problem here is that any group of related churches which find part of their reason for being a unity in the *opposition* to denominationalism have already *defined* themselves denominationally. An undenominational group has never survived, by definition, as a "non-denomination." As church historian Martin Marty put it so well:

> Stick around: a little longer look makes clear that there is no real, permanent, widespread "undenominational" group religion in America. Set yourself up against denominations, as parachurch, community church, or megachurch, and before long, *willy nilly,* you start acting like a denomination, looking like one, and being called one. Yes, and being one.[25]

One cannot, by definition, oppose denominationalism without becoming one. Those who are attracted to an anti-denominational status ultimately unite in their opposition. This requires mutual support and relationship, the earmarks of denominational relations. Toulouse points out how this shift took place within the Stone-Campbellite Movement in particular:

> By the time Disciples reached 165 years of age, they had gone through significant changes in their understanding of their own self-identity. In their infancy (1804-1830), they had seen themselves as a reforming movement within other denominations. Later, as they went through the toddler, adolescent, and teen years (1830-1875), they continued their call for the denominations to abandon denominational identifications while, at the same time, they recognized the need for increasing structure and cooperative endeavors among their own congregations. In their young adult years (1875-1919), they began to break out of their traditional isolationism in order to cooperate with other denominations in areas of social work and foreign missions, willing even to divide foreign areas of the work with those groups who baptized infants. During this period, they took on forms of denominationalism while many continued to insist their congregations did not constitute a denomination. The movement became known as "the Brotherhood." The name signaled Disciples' belief that the fellowship of the church represented God's intention for the human family. But the name also provided a denominational handle or reference for members without alluding to definite denominational status. . . . The effort known as "Restructure," accomplished by Disciples during the 1960s, finally brought Disciples to a maturity in church life comparable, perhaps to the maturity that is supposed to accompany senior adulthood [that is, they acknowledged at long last their denominational status.][26]

As noted earlier, the core problem with the entire issue is a failure to understand that the danger to catholicity is fundamentally *sectarianism* and not *denominationalism*. A return to a historic balance of denominationalism is the only means to counteract that and to regain a truly nonsectarian church catholic. But let me first clarify that issue by a review of the historic development of denominational theory of the church.

THE HISTORICAL PHILOSOPHY OF CATHOLICITY BEHIND DENOMINATIONALISM

For those who argue against denominationalism, the nature of historic denominational theory is all too often misunderstood. As noted earlier, church historian Winthrop Hudson identifies the source of denominational theory of church catholicity with the Dissenting Puritans who participated in the Westminster Assembly in England (1642–49).[27] The case for a denominational approach to catholicity they developed is based on six important factors:

1. Differences of opinion about the implications of the Christian faith for the outward life of the church are inevitable due to the weaknesses of human apprehension of the truth.[28]

The Fall of man and the noetic (mental) effects of sin mean that varieties of interpretive tradition are inevitable. We simply are not, nor can we become, infallible interpreters of the Word of God. This especially applies to areas which are less clear than others in Scripture, such as church polity. A chief spokesman among these Dissenting Brethren was Jeremiah Burroughes, who wrote, "If we consider things wisely, we have no cause to wonder that godly men in this their estate of imperfection should differ so much one from another as they do."[29] Further, he comments as follows:

> Every godly man prizes and seeks after knowledge. Others mind little but their own profit and pleasure. They trouble not themselves about knowing the things of God, except ambition puts them upon it. They care not which way truths go. But the godly man prizes every truth at a high rate, worth contending for to the uttermost. In the dark, all colors be alike; but in the light, they appear diverse.... When men discuss things and desire to see farther in them, it is impossible, considering the weakness of the best and the variety of men's apprehensions, but there must needs to be much difference in men's judgments. And then, considering [that] their consciences are engaged in it, that everything they apprehend to be a truth (at least thus far) that they must not deny it for a world, this puts men's spirits at a distance although both be godly, both love the truth equally.[30]

Clarence Goen thoughtfully comments about this Puritan notion (particularly as worked out later by Roger Williams) in these words:

> Because all people are sinners, and because vestiges of corruption remain even among the purest of the regenerate, every person's grasp of truth is limited, partial, even distorted and corrupted. It therefore little behooves any person to try to define other peoples'

religion for them; and if the definition is enforced by the power of the state—as is the case with an established church—only evil can result. As dissenters argued persuasively, coercion in religion can make martyrs or it can make hypocrites; it cannot make true Christians.[31]

2. Even though differences of opinion exist among Christians, they are not matters of indifference, but matters of conscience.[32]
Because of the desire to faithfully interpret Scripture in all matters and at all times, sincerely held and supported interpretive models must not be downplayed, because they become matters of personal obedience to conscience before God. To call another's doctrinal distinctives "matters of indifference" fails to take into account the latter's serious attempt to understand and appropriate the Scriptures in sincere obedience to God. Burroughes brings out this point as well:

> Godly men are free men. Christ made them so, and requires them not to suffer themselves to be brought under bondage. They must not, cannot submit their consciences to the opinions, determinations, decrees of any men living. They cannot submit to any as lords over their faith. This others can do. As for points of religion, say some, let the learned men judge of them; we will not be wiser than they; we will submit and others must submit to what they shall determine. This makes quick work of divisions, but this those who fear God cannot do. They must see everything they own as a truth with their own light . . . received from Jesus Christ.[33]

Certainly this must be the case. Consider the scenario of an ecumenist who would enjoy seeing denominational barriers removed. Would a Baptist, for example, really give up his understanding of the autonomy of the local church, or of a believer's church? Or would the (Plymouth) Brethren give up that which is most precious and dear to them, the weekly Breaking of Bread? Can you envision a Roman Catholic, an Orthodox, or an Anglican believer giving up his belief in episcopal succession? Or a Presbyterian giving up on divine sovereignty or election? Or how about a Pentecostal her belief in speaking in tongues? Each group (or at least the serious believers in each group) holds their peculiar distinctives as matters of conscience. They are not simply matters of indifference. One cannot simply assert that these things are negotiable.

3. Differences of opinion that are honestly held can lead to profitable and fruitful discussion out of which a fuller apprehension of the truth may emerge.[34]

Matters of conviction in interpretation must be held open to discussion with others who have alternate matters of conviction. Otherwise, parochialism develops. Sectarianism attempts to persuade me that the others are entirely wrong and I am entirely right; or worse, I and mine alone constitute the true church since we have more of the truth. A healthy denominationalism means that I must discuss with my fellow pilgrims from other denominations issues we disagree on, without ridicule and with full respect to them as brothers and sisters. Burroughes again states, through a few illustrations, this point:

> God hath a hand in these divisions to bring forth future light. Sparks are beaten out by the flints striking together. Many sparks of light, many truths, are beaten out by the beatings of men's spirits one against another. If light be let into a house, there must be some trouble to beat down [a place in the wall for] a window. A child thinks the house is beating down, but the father knows the light will be worth the cost and trouble. If you will have the cloth woven, the woof and the warp must be cast cross one to another. If you will have truths argued out, you must be content to bear with some opposition for the time. They who are not willing to bear some trouble, to be at some cost to find out truth, are unworthy of it. . . . We may well behold men's weakness in these divisions, but [we may] better admire God's strength and wisdom in ordering them to his glory and his children's good.[35]

4. Since no church has a final and unambiguous grasp of divine truth, the true church of Jesus Christ can never be fully represented by any single ecclesiastical structure.[36]

Matters of conscientious interpretation of Scripture will always yield differences in polity. It is wrong, therefore, to impose one form of polity upon all. Any changes of conviction must come voluntarily as a result of genuine interaction with alternate convictions. This is in fact to perceive catholicity as embracing them all. As another Westminster Dissenter, Henry Burton, stated it, "The Catholic Church . . . includes all true churches throughout the world."[37]

5. There are godly people on all sides of Christian divisions.[38]

In the heat of debate, it is all too easy to forget that godly

Christians can and will differ in matters of interpretation. That makes them no less godly. Burroughes states once more:

> Godly people are divided in their opinions and ways [but] they are united in Christ. Though our differences are sad enough, yet they come not up to this: to make us men of different religions. We agree in the same end, though not in the same means. They are but different ways of opposing the common enemy. The agreeing in the same means, in the same way of opposing the common enemy, would be very comfortable. It would be our strength. But it cannot be expected in this world. . . . [O]ur divisions have been and still are between good men; there are as many godly Presbyterians as Independents.[39]

And again:

> Though we are fully persuaded by God's Word and Spirit that this our Way is Christ's Way, yet we neither do nor dare judge others to be reprobates that walk not with us in it, but leave all judgment to God, and heartily pray for them.[40]

6. The mere fact of separation of the various Christian bodies from one another on the ground of conscience toward God does not constitute schism.[41]

Schism is a willful resistance to, and breaking from, legitimate authority. Excusing oneself from the rule of ecclesiastical authority on the grounds of obeying a higher authority when the ecclesiastical authority is understood to be erring doctrinally (following God as understood by conscience from Scripture) is not schism. Burroughes again writes how this connects with the very issue of catholicity:

> When men, who give good testimony of their godliness and peaceableness, . . . cannot without sin to them (though it be through weakness) enjoy all the ordinances of Christ and partake in all the duties of worship as members of that congregation where their dwelling is, they therefore in all humility and weakness . . . join in another congregation, yet . . . not condemning those churches they join not with as false but still preserve all Christian communion with the Saints as members of the same body of Christ, of the Church Catholic, and join also with them in all duties of worship that belong to particular churches so far as they are able — if this be called schism, it is more than yet I have learned.[42]

101

Further Factors to Consider in the Denominational View of Catholicity

In addition to the classic arguments raised by the Westminster Dissenters, there are further reasons to consider the validity of a denominational model of the church catholic. These further arguments include: (1) the inevitability of denominations; (2) the protective element of a denominational model; (3) the equalizing force of denominationalism; (4) the adaptability/changeability of denominationalism; and (5) the mediatorial function of denominationalism.

Denominations are inevitable. Those who would downplay the place of denominations must face up to the sober truth that denominations will occur inevitably. From the largest megachurch to the smallest autonomous congregation, a denomination will occur once that group develops enough of a sense of mission to support a church plant and to retain reciprocal fellowship with the daughter church. As noted earlier, uniting around a "nondenominational" platform does not preclude a group from becoming a denomination. It merely creates one. And one, at that, that could have dangerous sectarian leanings.

I believe this impetus for associations and fellowships of churches arises from the catholic spirit implicit in the saints to embrace "all those who in every place call on the name of our Lord Jesus Christ" (1 Cor. 1:2, NRSV). We cannot expect our local congregation, as important as it is for our Christian nurture, to be coterminous with our understanding of the church. Evil is too prevalent in our culture, the enemy too powerful. We instinctively reach out to link our hands and prayers with others who know our Lord. And the hands we reach out for most readily are the hands we know the closest, family members.

Further, denominations are simply groupings of groups of Christians. As such, they take on sociological dimensions.[43] Christians who gather in groups, just as all other human beings who do so, must organize. Just as the local church must become more organized the larger it becomes, so groupings of churches must become organized, the more churches they include. Institutionalization and bureaucratization (when the institution becomes more important than the people who make it up) are dangers in both situations, but effective and people-caring organization is inevitable, and even desirable, as groups grow.

Denominationalism can protect from sectarianism and cultic tendencies. Any denomination (if it does not correctly understand and balance the nature of its own traditions) runs the risk of reactionary groups pulling it away from its trend toward a fuller catholicity and urging a withdrawal into sectarianism: an overemphasis on the "biblical" nature of their distinctives at the cost of the commonness with others in the body of Christ. In fact, some denominations begin and sustain themselves on the basis of their claim to a fuller apprehension of truth than any other Christian group.

In part, this is inevitable in Protestant groups which assert *sola Scriptura* and the right of private judgment. Once an interpretation is legitimately arrived at, it must be conscientiously followed. And, unless that group can effectively distinguish between levels of tradition, it becomes a sect. Beyond that, it runs the risk of becoming a quasi-Christian cult that promotes heresy at the local level. Beginning with a core of orthodoxy and attributing an equally binding orthodoxy to its own traditions, the group becomes a sect. It alone has the entire truth. But all too often, this broader definition of orthodoxy involves the group so much in its own unique characteristics that, with time, the core of orthodoxy does not matter so much any more. The core elements are too "common." They no longer "distinguish" or justify the group's existence. In fact, such a group believes itself to have a better perception of even those common areas, and the entire historic church is judged to be wrong. Trinitarianism (as in the Jehovah's Witnesses) or monotheism (as in Mormonism) disappear, yet the claim to be fully Christian remains. That is how heresy slips in unawares, and how sects become quasi-Christian cults.

The danger of sectarianism and its tendency toward heresy may be illustrated in figure 3.1, on page 104.

As noted above, the problem lies with the tendency to see one's own group as the sole claimant to orthodoxy and thus the only proper claimant to the title of "the church," in opposition to all others. A narrowly defined orthodoxy, which includes areas outside of the reach of other groups (and which thus excludes them), all too easily allows one to redefine areas shared with them (core orthodoxy) and thus to slip into heresy. In this sense, an appropriate appreciation of the place of denominationalism can keep one within genuine catholicity and away from sectarianism and its trend toward heresy.[44]

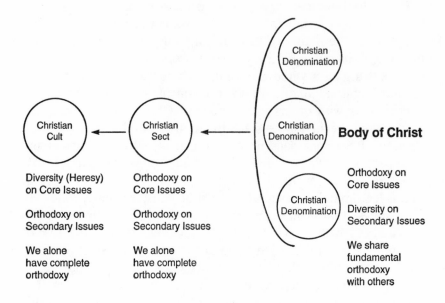

Christian Cult

Christian Sect

Christian Denomination

Christian Denomination **Body of Christ**

Christian Denomination

Christian Denomination

Diversity (Heresy) on Core Issues

Orthodoxy on Secondary Issues

We alone have complete orthodoxy

Orthodoxy on Core Issues

Orthodoxy on Secondary Issues

We alone have complete orthodoxy

Orthodoxy on Core Issues

Diversity on Secondary Issues

We share fundamental orthodoxy with others

Figure 3.1.
The Dangers of Losing the Catholicity
of Denominationalism

It is far better to retain a denominational model of the church catholic where a group carefully defines the core of orthodoxy and identifies its own traditions as valuable but secondary. Pannenberg states the following in this regard:

> The mutual relationship of the various regional or denominational traditions within the one Christian world should be thought of in terms of that type of multiplicity of concrete forms in which the catholic fullness of the church comes to expression. The multiplicity of such traditions in church order, doctrine, and liturgy does not exclude catholicity as long as each of them holds itself open, beyond its own distinctive features, for the Christian rights of the others and feels a responsibility, not just for its own tradition, but for the whole of Christian history and its heritage.[45]

In this way a group may retain its core of orthodoxy and take its place among other denominations in the great, universal body of Christ.

Denominationalism as a theory for the church catholic equalizes all groups. There is always an inherent potential for larger or more ancient Christian groups to feel a stronger sense of legitimacy for themselves than for smaller or more historically recent groups. This attitude, of course, is offensive to Christians who take conscientious exception to certain elements within those expressions of Christianity.

A denominational theory of the church treats all Christian groupings, even the most ancient or the largest, on an equal footing. They are all but parts (denominations) of the entire catholic church. They have no greater, nor any lesser claim to be called "church" than any other grouping of genuine Christians. Nor should they expect other Christian groupings to come and merge or be subsumed by them. Understanding this can lead to a fundamental paradigm shift in our thinking toward a broader catholicity.

Denominationalism is changeable and adaptable. Any denomination will change with the passage of time. Sometimes the factors that led to the formation of a given denomination will change, leading to a merger with the original parenting body. Sometimes further reflection will lead members of a given denomination to recognize that some of their distinctives (microtraditions) are not justifiable from the standpoint of a more rigorous hermeneutic. Sometimes a parent denomination will change, through the importation of too liberal or too conservative a theology and a fresh denomination will start. And this is not necessarily bad.

Sometimes a denomination refuses to change. It digs its heels in and doggedly claims that its distinctives, in all their glory, fully, solely, and more accurately reflect the true teaching of the New Testament. Such a group has either pointed itself in the direction of sectarianism, or will ultimately find itself devoid of younger, more educated types who want hermeneutical justification for given beliefs and practices.

But as a whole, the church, when understood as an aggregate of denominational expressions, will grow and change with time. Just as many denominational expressions which existed in the eighteenth or nineteenth centuries are no longer around, and many new ones have begun since, so (short of the Second Coming), one and two hundred years hence the overall configuration of the church, in its denominationally catholic sense, will be substantially different than it is now. The denominational theory of the church expects such change to occur and understands that as a positive development. It is an expression of the church's life and vitality. Single expressions of the church too quickly lose this, just as the old Catholic Church became locked into an historic cultural expression that froze its diversification. The Spirit of God is alive and working in this diversification just as He is in distributing spiritual gifts among the members. It is a good thing.

Denominationalism has a mediatorial function. The denomination preserves and passes on a distinct interpretive understanding of Scripture in its own characteristic doctrines and practices, known as distinctives. These distinctives, as will be pointed out in the next chapter, are really interpretive *traditions,* since they are not the core of orthodoxy that is shared by all denominations, but are rather elements that distinguish a group or denomination from all the others. This is not all bad, so long as we recognize that such traditions do not have the same binding authority that Scripture possesses. In fact, tradition serves as a kind of mediatorial function by which the truth of Scripture is communicated to people. Thomas Finger puts it this way:

> In speaking of revelation as historical and personal, if we overlook the function of tradition, then our understanding of revelation will be quite incomplete. We might well leave the impression that the Spirit simply picks up the written Word from the first century and drops it, unmediated, into our own. . . Tradition may well distort God's revelation in certain ways. Yet . . . we finite humans always begin to perceive revelation through the particular lens or angle of vision that tradition provides . . . Essential as it is to revelation's dynamics, tradition nonetheless adds no content to revelation's propositional truth.[46]

Dunning affirms this basic idea and identifies the value of the diversity of traditions that denominationalism represents:

> Within the basic Protestant commitment to the sola scriptura principle, where it is recognized that no tradition has an ultimately normative authority, the diversity of tradition does not necessarily need to lead to the abandonment of a self-conscious appeal to

one's own tradition. Within certain limitations, it is doubtless the case that each tradition witnesses to some important aspect of the biblical message, and all together witness to the inexhaustible riches of its truth.[47]

And Clark Pinnock is right when he observes:

Protestant as well as Catholic beliefs are ecclesiastically shaped. It makes me tend to suppose that in my theology I go directly and immediately back to the Bible, unaware of the fact that I read the Word in the context of a Christian community through which the message has been transmitted to me.[48]

Denominational tradition thus has a certain interpretive, transmissional value to it. It provides us with a distinctive lens through which the message of the Bible can meet us. That lens is not always clear, and sometimes it is colored inappropriately, but it does help us to see what we may not otherwise see. The only danger comes when we conclude that there is no lens, or that only our lenses are the correct ones. What we look at through them is the same, and without the lenses it would be very difficult to see in some ways what is there. And so, denominational tradition serves as a sort of mediatorial function for us in our understanding of Scripture.[49]

THE RISKS OF DENOMINATIONALISM

The denominational theory of the church has inherent risks in it, which are often pointed out as those things which are wrong about denominationalism.[50] It is, most importantly, a theory of *balance*. Each denomination must sustain catholicity in the middle of two extremes: If it *compromises* its core of orthodoxy in favor of more liberty, it slips into the left extreme of theological liberalism. If it *extends* its core of orthodoxy too wide in its attempt to submit to biblical authority and justify its distinctives, it slips into the right extreme of sectarianism. Balance is critical. A safe, denominational catholicity is the central point to which we must constantly return. This balance may be illustrated as shown in figure 3.2 on page 108.

A healthy denominationalism strikes a balance that takes great effort to maintain over the years. A cry for catholicity without orthodoxy leads to the latitudinarianism of liberal pluralism; a

Catholicity		
Growing Rigidity		*Growing Laxity*
Sectarianism ◄───	*Denominationalism* ───►	**Latitudinarianism**
Authority only	Authority and liberty	Liberty only
Everything matters doctrinally	Some things matter doctrinally	Nothing matters doctrinally
Enlarged core of orthodoxy	Historic core of orthodoxy	Diminished core of orthodoxy
Narrow ground of fellowship	Broad ground of fellowship	No ground of fellowship
Tradition ignored and confused	Tradition recognized and used	Tradition disregarded

Figure 3.2.
The Balance of Denominational Catholicity

cry for orthodoxy without catholicity leads to sectarianism. Of the two fundamental issues to be concerned with for Christians, love (relationship) and truth (core doctrine),[51] it is concern for love that protects catholicity from slipping into sectarianism; it is the concern for truth that keeps it from slipping into latitudinarianism. And there are many temptations to fall off balance in either direction. Denominational catholicity maintains concern for both issues.

So, in this important area of balance, there are important risks to watch out for. In the following pages, I hope to guide you through some of the risks.

The risk of substituting the denomination for the universal church. There are denominational structures which are more or less imposing on the churches which they serve. There are loose denominational structures, such as "associations" of Baptist churches (*The Conservative Baptist Association of America* being an example) or groups of Christian churches that have no parachurch service organizations at all, but simply have free-flowing congregational reception and uniform practices (such as the *Bible Fellowship Churches* spawned by Gene Getz and associates). The local congregation is the focus of this type of denomination. Beyond that there is little or no structure, but only informal relations between congregations.

On the other extreme, there are tight denominational structures, in which strong centralized organizational systems set standards and requirements for the individual congregation. That is, the local congregation simply becomes one of the many parts of the larger organization. This latter type of denominational structure (and, by the way, there are many types between these two extremes of denominational styles) tends to take on some of the centralizing characteristics of the ancient Catholic Church which, as we have seen, tended to inhibit a truly catholic understanding of the church (when combined with its clerical sacerdotalism).

This being the case, the danger here is for a congregation to look at itself more as a part of a whole organization (the denomination) rather than a part of a broader organism (the catholic church, of which the denomination is a part). This is intensified by the tendencies for denominations to use the term *Church* for their collection of congregations, rather than *churches*. So, for example, we have the Reformed *Church* in America; the Lutheran *Church*—Missouri Synod. Instead, these would more appropriately be called simply "Churches."[52] Each denomination is simply a collection (larger or smaller) of like-minded churches.

The risk of violation of conscience. Another risk of denominationalism is minimizing the content of "core orthodoxy" so much that there is nothing left of distinctive Christian teaching, either in its attempt to merge with others and grow larger, or to "modernize" through its control of theological training centers. The temptation is ever present within larger bureaucracies to lose sight of apostolicity as the core unitive orthodoxy that bound all diversity among Christians together. Reductionism of the Christian message to less than the minimum is the ever-present danger on the left, nurtured by denominational authority structures.

This, in fact, is what led to the fundamentalist exodus from the mainline American denominations in the first several decades of this century. The controlling centers of tight denominations adopted liberal theology from the "top," and those who saw the results of their influence, and the impossibility of turning it back around from within, felt compelled by conscience to leave.[53] Hudson again notes the following, in this regard:

The great temptation [of denominational approaches to catholicity] was to transform the denominational theory from a means of expressing unity into a means of securing unity—to seek to enlist all men of good will under the banner of righteousness by a progressive narrowing of the central core of the Christian faith until little remained that was theologically incisive or distinctively Christian. Thus it was a precarious balance that American Protestants were called upon to maintain with their concept of denominationalism.[54]

Sometimes this reductionism takes place in the attempt to minimize the real differences with other Christians, or with others who claim Christian faith but have themselves compromised on important matters in the process during merger or ecumenical discussions. Or, it may simply be that the authority structures of the denomination have become so institutionalized that the leadership elements in the denomination themselves no longer support a core of orthodoxy personally.

The risk of obscuring the visible city-church. As noted in chapter 1, the New Testament church was understood in three ways: (1) in its most intimate sense, as the house church in which a relatively small "family" of believers met weekly for Christian nurture; (2) the "city-church," made up of all the house churches at various locations within a city and its suburbs, which met together less frequently and only when a facility was available; and (3) the aggregate of all believers everywhere, which for practical reasons never met together.

Denominations, as noted, do not fit this model well, but serve instead as a sort of organizational or social subclass of the third element, the universal church. But the expansion of denominations into new locations is due to one of several factors: (1) there is no church in that area; (2) there is no evangelical church in that area; or (3) there is no church of my type (denomination) in that area.[55] The first ground for expansion is certainly viable, particularly if the fellowship of churches (denomination) is indeed evangelistic in its outlook. The second is viable on the understanding that any existing churches may have clearly compromised the Gospel or its witness through extensive theological liberalism, or if there is no church that understands the core orthodoxy of the Gospel; but the third type of ground for expansion is less understandable.

Certainly it could be argued that if a city or area has one or more evangelical gatherings of believers, it does not need a new "franchise" to move in to compete with it.[56] Unless, of course, there is much work to do and the incoming denomination sees itself cooperating with the existing elements of the city-church. But, unfortunately, new denominations starting up in a given city are not always begun altruistically. They are sometimes begun simply because of convenience (members of one denomination do not wish to travel so far as the next town to meet with those of like mind), an attitude of superiority, or even lesser reasons. But whatever the reason for the starting of a new group, if it can but see itself as a segment of the entire city-church first of all, rather than as a part of an outlying denomination (or as an independent church of some sort), then it can become a vital part of the work of God by the church catholic in that city to reach the unchurched with the Gospel.

The problem here is that, without this, there is the loss of the city-church and its effectiveness. Loyalties of congregations subsisting within the same city (the equivalent of the house churches in a given city) may be directed *outward,* toward the organizations and social linkages of the denomination, instead of *inward* and *sideward,* to the city itself—thus neglecting the need, in view of the staggering problems of urban America, to link hands with other congregations to reach the city for Christ. The problem may be illustrated in figure 3.3 on page 112.

The problem in the above scenario has been played out in many communities. The denominational, social, and organizational ties keep congregations of the same denomination related well to each other in a given city, but the ties cross-denominationally are nonexistent. In fact, the loyalties are more to congregations of the same denomination outside the city than they are to different denominations within the city.

And this is a great loss for the kingdom of God. The city-church was a functional organism in the first century, a viable connection for house churches, and enabled them to feel a joint responsibility for reaching their communities for Christ. But this is lost amid the intervening fabric of denominational loyalties and interdenominational competition within our cities. And, this is a key factor to overcome in developing a real sense of catholicity in the churches today.[57]

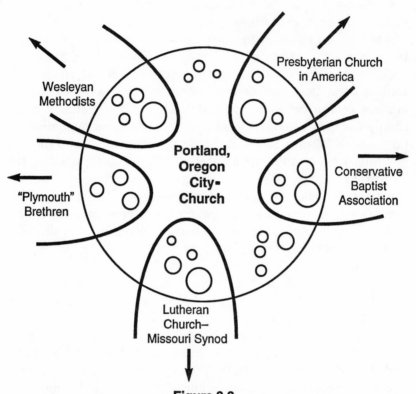

Figure 3.3.
Loyalty Tendencies of Denominational Churches

The risk of minimizing the local church as denominations be-come parachurch groups. Another danger of denominational models of the church was hinted at in the previous discussion. When denominations become such that they choose to organize themselves efficiently for joint efforts of any sort (missions, church planting, education, publishing, etc.), some sort of extra-local church mechanism becomes useful and therefore necessary to them. This is the development of a parachurch mechanism: organizations exterior to the local congregations are formed around a common purpose.

Parachurch organizations have been around for a long time (e.g., the numerous nineteenth century evangelical voluntary co-operative societies) and their more recent manifestations in specialty ministries such as *Campus Crusade for Christ, Inter-Varsity Christian Fellowship, The Navigators,* the *Billy Graham* and *Luis Palau Evangelistic Associations,* have armed the church with means outside of the local congregation to fulfill some of its evangelistic and discipleship mandates. And, as will be pointed out later, parachurch organizations can play a vital role in helping denominational churches toward a healthier catholicity. But parachurch organizations are not without their critics, who point out that such groups drain money, manpower, and other resources from the local congregations.[58] But the same critics do not often rain down their criticisms on denominational structures, which are simply the same sort of extra-congregational ministries that are controlled by like-minded congregations.

That is not to say that parachurch organizations are wrong any more than one would wish to say that denominational structures are wrong. Rather, it is to say that the greater the degree to which parachurch structures dominate a denomination, the more a congregation loses its *individual* focus and mission within its own geographical context. And in this there is great danger. For the local congregation of believers is precisely where Christian nurture takes place on the lowest and most real level from week to week. To minimize this element is to lose sight of the essence of Christian message: the salvation and transformation of human persons. The most effective denominational structures encouraging Christian nurture are those which place the needs of the local congregation as their highest priority.[59]

The role that parachurch structures (whether denominational or non-denominational) play within the church catholic may be illustrated by the diagram in figure 3.4, on page 114.

Parachurch organizations—whether denominational or nondenominational—are here to stay, and they have a vital place within the church catholic. But neither kind can replace the local church's role in developing Christian nurture. And individual members of parachurch organizations should align themselves with a local congregation in order to receive appropriate Christian nurture themselves.

The risk of ethnicity. Many American denominations were started by Christian immigrants, who sought to perpetuate the ecclesiastical structures of their homelands in the new country.[60]

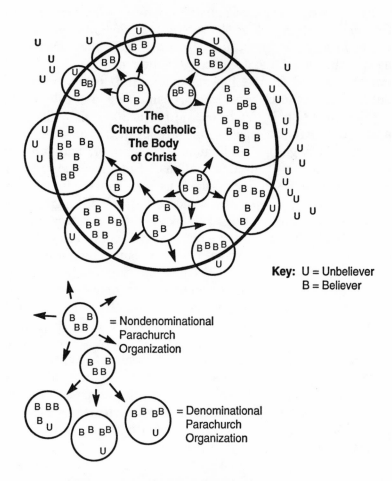

Key: U = Unbeliever
B = Believer

= Nondenominational
Parachurch
Organization

= Denominational
Parachurch
Organization

Figure 3.4.
Denominational and Nondenominational
Parachurch Structures

So began the *Baptist General Conference* among the Swedes in 1852, or the *Evangelical Free Church* among the same group in 1884, or the *Apostolic Lutheran Church* in 1872 and the *Suomi Synod of Evangelical Lutherans* among the Finns in 1889, or the *North American Baptist Conference* among the German immigrants in 1840, not to mention the numerous African-American denominations and congregations.[61]

Ethnic homogeneity in church planting is a common theme in

discussions of church growth today, and from the standpoint of ethnic outreach and evangelism, one can find little to argue against it. Ethnic ties between Christian and non-Christian immigrants can serve as a useful tool for congregational outreach, as long as this is understood to be a clear mission of the congregation. Most ethnic congregations and denominations outgrow their ethnicity as time goes on, immigration tails off, language and culture-learning needs diminish, and the process of normalization and integration into the cultural mainstream has been accomplished.

But in some instances, the ethnic elements are retained beyond their usefulness as a tool to reach immigrants for Christ. Individuals of *different* ethnic backgrounds are denied a part of the congregation, and a spirit of ethnic centricity or superiority develops. The congregation becomes a means of preserving a culture rather than of reaching a people. In this instance, the multi-ethnic nature of the church of the New Testament must take precedent over such a church or denomination. The church must welcome all and seek to minister to all, even though its target of ministry may be a select ethnic group.

The risk of independency. Denominationalism essentially finds its impetus in the critical factor of the individual human conscience before God. With this in mind, it tends to have a grassroots dimension to it. All denominations begin with a unique set of shared convictions before God that distinguish that group from others who do not share the same convictions. Because of this, the denominational theory of catholicity looks at catholicity as something that also begins at the bottom, with the individual and local church, and then works its way upward to various levels of acceptance and cooperation. It is not something that can be imposed from "above." Like racism or other forms of prejudice, legislation from above rarely touches it. Only changes from the foundational level can significantly affect the outlook in the long run.

But because the denominational theory of church catholicity begins at the grass-roots, conscience level, the risk of sustaining this model is the trend toward abandoning or obscuring a broader church view, through either an overly strong emphasis on the autonomy of the local church or on overestimating the value of a megachurch to the community.

Autonomy has certain implications in terms of understanding the catholicity of the church. In and of itself, the autonomy of the local church has certain values to it, although the biblical justification for this practice is not as clear as one would like. The primary value, of course, is in allowing the lordship of Christ to function at its most immediate level among the community of believers: over the individual congregation. Decisions are not imposed from above, but are worked out between the collective conscience of the weekly community of believers and lived out together under the lordship of Christ over them.

Freedom from external control and manipulation allows the congregations to seek the Lord's mind for its own future and direction. "Hyper-autonomy" is what I call the practice of over-emphasizing the autonomy of the local church. This is the danger of focusing so much on the centrality of the local congregation that one cannot or will not allow the church at large to minister to the congregation. When this occurs, the narrowest form of sectarianism has taken place. The horizons are limited to the local congregation and perception of the entire catholic church is lost. So, the very element that spawns a denominational model of catholicity (honoring the individual conscience) can lead to its own demise.

The other concern in terms of independency is the megachurch phenomenon.[62] The megachurch is a single local congregation whose membership is numbered in the multiple thousands.[63] This concept of the church is loaded with implications for catholicity. My point here is not a megachurch critique, for they can have an important place in the church catholic. Rather, the key factor is Christian nurture. If the factors necessary for Christian nurture can take place in the context of a single congregation of multiple thousands, then there is no fundamental objection. The concerns are in the area of catholicity.

First, is the tendency for a massively large congregation to perceive itself in competitive terms as the most effective church in the city. This can be detrimental for the congregation in the long term. For the entire local church is in fact made up of all the nurturing congregations in a city—large and small.[64]

Second, is the tendency for a megachurch congregation to understand itself as a full-service church, capable of meeting the needs of Christians more effectively than smaller fellowships.

With Christian rest homes, Christian day care, Christian retirement homes, Christian schools and colleges springing out of them, they offer much to their members. But in terms of catholicity, this full-service attitude is unsettling. No matter how large a single organization structure is of a local church, it is still but a fragment of the body of Christ and needs that entire body—in all its rich history and present extent—for spiritual depth and maturity. The megachurch can never be a truly "full-service" church.

Third, there is danger to the congregation in the nature of teaching received at the megachurch. The megachurch with a high-caliber senior pastor often yields relevant, biblically alert messages. However, in serving as CEO and chief teacher of the large corporation that a megachurch essentially is, the pastor can lose out in terms of peer accountability. Does the megachurch pastor view other pastors of the community as being peers, regardless of the size of their congregations, or does the megachurch pastor claim to be above peers in the community? If one understands this need for local, mutual accountability, then one is thinking with catholicity.

Both the autonomous tendency and the megachurch tendency arise from a model of independency that finds its roots in the historic denominational model of the church. Both aspects of independency are risks that those who support the denominational theory of the church catholic must face. Denominational catholicity spawns them, but they in turn can squelch the very model that produces them if the church catholic is not ever in the forefront.

The risk of Americanization. As we observed in the previous chapter, denominationalism as a theory of church catholicity came about as a result of the deliberate decision in American constitutional history to allow for the free exercise of religion in the new country, and therefore to avoid the establishment of a state church. This cut all of the distinct Christian denominations loose from any further vying for state support and sanction, and left them to compete among themselves. This "free competition" among the denominations in America has had distinct influences upon the very denominational system it spawned, just as the free enterprise system of economics influences many dimensions of American life.

But the church is not a civil or economic system. It existed for centuries before America came into political existence. Nevertheless, with the American system spawning the denominational model of the church catholic, there are several distinctly American dangers that very model must resist in order to retain its historic character as the people of God. I would like to suggest a few of these elements.

First, one risk of Americanization that denominational catholicity faces surrounds the very issue of competition as it relates to church discipline. The term this associates with is known as "voluntarism" or "voluntaryism."[65] There can be a tendency for denominational groups to compete with each other for members, since each group has its own distinctives and must appeal to the appropriate biblical basis for them.

This competition can lead to elements of self-superiority and inappropriate treatment of other groups which, after all, cannot really be described as "substantially the same as us." If they could, then why choose one group over another? Another problem connected with the voluntary principle is the lack of commitment to the local congregation. If the pastor or the program loses appeal, it is easy to lose members to the church-hopping phenomenon—sometimes described as "church-shopping," to use the marketing model.[66]

Pastors, in this regard, can end up building large congregations because they are popular or effective communicators and can attract people by their personalities and entrepeneurial efforts rather than necessarily by their faithful and careful exposition of Scripture. The need to always be a creative communicator lest they fail to attract and sustain their audience can place a heavy burden on pastoral leaders.

Voluntarism also makes church discipline a special challenge in American denominations. If an individual is disciplined in one denomination or congregation, he or she all too easily can slip into another one and cause similar problems, even if the problem is known to the leadership of the new congregation.

In view of this implicit danger, it is important for leaders to be imbibed with the principle of catholicity. Faithful interpretation of the Word under accountability before God must take precedent over building a larger congregation. If individuals leave our congregation, it is important to follow up, not necessarily to try to get them back, but to find out if there are unresolved interpersonal problems they must deal with, or to make sure that they are safely into another congregation (of whatever denominational connection) for the good of their souls.

Furthermore, church discipline and membership commitment must be carefully fostered. Pastors and other leaders must have a healthy concept of the church as the body of Christ. Their service must be understood as equipping people for ministry, rather than being the king or queen of all the church's ministries. Spiritual gifts must be taught and practiced by all the members of the congregation, and the notion of every-member ministry must be developed and practiced. When a moral or doctrinal violation occurs, and discipline ensues, it is important to follow up individuals as much as possible and communicate pertinent information to any new church they may associate with. In fact, to fully protect themselves, churches with a catholic outlook should not receive new members on a transfer basis without a letter of good standing from the leadership of their past congregation (whatever its denomination).

The voluntarism of American denominationalism can be addressed. The spirit of the culture in terms of competition and free market choice can be overcome in large part. But it takes effort and appropriate attitudes on the part of church leadership.

Another risk of Americanization of the denominational model is laicism.[67] Laicism is the opposite of clericalism and is a form of anti-clericalism. It is the tendency to pit "lay people against the clergy to the detriment of the whole church."[68] In reaction to the strongly clerical models of the historic church, the churches in America have tended to be strongly oriented toward lay leadership. In fact, many of the great evangelists in American church history (Charles G. Finney, Dwight L. Moody, Billy Sunday, Billy Graham) have been persons without formal theological training, that is, laypersons. Strong lay involvement is an important strength of the American churches,[69] especially as the place of every-member ministry is realized through the functioning of the spiritual gifts. Within my own movement, the nonclerical focus (that a clergyman is not necessary for the church to function) is all too often supplanted by an anti-clerical focus (that a clergyman is wrong).

But laicism is a cultural byproduct of the individualism and antiauthoritarianism implicit in American life. It is the almost plebeian dislike of anything that smacks of intellectual or spiritual elitism. We all expect a vote in this country. We all want an equal say. Equal education despite diversity of talent and intellectual capacity is expected. We assume our opinions will be heard. And we all resist despotism and any form of monarchical tendencies in our leadership. But the downside is to miss the fact that God has given the gift of leadership to certain individuals, and leadership requires a followership. We must learn to respect and obey leadership in the church of Jesus Christ, despite the cultural trends against it.[70]

Another risk of Americanization implicit in the denominational model is tendency toward pragmatism. Denominations can tend here to develop their rationale for existence on either *experience* (a theological nonintellectualism), or on quickly *demonstrable biblicism* (a nonhistoricism). A megachurch must be doing something right, it is said, because look at all the people! Too often it matters little whether the doctrine is correct or not, because if it works, it must be right. Others can't be bothered with the history of interpretation or exegetical methodology, because they can see exactly what the text is saying!

SUMMARY AND CONCLUSIONS

There are risks in the denominational model of the church. It is a factor of trying to balance between the pull of authoritarian sectarianism on the right and nonauthoritarian latitudinarianism on the left. But such a balance is not uncommon in healthy biblical theology and ethics. In theology proper, the doctrine of the Trinity balances in tension between unitarianism and tritheism. In ethics, Christian liberty is a balance between legalism on the one hand and license on the other. So denominational theory forces a balance, one that insists on a core of orthodoxy and allows for traditional diversity. Sectarians will tend to call the denominational catholic model around a core of orthodoxy "compromise," and latitudinarians will look at the core of orthodoxy expected and cry out "fundamentalist!" It is of utmost importance, therefore, to maintain the balance.

I have argued that historic denominationalism can be viewed as a healthy corrective to both sectarianism and latitudinarianism. In fact, the unique characteristics that each denomination brings may be viewed as its special "gifts" to the church at large for its enrichment. To deny the place of denominational distinctives would be unhealthy to the life of the church as a whole. We must agree with Pannenberg when he writes:

> It is easy to regard the various denominations as mere obstacles to Christian unity. On the other hand, it must not be overlooked that the content of Christian beliefs and the forms of Christian life and church organization are today overwhelmingly intertwined with the various denominational expressions of belief, practice, and organization. Thus there is a danger that a rejection of denominational forms of faith and life would mean the loss of that Christian content which has been preserved chiefly, or even exclusively, in the specific forms it has assumed in various denominations. Hardly ever does anyone contend today that one of the denominations is the exclusive expression of the truth of the Christian faith and does not require supplementation by the other Christian communities. In spite of the contrasts in the ways the denominations express their faith and life, they still preserve the substance of the traditional Christian faith. Therefore, the denominations are more than merely tenacious but outmoded remnants of a hopelessly backward phase of Christian history, characterized by ominous, even fatal divisions. At the very least, the denominations can play a positive role in the future development of Christianity if they regard themselves as custodians of a heritage that can be made a part of a new Christian unity. Viewed in this way, the multiplicity of denominations has a positive function today in the search for Christian unity. The challenge is to allow the Christian substance preserved in contradictory denominational expressions to help shape a new awareness of Christian community and share in the development of new forms of Christian life.[71]

While agreeing with his basic thrust, I would also argue that even today there is an ever present danger of sectarianism in denominationalism which can tempt each group to expand the core of orthodoxy to include all of those elements which are distinctive to them. After all, they are "clearly" demonstrable from Scripture! In view of the appeal of the diverse denominational groups to the same Bible to support their distinctives, the threat of sectarianism is ever present.

Finally, let me explain how our tour of cross-denominational renewal will continue. In the next chapter, I will suggest how we can address the above problem of sectarianism: by understanding the inevitable development of "tradition" within all denominational groups. In the following chapter, I will discuss means to determine our denominational traditions: we detect them by a practice of biblical hermeneutics influenced by catholicity. The understanding of the place of tradition and the use of hermeneutics protect our churches and denominations from the sectarian drift to the right. Then, in the succeeding chapter, I will address protecting ourselves from a drift to the left by defining a suggested "core of orthodoxy" around which we can agree and serve together as members of the church catholic.

Four

CATHOLICITY AND TRADITION: OR, DO PROTESTANTS HAVE TRADITION?

The question is really not "Do I believe in tradition?" but, "Which tradition will I follow?" Every evangelical subculture is laden with traditions peculiar to its own history.

—Robert Webber

 All denominations have their distinctives that mark them off from each other. The ability to wholeheartedly accept and work with other groups as genuine brothers and sisters in Christ is a mark of catholicity. To develop this attitude, however, they must address their distinctives seriously and attempt to draw a clear distinction between the core of orthodoxy which they warmly share with other believers and their own peculiar distinctives. My argument in this chapter is that these distinctives, characteristic of every denomination (that includes every Protestant denomination), should be treated at the level of "tradition." And unless we understand the reality and function of such traditions, we run the risk of confusing them with a core orthodoxy and moving away from our distinct denominational family members in the body of Christ toward the dangers of sectarianism.

Tradition? Tradition! The term reeks with negative connotations for many of us in the evangelical Protestant stream of Christianity. We recall poor Tevye in *Fiddler on the Roof* singing fervently in defense of the beloved Jewish traditions he saw decaying before his eyes: his daughters were marrying off one by one in ways contrary to long-established Jewish custom. To him tradition was to be valued, in part, because of the stability it brought to his little town of Anatefka. We as evangelical Christians, heirs of the Protestant Reformation, are taught to chuckle at such a quaint perception of tradition. We are urged to recall the resounding condemnation of tradition on the part of our Lord found in Mark 7. To us, tradition is supposed to be nothing but a negative idea. Scripture alone is to be our authority.

It is ironic that this evangelical strong-arm against tradition tends to backfire within our own congregations. Energetic visionaries among us have tended to take this tradition/Scripture bifurcation all too seriously. Observing what they perceive to be biblically unfounded practices, they become vocal dissenters. Reaching for an appropriate term for the doctrines and practices they observe among as biblically unjustifiable, they have labeled them for what they are: Tradition!

But they have gone a step further which is, in my opinion, going too far. They have sought to jettison those "traditional" practices implying that in *labeling* them as tradition they must be equated with the unbiblical tradition condemned by the Lord. They have followed the philosophy Alfred Kuen once suggested as a cure for Protestant confusion: "Burn tradition, or at least shake off its yoke in the measure that it tries to impose itself as a norm of faith next to the Scripture or above it."[1] Although not known for his inclination toward historic Christianity, Thomas Jefferson summed up the attitude of many Protestants:

> As to tradition, if we are Protestants we reject all tradition, and rely on the scripture alone, for that is the essence and common principle of all the protestant churches.[2]

Church historian George Marsden says much the same about American evangelicalism:

> It is remarkable that American evangelicalism has the degree of coherence it does. Little seems to hold it together other than common traditions, a central one of which is the denial of the authority of traditions.[3]

Thus, such denominational dissidents have either tried some sort of radical surgery within their denominational or local church structure to remove the infection of this fierce enemy (if they have the loyalty and determination to remain within those structures), or they have launched out to plant a new church that they believe will be free from the restraints of tradition once and for all.[4] Little do they know that the former course often creates nothing but alienation and division, while the latter course only creates new sets of tradition-structures that their own offspring will in turn critique. This is poor thinking and teaching about tradition on the part of pastors and denominational leaders come full circle.[5]

My point here is this: even if certain local church/denominational practices or teachings can be demonstrated, by careful biblical analysis, to really belong to the level of tradition (rather than explicit biblical teaching), *that does not mean they must automatically be jettisoned.* You see, some tradition may well be *good* tradition, tradition well worth keeping, if it is acknowledged and valued *as such.*[6] Let me explain.

DEFINING TRADITION

Tradition in general. To gain a clearer perspective on Christian tradition (especially as it relates to evangelical Protestant groups), it is important to get a broader notion of the idea of tradition itself, before thinking specifically of tradition in the church. What does tradition generally mean? In common American parlance (according to the *Oxford American Dictionary*), "tradition" usually means the following: "The handing down of beliefs or customs from one generation to another, especially without writing."[7]

There are three dimensions to tradition, as indicated by this definition: (1) the "handing down," or "passing on" *activity* association with tradition; (2) the idea of beliefs or customs as the *content* of tradition; and (3) the unwritten *nature* of tradition. I would therefore like to suggest a working definition that incorporates these three elements: Tradition, broadly speaking, is *any unwritten notion or habitually repeated activity that is deemed worthy of passing on to others.* Tradition in this broad sense is not restrictive to Christian, or even any general religious traditions. It includes personal customs or useful habits that most people tend to receive, develop, continue, and pass on. And this basic sense of "tradition" may have a quite positive connotation.

My wife and I have developed "traditions" in this sense, as have other families. Every year we have made it our tradition to get away to the Oregon Coast for two nights without the kids during Spring midsemester break. By that time we are typically worn out and we need and enjoy the break. It has become a "habitually repeated activity" that gives us refreshment and we look forward to it. We are not ashamed to call it our tradition, and friends and family honor it as such. And, should we miss it some year, we may feel a loss, but we would not feel we have "broken" any sort of obligation. After all, we established the tradition. We expect this activity and have come to depend on it, but we have no written document anywhere that formally established this custom. And, we would recommend it to our children as an example of a useful tradition for them in their future. But it is simply a custom, a "tradition" for us. Similarly, many families develop vacation, holiday, and special traditions as well.

In the New Testament, Pontius Pilate likewise had a "tradition" of this nonreligious sort. He made it his custom to release a prisoner to the Jews as a part of his annual Passover Amnesty. This was his habit, a regularly repeated action that people came to expect and depend on (and, it is doubtful that this was written down anywhere). In fact, the terms used for Pilate's "custom" are among the stock vocabulary words used in the New Testament to refer to tradition.[8] As a tradition it was neither good nor bad. It simply was a tradition. It was done repeatedly at regular intervals as a "custom" and one suspects the Jews would have expected this custom to be continued by any of Pilate's successors sent by Rome, that is, it would be expected to be "passed on."

Religious tradition. It is especially in terms of religious teaching and practice that tradition appears. Yet at this point those unwritten notions or habitually repeated activities that are passed on to others take on an added dimension: they are believed worthy of practice and promulgation precisely because such traditions are understood to be ordained by God in some sense. They tend to take on a nuance of divine authority. Thus I would define a *religious* tradition as any unwritten notion or habitually repeated activity that is deemed worthy of passing on to others *because it is believed to have been ordained by God.* And in this sense religious traditions often take on an authoritative dimension in and of themselves. And they are not unique to Christianity, but may be found in Judaism, Islam, and other religious movements as well.[9]

Christian tradition. But it is obviously a particular kind of religious tradition that we have in mind, that is, *Christian* religious tradition. This is where we as (Protestants) diverge in many ways from Roman Catholic theology, and its near cousin, Eastern Orthodoxy. The reason for this is that Eastern Orthodoxy and Roman Catholicism (from which Protestantism diverged), both acknowledge a twofold authority base for establishing doctrine: Scripture *and* tradition. Note, for example, the explanation of John Karmiris, an Eastern Orthodox theologian:

> The Church teaches and interprets those divine truths brought out in Holy Scripture and Sacred Tradition. *Scripture and Tradition, then, are equally valid, possess equal dogmatic authority,* and are equal in value as sources of dogmatic truth. The Church's teaching shows that the Scriptures are in complete harmony with Apostolic Tradition. This is because the word of God was *transmitted to the Church via two different media: written Scripture and oral Tradition.*[10]

Official Roman Catholic theology has very similar notions of authority. In response to the Protestant Reformation, the Council of Trent (1545–1563) was held in order to address many of the objections raised by the Reformers. In response to their critique of the church's use of tradition, Roman Catholicism formalized a binding response:

> This truth and discipline are *contained in the written books, and the unwritten traditions.* . . . [The Synod] following the examples of the orthodox Fathers, receives and venerates *with an equal affection of piety and reverence,* all the books both of the Old and of the New Testament—seeing that one God is the author of both—as *also the said traditions,* as well those appertaining to faith as to morals, as having been dictated, either by Christ's own word of mouth, or by the Holy Ghost, and *preserved in the Catholic Church by a continuous succession.*[11]

Although the focus has become a twofold dimension of a single revelation source, modern Roman Catholicism reaffirms this general idea that tradition has an authoritative aspect to it, as may be seen in their most recent conciliar statements found in the materials of the Second Vatican Council (1962–1965):

> Sacred Tradition and sacred Scripture, then, are bound closely together, and communicate one with the other. For both of them,

flowing out from the same divine wellspring, come together in some fashion to form one thing, and move towards the same goal. . . . Hence *both Scripture and Tradition must be accepted and honored with equal feelings of devotion and reverence. . . . Sacred Tradition and sacred Scripture make up a single sacred deposit of the Word of God, which is entrusted to the Church.*[12]

It is interesting to note that Roman Catholic and Eastern Orthodox notions regarding tradition are not unlike the contemporary Jewish notions of tradition. The prolific Jewish writer Jacob Neusner makes this revealing comment regarding Jewish thought on this very subject:

The central myth [belief] of classical Judaism is the belief that the ancient Scriptures constituted divine revelation, *but only a part of it.* At Sinai, God had handed down a *dual revelation:* the written part known to one and all, but also the oral part preserved by the great scriptural heroes, passed on by prophets to various ancestors in the obscure past, finally and most openly handed down to the rabbis who created the Palestinian and Babylonian Talmuds. *the 'whole Torah' thus consisted of both written and oral parts.*[13]

The similarities between this latter statement and the rabbinic teachings in our Lord's time, which saw the traditions of the Fathers as a second (albeit "oral," and only later written) voice that came from God through Moses are evident. Tradition and Scripture are thus understood as two equal elements of the voice of God, upon which all doctrine must be based. And in this, Eastern Orthodoxy, Roman Catholicism, and Judaism follow a similar pattern.[14] This understanding of tradition may be illustrated by the drawing shown in figure 4.1 on page 129.

EVANGELICALS AND TRADITION

Here we evangelicals, as heirs of the Protestant Reformation, vigorously disagree with Eastern Orthodoxy and Roman Catholicism. We argue that any time tradition is placed next to Scripture as an *equal* authority it all too easily takes on a *superior* authority to Scripture as the "fresher" voice of God.[15] And this is precisely the kind of problem that our Lord was facing when He blasted the Pharisaic approach to the traditions of their fathers (Mark 7:1-23; cf. Matt. 15:1-20).

As you may recall that incident, certain Pharisees and teachers

The Dual Model

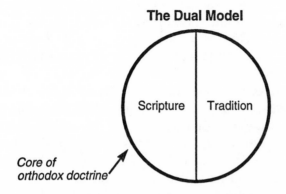

Scripture | Tradition

Core of
orthodox doctrine

Figure 4.1.
The Authoritative Voice of God

of the law had come from Jerusalem to see Jesus and observed that some of His disciples were eating food without first ceremonially washing their hands. Mark parenthetically explains for his readers the Pharisaic practice of tradition:

> The Pharisees and all the Jews do not eat unless they give their hands a ceremonial washing, holding to the *tradition of the elders.* When they come from the marketplace they do not eat unless they wash. And they observe *many other traditions,* such as the washing of cups, pitchers, and kettles. (Mark 7:3-4)[16]

Our Lord was quick to attack the Pharisees' tradition at this point. Citing Isaiah 29:13, He called them hypocrites who "have let go of the commands of God and are holding on to the traditions of men" (Mark 7:8). Then He added, "You have a fine way of setting aside the commands of God in order to observe your own traditions!" (Mark 7:9) Citing the practice of *Corban,*[17] which in Pharisaic tradition allowed a man to dedicate to God money which might otherwise be used to support an aging set of parents as required by the fifth commandment (Ex. 20:12; Deut. 5:16), He capped His argument again with the final refrain: "Thus you *nullify the Word of God by your tradition that you have handed down.* And you do many things like that" (Mark 7:13).

Jesus' point is clear. There is religious tradition which is *bad*

ONE LORD, ONE FAITH

ONE LORD, ONE FAITH

tradition. Tradition which "nullifies" or "invalidates" the written Word of God is *bad* tradition.[18] This tradition must be rejected. The normative voice of God must therefore come from Scripture alone, and all other claims to divine authority, especially the traditional, must thereby be judged.

Martin Luther and other early Protestants recognized how the development of extensive, controlling ecclesiastical tradition in their day (and especially the "dual voice" model) had demeaned and contradicted the Word of God. That is why they drew a clear line of ultimate authority at the written Word alone. They saw that ecclesiastical tradition had evolved into the very thing that Jesus had critiqued among the Pharisees of His day. And, although they did not deny tradition a place within the church, they would never give it a place *alongside* Scripture as an *equal* authority.[19] So, the watchcry of the Reformation which encapsulated their beliefs about the source of divine authority was simply *"sola Scriptura"* (Latin for "Scripture alone").[20]

Evangelicals love to recall with relish, on this point, the affirmations of Martin Luther at the Diet of Worms on April 18, 1521:

> Your Imperial Majesty and Your Lordships demand a simple answer. Here it is, plain and unvarnished. Unless I am convicted of error *by the testimony of Scriptures or* (since I put no trust in the unsupported authority of Pope or of councils [tradition!], since it is plain that they have often erred and often contradicted themselves) *by manifest reasoning I stand convicted by the Scriptures to which I have appealed,* and my conscience is taken captive by God's word, I cannot and will not recant anything, for to act against our conscience is neither safe for us, nor open to us. On this I take my stand. I can do no other. God help me. Amen.[21]

We therefore share in the heart of the Protestant Reformation by giving tradition no place at all alongside Scripture as if it were in any way an authoritative part of God's voice.[22] But the Reformers even went a step further. They argued that this primacy of Scripture was the historic position of the ancient church and that it was the Roman Church, and not the Reformers, who deviated into abnormality in their treatment of tradition.[23]

The Protestant (and evangelical) pattern, at least conceptually, would be represented more like the illustration given in figure 4.2 on page 131.

The Singular Model

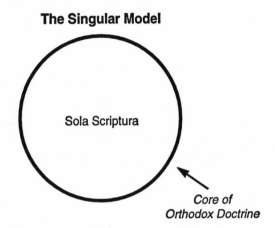

Sola Scriptura

Core of
Orthodox Doctrine

Figure 4.2.
The Authoritative Voice of God

The early Reformers spoke out against Roman Catholic dogma which appealed to a "dual voice" much like our Lord did against His Jewish contemporaries: such a pattern of authority would inevitably "nullify the Word of God" (Mark 7:13).[24] Again, like the Lord, they spoke boldly to those who would hold to unbiblical traditions: "You have let go of the commands of God and are holding onto the traditions of men" (Mark 7:8).[25]

As heirs of the fundamental thought and theology of the Reformation, evangelicals instinctively return to this model as a doctrinal base, since we see no ground in Scripture, early church history, or manifest reason from Scripture to doubt this model. But, lest we be a bit smug in our correct conceptualizations, it is important that we take a look at the tenacious and inevitable tendency for tradition to arise in evangelical Protestant groups as well.

EVANGELICALS AND TRADITION: ANOTHER LOOK

I would like to suggest that there is an *equal* if not *greater* danger for evangelical Protestants to be controlled by tradition. The reason for this is the *claim* that we do not develop traditions at all, but that *all* our doctrines and practices are directly attributable to Scripture alone. This is belied by one simple factor: Protestant faith and practice is *not entirely uniform,* despite the consistent plea that we each base all our faith and practice solely on a biblical foundation. Why the differences? Several factors come into play here.

1. Evangelical Protestant tradition often arises in areas of lesser scriptural clarity.

Of fundamental importance here is what must be a truism: the Scriptures do not speak with equal clarity on all matters that they touch upon.[26] This is why it is so important from an interpretive standpoint not to build major doctrines on unclear or obscure passages.[27] Issues of church polity are a classic example of the problem here.

Within Protestantism there is quite an array of interpretations and therefore practices in terms of what constitutes biblical church organization and structure. Episcopalians argue for an episcopal hierarchy that extends beyond the local church. Presbyterians argue that the Scriptures teach that local church government should consist of a plurality of elders governing a group of congregations. Others (like the Brethren) argue for a plurality of elders in a single congregation. Baptists and many other free church Protestants argue for a single pastor and for autonomy of the local church. All of them use the same Bible as a base. However, the Bible is not crystal clear on the issue of church polity or whether God intends one form to be normative at all.

Henry Craik, a uniquely clear thinker within my own tradition, put it well at the end of the last century:

> I may be regarded as advocating very latitudinarian opinions, but *I am disposed readily to admit that there are passages in the inspired writings that seem, to some extent, to favour a species of Episcopacy; others that may appear to support Presbyterianism; very many, again, that uphold Congregationalism, and others, as clearly teaching what may be described as less systematic than any of the above organizations. . . . It appears to me that the early Churches were not, in all places, similarly constituted.* The epistle to the church at Corinth contains no reference to official persons bearing the name of Bishops or Elders, while the epistle to the Philippians expressly makes mention of the Bishops and Deacons as distinguished from the other members of the church. I believe, in short, that, as time went on, even during the Apostolic age, the orderly organization of gathered believers became increasingly the rule, and that only in the very infancy of Christianity do we find evidence of the absence of Presidents or Overseers.[28]

Craik's observation deserves careful consideration. It is arguable that the New Testament does not necessarily present a uniform mandate in terms of church polity.[29] Yet each denomination tends to rely on those passages which support its system to the exclusion or minimization of others. But since there is no uniformity of opinion or teaching on this matter, what right does any group have to expect conformity of other groups to their own viewpoint on these matters?

Church polity is only one of many issues where the Scripture is not clear in terms of its mandate. Other issues include the mode and legitimate recipients of baptism, the finer points of eschatology, the normative roles of men and women, the manner of creation, and the continuity of spiritual gifts, to name a few. There is clearly warrant for drawing a distinction between issues of orthodoxy, issues of conscience, and issues of preference. Issues of orthodoxy must be limited to those historic and fundamental doctrines shared by all who genuinely believe, in what I have referred to as "core orthodoxy." But to place all of any group's teachings at the same level of orthodoxy is to run the danger of what Robert Webber calls "theological legalism," or what Donald Bloesch calls "orthodoxism."[30] That, as noted earlier, is the seed of sectarianism. It is a failure to realize the fundamental notion, written by some dear friends into the flyleaf of my first Bible: "What is clear in this book is vital; what is not clear in this book is not vital."[31]

2. Evangelical Protestant tradition is most often found in the distinctive teachings of each evangelical group, as set forth by those who inaugurated the group.

In many ways our denominational distinctives are merely traditional interpretations, that is, interpretations on certain issues which have become normative within the group of which we are a part. And, as noted earlier, they derive in large part from the interpretation of passages which are either unclear or not so clear as we would like, at least perceiving it from the eyes of other Protestant groups.[32] We sometimes even tend to focus on certain passages we consider "undiscovered" by other Christian groups. Yet we claim that these practices derive "from the Scriptures alone."[33]

Where do these Protestant interpretive traditions come from? They derive from the teachings, in many instances, of denominational founders which have, in succeeding generations, been normalized (whether in creedal or unwritten form) as the only proper interpretation of the Bible on the matters addressed. F.F. Bruce pointed this out in his classic work *Tradition Old and New:*

> Where subordinate standards [such as creeds] are not recognized, it does not follow that there are no such guidelines: guidelines and even more precise canons are quite likely to be laid down, but because they take the form of unwritten tradition, their true nature may be overlooked. Indeed, in some more enclosed traditions the authority of *Scripture will be identified with the authority of the accepted interpretation and application, because it has never occurred to those inside the enclosure that Scripture could be interpreted or applied otherwise. . . .*[34]

Among the Brethren, the teachings of John Nelson Darby have carried more than their share of influence.[35] Among the Presbyterian and Reformed groups, John Calvin's theological ideas have dominated. Among the Lutherans, Martin Luther and Melanchthon have carried the day. Baptists dare not forget Roger Williams. In the Campbellite tradition, Barton Stone and Thomas and Alexander Campbell are paramount. And the list could easily be multiplied to include leaders from most every group. Alfred Kuen notes well this problem:

> The notion of tradition is not confined to Roman Catholicism. There are Protestant traditions just as tenacious and dangerous as those of the Catholics when they come between the Bible and the church. *The words of a great man, whether it be Luther, Calvin, Zwingli, Wesley, or Darby, and the decisions of such and such a synod or conference often dispute the authority of the Bible.* A certain spiritual guidebook by a highly esteemed leader, a certain experience common to a great number of Christians, a certain practice which is venerable because of its antiquity and the number of its followers—these easily become the norms of a whole Christian circle. . . . *Instead of having one infallible pope, we [Protestants] have an infinite number of those who are semi-fallible but whose authority is nontheless absolute over their circle of followers where they rule. Many theologians, pastors and evangelists have their groups of disciples who see only through their leaders' eyes and who consider all of their affirmations as gospel truth.*[36]

As Kuen acknowledges, this is tradition, plain and simple, despite our disavowals. And a sure indicator of the presence of our own distinctive traditions is simply to review who it was that founded our movement or group and what his/her distinctive teachings were.

It is far better, in my estimation, to classify denominational or local church distinctives simply as elements of the different Protestant traditions: The Presbyterian tradition, the Baptist tradition, the Grace Brethren tradition, the Evangelical Free tradition, the Christian Brethren tradition, the Bible Church tradition, and so on. And beyond these specific denominational distinctives are broader interpretive traditions which often connect denominational distinctives into *schools* of interpretation. Among these are the Dispensational interpretive tradition, the Pentecostal interpretive tradition, the Wesleyan/Arminian interpretive tradition, the Calvinistic or Reformed interpretive tradition, and so forth. And these traditions may all be legitimate variations that are not particularly worth quibbling over at those times when they obscure the theological core of orthodoxy which unites us all.[37]

3. Evangelical Protestant tradition is unavoidable.

Not long ago I was invited to preach at a local Baptist church. The church was without a pastor and I was one of several they called on for pulpit supply in the interim. I enjoyed my time among this congregation, so when I was asked to come back, I accepted with joy and anticipation. Before I hung up the phone, my contact made one parting comment which caused me to pause however: "Oh, by the way, it will be communion Sunday for us, and we would be delighted if you would serve communion to us."

I took a deep breath. "Thank you for asking," I replied, "but you do remember that I am not a Baptist? Wouldn't you be better served by one of your deacons or other leaders who understand the Baptist style of breaking bread?" He insisted that I could do it. After all, what could go wrong? I was a biblicist, a teacher of Bible and Theology. And Baptists were biblicists. I agreed (despite his misunderstanding on the relationship of one's biblicism and tradition) on one condition: that before I lead I receive an explicit order of service, including *who* does exactly *what.* You see, I am well aware of the fact that every group has their own style (read: "tradition") of practicing the Lord's Supper, which is always very sacred to them. And my dear Baptist friends are no exception. So, on receiving the "obvious" order of service, I successfully led my first Baptist communion service.

The expected order of service is tradition. It is custom. There is nowhere in the Bible that gives us anything about the *how* of communion services, only *that* it is to be done. All else is diversity. All else is tradition.

So, if we are honest, we will need to admit with Baptist historian Bruce Shelley that "complete rejection of tradition is an impossibility. Any biblicist who will carefully examine his own denomination will find certain characteristics that fail to rally explicit New Testament support."[38] These "characteristics" are in fact "tradition." Similarly, Robert Webber states in this regard:

> It is impossible to deny the presence of tradition in faith. The question is really not "Do I believe in tradition?" but, "Which tradition will I follow?" Every evangelical subculture is laden with traditions peculiar to its own history.[39]

Tradition is thus inevitable even within evangelical Protestantism.[40] It is inevitable because Christians *must* interpret the Bible into their life context. As Clark Pinnock noted:

> Protestant as well as Catholic beliefs are ecclesiastically shaped. It makes me tend to suppose that in my theology I go directly back to the Bible, unaware of the fact that I read the Word in the context of a Christian community through which the message has been transmitted to me.[41]

None of us interprets the Bible in a vacuum. We interpret *out of* a cultural, historical context, *through* an ecclesiastical context, *looking for* the Bible's relevance to cultural problems.[42] Since the cultural context and problems change, what we *look for* in the Bible changes, even though the text remains the same. Brown is right when he says that the "leapfrog" model of interpretation which asserts we can go directly, uninfluenced by tradition to the Bible is wrong, for two reasons:

> (a) it ignores the fact that people inevitably read the Bible in the light of a denominational or theological heritage, and (b) it ignores the fact that they read it in the light of their contemporary situation.[43]

Thus, interpretive traditions are unavoidable even for the most ardent evangelical student of the Bible. And beyond that, we really stand on the shoulders of interpretive work done by Christians centuries before our time—not to mention the work of the originators of our own denominational subgroup.[44] This is not to say that reading Scripture from the standpoint of an inherited tradition is wrong (it definitely *can* be if it is unrecognized and therefore confused with biblical authority), but it is only to say that doing so is inevitable. In fact, sometimes a given tradition can draw out some nuances from the text that is lost to other traditions.[45]

4. Evangelical Protestant tradition can have extremely dangerous implications.

First of all, it can have implications for biblical authority. The danger in all I have said comes not from *having* traditions (remember: that is unavoidable), *but from being unable to distinguish our traditions from the clear teachings of Scripture.* We thus confuse our more subtle doctrines (often described as "distinctives") with the voice of God by denying their identity as "tradition" or "traditional interpretation." We thus tend to equate our tradition with the authoritative teaching of the Word of God. John Van Engen was correct when he wrote the following insightful words:

> In practice, most Protestant groups formed traditions nearly as binding as the Catholics and established similar sets of authorities: ecumenical councils, confessional creeds, synodical legislation, church orders, and theologians (especially founders) of a particular church. *Those free churches, particularly in America, that claim to stand on Scripture alone and to recognize no traditional authorities are in some sense the least free because they are not even conscious of what traditions have molded their understanding of Scripture.*[46]

Robert Webber makes the same observation:

> Although few evangelicals will allow the Roman Christian such an assertion [two sources for truth—scripture and tradition], the strange fact is that many American evangelicals function with a similar attitude toward their tradition. One only has to look at the heated discussions among Calvinists and Arminians, premillenarians and amillenarians; dispensationalists and covenant-

alists; charismatics and noncharismatics. . . . *This attitude forces us to conclude that some evangelicals act as though there are two sources of truth: The Scriptures and the particular tradition of the subculture, i.e., "I believe in the Scriptures and the Calvinistic interpretation of it."*[47]

The Protestant situation is thus rather more dangerous than the Roman Catholic one which evangelical Protestants are concerned to avoid. The problem is that once *all* of our practices are perceived to have come directly from Scripture, they then all take on *the same note of authority.* This is to extend the authority of the Word of God to matters which have no such authority. John Jefferson Davis notes that "traditional interpretations tend, in the mind of the holder, to become fused with the text itself, and thus to be given a spurious legitimacy and authority."[48] And that is the precise extension of Roman Catholicism and Eastern Orthodoxy that *sola Scriptura* is intending to avoid in the first place: confusing the voice of humans with the voice of God.

Second, there are implications for sectarianism. As noted above, all evangelical groups believe that their *distinctives*—where they differ from other Bible-believing evangelicals—are "clearly" biblical! But we cannot *all* be right, especially when our distinctives are mutually exclusive. My fellow evangelical friends who are Baptists argue for congregational rule, including elections by voting, on the basis of certain passages from Scripture. My Grace Brethren friends practice footwashing and trine immersion with (what is at least in their minds) clear scriptural support. And my charismatic friends argue for the biblical teaching of certain miraculous sign gifts of the Spirit for today. And all three groups would disagree with each other on numerous points akin to these. And I, the local Christian Brethren representative, disagree with them all—on scriptural grounds, of course. Yet we all would affirm that tradition has no place in determining doctrine and that true doctrine (including these distinctives) can only be derived from the Bible alone.

Rather than traditional interpretive matters (which, as was noted earlier, are unavoidable), the issue is *how we perceive and treat the other groups in view of their disagreement with us on those interpretive matters.* These distinctive traditional interpretations can, depending on one's attitudes toward them, be viewed as "one of the most dangerous tendencies of Protestantism, and certainly the greatest obstacle to the unity of real Christians."[49] As Robert Webber points out, "The exclusiveness and party spirit which denominational distinctives create is rooted in the conviction 'I have the truth and you don't.' "[50] *That* is sectarianism. And that has a terrible effect on the catholicity of the church.

In summary, the key issue in the above discussion is the necessity to recognize that we evangelicals develop interpretive traditions as well. Although we share a mutual core of doctrinal orthodoxy (C.S. Lewis' "mere" Christianity), we differ from each other in the way we develop certain biblical values or doctrines. A more consistent biblical model, in my opinion, which reflects the place of the traditional in evangelical Protestantism, would be something like that shown in figure 4.3 below.

The Singular Model Interpreted

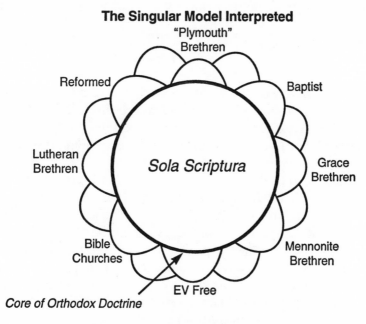

Figure 4.3.
The Authoritative Voice of God[51]

The first step in keeping tradition from controlling our biblical interpretation is to *recognize* that evangelicals inevitably develop traditions as well. Unless we acknowledge that we *have* traditions, we will all too easily *confuse* them with the voice of God.

But if we recognize their existence, then we can place them in a subsidiary category for evaluation and enjoyment (if they do enhance the Word of God) or modification/dismissal (if they do not enhance the Word of God). Only when we have separated out what is traditional can we be allowed to hear the crisp, unadorned voice of God ringing out from Scripture alone.

I did not say that the way to keep tradition from controlling our interpretation of Scripture is always to *dispense* with tradition. Rather, it is to *recognize* the presence of such, since the inevitability of our developing traditions keeps us from having a tradition-less faith as a goal. But even more should come into play here, for, you see, I am convinced not only that the Bible recognizes that we all tend to develop traditions (regular habits and customs that we pass on to others), but that *it allows a place for tradition when rightly viewed as such.* Let me illustrate from Scripture.

POSITIVE TRADITION IN THE NEW TESTAMENT

Positive tradition and the Lord Jesus. Our Lord Jesus did not simply attack tradition whenever and wherever He found it. On the contrary, He only attacked *some* traditions. Other Jewish traditions He seems simply to have practiced without critique. In Luke 4:16, for example, we are told that Jesus entered Nazareth and went into the synagogue on the Sabbath *according to His custom.*[52] Elsewhere the New Testament shows our Lord regularly participating in synagogue practices.[53] The point is this: The synagogue and its associated practices cannot be found "taught" anywhere in the Hebrew Scriptures; instead, the synagogue system is likely to have developed sometime in either the exilic or postexilic period.[54] Yet Jesus did not for that reason reject the synagogue practice out of hand. Instead, He participated in the synagogue service and supported its use.

Why would Jesus support and practice this tradition, while rejecting other traditions (such as the *Corban*)? Because the synagogue tradition did not detract from ("nullify") the Word of God. Rather, it *enhanced* the place and teachings of the Word of God. It was in the synagogue where the Scriptures were taught and applied most consistently and regularly. It was there that the covenant community of Israel kept itself nourished in matters of faith. But nonetheless the institution of the synagogue *is* a tradition unfounded in the Scriptures. And yet Jesus found it worthwhile. So, while Jesus vociferously rejected the Pharisaic tradition of *Corban* in Mark 7, He actively supported the tradition of the synagogue. Jesus supported *some* traditions and rejected *others*.[55]

Another example of Jesus' support and practice of extra-biblical traditions is His apparent participation in the Feast of Dedication (John 10:22-23).[56] The Feast of Dedication is *not* a Jewish feast derived from the Old Testament Scriptures. It is unquestionably the winter commemoration of the cleansing of the temple from its terrible defilement by Antiochus IV Ephiphanes in 167 B.C. by Judas Maccabeus, still celebrated by observant Jews today as *Hanukkah*.[57] It was a tradition created between the testaments, if you will. It was not envisioned at all by the Scriptures that the Jews revered. In fact, it neither enhanced nor detracted from the Scriptures. It was simply a tradition that remembered a mighty act of God. And yet Jesus did not attack the custom as "unscriptural," but like the tradition of the synagogue He participated in it.[58]

Thus in both instances the practice of our Lord indicates that traditions, per se, are not bad. Only bad traditions are bad. And bad traditions are those which nullify the clear teaching of the Word of God. If they do not nullify it, or if they directly enhance it, they are legitimate traditions.

Positive tradition and the Apostle Paul. Sometimes we get the impression that Paul was an implacable foe of all Jewish tradition. But this is surely a shallow reading of the New Testament representation of his teaching and life. Several items call for attention in this regard, even apart from the obvious factor that Paul, like Jesus, did not eschew the use of the synagogue. First, Paul did not reject Jewish tradition as inappropriate for all Christians. Although he may have felt that much of his Jewish tradition was *unnecessary* for a new life in Christ, he did not always support the notion that all Jewish tradition was *wrong*. For example, although he was steadfastly opposed to the notion that Jewish circumcision or lawkeeping was necessary for one who came to faith in Christ (that would impinge on the Gospel of grace), Paul still felt free to live at will under certain Jewish traditions.

Before Paul left for his second missionary journey, he added Timothy to his party, but not without circumcising him (Acts 16:3).[59] In Acts 21:17-26, Paul is depicted as participating in certain Jewish purification rites in the Herodian Temple[60] in order to demonstrate that he did not dissuade Jews from practicing their customs at the same time that he protected Gentiles from being bound by those Jewish customs.[61] Surely these are examples of Paul's implementations of the principle found in 1 Corinthians 9:19-21:

> Though I am free and belong to no man, I make myself a slave to everyone, to win as many as possible. To the Jews I became like a Jew, to win the Jews. To those under the law (though I myself am not under the law), so as to win those under the law.

Paul's intent here in freely practicing Jewish law and custom was not particularly out of personal preference in all instances, but rather utilitarian. He was free to practice those laws which he was not personally bound to if by doing so he could win others to Christ without offending them. But the point must be clear: Paul's freedom to practice certain Jewish customs that he knows are not required of him by God indicates that Jewish tradition is not wrong in and of itself; it is wrong only insofar as it violates the clear teaching of the Gospel (that is, if it is made an obligation and thus opposes itself to the grace of God).[62]

Second, Paul's teaching regarding the function of areas in which genuine believers differ has relevance (1 Corinthians 8–10; Romans 14–15). Paul recognized that there were areas of Christian practice (eating of particular foods, honoring of certain days) where believers would come to differing convictions due to the lack of clarity from Scripture, or due to personal background. His point is the need for tolerance and mutual respect: allowing each person's conscience its own inviolability so that areas of scruples or freedom are not imposed by example or coercion on others who may differ. Certainly Jewish tradition comes to play here, particularly dietary and calendar restrictions. And Paul is saying quite clearly: allow those who practice such restrictive behavior out of conscience toward God to continue to do so if they so desire.[63] This is much more akin to the synagogue function than the *Corban* function of tradition.

In summary, Paul, like the Lord, allows a place for those things that are not taught by Scripture as long as they do not detract from or contradict the clear teachings of Scripture. There is such a thing as acceptable tradition. But tradition that conflicts with the Word of God (the Gospel) comes in for scathing denunciation, just as it did for our Lord in His response to the *Corban* law.

POSITIVE TRADITION AMONG THE REFORMERS

It is clear that Jesus and Paul critiqued only certain *kinds* of traditions, that is, any one which nullified the clear teaching of the Word of God. It is also clear that neither Jesus nor Paul dispensed with or critiqued all of the Jewish tradition of their day, but actually allowed by their own practices certain Jewish traditions not found in the Word of God. But that leaves us in a bit of a quandary. If their practice actually justifies biblically unsupported tradition, how can we justify the Protestant claim of *sola Scriptura?* Some practices apparently may well be kept without direct biblical support. Does this run counter to the claims of Protestantism?

Reflection on Protestant thinking in the Reformation era indicates that many of the Reformers concluded that there was a place for any received tradition that did not run counter to the clear teaching of Scripture.[64] The key idea was that if any elements of practice did not deny a teaching of Scripture, even though that practice was not taught in Scripture, it may be allowed. It was considered *adiaphora* (indifferent things).[65] When Scripture did not address something, it was a matter of freedom rather than restriction. A number of the Reformers adopted this model, which deals with what I have called micro-tradition, or denominational distinctives.

The Lutheran *Augsburg Confession,* for example, in discussing the genuine unity of the Church, notes the following:

> And unto the true unity of the Church, it is sufficient to agree concerning the doctrine of the Gospel and the administration of the Sacraments. *Nor is it necessary that human traditions, rites, or ceremonies instituted by men should be alike everywhere,* as St. Paul saith: "There is one faith, one baptism, one God and Father of all."[66]

Article XXIV of the *Thirty-nine Articles of the Church of England* captures this as well. It demonstrates a mature understanding that Christian churches develop traditions, and warns both against giving that tradition final authority, and against lightly dismissing it. Tradition may be changed, but it should not be treated lightly:

> *It is not necessary that Traditions and Ceremonies be in all places one, or utterly like;* for at all times they have been diverse, and may be changed according to the diversity of countries, times, and men's manners, so that nothing be ordained against God's Word. *Whosoever, through his private judgment, willingly and purposely, doth openly break the Traditions and Ceremonies of the Church, which be not repugnant to the Word of God* [that is, on my definition, Good Tradition], *and be ordained and approved by common authority, ought to be rebuked openly* (that others may fear to do the like), as he that offendeth against the common order of the Church, and hurteth the authority of the Magistrate, and woundeth the consciences of the weak brethren. *Every particular or national Church hath authority to ordain, change, and abolish, Ceremonies or Rites of the Church ordained only by man's authority, so that all things be done to edifying.*[67]

In fact, the Reformers, to stay the criticism that they promoted something altogether new and therefore heretical, argued that their teachings were actually supported by the ancient teachings of the church, and that Rome was in fact the innovator and had departed from apostolic doctrine. As A.N.S. Lane pointed out:

> It is significant that the Reformers repeatedly sought to use tradition on their own side. The prime enemy was not tradition, not even supplementary tradition, but the teaching of the contemporary (Roman) church.[68]

But there were also matters apart from Scripture that were not "indifferent things" but were in fact valid authorities, even though derivative, such as the creeds of the first five centuries.[69] Here the Reformers made their clear distinction between Scripture as *norma normans* (the rule that rules), and (macro-)tradition as *norma normata* (the rule that is ruled).[70]

LOOKING AGAIN AT TRADITION

That leads me to a consideration of what we observed earlier regarding the relationship of tradition to the voice of God. The Roman Catholic and Eastern Orthodox churches, in my distinctly

Protestant opinion, are clearly off base when they see the voice of God conjointly in both Scripture and tradition and especially when they view Scripture as a subcategory of tradition. Yet we must not be too critical. They at least *acknowledge* the fact that they have practices which derive from tradition rather than Scripture. They err in giving that tradition equal or superior authority to Scripture, but *at least* they admit the existence and use of tradition in their thinking.

Evangelicals run an even greater risk because we are *too unable to recognize the presence of tradition among us.* We insist so strongly that everything we do derives directly from Scripture alone that we are unable to see that what makes each evangelical group distinct in many instances is the existence of unique interpretive traditions.[71] Some of these traditions are helpful.[72] Helpful, that is, if they (like the synagogue) enhance the teachings of the Word of God or even illustrate them. Examples of traditions of this type may be the use of Sunday Schools (not taught in the New Testament, but useful), Missionary Societies, the celebration of Christmas or Easter, the use of liturgy in worship, the practice of using the sign of the cross or kneeling in worship, or the use of instrumental music.[73] Others may be directly opposed to the Word of God and must be (like the *Corban)* either modified or dispensed with.

But either way, no group by claiming a market on New Testament truth should ever use their distinctive teachings as a wedge to separate from brothers and sisters in other traditions. That is raw sectarianism, laying claim to exclusive possession of the truth. And, sad to say, church history shows that many groups may be charged with erring in this regard.

LEVELS OF CHRISTIAN TRADITION

Thinking about tradition as we have, it is important to draw some careful distinctions in the *kinds* of tradition we are talking about and which kinds may or may not be helpful. In this regard, it would do us good to distinguish carefully between what we may refer to as *interpretive* tradition and *external* (or non-interpretive) tradition.

Interpretive tradition. Interpretive tradition claims to be based directly on the interpretation of the Bible. In Protestant circles, it is the one least likely to be called "tradition," since a given interpretation is often perceived to be the "plain teaching of the Bible." This is not at this point a value judgment in terms of the validity of a given interpretive tradition, simply a statement that traditions of this sort may claim their validity by appeal to the Bible. This is what van Engen had in mind when he wrote:

> Scripture has never existed in a vacuum and never will. It must be interpreted, and its truths passed down, its teaching lived out. The process of interpreting, passing down, and living out takes place in community and results in what historians and theologians call "tradition."[74]

Examples of this kind of tradition are the competing claims over the various types of church polity, the appropriate mode of baptism, the ongoing validity of all of the spiritual gifts, and others. The chief characteristic of this kind of tradition is the appeal to the Bible for support.

Similarly, *systems* of interpretation of the Bible would fall under this rubric, such as the Reformed, dispensational, Wesleyan, or Pentecostal interpretive traditions. It is because these systems claim biblical support that they are called *interpretive* traditions. The claim to correctness here is grounded only on the legitimacy with which one system or another may lay claim to appropriate use of biblical hermeneutics. That is, there are legitimate and illegitimate interpretations of the Bible, if one may use a consistent hermeneutic to be the standard. But one must call every system an interpretive tradition to the degree that they lay claim to biblical support. And, at least in theory, without biblical support, such traditions would be minimized or abandoned.

The problem with this level of tradition is the temptation for it to be invisible to the interpreter. As mentioned earlier, this is the constant temptation to Protestant interpreters with their emphasis on *sola Scriptura*. Again, the presence of interpretive tradition does not mean that interpretive tradition is wrong. The wrong is in confusing unchecked interpretive tradition with the Word of God.

External tradition. External tradition, or non-interpretive tradition, does not lay claim to any direct biblical basis. It sometimes appeals to ancient Christian practice, or (more often) to apostolic tradition transmitted apart from the Bible. Examples may be the Christian liturgy in use in many historic churches (e.g., Catholic, Episcopal, Orthodox, Lutheran) or the use of the sign of the cross.[75] If a tradition is practiced, and justification for its practice is church tradition or ancient practice or the like (or even, may I say, "we've always done it that way") rather than the Bible, then we would call this kind of tradition external tradition. Again, this is not to place a value judgment on such tradition at this point, but only to distinguish between the two major types. Even external tradition is only bad tradition if it undermines a clear teaching of the Bible.[76]

The problem with this level of tradition is not so much that it claims to be a binding interpretation of Scripture at all, but that it is sometimes held to be binding upon all Christians simply because such a practice is ancient within the church. No such binding authority can be given to these traditions. They cannot be *proved* to derive from the apostles at all, no matter how ancient they are, if they cannot be shown to derive from apostolic Scripture. They may be *enjoyed* (if they do not conflict with Scripture) just like other forms of traditions may be enjoyed, but they must not be *enjoined* as a divine mandate required of all Christians everywhere.[77]

SUMMARY AND CONCLUSIONS

Here, in summary fashion, is what I have been arguing:
(1) Tradition is inevitable in any Christian community.
(2) Tradition is condemned *only when it nullifies the Word of God.*
(3) Not all tradition nullifies the Word of God (as seen in our Lord's practice).
(4) Thus there is tradition that is not condemned (some is acceptable).
(5) When a tradition actually *enhances* the Word of God (some teaching or value therein), then it is a good tradition (it is acceptable).
(6) Tradition in evangelical Protestantism is even more dangerous than tradition in Judaism, Roman Catholicism, or Eastern Orthodoxy in that it is often unnoticed and unrecognized, yet it is invariably present and thus unconsciously can become confused with and nullify the Word of God.

(7) To avoid our Lord's condemnation of tradition which too easily overrides the Word of God, we as Protestants must first of all *become aware* of our interpretive traditions.

(8) Once we are aware of our interpretive traditions, then we can either:

(a) appreciate them for what they are *if they enhance a biblical teaching,* or

(b) consider ways to dispense with or modify them *if they detract from a biblical teaching.*

(9) But once we have recognized our distinctive teachings as tradition, we have no right to hold them as intrinsically biblical and therefore superior to those of other evangelical groups. They become a matter of "perspective" or "preferences" which may be fairly passed on as valid tradition.

The key question, of course, is how can we ever become *aware* of the existence of tradition within our specific evangelical traditions. More specifically, how can we evangelicals, who have been taught regularly that we have a set of distinctives which are uniquely "New Testament truths" ever recognize whether some or all of them are simply traditions or traditional interpretations which have been passed on to us?

It apppears that the only clear way to do so is to examine our distinctives in the light of a fair and cooperative use of the principles of biblical interpretation, or *hermeneutics.* If some or many of our practices turn up in the "tradition" category through a consistent use of good hermeneutics, then it is not our duty to automatically dispense with them at all. Instead, we must ask a further question. Does this tradition *enhance* or *detract* from a clear biblical truth? If it enhances one, then we can be free to enjoy it as a useful tradition. If it detracts from one, then we are duty bound before our Lord to modify or dispense with that tradition. But, as I said, the first step is to examine our practices in the light of the principles of biblical interpretation, so as to distinguish clearly taught doctrine from denominational distinctives which may lie in the realm of the traditional.

With that, we will move to the next chapter, which is a treatment of fundamental interpretive guidelines crucial for detecting tradition. Once our denominational distinctives can be identified as "tradition," then they can no longer be used as "truth-clubs" to attack our fellow Christians. We will then need to embrace each other more completely around a core of orthodoxy which we share. Again, understanding our unique traditions keeps us from drifting into sectarianism; the core of orthodoxy which binds us all keeps us from drifting into liberalism. So, let us take a look at the tool with which we may examine our own distinct teachings in an effort to distinguish what is core from what is traditional.

Five

BIBLICAL HERMENEUTICS AS THE KEY TO TRADITION AND CATHOLICITY

Tradition is the process of interpreting and transmitting the Word. It is not simply the process of deformation, but more often it is the history of heroic hermeneutical achievement.

— Clark Pinnock

After my conversion in 1968, I joined the evangelical Christian community of the person who led me to Christ. The group happened to be the Christian Brethren. Although I had minimal exposure to any churches up to that point, I soon recognized that this group was insistent on affirming its own unique characteristics. For one, they had a special meeting entirely devoted to remembering Christ's death every week, while they tended to look down somewhat at other groups and denominations that only had communion once per month, or worse, quarterly or less. Although I could see much of the value placed on this doctrine, before long I became curious about applying one of the cardinal rules they had taught me regarding this unique characteristic, namely, that any Christian practice was only justified insofar as it was demonstrable from Scripture.

So I asked a venerable older saint what Scriptures supported the idea that we were to break bread to remember the Lord every week. His response was to the point: "1 Corinthians 11:26 says 'For as *often* as ye eat this bread, and drink this cup, ye do show the Lord's death till He come' [KJV]. It is not possible that breaking bread once a month or once a quarter could be considered *often*." It did not matter to him when I suggested that the text did not say *how* often, that it simply said "as often." To him what it said was what it meant. Often meant *often*. To suggest otherwise was to question what the Bible plainly said.[1]

Many people have had similar experiences within their own denominational or other Christian fellowship structures. People sometimes claim that the Bible's meaning is found clearly on the surface of the text and that wrangling about the meaning is simply a way to get away from obeying the plain sense of the words.[2] However, that is simply not the way language operates. Anyone who has ever misunderstood another person must recognize that ambiguity in human communication occurs, and inquiring carefully into what another *meant* by the words they used can often clarify communication rather than obscure it.[3] Inquiring into what the Bible means by what it says, and in particular *how we know* what it means by what it says, is a critical task, and although it may be used by some as a way of rationalizing away one's need to obey the text, it cannot be dispensed with in any cavalier way. We *all* interpret the Bible if we read it. It would do us all well then to think about whether we are doing so appropriately or not.

I argued in the previous chapter that the key to recognizing sectarian tendencies is to determine how many of our denominational, parachurch, or local church distinctives are treated by us *as if* they were New Testament mandates (when they are not), and thereby serve as sectarian or organizational ammunition against other Christians who do not quite hold to these truths.[4] The problem comes when we emphasize our distinctives, derived from our unique ways of interpreting the Bible, *at the expense of* our commonness. All too frequently the result is a pure sectarian exclusiveness: a violation of the New Testament teaching on the one body of Christ.

But what drives us to emphasize our distinctives is the notion that they are just as "clearly taught" in the Scriptures as those elements which we have in common with other evangelical groups. To us, they often appear plain as day. The Bible simply *couldn't* mean anything else. But how does this explain such diversity of practice? Can we (as is often done) merely appeal to the biblical ignorance of others who read the same texts but do not see the meaning we attribute to them? I think not. The mutual exclusivity of interpretation demands that we take a closer look at *how* we interpret, to see if our specific interpretations belong to what I have described in the preceding chapter as *tradition*. Only then can we accept them at that level and cease to treat them as doctrinal mandates requiring obedience of the whole church, but view them merely as (1) good tradition to be enjoyed but not foisted upon other Christians, or (2) bad tradition that hinders the Word of God and must be modified or dispensed with. The key tool here which enables us to distinguish "what is taught and what is not" in the Scriptures is known as biblical *hermeneutics,* or the study of how we interpret and apply[5] the Bible.[6]

HERMENEUTICS AND PRIVATE JUDGMENT

An important preliminary issue should be addressed "up front." That is the issue of denominational proliferation, the "sufficiency" of the Bible, and the so-called "right of private judgment." As noted earlier, traditional Roman Catholic theology objects to the Protestant demand for the sufficiency of Scripture. Without the church to tell them the *meaning* of the Bible, they say, Protestants devolve into a quagmire of "private judgments" about the meaning of the Bible with no standard for judging between competing claims. During the Reformation era, the Roman Catholic Council of Trent warned against this in the following words:

> Furthermore, in order to restrain petulant spirits, it [the Council] decrees, that no one, relying on his own skill, shall—in matters of faith, and of morals pertaining to the edification of Christian doctrine,—wresting the sacred Scripture to his own senses, presume to interpret the said sacred Scripture contrary to that sense which holy mother Church,—*whose it is to judge of the true sense and interpretation of the holy Scriptures,*—hath held and doth hold; or even contrary to the unanimous consent of the Fathers; even though such interpretation were never [intended] to be at any time published.[7]

The argument contends that the very diversity found in Protestantism necessarily results from abandoning the authority of the one Roman Church, whose right it is to authoritatively interpret the Scriptures. Once this private judgment was begun by the Protestants (that is, that the Bible may be interpreted by individuals) then diversity of denominational interpretation was inevitable. Some ecumenists argue similarly. Morrison wrote that the same kind of interpretive "private judgment" has caused the problem of schism and denominational division:

> In the New World their [Protestant immigrants] sense of denominational independence was reinforced and stimulated by their consciousness that a great ocean separated them from the milieu in which their ecclesiastical independence had been achieved. They were now on their own, completely detached from any disciplinary restraints. For them, the Bible completely supplanted history, tradition, heritage, catholicity. The right of private interpretation was the principle upon which they had won their independence. Over against this private right there was no adequate counterweight of discipline to inhibit defection and secession from an existing denomination. In the intense controversies over the meaning of Scripture, new denominations arose, all justified by their private interpretation of the Bible. Thus the soil and atmosphere of American freedom encouraged the anarchic proliferation of denominationalism.[8]

Morrison's assessment is perhaps a bit too bleak, and colored by his desire for structural unity. But it is essentially the same one that has been heard from Rome since the time of the Reformation. And the alternative is an authoritative interpretive tradition passed on through the hands of an infallible teaching office (the "magisterium"). But who possesses this? Rome? Constantinople? Geneva? Once one claims to be the sole authoritative interpreter of Scripture, then *any* who depart from that authority can be accused of producing unwanted diversity!

Protestants, on the other hand, appeal to the sufficiency of Scripture and the priesthood of all believers as bases for placing the Bible in the hands of the people. They also acknowledge the place of Spirit-gifted teachers. Protestants simply do not allow the teaching office to have the final say. The text itself is the final authority, and the only appeal is to objective standards of literary interpretation used with any similar literature. "The right of private judgment" becomes as much a *responsibility* as it does a right, which must be weighed against the work of *other* teachers throughout the church, and assessed in view of fair principles of biblical interpretation.[9]

Bear in mind that to Protestants, in particular, hermeneutics is a particularly critical endeavor. Since Protestant theological formulation is based on the mind of God as revealed in the written Word of God alone, the critical link for any Protestant group is interpreting what the Bible really means. To minimize the role of tradition in interpreting the Bible (its presence cannot be *denied)* is not to maximize private judgment, but rather it is to maximize the role of hermeneutics, the principles by which we determine meaning and application in Scripture. The Scripture is *perspicuous* or clear enough to understand its message.[10]

Further, Protestants do not mean to say by this that everything in Scripture is *equally* clear.[11] That would be patently untrue. But, on the other hand, to say that *nothing* is clear, that we always approach the text with preunderstanding that negates our ability to gain any understanding of its objective access to original meaning, is to lead to despair and a frightening hermeneutical agnosticism.[12] Either that, or it leads to an authority considered higher than the Bible itself.

So, with these preliminary issues in mind, it is time to address the issue of hermeneutical principles themselves. This will only be an overview and in no way exhaustive. Many fine works on the process of biblical interpretation are readily available.[13] One would do well to review them, or read several if you have not yet done much thinking on interpreting the Bible. But here I am trying to catch some of the broad, common sense principles we all use when interpreting any written document, and then to apply them to our own inevitable development of tradition. Again, these are "common sense" interpretive tools we use every day to interpret written documents we see. That these apply equally well to the Bible is based on the understanding (a correct one, I believe), that God gave people the Bible not as some mystical document fully understood only by those initiated in its secret codes, but as a clearly understandable document that people can interpret with simple human common sense.[14]

The diversity among Protestant denominations is due at least in part to the fact that, although all groups subscribe to *sola Scriptura*, they diverge at a number of points in their interpretation of that Scripture. Those divergences comprise a diversity of interpretive traditions. But, in a sense, one might argue that if there were common ground in terms of the principles of hermeneutics among all Protestants, then there would be more commonality in terms of the understanding of the meaning of the text of Scripture, and thus less diversity.[15] That is the purpose of this chapter. It is an attempt to identify certain "common sense"[16] rules of interpretation with which we may examine our own denominational distinctives, which are, at the bottom line, interpretational differences of understanding the Bible. Then, given an understanding of these, the grounds for classing some of our distinctives as traditions (traditional interpretations which may then be assessed as either good or bad traditions and retained, modified, or dispensed with) may be more easily accomplished. We may then accept our legitimate traditions as patterns of diversity and enjoy ours, and others' as such.

To help broaden our appreciation for our own traditions as well as those of other groups, it is my desire to do two things in this chapter. First, I lay out some fair and foundational "common sense" interpretational principles, essential to investigating the meaning of Scripture and discovering our own interpretational distinctives. Second, I suggest some practical means to employ in order to broaden our understanding of the breadth of the church's alternative traditions and understandings, and thus to begin our practice of recovering a renewed cross-denominational catholicity in the church today. I will investigate these ideas under two categories: (1) the church as a community sharing general interpretive principles, and (2) the church as a community learning from and sharing each other's interpretive insights.

THE CHURCH AS A COMMUNITY SHARING
GENERAL INTERPRETIVE PRINCIPLES

The church has not always agreed on *how* to interpret the Bible, but it has tended to affirm very clearly what it understood to be the *content* of the teachings of the Bible on the Christian faith — the authoritative apostolic faith. These affirmations of the church in terms of the teachings of the Bible are found in the ancient creeds and confessions, a pattern supported and followed by the Reformers.

The difficulty in interpretation comes when one adopts the Protestant notion of *sola Scriptura*, coupled with the notion of the priesthood of all believers with its corollary, the "right" of private judgment. Two problems immediately arise: (1) What method can legitimately be used to help tell what the Bible means (since its meaning is no longer taken by faith from any authoritative ecclesiastical affirmation such as the creeds)? and (2) What do we make of the ancient affirmations? Are they some sort of guide to interpretation, or are they irrelevant to interpretation?

I will briefly interact with the second question before taking on the first one in the rest of the chapter. In short, *sola Scriptura* and its corollaries requires some sort of inductive, objective approach to the Bible as Scripture apart from the direct interference of any sort of creed or dogma. Otherwise, one risks being locked into some sort of *eisegetical* rather than *exegetical* method that looks for meaning in the text rather than drawing meaning from the text.[17]

On the other hand, the place of interpretation, particularly the ancient interpretation of the text cannot be ignored and dismissed out of hand since that is part of a broad-based (macro-) tradition of the church catholic, of which I am a part by faith. Ancient interpretational statements (as well as more recent ones) can serve as a *check* on interpretive conclusions rather than as a *guide* to those conclusions.[18] As stated earlier, if Scripture is *norma normans,* then this interpretive macro-tradition is *norma normata* — a very important check.[19]

If we draw radically different conclusions from that which the church has understood its own Scriptures to teach for centuries, we can probably assume we may have missed something in our own procedure. It could be rather arrogant to assume that our "insight" into the text is always clearer and more authoritative if it conflicts with centuries of Christian interpretation. We should therefore be forced back to our work once again.[20]

With that in mind, the first question must be addressed. What means do we have for determining the meaning of the text in any appropriate fashion, so that it can serve as the norm to not only assess the legitimacy of macro-tradition (the creeds and confessions), but especially (as we look at its importance for catholicity), to detect and assess our own denominational/local church micro-traditions?

Theological assumptions about the Bible. There are certain assumptions which we all bring to the text in interpreting it. It is good to get those assumptions out in the open to begin with so that we can address them. The first assumption (an ancient one) is that each book in the Bible has *two* authors: God and a human author. The Bible is the confluent work of both divine and human authorship, yet the biblical writers indicate that the primary agent in the process of the Bible's production as Scripture is God (2 Tim. 3:14-16; 2 Peter 1:20-21).

A second assumption is that the Bible is an *intelligent communication* from God. In sponsoring the production of the Bible, He was intending to communicate rather than obscure.[21] God therefore communicated in language forms that would have been intelligible to the original audiences of each piece of biblical literature.

A third assumption is that divine meaning is to be found in the *expressed intent* of the human author in addressing his audience by using common language patterns and literary forms of his day and culture, and not in some mystical meaning that superseded the normal communication forms of the human author. These ideas will be expanded in what follows.

The Bible has historically been considered the Word of God written through the hands of men. Yet there are two extremes in viewing these aspects of the Bible that interpreters tend to take. Both of these extremes can lead into error. The one extreme is to see the Bible as solely the word of man (the extreme of some theologically liberal interpreters). The other is to see it solely as the Word of God (the extreme of some theologically conservative interpreters). It is, however, both. Either extreme can lead to interpretive error in the long run.

Those who go to the first extreme are often careful to look at the historical factors behind the production of each book of the Bible, but care little about any normative, divine authority it may have for the church today, or for their own lives for that matter. God's activity in the production of the book is, at best, downplayed; at worst, it is denied all together.

Rationalism of the eighteenth century injected this attitude into modern biblical studies. As a result, many liberal seminaries offer their students (and thereby their congregations) a Bible to read that is little more than mere religious opinions of ancient peoples. That is why preaching and interpretation in these churches is often so theologically thin — often focusing instead on contemporary social and moral opinions rather than any form of authoritative biblical interpretation and application. Also, that is why fervent interest in personal Bible study is all too often missing among these congregations. After all, of what relevance are the opinions of such ancients to complex contemporary moral and social problems? Certainly biblical interpretation will take a rather different approach when the relevance of the Bible itself to modern moral and social issues is understood to be limited.[22]

But the other extreme is more subtle. There are those, even from conservative interpretive traditions, who tend to view the Bible only from the standpoint that it is the Word of God. The historical, cultural, linguistic factors are of far lesser relevance than the immediacy of the voice of God to one in the here and now. Bible study is reduced often in this perception to searching for daily "blessings," and preaching is diverted into sentimental devotionalism. What it means "to me" becomes more critical than "what it means, period." Or, as has tended to be the earlier history of my own tradition, the typological or pragmatic becomes more important than the historical.[23] Beyond this, the desire for infallible meaning from an infallible God tends to compel some preachers and teachers toward greater certainty than is really available in the text. The minimally attested is given eternal authority simply because it is found in the Bible. Living with any degree of ambiguity or uncertainty for such persons becomes a frightening or unsettling experience.[24]

But so often popular biblical interpretation reduces to finding a meaning that may have little or no connection with the meaning intended by the original writer. The "meaning I get out of it" is considered the more important, practical, and personal dimension to Bible study. But can we really be confident in this sense that we have discovered *the* meaning of the text? Must we not return to the meaning put there by the writer? And we dare not claim that God may well have meant something other than the biblical author meant by the words and syntax he employed. If that were the case, then we would do well to wait on those who have more immediate access to the divine throne to tell us what God wants us to do, rather than to deal with the Bible at all.[25]

Balanced biblical hermeneutics begins with the theological foundation that the Bible is both the Word of God *and* the word of men. It has full authority, absolute inerrancy, and universal applicability as the Word of God and it has historical, cultural, literary, linguistic, and particular sense as the word of men.[26] In fact, unless God is trying to hide something *from* us rather than reveal something *to* us in the Bible, then we must admit that the *only safe way to understand what God means in the Bible is to focus on understanding what the human author of Scripture meant by what he wrote.*[27] God means (at the very least) what the human author means. To seek further meaning is unverifiable and therefore must be held suspect to a certain degree. We should therefore be wary of trying to find a "higher" or "spiritual" meaning. How could we ever check that out? All we have are the words the human author left us, by the providence of God. So we must focus our efforts at finding God's meaning on finding the human author's meaning.

And we must let that author give us the key to what he means, not what we may want him to say.[28] We cannot read into the text some meaning that we think God wants us to put there if it conflicts with the human writer's intention, nor can we attribute a current, contemporary meaning that we get out of the text if it conflicts with the writer's intended meaning. Let me give you an example from contemporary life.

In the early 1960s the folk musical group known as Peter, Paul, and Mary sang a song written by Peter Yarrow called "Puff the Magic Dragon." It is a beautiful, sentimental song about the playful imaginary world of a young boy which sadly falls aside as he grows into manhood. But when I first heard that song in junior high school, my friends told me it had a hidden meaning about marijuana. The "magic dragon" was supposed to be marijuana, which, of course, you "puff" on. We all bought into this secret meaning because it was not unlike contemporary musicians to hide protest or countercultural messages between the lines of their songs. That, to us, was what the song meant. But is that really what the song *meant?* What made our interpretation so special, and what if another attached a different meaning to it?

Peter, Paul, and Mary had a thirty-year reunion tour, which was videotaped and later televised. Late in the program, Peter Yarrow was about to lead the audience in singing "Puff," which had since its debut become a popular American folk song. But he prefaced his remarks with an illuminating comment, to this effect: "Many people thought that this song was about drugs. But it never was. It was a simple song about a boy and his dragon, and the sorrows of leaving boyhood. I know. I'm Puff's daddy."

Now we could go on to argue that it doesn't matter what Peter Yarrow meant by the words of the song he wrote, that there is a "higher" meaning. But if Peter Yarrow cannot tell us what he meant by the words *he wrote,* then who could ever say with any degree of certainty what the meaning really is? Words *must* be linked in their meaning to what is intended by the person who originally spoke (or wrote) them.[29] Otherwise, any certainty of ascertaining meaning is lost. Demonstrating that a suggested meaning is the author's expressed intent is the only way to objectively validate an interpretation.[30]

For proper hermeneutics this is critical. If I can (with a fair degree of objectivity) determine from context, flow of thought, and historical studies that *this* is what the human author is saying by a given passage, then I have the objective basis for demonstrating that my interpretation is valid. Of course, the Spirit of God is there to grant me enlightenment in terms of my own objectivity (or lack thereof), and to enable me to *believe* the supernatural message I find there. But I cannot call on Him to tell me what He is saying *apart from the text of the Bible itself.* Any impulse I may understand to be from the Spirit of God in terms of meaning I must, in the final analysis, confirm or deny on the basis of the *text.* That alone is the normative Word of God for today. And that we must study carefully.[31]

The single meaning of the text. Closely related to the above discussion is the need to understand the "single meaning of the text." Given the assumption that the Bible was given to humankind through the confluent process of divine and human authorship, and given the fact that the divine meaning must be found *in* (and not apart from or above) the human author's meaning, then we must also begin to assume that the basic elements of any human communication process holds true. The first of these is what the Reformers referred to as "unity of meaning," or the single meaning of the text.

All this means is that humans typically mean something by what they say. They *intend* to communicate something. And, unless they are playing with words (such as a pun or *double entendre*), they mean only one thing. Otherwise, communication would be impossible. With a biblical writer, we must allow the same human principle. The biblical writer (Paul, David, Moses, Isaiah) wrote words that he meant to be understood. Only in those instances where he is playing with words does he ever imply more than one sense — but even so his single meaning is a "double sense." He means in that instance to give us a double sense.[32]

In terms of biblical interpretation, this means that we have no right to play "biblical roulette" in a group Bible study ("What does it mean to you? And you?"). We must work hard on a single goal: the intended meaning of the author. And we must not rest until we have gathered enough data from the type of literature a biblical writer has produced, from the flow of thought and context, and from even a reference to the way his language operates as opposed to ours.[33] Our goal as students of the Word of God is to sweat hard over it until we can, to the satisfaction of ourselves, our peers, and our audiences (if we preach) demonstrate from the literary factors of the text that this—and not that—is what a biblical writer meant. Because what *he* meant is what *God* meant. And God is trying to communicate and not trying to obscure. In reviewing our denominational distinctives, this is a key factor. There are passages used to support our distinctive teachings. Are those passages interpreted in such a way that the meaning ascribed can be demonstrated to be the single meaning intended by the biblical writer?

Literal interpretation. The notion of "literal interpretation" has been grossly misunderstood by the critics of historic Protestant evangelicalism, and not without justification. Some evangelicals and fundamentalists, reacting to those who explain away the miraculous as myth or allegory, insist not only on understanding them literally, but on denying the presence of figurative language altogether in the Bible. But this is really a set of extreme reactions. The liberal sees the figurative in the Bible, but simply misapplies it in the case of the miraculous (often based on false philosophical assumptions); the conservative sees this misuse of the figurative and denies its presence altogether. Both of these extremes are wrong.

Literal means, first of all, the "simple" or "normal" or "common" sense.[34] It does not deny the place of the figurative, but simply expects that the normal use of language must determine when a figurative is being employed. That is, "literal" indicates that the language of the Bible operates in the normal way language does (particularly, the way the writer's language operates). We are not to impose a figurative sense when the author was intending an historical description, nor to demand a formal sense when he was using symbol. It is to recognize that each language and culture has its own idioms, grammar, and vocabulary, and the languages and culture of the Bible are no exception. Literal interpretation is thus a dimension of understanding the original author's intention in the language and literary forms he chose to use.[35] It leaves the meaning with the author as expressed in the text, rather than detaching the text from the author.

Furthermore, when we use the term *literal* we must take into account the method by which we understand language in the presence of a plethora of figures and idioms. In both written and oral communication, we tend to understand the language used in a literal way unless we receive clear clues that one is departing from normal ways of communicating or using a stock figure of speech that we already understand to be such. That is the way we humans talk. That is not to say that we do not use figures of speech, nor to say that the Bible does not contain them. In both instances the presence of both literal and figurative meaning is manifold. But the figurative depends in many ways on the literal for its detection.

When I say, "I'm going to bat for you" and we are standing in the dugout of a baseball field, you understand me in a normal, literal way: I am informing you that the manager has asked me to pinch-hit. When you are told that in another context, such as in the business world, you understand it in the figurative sense it has taken on in our culture: I mean that I am going to "put in a good word for you" or "I am going to stick up for you." One knows that because of the context in which it is said and would rarely be confused by that sort of idiomatic expression.

Our language is filled with figures of speech that have crept in from the sports world ("I *struck out* on that one."), aviation ("We'd better *bail out* of this situation."), show business ("She's quietly serving the Lord *behind the scenes*"), seafaring ("Is our church *in the doldrums?*"), technology ("We'd better *interface* the two."), travel ("You sure *missed the boat* on that one."), and others. But that does not mean that we cannot understand each other. We assume the literal as basic and are "tipped off" to the existence of a figure of speech when the literal makes no sense at all in a given situation. Often we are so accustomed to the automatic nature of this process, that we forget how many figures of speech we use in a day.[36]

In this same way we must, in our practice of biblical interpretation, force ourselves to be more literal than is normal in order to detect the presence of the figurative. We need to be more literal than normal in reading Scripture, but only in a methodological sense. Working from the strictly literal can force us to detect when a given writer is tipping us off that he is using a figure of speech. Paul, for example, must be taken in a plain, literal, normal sense when he talks of seeing the risen Lord. But when he refers to Peter and James and John as "pillars" of the church of Jerusalem (Gal. 2:9) he has alerted us to the presence of a figure. The literal would produce an absurdity. Living human beings do not typically hold up buildings (Samson aside). Further, the church in Pauline theology does not refer to a building at all, but to a community of God's people. But we do not abandon the literal even here. We are "tipped off" by the literal. And thus we understand that "pillar" in this context is a figure of speech for a person who is critical for the holding together of the Christian community.

So in studying the Bible we need to take it in a normal sense. The preference for the literal is primarily methodological and helps us to detect the figurative. That is simply the typical way humans communicate. When we have detected a figure of speech, we must enjoy it as such, but seek to determine the singular intent behind the figure.[37] The figure thus serves as sort of multidimensional enrichment that adds flavor to the author's meaning. It is the extensive use of figures of speech that makes the hymnic and prophetic literature of the Bible such a pleasure to read — and, unfortunately, also makes those sections such a difficulty to interpret. And it is attention to this element of hermeneutics which again can help us assess the fairness of our denominationally distinct texts.

The historical element. The United States recently celebrated the two-hundredth anniversary of its Constitution. But the Constitution, like any other type of literature, must be interpreted. And some modern interpretations of the Constitution, especially the First Amendment and the Bill of Rights, would have surprised its original framers. Unfortunately for life in modern America, the Constitution has been interpreted to teach freedom *from* religion rather than freedom *of* religion, the freedom of women to terminate human life in their wombs, and in other equally nonhistorical ways.[38] But the Constitution is a 200-year-old document. As some voices have been crying out in the current interpretive wilderness, that document too must be interpreted in the light of the intention of the original framers — otherwise we are not letting *it* guide us at all; we are simply shaping it to fit our own preferences.[39] Such studies have led to some rather startling conclusions.

So it is in interpreting the Bible. We must let the Bible mean first what it meant to the original human authors and readers. Only then can we properly and carefully apply it to our own context. If we begin with our context and work backward, we run the risk of shaping the Bible to our own preferences rather than shaping our preferences to conform to Scripture.

This process of asking first what the Bible meant to the original reader is sometimes known as "distanciation" or "distancing" ourselves from the text of the Bible.[40] This is done just long enough to hear as much as possible what the author meant to his contemporaries. Then we can more objectively draw the Bible near to us to know more accurately what God means to say to us today. In distanciation, several factors must be bridged: the historical gap, the linguistic gap, the cultural gap, and the literary gap. This is only to say that the biblical writers wrote in a different period of history than we do, using different languages than we speak, familiar with different cultural practices than we use, and often with different ways of writing from us. Moisés Silva notes well that:

> We do not indeed need help because the Scriptures are inherently obscure but because we are far removed from the biblical writers in time and culture. Even a document written carefully in clearly formulated English, such as the Declaration of Independence, can *appear* obscure two hundred years later.[41]

The first gap that we must overcome in interpreting Scripture is the historical gap. When Moses wrote, the world was dominated by Egyptian and Mesopotamian superpowers. He knew nothing of Romans and Greeks. When Paul wrote, he knew of the historical past up to the point in which he lived. To him, Abraham was some 2,000 years in the remote past; the Exodus took place some 1,500 years earlier; David was 1,000 years past; and Ezra, the most recent of biblical characters to him, was some 500 years in history to him. But he knew nothing about nuclear weaponry, automobiles, or two world wars—not to speak of the Council of Nicea, Charlemagne, the Crusades, or the Renaissance.

To be sure, the God who moved them to write Scripture knew all of these things. But apart from the genre of prophecy, inspired revelation, as we must know, is not predominately predictive in nature. It is, instead, primarily contemporary: God speaks to a given people in time, space, and history in ways they can understand because He wills to reveal and not to conceal or simply to impress.

Secondly, there is a language gap. Moses spoke and wrote Hebrew, a Semitic language which was akin to various languages spoken in Canaan and the surrounding regions. Paul knew Hebrew (as a rabbi trained in the original language of his Scripture), but he spoke Aramaic and Greek. Aramaic, akin to Hebrew, was his native tongue—adopted by his people as a result of foreign influence during the Babylonian captivity. Paul learned Greek from his youth due to the predominate use of that tongue in his native land ever since King Alexander's conquests some 300 years earlier. Each language has its own vocabulary, pronunciation, and syntax.

The third gap we must bridge is a cultural gap. Cultures are different. One of the most difficult elements of moving to a different country is not so much the language learning, but the adjusting to significantly different ways of doing things, and doing them with different tools. My Canadian students face a cultural diversity just by living with us south of the border. One can experience a similar feeling by taking a vacation to Canada. Try to adjust yourself to speed limit signs posted in kilometers per hour instead of miles per hour and to purchasing fuel for your car in imperial gallons rather than U.S. gallons. Have you ever seen the puzzled look on people's faces in a Canadian airport or train station when you ask for the "restroom," or worse, "bathroom"? Or did you take the opportunity to review your French on all the signs and consumer labels? Let's face it: Canada has its cultural differences from the United States. And getting along well in Canada depends in the long run on learning and adapting to those customs.

The same is true in dealing with the Near Eastern cultures of the Bible. There is Egyptian culture that the Hebrew culture had to relate with, as well as the Babylonian culture later on. The Assyrians made their mark, as did the Persians. The Greeks were there (hidden, in large part, between the Testaments),[42] and of course the Romans. Each one had its own material culture, as revealed in its implements of daily life; as well as immaterial culture, as seen in its customs. Sometimes the Bible brings these customs to light; at other times the customary nature of the practice is less transparent.[43] But either way, we must make our adjustments and not transpose the material world of our time into the biblical era.[44]

In many of these areas, especially the language gaps, we can confidently rely on good translations for resolution. But we must be ever alert to the historical time gaps and progressions of events. And we must be careful in interpreting specific types of biblical literature without paying attention to the way in which the writer followed the literary norms of his time.

And the key issue in applying these factors to our favored denominational texts is clearly this: What was it that the biblical writer meant in the context in which he wrote? Do our favored passages mean what they meant to the original writer?

The genre element. In writing a letter to a friend, we communicate in a certain format. We begin with a greeting and end with a closing, following a common literary convention. The first century New Testament epistles followed a different format. It was fairly consistent, since the thirteen letters of Paul all follow a very similar pattern, as do the general epistles. That is because there was a certain way in which a letter was to be written in the first century. It wasn't a law, just a "convention," and could be adjusted according to individual taste, just as we vary the modern letter writing convention today.

But the Bible contains more than just letters. Our Scriptures are a rich library of God-breathed literature of several types: civil and moral law (legal literature), history (historical literature), prophetic revelations and apocalypses (prophetic literature), poetry and hymnody (poetic literature), and proverbial sayings and explorations into the nature of true wisdom (*hokmâ* or wisdom literature). We ought to thank God for giving us such a rich treasure of variety in His revelation, but there is a slight catch.

The problem arises in the tendency to treat the Bible as if it was made up of one variety of literature (e.g., a divine law book, or a divine love letter). Therefore, our hermeneutic skills need to be more carefully honed so as to treat each book (or section) of the Bible as the kind of literature that it really is. We do not read a book of poetry with the same sort of critical historical acumen as we do an historical work. True, they both may teach truth, even historical truth, but they do so in different ways. One uses images and figures to give the emotive sense of an event. The other tends to use raw data to give the narrative content of an event.

We don't expect a personal letter to follow the format of a legal briefing. They have different functions as well as different forms. Further, the forms are not exactly the same. When David wrote poetry, for example, he was following the conventions of a Hebrew poet of the late eleventh century B.C., and not the conventions of a twentieth century American poet. They did it differently.[45] When Luke wrote Acts, he was not writing quite the same as a modern historian would, although there are similarities. He was not intending to be exhaustive. He had a specific point to demonstrate, and so he selected a number of events from the history of the early church to prove that point. The Gospel writers themselves show that, although there were many other events known about the life of our Savior in the first century church, each of them selected only those sayings and deeds of our Lord he wished to highlight. The Gospels were written with specific intent.

Again, there is a fundamental issue at stake in looking at the various genres in the Bible. This is what is known as the "is/ought" issue. That is, how much of the Bible is describing what took place without necessarily recommending what ought to be followed at all times and at all places. Judas, for example, is described in the Bible as hanging himself, but that does not mean that the Bible teaches us that suicide is acceptable. Many prominent men in the Old Testament, even before Sinai, are described as having multiple wives, but that does not mean that the Bible teaches polygamy. In this sense, narrative literature such as the historical books of the Old and New Testaments most often describe covenant life, sometimes to show error as much as to show obedience. But it is from other didactic sections, such as Law, Prophets, and Epistles, that we derive the doctrinal content from which to evaluate these. More could be said on this issue of the place of literary genre in hermeneutics, but there are other fuller treatments of the subject.[46]

Some derivative hermeneutical mistakes. Although there are many other interpretive principles which we could address here, a few common interpretive mistakes that evangelicals make must be outlined.[47] Two that need to be singled out are what I call the "negative hermeneutic" and "patternism." Let me briefly explain.

The "negative hermeneutic" says that because something is *not found* in the New Testament it is inherently wrong and unbiblical. Thus, by implication, anyone who practices something that is not found in the New Testament is somehow out of line with proper biblical teaching.[48]

On reflection, of course, this is a rather absurd interpretive notion. Who would say, for example, that because a person's name is "not found" in the phone book she does not exist, or that because certain practices are not explicitly *allowed* in the laws of our country they are automatically *prohibited?* This is simple nonsense, is it not?

When something is "not found" in a thing it is simply because it is not found there. It does not explain *why* the thing is not found, nor does it mean that it is not there in actuality. It *may* mean that it is not there, but it may also mean that it simply was not recorded, or that it was in fact permitted. And so it is with God's Word. Because a thing is not found in the New Testament does not automatically prohibit it. It may just as likely mean that God is giving *freedom* in that area.[49]

An honest look at evangelical Christians reveals that most instinctively operate in the above way in other areas of church practice. Few churches prohibit the use of a Sunday School program, but any of us would be hard pressed to find a Sunday School in the New Testament. But Sunday Schools have value in the instruction of children in the Word of God, and hence they are perceived to have value even if they do not rally explicit biblical support. This is, as we said in the previous chapter, an example of positive tradition. It is an example of something valuable that is practiced by many churches, though not found in the Bible.

Similarly, most churches freely condone other elements which we cannot demonstrate were a part of the New Testament church at all: the use of a pulpit, the ownership of a building, the wearing of coats and ties by men, the use of certain theological terms (e.g., "trinity" and "rapture") none of which are "found in the New Testament." So we have a contradiction in practice as well as an unsupportable hermeneutical idea. The bottom line is simply this: if a thing is not found in the Bible, *it is not necessarily prohibited.* Unless it violates a clear command of Scripture, perhaps it is really a matter of the individual local church or denomination to operate under the lordship of Christ and the freedom of the Spirit of God. One simply cannot argue from what the Bible does *not* say. How is one to understand the intent of the author of Scripture when he has left *nothing* to express his intent?

The other common hermeneutical mistake that I wish to address is what I call "patternism." This interpretive mistake asserts that the *way* a thing was done by New Testament believers is the *way* that it is to be done by all Christians at all times and at all places, particularly if that *way* is recorded in numerous places. But this is another example of a hermeneutical error. It is mixing up what *happened* in the New Testament with what *ought* to happen (as discussed under the issue "genre"). But even so, it is sometimes argued that, if a practice is shown *enough* times in the Bible, a pattern emerges and a precedent is set. Since the Holy Spirit has recorded for us that the early church did it this way, then He is providing for us a precedent that we should follow, even if there is no direct command to do so.

But on reflection this is not an appropriate approach to interpreting the Bible. For example, the New Testament reveals a number of things about Paul. First, he regularly relied on sea or land travel for his missionary journeys. Are we to require this of our missionaries today and prohibit air travel because flying is not the New Testament pattern for missionary travel? Further, Paul always went to the Jews first in his evangelization of new territories. Does that mean that modern missionaries are always to do the same? Again, Paul regularly went to major metropolitan areas to preach. Are we, for these reasons, to avoid third and fourth world cultures that are predominantly nonurban?

The answer to the foregoing questions is simple: of course not. We may learn much from what appears to be Paul's strategy, but to construe that as the God-given strategy for all times and all places would be foolish. What we find in the New Testament was Paul's plan for reaching an urban Greco-Roman world with a large Jewish Diaspora, but that does not at all imply that an identical plan for reaching the world should be used in a different time, culture, and place. These things are *found* in the New Testament but are not *mandated* by the New Testament. No matter how many times an "is" is shown to us in Scripture, we cannot take it as any sort of divinely mandated precedent, an "ought," *unless* it can be demonstrated that it was the intent of the human author of that book to set us a precedent. If we can demonstrate that, then we can confidently affirm that God has set such a precedent. But that is not an easy task.[50]

Conclusions. We must let the Bible be understood as it was understood by those who wrote it and to whom it was originally written. We have no right to try to force God's Word to act as if it were written personally to us — on our own terms. It was written *to* others, but *for* our benefit as well. We ultimately were within the scope of God's plan as beneficiaries of His Holy Word, but it was not given to us in our time, space, and history. He has seen fit to preserve it for the use of His church throughout the ages, and His breath is seen in its pages, but we must force ourselves to work hard to understand it as it was given originally.

We cannot automatically assume that those who began to read Scripture afresh in the sixteenth century to spawn the Reformation, as bright and zealous as they were, were given all of the hermeneutical answers. And we cannot assume that our denominational or Christian organizational forebears were given them either. On some things they simply did not dig deep enough. On others, they found some clean, fresh insight. But we must discipline ourselves to find answers, historically, as God gave them. And we must not simply assume that we have automatically arrived at the truth (or, "sound instruction") simply because we are reading a "safe" or "doctrinally sound" writer. God's Word is an immense well to draw from. We need not be satisfied with water others have drawn for us. Let us demand that we throw the bucket in for ourselves. That is what occurred within my own tradition in the nineteenth century, as well as in countless other renewal movements throughout church history. Let us all imitate our forebears' zeal for fresh biblical knowledge. To do that, we must apply a fresh, clean, historical, "common-sense" biblical hermeneutic once again.

THE CHURCH AS A COMMUNITY SHARING HERMENEUTICAL PRACTICE

As noted earlier, part of the problem in seeking the meaning of the biblical text is that we interpret the Scriptures from within a particular ecclesiastical tradition. Even when we are attempting to use fair hermeneutics on the text in order to detect the traditional in our own denominational thinking, we sometimes simply cannot avoid the influence of the very tradition that we are trying so hard to detect. We are not unlike fish trying to notice they are surrounded by water. The water upholds, infiltrates, and feeds them, but they do not even notice that it is there. So it is with our own interpretive traditions. Though we may study hermeneutics and use it on the text arduously, as long as we continue to interpret solely from within our own ecclesiastical framework we run the risk of being controlled by traditional presuppositions.

That is not to deny that our own ecclesiastical tradition may have the correct interpretation of a certain point, but the problem we face is just how much we are unconsciously influenced by our tradition. How can this be resolved, so that we can become more aware of our own interpretive biases? Furthermore, how can we avoid coming up with unique and bizarre "private" interpretations that lead to exclusivistic sects that hold all other Christians wrong? The answer to both questions is the same.

I would like to suggest that a key factor here is learning to practice *community exegesis.* We must allow the thinking of others outside our traditions to become involved in the confirmation of our interpretive processes. Those operating outside our own ecclesiastical grid can help us to see our own biases.

Two primary concerns must be addressed to effectively practice community exegesis. The first is to understand well our own specific denominational interpretive traditions, and the second is to make good use of the broader interpretive traditions (historic and contemporary) outside our own. These two concerns actually feed each other, and both are necessary. As I understand the role of my own tradition with both its strengths and its limitations, I am pushed outward to appreciate and learn from the traditions of others. As I interact with the traditions of others, I am better able to understand the role of my own tradition with both its strengths and limitations. But it does not matter where we begin. To be alert to the influence of traditional presuppositions regarding the text, we must incorporate these elements to do a better job of inductively seeking the meaning of Scripture.

Hermeneutics in the macro-community: understanding your own tradition well.
1. Know the history of your own denominational tradition.
Each denominational tradition began to provide something that was believed to be lacking in the emphases or teachings of the church at large, or of a parent denomination. The emphasis of that "movement," denomination, or sect's distinctive teachings focused on solving that problem. For Presbyterians and Lutherans (as well as any other Protestant denomination), the Protestant Reformation should be their forte. John Calvin and Martin Luther's thinking and interpretive approaches to the Bible should be areas of expertise. Baptists must read their history to understand the great men and women who gave their lives and efforts to champion the characteristic Baptistic distinctives. Methodists must study and understand the impetus behind the development of Methodism and what drove men like John and Charles Wesley and Francis Asbury. Those in my Christian Brethren tradition must understand the backgrounds to the movement in the early nineteenth century and personalities like Anthony Norris Groves, George Müller, Henry Craik, and John Nelson Darby.

And, of course, the list goes on. Be sure to find (1) a definitive history or two of your own tradition, written in a sympathetic but careful style (and perhaps some sharply critical works as well); and (2) any original documents that may identify key Scriptures and theological ideas which drove the founders of your group. If you have access to a theology school affiliated with your church, instructors of denominational history there could be of good help to you.

2. Identify the distinctives of your denominational or local church tradition.
The key issue here is the reason for a group's existence. What factors were important to the early leaders of this group? Why

did they carve out a distinct movement, rather than simply stay-
ing with the existing institutions of the time? What characteristics
mark this group's identity? Can you identify key, original historical characteristics which marked off this group that may be different from secondary characteristics which have developed in
subsequent years? Sometimes these questions can be answered
by books describing the origins of the movement, or they may be
answered by obtaining materials from a denominational
headquarters.

*3. Identify the key Scriptures and rationale used to support the
distinctives of your own tradition.*
Of course, the key element here is to find out what Scriptures
are used to support a given tradition. In Protestant groups, this is
an appropriate question, since all practice and doctrine (based
on the mutually embraced notion of *sola Scriptura*) must be demonstrated from the Bible. Typically books on doctrine from your
tradition, or on denominational distinctives, will give both the
distinctive doctrines and the Scriptures used to support those
distinctives.

*4. Assess the Scriptures and rationale from the standpoint of
hermeneutics. Have these Scriptures been appropriately interpreted in
the history of your own tradition?*
Here is where the application of the principles of hermeneutics
reviewed in this chapter must come into play. For this to be of
optimal value, honesty and humility must accompany a sincere
desire on the part of the interpreter to find out the intent of the
biblical writer in each given passage. Of course, looking carefully
into the interpretive approach of others must be a part of this
(see the second part, below).

*5. If the Scriptures used to support a distinctive are not appropriately
interpreted, determine whether these "traditional" interpretations are
helpful or harmful ones.*
If the Scriptures used to support a given element do not affirm it
at all (e.g., a mode of baptism, or a type of polity), then the
interpreter must ask if the practice detracts from or enhances a
biblical truth. If it is *neutral,* then it need not be addressed further, but may simply continue to be practiced as a denomination-

al tradition—as long as it is clearly and honestly recognized as such. If it is harmful, however, by undercutting a clear teaching of the Scriptures elsewhere, then the next step must be followed.

6. If it is your assessment that these "traditional interpretations" are harmful, then develop a plan for addressing them with integrity.
This is a difficult step, requiring integrity and commitment on the part of the individual. If you are a part of a group which embraces and practices a harmful tradition, then you must determine how critical it is to the group: Is it a foundational, or peripheral tradition—that is, does it touch a core value of the group, or is it a secondary value? If it is a core value that *must* be held, then one must acknowledge his or her divergence from it to one's fellow superiors and colleagues, and leave the judgment up to them. But at that point, one must be prepared to realign with a group that shares more consistently his or her belief system. Teaching one's incompatabilities to dissuade others without discussing it frankly and openly with one's superiors is a dangerous practice. And it is even worse to teach contrary to an accepted teaching despite the opinions of one's superiors.

7. Identify and affirm those "traditional interpretations" which are beneficial.
It is important, at the same time, to not communicate the need to subvert all those traditions for which one cannot find explicit biblical support. Identify those traditions which are helpful, and emphasize them as helpful traditions. This not only reaffirms the value of the group's uniquenesses, but can emphasize its distinct contribution to the *entire* church, of which each denominational group is but a part.

Hermeneutics in the macro-community: learning from the traditions of others.
1. Cultivate an attitude of hermeneutical humility.
We must recognize the possibility that our own background may unduly color our ability to read Scripture. Hermeneutical humility, as I am using the phrase, means that we can expect to learn from other believers *outside* of our tradition something of the meaning of the Bible. It is not the same as hermeneutical agnosticism, that we can never really know for certain the Bible's

meaning. We can, instead, seek to obtain certainty with a humble ear to saints of all persuasions, all generations past, and all denominational traditions. Unless we have heard, we cannot be sure that we have understood. If we have not understood, then we cannot evaluate whether an interpretation, be it ours or theirs, is consistent with biblical authorial intent. And one can learn something of the Bible's meaning not just from those who are intellectually astute or theologically trained. We can learn from any genuine believer whom God has taught in His Word.[51]

2. Study the Bible with others and not just privately.
Too often, those with formal theological training end up serving in churches where they are looked upon as "resident experts" on the Bible. Unfortunately, this leads to a Lone Ranger approach to interpretation. The leader studies the Bible and then dispenses the meaning to those who need to hear it. But humility must teach us that those with theological training are not the only ones who can hear and understand the meaning of the Bible. A layperson's lack of precise training may lead to some overt interpretive errors, but who is free from such errors?

Humility ought to teach leaders that the Spirit of God can use even the least theologically trained believer to reveal some new angle of understanding from the text. Rather than experts, leaders ought to think of themselves as eager *students* of the text, whose desire to learn the meaning of Scripture is so infectious that others become avid students as well. This should occur at several levels. Most importantly, this attitude should be modeled by the pastor/elder from the pulpit in the context of leadership meetings. Secondly, this can naturally occur in the setting of the home Bible study or small group experience.

3. Use commentaries, journals, and theological study tools of those outside your interpretive tradition and your generation.
Each interpretive tradition tends to have commentators and theologians which it reveres as best encapsulating its teachings. Wesleyan Arminians have writers and commentators which they utilize and respect, while Reformed believers look to others. Dispensationalists and Covenantalists each have their own favorites as well. Even though Roman Catholics have been producing some fine commentaries ever since Vatican II freed them up,

Protestants still generally tend to read only Protestant interpretations—and Catholics stick with their own. And which of either has a sense of Eastern Orthodox interpretation on biblical and theological themes? And, as much as evangelicals hate to admit it, they can even learn about some of their biases from theologically liberal interpreters who care little about biblical authority, but only study for historical or literary interest. Brown is certainly correct when he says:

> There is another thing we can do, and it too takes courage. *We can listen to the interpretations of Scripture that come from traditions other than our own.* There is something salutary about the fact that in the ecumenical movement Baptists must now be exposed to Anglican treatments of the New Testament doctrine of the ministry, and that Lutherans must listen while Methodists explain how their social activism is rooted in the Bible. There is no longer any excuse for pockets of Christendom to remain uninformed about the way other Christians interpret Holy Scripture. Denominational exegesis exists to be challenged. *The wider the scope of the church's listening, the better the chances for the corrective power of the Holy Spirit, speaking through Scripture, to break down the barriers men constantly erect so that they will not have to heed his disturbing voice.*[52]

So, to be careful interpreters who are less hindered by our own ecclesiastical traditions, we must read broadly within other traditional interpreters on given passages, both historical and contemporary.[53] The Bible was given to the *whole* church, and it is the epitome of sectarianism to assume that our group—or generation—only has a market on interpreting the Bible rightly.[54] We may find that other groups and generations are interpreting the text much as we do, or we may find them interpreting the text much differently than we do. And we always must be aware that they may be interpreting out of a bias as well. But we may just discover a fresh interpretive approach that is far more in keeping with the intent of the author of the text than the one that we have always believed to be there.

4. Make use of theological educational opportunities at an interdenominational or nondenominational Bible college or seminary as much as possible.
Often young people are sent by parents or their church to a denominational college or seminary for their theological training.

There they are taught Bible and theology from what is an accepted (traditional) framework. This is not necessarily wrong. But in some instances, it may lock students into one carefully prescribed model of biblical interpretation, where all that is heard of alternative interpretations is the predigested explanation of those positions by the instructor, who does not believe or sanction (or sometimes even understand) those alternatives at all.

Again, this is not always the case. Some denominational institutions provide a healthy, honest interaction with alternative systems of interpretation. However, sometimes one may be better served at an alternative denomination's school, or at an interdenominational school if one's goal in training is hermeneutical catholicity.

5. Join and participate in a theological society.
Theological societies are a place where dialogue can take place in an unthreatening context on fairly objective grounds. Theological and biblical papers are read and critiqued in a more or less objective atmosphere. If an individual suggests an interpretation that is unduly influenced by his or her own tradition, without adequate interpretive evidence, it will be quickly pointed out by colleagues from other traditions. Pastoral leaders can certainly find a context for such discussion and should not be frightened away from these meetings by the presence of theological academes.

Among the more active contemporary societies are the *Evangelical Theological Society* (with national and regional meetings), which has as its operating premise the doctrine of biblical inerrancy, and (for those who can deal with liberal theological presuppositions) the *Society of Biblical Literature,* which does not have a particular doctrinal or bibliological commitment and therefore contains a large proportion of liberal theologies. But either way, if the premises of a group are understood, then interaction with the meaning of the text may occur and our own preconceived interpretations may more easily give way for open discussion and either be confirmed or invalidated.

6. Develop an interdenominational prayer and support group.
Bible interpretation was intended to take place *within the community of faith,* not simply among the "objectivity" of academia.

To encourage this spirit, I suggest making it a point, as the opportunity arises, to visit churches of other traditions—not to look for proof that we are right and they are wrong, but rather to look for genuine expressions of faith in that other context. We never really know our own language—as a language—until we take time to learn another. So we never really know our own tradition—as a tradition—until we take time to learn another.

We need to give and receive the support of brothers and sisters outside of our own comfortable cloister. We need to get back to basics—that despite our differences, we are not persons "of a different religion." We pray to, worship, teach, and evangelize in the name of the same Lord. We need to know each other's needs and struggles and get back to the true basics of the Christian faith we share with one another. There is something about genuine *koinonia* within the Christian community that brings us back to those basics.

SUMMARY

This chapter was primarily intended to lay out an agreeable means by which we can detect the presence of traditional (nonauthoritative) interpretations within our denominational, local church, and Christian organizational contexts. Through a fair application of normal "common-sense" hermeneutics, and with the help of others outside our own tradition, we can more easily detect the presence of tradition among us. In doing so, we can appropriately call it such. Again, since tradition is inevitable and neutral (unless it nullifies the Word of God), recognizing its presence has enormous practical value for developing a sense of catholicity and curtailing the tendency toward sectarianism.

The development of a healthy hermeneutical practice, as suggested above, can help to more realistically display the presence of the traditional among us and to free us to distinguish it from a core of shared orthodoxy binding us with all true believers beyond our own denominational distinctives. This will help center us in denominationally spawned catholicity and away from a drift to the right, and the danger of high authoritarian sectarianism.

In the next chapter, the key issue in avoiding the other extreme of denominational catholicity (low authoritarian liberalism) will be addressed. That key, as mentioned, is to look toward a core of orthodoxy that all who truly believe will share.

Six

THE SEARCH FOR A CORE ORTHODOXY FOR CATHOLICITY

Beloved, that that makes a church to be a catholic church . . . is the catholic faith.

— Richard Sibbes

 It is a rare Christian on the modern scene who has not been impacted by the writings of British literary scholar and apologist C.S. Lewis. The first of his books that I ran across as a new university student and young Christian was *Mere Christianity.* Originally broadcast over the radio during World War II, these programs were later edited and issued in book form as *The Case for Christianity, Christian Behavior,* and *Beyond Personality* in the later 1940s. In 1952 they were combined, re-edited, and given a new preface by Lewis under the title of *Mere Christianity.* And in that form it waited for me to discover the book some twenty years later.

What struck me right off was Lewis' basic portrayal of such a thing as "mere" Christianity. What did he mean by that phrase? Simply "the belief that has been common to nearly all Christians at all times."[1] Mere Christianity is the "core orthodoxy" around which all Christians gather. It is the *sine qua non* of Christianity. It is the essential doctrinal core, from which diversity must be disallowed. To *have* mere Christianity is to have Christianity— regardless of a myriad of differences in other matters of faith and practice. *Not* to have mere Christianity is not to have Christianity at all.

Thinking in terms of what was earlier discussed as "tradition," core-orthodoxy may rightly be termed macro-tradition as opposed to micro-tradition. Macro-tradition is the broad, well-accepted, interdenominational interpretative tradition of the church as a whole as opposed to micro-tradition, which is the interpretative tradition of a smaller segment of the church (a theological tradition, movement, denomination, or local church). Macro-tradition is that which unites us in genuine catholicity; micro-tradition is that which divides us into our distinctive groups. As Thomas Ryan has said, "The Gospel of Jesus Christ asserts that our real identity is not at the edges of our Christian existence where we can brag about our specialties, but at the center where we are rooted in Christ and where the bond of the Spirit yokes us together."[2]

As Andrew Walker notes, there is a focus that all genuine believers must and can agree on, one that avoids the dangers of the sectarian overemphasis on micro-tradition and a wishy-washy liberal notion of complete doctrinal pluralism without an adequate core of truth:

> This ground is no less than the high road of basic orthodoxy: the common, yet holy tradition of Christian Theology and spirituality that spans the ages from the New Testament to the present day. C.S. Lewis saw this mere Christianity, metaphorically, as the "main road"; in another apt image he talks of the great level viaduct that stands firm and sure over the dips and valleys of apostasy and heresy. It is the road that stands for the sacredness and truth of the Holy Bible. The road incorporates and is directed by the ancient creeds and the great councils of the early church and by the undivided ecumenical church of the first millenium of Christendom, which sought to bear witness to a trinitarian God and the risen Jesus who was both God and man. It is the road of Christian pilgrims everywhere who press on believing in not only a God of miracles and revelation but also one of personal encounter.
>
> This road, this great viaduct, is the infrastructure of all mainstream Christianity—even though Christendom has been broken by schism and division. The orthodox believers—or to use the Greek meaning, those of true faith and worship—can, or rather should, be able to recognize one another across the broad expanse of the main road because they are members of the same family: of one blood and one body.[3]

Andrew Walker is certainly correct in his assessment of need, especially in view of the attacks at the foundations of this "great viaduct" by existential philosophy, New Age mysticism, and secular humanism while we twitter away at our own micro-traditional duct-work of peripherals. But acknowledging the *need* for a core orthodoxy (the importance of a common macro-tradition) and coming to an agreement on the *identification* of this core orthodoxy are not always the same thing. There is the danger of excluding, by one's definition, genuine believers in the faith (the danger of sectarianism); or of defining so broadly as to lose the historic, definitional core of Christianity (the danger of theological liberalism's doctrinal pluralism).[4]

OPTIONS OF A CORE ORTHODOXY

There have been many proposals for a core of orthodoxy over the centuries. In fact, one could almost suggest that every doctrinal statement, every creed or confession, every systematic theology ever written offers itself as a statement of orthodoxy. Granted that factor, our task is overwhelming indeed! But as was pointed out in our discussion of interpretative tradition, there are areas of serious and conscientious disagreement on the interpretation of a number of matters pertaining to Christian doctrine and lifestyle. The very fact that sincere, godly Christians differ in their attempt to be faithful to their understanding of Scripture forces us to look for that which is common—for shared beliefs.[5] And there are fewer options to consider when that is concerned. Let's take a look together at some of these options.

The Bible alone is sufficient for a core orthodoxy. In the century after the Reformation, Anglican apologist William Chillingworth (1602-1644) argued against any infallible guide except the Bible, stating "those truths will be fundamental, which are evidently delivered in Scripture, and commanded to be preached to all men."[6] These fundamental truths were those that defined the church and guaranteed salvation, although there may be great latitude in more obscure questions. Chillingworth again states:

> By the religion of protestants, I do not understand the doctrine of Luther, or Calvin, or Melanchthon; nor the confession of Augusta, or Geneva, nor the catechism of Heidelberg, nor the articles of the church of England, no, nor the harmony of protestant confessions; but that wherein they all agree, and which they all subscribe with a greater harmony, as a perfect rule of their faith and actions; that is, the Bible. *The Bible, I say, the Bible only, is the*

religion of the protestants! Whatsoever else they believe besides it, and the plain, irrefragable, indubitable consequences of it, well may they hold it as a matter of opinion; but as a matter of faith and religion, neither can they with coherence to their own grounds believe it themselves, nor require the belief of it of others, without most high and most schismatical presumption. I, for my part, after a long, and (as I verily believe and hope) impartial search of the true way to eternal happiness, do profess plainly, that I cannot find any rest for the sole of my foot but upon this rock only.[7]

And again:

I am fully assured that God does not, and therefore that men ought not, to require any more of any man than this—to believe the Scripture to be God's word, to endeavor to find the true sense of it, and to live according to it.[8]

Chillingworth's notions are dear to the heart of many Protestants and are a logical extension of two key Protestant ideals: *sola Scriptura* and the priesthood of all believers. These, in turn, developed into the basic principle of the right of private judgment (that each believer can, unaided by priestly intermediaries, understand the basic message of the Bible).

A parallel notion to Chillingworth's idea that the Bible alone is the religion of Protestants is found, for example, in the unstated assumptions of groups such as the Evangelical Theological Society (ETS). The sole doctrinal basis for membership with this group of biblical scholars ever since its inception in 1949 has been: "The Bible alone, and the Bible in its entirety, is the Word of God written and is therefore inerrant in the autographs."[9] Certainly this appears to be a fair rallying point (though some dispute the focus and negativity of the term "inerrant"). Within this society, evangelical biblical scholars from widely variant interpretive positions (Calvinist, Arminian, Dispensationalist, Wesleyan, Pentecostal, etc.) have found grounds for discussion on the meaning and implication of the biblical text with relatively free interchange of ideas. Regardless of who reads a paper, the issue can always be evaluated based on the adequacy of the use of hermeneutics. The same epistemological base is granted by all, so this appears to be an adequate ground for a core of doctrinal orthodoxy. Or is it? Several problems arise with assuming that acknowledging the authority of the Bible alone is an adequate statement for Christian doctrinal orthodoxy.

First, there must be consistent agreement on what the Bible means as a ground of fellowship; otherwise we simply gather around a meaningless (though authoritative) book. Those groups which affirm that their only doctrinal statement is Scripture have been able to maintain that and at the same time to drift into a denial of such rudimentary Christian things as the Trinity and the Incarnation. When the Northern Baptists in America drifted into theological liberalism, both the conservatives and liberals agreed on the Baptistic tenet of *sola Scriptura* (with the Baptistic focus on the Bible as the *sole* authority of faith and practice, not simply the *supreme* authority of faith and practice). In 1922, when the conservative Fundamentalist Fellowship of the Northern Baptist Convention proposed that the Convention adopt the historic, conservative New Hampshire Confession of Faith of 1830, the reaction of the liberals was typically Baptistic, however unhelpful: We have no creed but the New Testament.[10] The problem is that the Bible alone is not an adequate creed, no matter how important it is as a foundational basis for a creed. It *must* be interpreted.

Similarly, the ETS in recent years discovered an unanticipated problem with their "Bible alone" statement: Jehovah's Witnesses were beginning to appear at society meetings, claiming that they too could sign the doctrinal statement of the Society. They agreed with inerrancy. They simply *interpreted* the Bible differently than most all other Christian groups (not to mention translating it uniquely).

The ETS finally concluded that their "Bible alone" creed would need to be expanded to make explicit an assumption that was implicit with their founders. In their San Diego meeting in November of 1989, the society voted to add a further phrase to their formula, now appended to the "The Bible alone" statement of old: "God is a Trinity, Father, Son, and Holy Spirit, each an uncreated person, one in essence, equal in power and glory." So, after forty years of operating with an assumption that the Bible alone is adequate as a statement of faith, it turns out as not quite so adequate.[11] The Bible must be *interpreted*. And there must be fundamental agreement on its interpretation. The Bible alone is simply not enough to serve as a core creed, a core orthodoxy.

Second, the Bible as the definition of core orthodoxy was not what the Reformers meant by *sola Scriptura*. Martin Luther and the other Reformers affirmed the great creeds of the church and agreed that there was a *magnus consensus* (great consensus) of doctrine from which the Roman Church had departed, and to which they were returning. Belief in the sufficiency of Scripture did not dispense with the need for creed or tradition. As Lowell Green points out:

> In spite of the popularity of that cliché, the term [*sola Scriptura*] can hardly be found in any writing by Melanchthon or Luther, and the idea of an exclusivistic appeal to the Bible does not accord very well with their respect for tradition. They both made of Scripture the final judge, rule, or norm of tradition, but this in itself shows that tradition kept its place.[12]

Again, in the face of the conflict within the traditions of the church, Luther himself did not *dispense* with traditions, but merely developed guidelines to *evaluate* them.

> Luther held to these two principles: the more ancient pronouncements took precedence over those which were more recent, and all opinions, no matter how well attested, were subject to the final judgment of Scripture. We should note that here is no biblicistic *sola Scriptura*. Luther did not reject tradition, he only made it subordinate to the Bible, thus leaving room for the *magnus consensus*.[13]

This understanding certainly accords well with the Lutheran *Augsburg Confession*, which at its outset confirms the Nicene and Apostles' Creeds.[14] In fact, the very existence of confessions of faith among the Reformers indicates that there is need to articulate and defend what one believes about what the Bible is teaching. The point is clear. The Bible alone is not the issue of core orthodoxy for the Reformers.

In view of these factors, Hanson and Hanson were certainly correct when they observed, "It is not the Bible that unites Christians, but the church's tradition in *interpreting* the Bible. . . . What we need is agreement on doctrine, on what we teach when we are not just repeating the words of the Bible."[15] Belief in the foundational function of the Bible in doctrine does not remove the need for explaining its meaning in some sort of formulation.

We must certainly include the vital role of Scripture in our understanding of core orthodoxy, but simply *acknowledging* its centrality, superiority, or sole authority will not suffice in terms of defining orthodoxy. We must elaborate its meaning and then see if we agree on that elaboration.[16]

The "fundamentals" define core orthodoxy. Modern evangelicalism and fundamentalism both trace their roots in this century to the publication of *The Fundamentals,* a twelve-volume set of paperback books financed anonymously by wealthy California oil capitalists Lyman and Milton Stewart. Some three million volumes were sent out free of charge to Protestant pastors and missionaries all over the world between the years 1910 and 1915. The purpose of this publication was to combat the anti-supernaturalist developments of religious liberalism, which had taken deep root in American Protestant institutions over the half century since the end of the Civil War.

What are the "fundamentals?" Defining them clearly is not easy, since the original volumes contained some ninety different articles dealing with various subjects that had been discarded or minimized by theological liberalism.[17] Even the estimates of which specific items are to be classed as a "fundamental" by fundamentalists varies, but historically speaking, these are the original fundamentals as they were defined as a result of the original controversy:[18]

1. The inspiration and infallibility of the Bible.
2. The deity and virgin birth of Christ.
3. The substitutionary atonement.
4. The literal resurrection of Christ.
5. The literal return of Christ.

I would not quibble here with the importance of these doctrines, nor would I argue with the notion that a departure from these doctrines challenges the very essence of historic orthodoxy. But I would differ in whether these doctrines are adequate to portray a core of orthodoxy. *The Fundamentals,* it must be remembered, were produced in the heat of theological reactionism and do not present a reasoned, balanced reflection on the *essence* of orthodoxy. Men and women were firing from the hip at anyone and everything that smacked of a slip from the received orthodoxy of the time.

Those of evangelical faith were simply overwhelmed by the sheer strength liberalism had gained so rapidly in their schools and pulpits. As a result, central historic affirmations were overlooked while other, more pressing needs, were addressed. Where, for example, is historic trinitarianism addressed? And why (in the volumes) is the authorship of Isaiah placed at the same level of fundamental treatment as the deity of Christ? This may be important, but is it of fundamental importance?

Furthermore, although the fundamentalist movement and the evangelical movement share common sympathies in this group of documents, the chief distinguishing characteristic between the two is the philosophy of *separatism*. Fundamentalist evangelicals tend to defeat the very essence of catholicity by their constant vigilance to separate from what they perceive to be false teaching rather than to gather around a core of true teaching.[19] For this reason, it is very difficult to see fundamentalist type of thinking helping us find a core of orthodoxy for cooperation and intermutual support.[20] It is too exclusivistic to really perceive the church catholic in all its fullness. We will need to look elsewhere for a core of orthodoxy.

The great creeds of the undivided church define core orthodoxy. Another option harkens back to earlier church history—the ecumenical creeds of the united church. Roman Catholics have held numerous "ecumenical (church wide) councils" *since* the Great Schism of 1054 (the most recent being Vatican II during the 1960s), and, because it perceives itself to be the one church established by Peter, it believes that those councils have binding force for the church. But these subsequent councils were not truly ecumenical, in the sense of having representatives of the *entire* church.

So, it is sometimes argued that the united opinions of the church as a whole *before* divisions set in (usually dated prior to the Great Schism of 1054) should serve as an adequate statement of core orthodoxy for the *entire* church. In Greek Orthodox thinking, this would include the teaching of the first Seven Ecumenical Councils.[21] Protestant groups that adopt the traditional creeds do not accept all seven of these Councils, however. In Anglican/Episcopal thinking, the appeal is to the theological consensus of the first *four* ecumenical councils.[22] Lutherans[23] and

Presbyterian/Reformed (Calvinist churches) argue similarly.[24]

The divergent thinking between these Protestant and the Eastern Orthodox groups, of course, is based on the notion of the relation of tradition to Scripture. To the Eastern Orthodox, Scripture derives from tradition, and therefore these councils, as a part of tradition, are perceived as having intrinsic divine authority. To the Protestant Reformers, tradition must be confirmed by Scripture to be valid tradition. But if it is confirmed by Scripture, then it is surely to be believed. And Anglicans, Lutherans, and Reformed groups, like other Protestants, find far less *scriptural* support for the conclusions of the final three of the Seven Ecumenical Councils, and hence do not support them.

The problem with this approach to defining a core of orthodoxy, however, is as follows. First, where and on what grounds does one draw the lines *historically* in terms of nonorthodoxy? Certainly the Anglicans, Lutherans, and Calvinists can argue for the first four councils on the basis of a Protestant view of the priority of Scripture (Scripture can authenticate the councils for them), but is it fair to say that the Protestant view of the priority of Scripture itself should be included *within* orthodoxy when it is not significantly addressed creedally during those early centuries? Not by any stretch of the imagination did the doctrine of the full sufficiency of Scripture (*sola Scriptura*) achieve dogmatic formulation until the sixteenth century. So limiting the core of orthodoxy to traditional statements of the first five centuries runs somewhere afoul of the formal principle of the Reformation itself.[25]

Secondly, are the creeds saying *more* than core orthodoxy? If the message that saves is the Gospel, does one need to understand, say, trinitarian thought, or the hypostatic union[26] to respond to the Gospel and so be saved? One may have woefully inadequate perceptions about the structure of a bridge and what makes it hold people up, and still have sufficient trust in that bridge to make it across the river. That is not to say that there are incorrect perceptions of the structure of the bridge, or that correct perceptions are unimportant for the maintaining of the bridge for future generations. Right theology *is* important. And a correct and clear understanding of the basics of that theology must be communicated in the process of evangelization. But the *quantity* of understanding of the person of Christ necessary for adequate faith to be expressed may be significantly less than we sometimes imagine.

Further, in view of the numerous factions within the church even in the earliest centuries, Lutheran writer Hermann Sasse even goes so far as to ask when in fact there ever *was* an "ancient undivided church."

> If in such schismatic or even heretical bodies [as in the Coptics, or Jacobites, or Nestorians or Armenians who did not deny Christ during Turkish persecution] there can be the crown of true martyrdom, if true loyalty to Christ can co-exist with christological heresies, then we Lutherans must confess that also in them the true Church of Christ exists, just as we believe that the true church exists also in the Eastern Orthodox Churches and in Rome despite all errors and heresies. We believe that the Una Sancta is hidden in the outward organizations that claim the name "church" wherever the Gospel of Christ is still being proclaimed and His sacraments are administered. This is, indeed, a dogmatic statement. But it seems to be consistent with the facts of church history. No one has so far been able to show what time the "ancient undivided church" was divided.[27]

Why, if Sasse's observation is correct, would one suggest that an "undivided" church existed until the Schism of 1054? Was that not merely the largest of the schisms to date? Is that not to say that the Novatianists and the Donatists were outside the church despite their orthodox faith? And what of the departure of the Monophysites in Egypt and Syria, which continues to this day in the Coptic Church? If, in some sense, genuine faith exists in all these groups, then one must look at a more fundamental level for a core of orthodoxy than to statements offered by a structurally united church.

The Vincentian view: core orthodoxy is theological consensus. Another understanding of core orthodoxy has arisen in recent years that is parallel to the previous one. This does not focus on the historical formulations of correct doctrine, but argues instead for a sort of "theological consensus" of *all* true believers. Anything *outside* this consensus is considered peripheral; anything within the consensus is orthodox doctrine. This, of course, is really a functional attempt to use the fifth century Vincentian canon to determine core orthodoxy. It is an attempt to use catholicity to determine the content of apostolicity/core orthodoxy/ macro-tradition.

As we noted earlier, the canon of Vincent of Lérins is essentially "what all men have at all times and everywhere believed." The rest of his text reads like this:

> That is truly and properly "Catholic," as is shown by the very force and meaning of the word, which comprehends everything almost universally. We shall hold to this rule if we follow universality, antiquity, and consent. We shall follow universality if we acknowledge that one Faith to be true which the whole Church throughout the world confesses; antiquity, if we in no wise depart from those interpretations which it is clear that our ancestors and fathers proclaimed; consent, if in antiquity itself we keep following the definitions and opinions of all, or certainly nearly all, bishops and doctors alike.[28]

This canon, as we noted, is the kind of thing C.S. Lewis had in mind when he spoke of "mere Christianity." And, if one can in fact obtain access to "what all men have at all times and everywhere believed," then certainly this would have much to commend it. One who has in fact adopted this Vincentian canon for a working model of doing theology is Thomas C. Oden, who recounts his journey from radical liberal Protestant theology to historic orthodoxy in *After Modernity . . . What?*[29] Oden relates, frankly, his discovery of Vincent's ideal:

> It was while reading Vincent of Lérins fifth-century aids to remembering (*Commonitory*) that I gained the essential hermeneutical foothold in defining generally received teaching under the threefold test of catholicity as "that which has been believed everywhere, always, and by all" (*quod semper, quod ab omnibus creditum est*). From then on it was a straightforward matter of searching modestly to identify those shared teachings.[30]

As a result of this search, Oden has written a massive, three-volume work that attempts to display this theological consensus.[31] Oden asserts regarding this project:

> My purpose has not been to survey the bewildering atonalities of dissent but to identify and plausibly set forth the cohesive central tradition of general lay consent to apostolic teaching, not its centrifugal variations but its centripetal centering. . . . My purpose is

not to seek to establish by rational argument that [for example,] the Son is God and the Spirit is God but rather to show textually that this has indeed been confessed by witnesses of countless cultural settings and times and social locations.[32]

One can do nothing but praise Oden for his energetic pursuit of this Vincentian ideal, but it is an incredibly Herculean task! One wonders how any living human being could gain a feel for genuine consensus when so much has been written in so many areas from so many writers for so many centuries. Oden instinctively recognizes this, and identifies the narrowing and selectivity of sources he employed.

Who are those principal consensual exegetes to whom irenic, classic theology so frequently turns? Above all they are the seven leading ecumenical councils received by patristic, medieval, Lutheran, Calvinist and Anglican consent, and supplementary early synods that came to be decisively quoted as effectively representing the mind of the believing Church; and the four great doctors of the eastern church tradition (Athanasius, Basil, Gregory Nazianzen, John Chrysostom) and of the west (Ambrose, Jerome, Augustine, Gregory the Great), as well as others who have been perennially valued for accurately stating certain points of general lay consensus: Cyril of Jerusalem, Cyril of Alexandria, Hilary, Leo, John of Damascus, Thomas Aquinas, Luther, Calvin.[33]

The selectivity, of course, does beg the question a bit. If the methodology of Vincent is used (*everyone, everywhere,* at *all* times), why then the selectivity?

A second limitation of this approach is in terms of subject matter. If one limits oneself to Theology proper, or Christology, or to Pneumatology, it is fairly clear that one can find a running consensus among all those listed. But what happens when one moves into areas of Soteriology? Or areas of religious authority? Certainly at this point the Reformers seem to be a bit on the outside of the mainstream here. Or are they? They claimed to be recovering what was lost in the development of the Roman ecclesiastical monolith.

In fact, one wonders if counting heads is the correct approach to determining doctrinal core orthodoxy any more than counting manuscripts is the best way to tell which text is original to the New Testament. One suspects that, at any given point in the history of the church what is believed "by everyone, everywhere, at all times" may be subject to variation, because new formulations (even if correct) take *time* to be understood and accepted broadly.

Another concern with the Vincentian method is the implicit assumption that the fathers are culturally *unconditioned* when they interpreted the Scripture and therefore their interpretive conclusions are always to be accepted. As Plantinga has pointed out:

> I think it is doubtful that we must accept the patristic consensus without question. After all, the Church fathers and mothers knew not only Bible but also philosophy and, in particular areas, did not hesitate to shape theories accordingly. . . . No. We receive the classical consensus with deep respect and hospitality, but also with a proper Biblical and scholarly reserve. We cannot assume that the patristic consensus gives us Scripture unalloyed. . . .[34]

Plantinga undoubtedly is correct. We are not the only generation of Christians who have the tendency to define our faith in terms of prevailing thought forms. Yet, as he admits, there is a depth of appreciation for the authority and teaching of Scripture as a whole that is lost in modern rationalistic, anti-supernaturalistic liberal thinking.

So, as much as the Vincentian canon has appeal as a focus of a core of orthodoxy, it is really an unreachable ideal that by the very nature of the case, must leave doctrinal development and maturation out of the question. A core orthodoxy must be sought, I am afraid, in other quarters.[35]

Where, then, are we to look in terms of defining a core of orthodoxy? I wish to argue that the genuine core of orthodoxy surrounds issues pertaining to the Gospel itself. What the church must gather around is that which makes the church: the *Gospel message*. What unites Christians is that which saves them and gives them life and a mission.

THE GOSPEL: EVANGELICAL FAITH DEFINES A CORE ORTHODOXY

This notion of a core orthodoxy with its focus in the Gospel and therefore in evangelical faith finds its clearest expression during the Reformation period. Paul Avis, in his study of the ecclesiology of the Reformers, said it well:

> The concept of the Church which was fundamental to the thought
> of the Reformers (including of course the Anglicans)—namely,
> that *only the Gospel* was of the *esse*—had profound implications
> for the doctrine of succession and with it the key concept of
> catholicity, one of the four creedal attributes of the Church. Here
> a radical reinterpretation was effected. . . . By making *the gospel
> alone the power at work in the Church* through the Holy Spirit, the
> Reformers did away with the necessity of a doctrine of apostolic
> succession, replacing it with the notion of a succession of truth.
> Correspondingly, *the gospel of truth was held to be sufficient to
> secure the catholicity of the Church.* The Reformers believed with
> all of Christendom that the Church was one, holy, catholic, and
> apostolic, but this was understood in a radically new sense in
> which the *gospel itself* became the decisive and dominant
> criterion.[36]

Further, as Robert Webber aptly pointed out, such faith is
really the ancient faith of the church and is only quickened by
the Reformation.[37] Evangelical faith argues for the centrality of
the Gospel as the means by which salvation is attained, and for
the familial interrelatedness of those who receive the Gospel
regardless of doctrinal diversity on subsidiary matters. It argues
that the Gospel *produces* the church.

And, it must be remembered, the Reformers themselves argued strongly that they were introducing nothing new with their
emphasis on the Gospel, but rather were reintroducing the faith
of the ancient church that had been lost in the innovative traditions of the medieval period. In a stimulating article, Alan K.
Scholes and Stephen M. Clinton conclude similarly regarding the
soteriological focus of core orthodoxy from a review of the New
Testament emphases:

> . . . we also propose that the proper dividing line between such
> persuasions [matters of difference among Christians] and deeper
> convictions [core orthodoxy], which would warrant confrontation
> and a risk of division, should be whether the beliefs in question
> are essential to having a right relationship with God, i.e., to the
> doctrine of salvation.[38]

Similarly, John Frame argues for this in his search for a common core. Frame affirms that the conditions for church membership should be no narrower than the Scriptures' conditions for
belonging to the kingdom of God. The basic confession, as he

sees it, normally involves "the willingness to confess that Jesus is one's own Lord and Savior: that Jesus, who is both God and man, died for the sins of his people to bring them forgiveness, and that he now has full authority over our lives as the resurrected, living Lord."[39] There is no better way to describe the objective and subjective content of the Gospel. This is evangelical faith.[40]

BASIC ELEMENTS OF THE GOSPEL

The issue then becomes: what *content* does the Gospel, or evangelical faith have? To this may be responded: evangelical faith has an *objective* content and a *subjective* content, supported by a *structural* content. The *objective* content to evangelical faith is the core facts related to the Gospel: the incarnation and sinlessness of Christ as the eternal Son of God, the sacrificial death as atonement for sin, and the resurrection. The *subjective* content of evangelical faith is the need for a personal faith-response to the objective content of the Gospel (the conversion, or "born-again" experience; justification by faith). This subjective necessity is what impels those of evangelical faith toward evangelism and mission. Those who have been converted by the Gospel have an intrinsic desire to "pass on" the life-change the Gospel has brought them. Further, the *structural* framework which upholds and feeds evangelical faith is the necessity of acknowledging the final apostolic authority behind these elements. These three elements would translate into the formal and material factors of the Reformation.[41]

It is important to keep these three elements together in proper balance. An emphasis on the faith-response to the Gospel is crucial. But if the faith-response is the only element, then evangelical faith devolves into mere sentimentality and pietism, and opens the door for experience to be the sole definer of orthodoxy—which it can never be. The focus on the Bible alone or its inerrancy, although important for the epistemological base for any expression of evangelical faith, is not adequate (as pointed out before) in that one's understanding of the meaning of the Bible must be an indicator of orthodoxy, not one's belief in the Bible alone. And orthodoxy of content without the faith-response choice of the individual can lead to a dry, formal orthodoxy without a genuine, vital faith eager to be shared with others.

There are several factors which argue for the Gospel/evangelical faith as the core element of orthodoxy. First, the Bible itself does this. The Apostle Paul even goes so far as to raise the Gospel above his own claim to apostleship: "But even if we or an angel from heaven should preach a gospel other than the one we preached to you, let him be eternally condemned!" (Gal. 1:8)[42]

Second, the Gospel itself (as derived from Scripture) serves as the confirmational factor supporting the ancient Christological creeds. That is, the creeds can easily be seen to arise from Scripture and the Gospel message of salvation. Indeed, their pastoral concern and soteriological focus comes quickly into view.

Third, evangelical faith actually has served as a significant rejuvenating factor in established churches due to its focus on the *core* of faith rather than external expressions.[43] Although those who have come to an evangelical faith-decision have often found the dominant evangelical "free-church" approach dissatisfying in the long run for nurturing a broad historical sense of the church as a whole, it should be noted that those evangelicals who return to the liturgical structures often found evangelical faith not within, but *outside* those structures.[44] Evangelical faith, by its very nature, provides an intrinsic commonality in the Gospel among those who have responded regardless of external confessional boundaries and denominational ties.[45]

A brief focus on these core elements will help to illuminate their centrality as a core orthodoxy for genuine catholicity.

The objective content of the Gospel message. One cannot doubt that the New Testament attests to the centrality of the Gospel message as the minimal "gate" through which one passes from death to life. Paul is not ashamed of this message, because it is God's power for the salvation of all people (Rom. 1:16-17). It is the message he passed on to the Corinthians "as of first importance" (1 Cor. 15:1-8). Yet the full content of the Gospel message is not contained in any one verse or group of verses in the New Testament. The reason, of course, is that the New Testament literature was not written as *evangelistic* material, but as *instructional* material for those already converted. Nevertheless, allusions to the Gospel are plentiful enough (in, for example, the evangelistic messages in the Book of Acts and in direct references to the Gospel in the Pauline epistles) to make a reconstruction of its core details relatively easy. Collecting these into one convenient statement, one could say that the Gospel message is simply this:

> *God sent His Son into the world*[46] *to die as an atonement for sin,*[47] *and God raised Him from the dead,*[48] *so that anyone who places faith in Him*[49] *receives the free gift of salvation.*[50]

Each of these statements has several levels of presuppositions and implications, which would be developed in many ways by the church in succeeding centuries. I will refer to the fuller implications that are not worked out within the New Testament itself as a "level II orthodoxy," or a "sustaining orthodoxy" to be discussed later in this chapter. But there are also some clear presuppositions and implications of the Gospel message that are demonstrable from the New Testament itself. That is, its writers meant certain things by the terminology they employed in communicating the Gospel; and they understood the Gospel to have certain important implications. It is the Gospel and its presuppositions and implications, as understood by the New Testament writers, that serves as the "level I orthodoxy," or core orthodoxy around which the church catholic centers itself.

In contrast to the term sustaining or level II orthodoxy of subsequent centuries, level I orthodoxy (core orthodoxy) we will call "saving orthodoxy." The reason for this latter terminology is due to the pragmatic elements connected with the nature of the Gospel: it *saves* people. Level II, or sustaining orthodoxy, is the subsequent reflection on the saving orthodoxy of the Gospel that enables us to understand *how* and *why* it saves people, but the Gospel can save without an understanding of these elements. But an incorrect explanation of the how and why can lead to serious error and distortion of the saving message of the Gospel. Both dimensions are therefore important, but the pragmatic tilt must be given to level I, or saving orthodoxy as outlined in the brief statement, along with its New Testament presuppositions and implications.

If we were to unpack this Gospel statement, then, the presuppositions and implications according to the New Testament writers would be these:

God sent His Son into the world. The presupposition is, of course, that the God who saves is the God of Israel, Yahweh, the only infinite and holy Creator of all that exists, and the saving and covenant-making God of the Old Testament.[51] The obvious implication here, seen at times in the New Testament, is that God must have had a Son in order to "send" Him, that is, the Son must have been preexistent: He existed prior to His birth as a baby in Bethlehem. This indeed is the uniform witness of the New Testament documents.[52] Further, the New Testament teaches that He existed prior to the creation of the material universe. And, He was preexistent because He is the *eternal* Son.[53] Since eternality is only appropriately spoken of God, that is why the term "God" is applied to Jesus in the New Testament.[54] This also means that He genuinely became flesh, for the way in which God sent His Son into the world is via the incarnation.[55] The incarnation took place, moreover, in the virgin's womb.[56]

Further, the fact that Jesus is the "only" Son of God indicates the reason He can be referred to as eternal and preexistent and why the term "God" and "Lord" was happily applied to Jesus: for God to have a "Son" after all, means that the Son must be deity. Jesus making a claim to being God's Son was therefore understood by His auditors as making a claim to equality with God.[57] The Old Testament concept of the one God is the presupposition to this first statement of the Gospel. The implications to this statement are the eternal preexistence of the Son as God and His real incarnation into humanity.

To die as an atonement for sin. There are two key presuppositions that the New Testament writers work from here, which supply the need for the atoning death of Christ. The first is that the one God of Scripture (the Old Testament) is *holy* and cannot tolerate sin. Further, He is *just* and will punish all sin. The second key presupposition is developed by Paul in Romans 3:9-18 and Ephesians 2:1-3, namely, that all human beings are deeply *sinful* and helpless to solve this dilemma.[58]

The incarnation then, sets in place the means by which God provides salvation for humanity in the face of this dilemma: the voluntary sacrificial death[59] of the incarnate Son of God to atone for human sinfulness. Without this atoning death, salvation and reconciliation with the God understood by the New Testament writers would be impossible.

God raised Him from the dead. This is the uniform statement in apostolic preaching. Numerous implications are drawn from this element of the Gospel in the New Testament. First, it serves as the certification of the claims of Jesus as to His divine sonship.[60] Further, it means that belief in Jesus is belief in a living Lord rather than in historical facts alone.[61] Finally, the resurrection becomes part of the Christian's hope: the living Jesus will return, and His resurrection gives believers the hope of their own resurrections. The resurrection turns the Christian faith into an anticipation of Christ's return.[62]

So that anyone who places faith in Him. The offer of salvation is open to all human beings. It is not restricted to any special people grouping, whether it be social, racial, or religious.[63] This does not address the issue of the notion of human inability requiring divine election. Calvinists and Arminians work this out differently. And, unless either interpretative tradition is willing to "unchurch" or "dechristianize" the other tradition, both must allow that their respective tradition (no matter how well supported in their thinking) is in fact secondary to a more core Gospel issue. In practice, both groups of Christians are much the same in their communication of the Gospel.[64] The more vital issue is the sacrificial work of Christ on the cross for the universal human condition of sinfulness.[65] That dividing line between Calvinists and Arminians cannot serve as an element of genuine core orthodoxy. But what is critical is the passage from death to life with the presence of faith.

Receives the free gift of salvation. Salvation is the general term under which several New Testament notions are hung, including such elements as forgiveness,[66] or the judicial release from guilt (often discussed under justification),[67] regeneration,[68] or the transformation of the soul, and eternal life, or the future presence of the believer with God. Regeneration (new birth) has an important implication in that the Holy Spirit becomes active and resident in the life of the believer.[69] The New Testament implication of this vital work of the Holy Spirit is that the Spirit, along with the Son, is understood to be a divine Person.[70]

The presence of the Holy Spirit in the life of the believer also indicates that there is a process-dimension to salvation subsequent to conversion.[71] It asserts that the Gospel message has as its focus those elements associated with the call to conversion. Salvation in its conversion-dimension means that salvation is received as a gift from God, whole and complete, at the point of genuine conversion.[72]

The subjective content to the Gospel: the response of faith. Acknowledging the centrality of the Gospel message and its call for faith is not enough. The message expects a *decision,* a choice to *place faith* in Christ.[73] Unlike traditional Roman Catholic sacramentalism, in which the sacraments are understood to be effective in administering divine grace *ex opere operato,*[74] evangelical faith can allow for sacramental thinking or non-sacramental thinking as long *as priority is placed on responding to the Gospel message as a distinct event* — a decision on the part of the individual to place faith in Christ alone for salvation. It is *genuine faith* which is the focus.

It is the faith itself which serves as the appropriator of the righteousness needed by the believer to stand before God in Christ, which inaugurates the presence of the Holy Spirit in the life and His subsequent regenerative "life-change," and which guarantees the future hope of the believer.

Of course, understanding the nature of saving faith is the central item here. Faith is not understood to be merely assent or cognition or affirmation of facts, although the assent to certain facts of the Gospel is necessary as a prerequisite (the Gospel facts indicate what we are to place our faith *in*). Faith is understood to have its primary focus of "trust" or "confidence" in the promise of God in Christ.[75] It is trust in a person.

Faith, in this sense, is contrasted in the New Testament to "works" or human effort to obey God and hence to gain His favor. Genuine faith exists *prior* to those works, and yet works indicate the genuineness of that faith.[76] It is not the works that save, it is the faith that saves. And salvation occurs from the moment that genuine faith occurs, and yields an inner confidence borne of the biblical promise of eternal life.

The structural underpinnings of the Gospel: apostolic authority. To evangelical faith, apostolic authority is the final arbiter in matters of faith and practice, since our Lord transmitted His authority to the apostles in charging them to communicate the Gospel to every creature. Since Scripture is given by divine inspiration and is therefore inherently authoritative (2 Tim. 3:15-16), and the New Testament writings are the ongoing, objective locus of apostolic authority, then apostolic authority must find its *ultimate* center in Scripture. This focus on Scripture (as apostolicity in its objective, abiding expression) serves as a critical backbone to the central apostolic message. It therefore undergirds the message of saving orthodoxy, which will not survive long without affirming its basis in this apostolicity.[77]

While those of evangelical faith may differ as to whether Scripture is the "sole" or "supreme" authority of faith and practice, the issue remains that the sustainer of evangelical nourishment and faith is a very high view of Scripture as the locus of apostolicity.[78] And there is the ever-present danger (especially in Protestantism) to confuse the authority of Scripture with a given line of interpretation that is not widely supported and imbue that interpretation with divine authority. This is the stuff of tradition, mentioned in earlier discussions. But without this basic understanding of the overarching authority of the Bible over all our distinctive traditions, core issues of the Gospel itself are all too quickly obscured.

So the core of orthodoxy in the New Testament is what I would call saving orthodoxy. That saving orthodoxy is the Gospel, with its New Testament presuppositions and implications.[79] The three elements of that Gospel are the objective content, the subjective application, and the undergirding apostolic authority. I would suggest that the ground of genuine Christian fellowship and cooperation must exist in relation to these elements of saving orthodoxy.

THE DEVELOPMENT OF MACRO-TRADITION: A SUSTAINING ORTHODOXY

We now need to address level II, or sustaining orthodoxy. Sustaining orthodoxy is the church's subsequent reflection on the implications of the Gospel and its elements.

A core, saving orthodoxy as outlined above demands further reflection on the explicit statements of Scripture which yield them. If Jesus is God's Son, what does that mean about His relationship to the Father? And if Jesus is in fact God, and if the Father is God, and if the Holy Spirit is God as the Gospel indicates, then how can we affirm that there is but one God? If Jesus became incarnate, what does that mean about the relationship of His deity to His humanity? If Jesus was a sacrifice for sins, *how* was He one? What is the nature of faith, since it is so crucial to the appropriation of salvation? Such questions cry out for explanation and integration. This integration and explanation is what we can call the *formulation* of faith. And, based on the elements of the Gospel, there are both orthodox and unorthodox formulations. Orthodox formulations are those which do justice to the core elements of the Gospel as laid out in Scripture. They are true to the apostolic intent as the explication of the Gospel's meaning in the face of heretical alternatives. Unorthodox formulations are those which minimize or deny certain elements of evangelical faith.

Sustaining orthodoxy of Gospel content: Christological. Saving orthodoxy of content, as far as the Christological elements are concerned, was developed into a sustaining orthodoxy of content, in part, in the great Christological Creeds of the first five centuries and is therefore enshrined in many historic liturgies as expressions of worship. Because of the clear explication of the Christological elements of the Gospel, those of evangelical faith have little trouble affirming the *Apostle's Creed,* the *Nicene Creed,* the *Athanasian Creed,* and the *Chalcedonian Definition.*[80]

These creedal formulations "fit," for the most part,[81] in their elaboration of the apostolic affirmations about the Person of Christ: He is "God of God," "Light of Light," "Very God of Very God," "Begotten, not made," "Of one substance with the Father," "of one substance with the Father as regards his Godhead, and at the same time of one substance with us as regards his manhood," and the like. Evangelical faith does not acknowledge these because the councils that produced these statements had intrinsic authority, but because these "level II sustaining orthodoxy" formulations square clearly with scriptural teaching on the Gospel.[82]

They are sufficient in what they do, and can wholeheartedly be affirmed. But they do not adequately affirm some issues of Gospel content (the atonement is notoriously unformulated), nor do they clearly affirm orthodoxy of application (justification by faith) or orthodoxy of source (priority of scriptural apostolicity). Their focus was predominantly on Christology. This is critical, but it is not the complete elaboration of Gospel content.

Formulations of the Reformation Era, however, despite their strong words against contemporary Roman Catholic teachings in some areas, consistently address these other issues of sustaining orthodoxy. First, the Reformers (as noted) affirm the first four ecumenical creeds. But beyond these, we may observe several statements from the Reformation period that elaborate on (1) the atonement; (2) justification by faith (the other aspect of the objective content of the Gospel, and the subjective content of the Gospel); and (3) the superiority of Scripture to tradition (the underpinning of objective apostolicity).

Sustaining orthodoxy of Gospel content: the atonement.[83] The *Heidelberg Catechism,* a Lutheran teaching tool dating to 1563, addresses the centrality of the atonement in its discussion of the sacraments:

Question 67.
Are both these, then, the Word and the Sacraments, designed to direct our faith to the sacrifice of Jesus Christ on the cross as the only ground of our salvation?
Answer.
Yes, truly; for the Holy Ghost teaches in the Gospel, and by the holy Sacraments assures us, that our whole salvation stands in the one sacrifice of Christ made for us on the cross.[84]

In a later section, some more questions were added after the Council of Trent was over in December of that year:

Question 80.
What difference is there between the Lord's Supper and the Popish Mass?
Answer.
The Lord's Supper testifies to us that we have full forgiveness of all our sins by the one sacrifice of Jesus Christ, which He Himself has once accomplished on the cross.[85]

The centralization of the forgiveness of sins as a completed act on the basis of the atoning work of Christ is a key theme in these Reformational formulations. This can be seen as well in the Anglican *Thirty-nine Articles* of 1563/71:

XXXI. Of the Oblation of Christ finished upon the Cross.

The offering of Christ once made is that perfect redemption, propitiation, and satisfaction, for all the sins of the whole world, both original and actual; and there is none other satisfaction for sin, but that alone. Wherefore the sacrifices of Masses, in the which it was commonly said, that the Priests did offer Christ for the quick and the dead, to have remission of pain or guilt, were blasphemous fables, and dangerous deceits.[86]

From the Calvinistic sector, we find the same theme in the classic *Westminster Confession of Faith* of 1647:

Chapter XXIX. Of the Lord's Supper.

II. In this sacrament Christ is not offered up to his Father, nor any real sacrifice made at all for the remission of sins of the quick or dead, but only a commemoration of the one offering up of himself, by himself, upon the cross, once for all, and a spiritual oblation of all possible praise unto God for the same; so that the Popish sacrifice of the mass, as they call it, is most abominably injurious to Christ's one only sacrifice, the alone propitiation for all the sins of the elect.[87]

The atonement is thus located in these Reformational formulations in the cross of Christ alone. There is no continuous reenactment of the sacrifice of Christ, since that act of salvation was done once for all on the Cross. That was where sin was totally and completely atoned for. This formulation is a clear development of the Gospel focus on Christ's sacrificial death.

Sustaining orthodoxy of the Gospel application. The second Gospel element, the subjective element of the human response of faith that yields complete salvation (justification, in most Reformational emphases), based on Christ's work rather than human effort was also formulated often during the Reformation era.

Once again, the Anglican *Thirty-nine Articles* makes this clear:

XI. Of the Justification of Man. We are accounted righteous before God, only for the merit of our Lord and Saviour Jesus Christ by Faith, and not for our own works or deservings. . . .

XII. Of Good Works. Albeit that Good Works, which are the fruits of Faith, and follow after Justification, cannot put away our sins, and endure the severity of God's judgment; yet are they pleasing and acceptable to God in Christ, and do spring out necessarily of a true and lively Faith; insomuch that by them a lively Faith may be as evidently known as a tree discerned by the fruit.[88]

We may also observe a classical Lutheran statement on this subjective application of the Gospel in the *Augsburg Confession* of 1530:

Also they [our churches] teach that men cannot be justified [obtain forgiveness of sins and righteousness] before God by their own powers, merits, or works; but are justified freely [of grace] for Christ's sake through faith, when they believe that they are received into favor, and their sins forgiven for Christ's sake, who by His death hath satisfied for our sins. This faith doth God impute for righteousness before him. Rom. iii. and iv.[89]

And finally, two expressions of classical Calvinism:

Justification is an act of God's free grace, wherein He pardons all our sins, and accepts us as righteous in His sight, only for the righteousness of Christ imputed to us, and received by faith alone.[90]

Those whom God effectually calleth He also freely justifieth; not by infusing righteousness into them, but by pardoning their sins, and by accounting and accepting their persons as righteous: not for any thing wrought in them, or done by them, but for Christ's sake alone; nor by imputing faith in itself, the act of believing, or any other evangelical obedience to them, as their righteousness; but by imputing the obedience and satisfaction of Christ unto them, they receiving and resting on him and his righteousness by faith; which faith they have not of themselves, it is the gift of God.[91]

The foregoing are clear sustaining orthodoxy statements that explicate two critical elements of the saving orthodoxy Gospel message: salvation is by faith and not works, it is based completely on the work of Christ once for all on the cross, and its benefits are enjoyed immediately upon expressing genuine faith (justification).

Sustaining orthodoxy of apostolicity framework. Here the issue again is the apostolic authority that sustains the elements of the Gospel. The issue for the Reformers was Scripture itself. Other claims to apostolicity, such as church tradition, must submit to the objectivity of Scripture. The Lutheran *Formula of Concord* (1576) starts us out:

> We believe, confess, and teach that the only rule and norm, according to which all dogmas and all doctors ought to be esteemed and judged, is no other whatever than the prophetic and apostolic writings both of the Old and of the New Testament, as it is written (Psalm cxix. 105): "Thy word is a lamp unto my feet, and a light unto my path." And St. Paul saith (Gal. 1:8): "Though an angel from heaven preach any other gospel unto you, let him be accursed."
>
> But other writings, whether of the fathers or of the moderns, with whatever name they come, are in no wise to be equaled to the Holy Scriptures, but are all to be esteemed inferior to them, so that they be not otherwise received than in the rank of witnesses, to show what doctrine was taught after the Apostles' time also, and in what parts of the world that more sound doctrine of the Prophets and Apostles has been preserved. . . .
>
> In this way a clear distinction is retained between the sacred Scriptures of the Old and New Testaments, and all other writings; and Holy Scripture alone [*sola Sacra Scriptura*] is acknowledged as the only judge, norm, and rule, according to which, as by the only touchstone, all doctrines are to be examined and judged, as to whether they be godly or ungodly, true or false.[92]

The French Protestant *Belgic Confession* of 1561 strikes on the same notes:

> We believe that these Holy Scriptures fully contain the will of God, and that whatsoever man ought to believe unto salvation, is sufficiently taught therein. For since the whole manner of worship which God requires of us is written in them at large, it is unlawful for anyone, though an Apostle, to teach otherwise than we are now taught in the Holy Scriptures. . . . Neither may we compare any writings of men, though ever so holy, with those divine Scriptures; nor ought we to compare custom, or the great multitude, or antiquity, or succession of times or persons, or councils, decrees, or statutes, with the truth of God, for the truth is above all: for all men are of themselves liars, and more vain than vanity itself. Therefore we reject with all our hearts whatsoever doth not agree with this infallible rule. . . . [93]

Similarly, the Anglican *Thirty-nine Articles:*

> Holy Scripture containeth all things necessary to salvation: so that whatsoever is not read therein, nor may be proved thereby, is not

to be required of any man, that it should be believed as an article of the Faith, or be thought requisite or necessary to salvation.[94]

And finally, the *Westminster Confession of Faith,*

The authority of the holy Scripture, for which it ought to be believed and obeyed, dependeth not upon the testimony of any man or church, but wholly upon God (who is truth itself), the Author thereof; and therefore it is to be received, because it is the Word of God. . . .

The Supreme Judge, by which all controversies of religion are to be determined, and all decrees of councils, opinions of ancient writers, doctrines of men, and private spirits, are to be examined, and in whose sentence we are to rest, can be no other but the Holy Spirit speaking in the Scripture.[95]

These Reformational formulations are classic statements of the importance of an objective locus for apostolicity that could affirm the genuineness of the saving Gospel.

It is safe to say that *all* aspects of sustaining Gospel orthodoxy were not fully formulated by the fifth century. Christology, though critical, was the primary focus for the church at that time. And they *did* formulate an orthodox Christology. But they did not address the other elements of the Gospel and their perpetuation. Level II formulation, sustaining orthodoxy, was therefore not completed at an early stage in church history, but rather was an ongoing process.

The Reformers accepted those level II formulations of the first five centuries because they believed them to be correct according to the apostolic testimony of the Scriptures. They developed for themselves level II orthodox formulations of their own to fill in the missing dimensions in terms of the atonement and apostolic authority finding its locus in Scripture.

But remember: it is level I orthodoxy (the elements of the Gospel) which defines a core orthodoxy in its most fundamental and functional sense. That is where saving orthodoxy may be found. And this saving orthodoxy is what serves as the centripetal focus of genuine catholicity, around which hover the varieties of Christian tradition, the closest of which are the early Christological creeds, followed by the soteriological and biblical formulations of the Reformation period. This sustaining orthodoxy tradition is important and inevitable, but it is definitely secondary to the binding core of saving orthodoxy found in apostolic Scripture. Perhaps figure 6.1 may show this better:

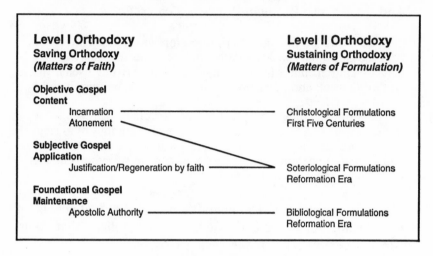

Figure 6.1.
Levels of Orthodoxy

OBJECTIONS TO THE GOSPEL AS ORTHODOXY

However, a question naturally arises. If evangelical faith (the Gospel) is the core element that serves as a fundamental saving orthodoxy, what of those groups (particularly Roman Catholics) which deny the function of the Reformation as a late intrusion into a constant tradition and unity up until that time, or of those groups (particularly Eastern Orthodox) which received no real part in the Reformational emphasis on evangelical faith? Do they not partake in the core orthodoxy formulation that antedates the Reformation?

Yes, in the sense that they affirm certain content elements of sustaining orthodoxy (the Christological creeds). And yes, in the instances that they affirm a high place to apostolic Scripture.[96] But no, in the formal teaching on the aspects of the atonement and its application to the subjective elements of justification by faith. The sacramental approach used in particular by Roman Catholic theology has robbed the Gospel of its saving power in many ways. This needs to be remedied.[97]

Remember, the Reformers did not innovate when they proclaimed the evangelical faith. They carefully documented it as in fact the apostolic message of the Cross, found in the pages of the New Testament. They created nothing new and claimed as much. They were simply reaffirming the long-obscured Gospel message. They claimed that while the Roman Church innovated and became sidetracked, they, on the other hand, were simply proclaiming the ancient faith.

Second, regardless of official teaching, where the genuine Christ is understood, genuine faith is possible and therefore so is genuine conversion. And sustaining Christological orthodoxy *is* present in the teachings of both Rome and Constantinople. Despite many elements which the Reformers and subsequent Protestants cannot condone within these historic churches, one must admit that legitimate, saving faith can occur within them. One appears to find saving faith in some surprising contexts.[98]

But all this means is that sometimes salvation is obtained *in spite of* official teaching of a given Christian group rather than *because of* it. And the same could be said for some forms of Protestantism, where aberrations of the Gospel message all too easily alienate rather than arouse one to converting faith. But because justification by faith is weakly communicated in these historic groups (as sanctification is weakly communicated in some Protestant circles), the call to faith and conversion is too easily lost (apart from evangelical renewal).

And, because the Bible plays a lesser role, the protection of the evangelical message is easily obscured for the long haul in these groups. That is why one wonders whether the newer evangelical thrust in these groups will have any long-term effect.

With the fact that the Gospel or evangelical faith and formulation are separable, and that the earliest formulations of the church were entirely adequate Christologies but went little beyond that, a true statement of formulation which integrates both the Reformational explications of the Gospel as well as the focus of the ancient Christologies might be desirable.[99] But such a formulation would need to take into account the different arrays of evangelical Protestant formulations. A statement of faith which is produced by a consensus of evangelical communities would likely be a good place to start as a centering place for cooperation and evangelistic effort.[100]

In addition, evangelistic parachurch organizations, such as

InterVarsity Christian Fellowship, the *Navigators,* or *Campus Crusade for Christ* similarly can yield models of sustaining orthodoxy formulations in which the functional centrality of the Gospel is present. This can serve as a help in core orthodoxy formulation. The contemporary formulation, which is a truly catholic one, must take into account not only the great, historic Christological creeds, but that which is common to all the classic Reformation statements on those issues pertaining to the Gospel, particularly justification by faith and the importance of Scripture over tradition in affirming genuine apostolicity. Such contemporary, catholic, widespread acceptance of a core evangelic orthodoxy will best take place in broad interaction rather than in narrow, denominational discussions.

CONCLUSIONS

Although saving orthodoxy becomes the critical criterion for working together as believers, sustaining orthodoxy must be taken very seriously as the uniform expression of the church's reflection on the implication of the Gospel. Saving orthodoxy arises directly from Scripture (*norma normans*); while sustaining orthodoxy is part of the macro-tradition of the church (*norma normata*).

Matters not contained in core orthodoxy—either saving or sustaining—must be relegated to a secondary position (traditional interpretation) and must not hinder Christian fellowship and co-operation. Things beyond these are matters of micro-tradition. That does not mean that these issues are unimportant, nor does it mean these issues are not worth further debate and discussion, but it does mean that they are not part of *core* or saving orthodoxy. And therefore, they are not to hinder interaction and mutual support and service. The Gospel is functionally central; its later formulations are important in understanding and sustaining the essentials and implications of the Gospel, but the Gospel is central.[101] And all other issues must be considered to one degree or another as matters of conscience but not matters of creed for the church.

Christians who agree on the Gospel as God's unique tool to grant complete forgiveness to sinners through the shed blood of the incarnate and resurrected Son of God will differ on the frequency and the sacramental value of the Lord's Supper; they will disagree on how the church should be organized and run. They will differ on matters pertaining to human free will and its relation to divine sovereignty; they will differ on the function of spiritual gifts today, and whether a believer, once saved, is kept saved. Genuine Christians will also differ from each other on matters of eschatology.

And in all these areas, genuine Christians have deep convictions, since they base their beliefs on the fact that these matters are derived from Scripture. But that is precisely why these areas must be discussed further. They fall in the realm of traditional interpretation. And, as I argue, we are obligated to assess our own unique teachings and evaluate them from the standpoint of a fair application of biblical hermeneutics. They are in large part probably micro-traditions which may never be resolved in our discussions. They must be talked over, but they must not be used to divide us, for they are no part of core orthodoxy. The Gospel is the core orthodoxy to which we all must return.

Seven

DETECTING DENOMINATIONAL TRADITIONS, PART 1: AN HISTORICAL FIELD TRIP TO THE BRETHREN MOVEMENT

The Brethren are a remarkable people for rightly dividing the Word of Truth and wrongly dividing themselves.

—W.H. Griffith Thomas.

During my college years, I spent several summers working at a lodge in Grand Teton National Park. During those summers the genuine believers I encountered were gems to be cherished, since the predominate atmosphere of the employee villages was either staunch Mormonism or rank hedonism. So, it did not matter so much whether the weekly Bible studies were comprised of a Baptist or two, a Pentecostal, a Presbyterian, a charismatic Roman Catholic, and a few independent Bible church folk. We differed with each other on many things, but we could celebrate a sincere and common faith quite readily in that environment. We were eager to have a weekly time of fellowship, Bible study, and prayer to support each other in our attempts to witness in a rather hostile or indifferent environment. We even broke bread together occasionally in marvelous catholicity.

One summer I discovered something rather unheard of in my past experience with other Christians at the park. I ran across a new fellow worker in the employee village who was a believer. As she shared with me the type of church fellowship she was involved with back home, things began to sound strangely familiar. It continued to click, so I pursued a bit, "Do you have a group of leading men, or elders, rather than a single pastor and call your group an 'assembly' rather than a church?" "Why, yes," she replied. "You don't happen to be 'Plymouth Brethren' do you?" I asked. "No, not at all," she replied.

"OK, let me ask you a few more questions," I teased. "Do women there wear some sort of head covering?" "Yes," came the response. "Do they keep silent in the public meetings?" "Uh-huh." "Do you break bread every week, with a nonstructured format, where any of the men may participate?" "Yes, we do!"

"I honestly think you may really be going to a Brethren assembly," I replied. She was adamant, "Oh, but we're *not* Plymouth Brethren." Somehow I knew that she had been warned about that label before. So, I teased on just a little bit further, "Do you happen to use two hymnals, one a large blue one and one a thinner, black one?" "Yes, but how did you know that?" she finally asked. Beaming a bit, I replied: "I fellowship among the Plymouth Brethren, too." I was surprised by her response, but I shouldn't have been. She responded both indignantly and firmly, "Oh, but no—we're *not* Plymouth Brethren."

The preceding story quickly acquaints the novice with just a few of the distinctive characteristics of my own denominational background. I offer it as the first leg of a personal field trip we will be taking in chapters 7 and 8.

My purpose in this chapter is to bring some of the book's main themes into sharper focus. We will do this by frankly discussing the way in which catholicity has been affected in at least this one free Protestant group, my own Christian (or Plymouth) Brethren.[1]

Prominent twentieth century churchmen who have come from a Brethren background include: the expositor of the previous generation, H.A. Ironside;[2] missionary martyr Jim Elliot;[3] InterVarsity Christian Fellowship's Paul A. Little (of *Know Why You Believe* fame); British scholar F.F. Bruce;[4] New Testament scholar W. Ward Gasque; Canadian evangelist Terry Winter; Christian counselor and author Larry Crabb; international evangelist Luis Palau; Ontario Theological Seminary president Bill McRae; and satirist and writer Garrison Keillor.[5]

The Brethren, as noted earlier, are in some ways a "restorationist" group who perceive themselves as having recovered a more biblical understanding of church truth than other groups. Further, the Brethren have had two contrasting streams from their earliest days: one a highly separatistic and sectarian stream (which has in some extreme expressions—not all!—become rather cultic), and the other a highly catholic and warm-hearted stream. In both streams, however, there is a tendency to disdain denominationalism. But the Brethren are (as I have defined it) clearly a denomination. They have informal links with one another and a shared history and set of doctrinal distinctives. The question is whether they are wanting to continue to deny that fact and actually drift toward sectarianism, or whether they will accept that and return to their historic bent toward catholicity.[6]

The key, in my thinking, is for the Brethren—as with all groups—to carefully assess their distinctive doctrines hermeneutically—with the help of the rest of the Body of Christ—so as to recognize the degree to which those distinctives actually fall under the rubric of "tradition." Further, they need to accept that although many of their traditions may have abiding value, they are at last *no more than traditions*. Even *more* important in the long run is what they share with the rest of the body of Christ in terms of the core of Gospel orthodoxy.

This scenario is not unique to the Brethren, so assessing them through the principles developed in this book should serve others in evaluating the distinctives of their own denominational backgrounds. My intent is not to bare our interpretive "dirty laundry" so as to deride this rich Brethren heritage, nor is it to single out the movement to extol it in some way. My intent is to show in a practical way how applying the principles of sound, broad-based hermeneutics can surface elements in a Christian group which must fall into the realm of tradition, despite that group's claims to a more complete understanding of biblical truth than other groups. And, although I am singling out only one segment of the free church movement, others may recognize some of the arguments Brethren use from their own practices in their own denominational contexts.

Please understand, what I do here is risky. I have long-standing friendships and relationships among the Brethren, and I may be held suspect by some who will think that by going through this exercise I am "betraying" the Brethren or "abandoning New Testament principles."[7] I am doing nothing of the kind. I am, rather, asking fundamental questions so that I can (1) affirm the Brethren tradition for what it is (2) enable them to think more broadly of the larger church as a number of the original prime movers did, and (3) give those in other traditions a glimpse into our interpretative problems with an eye toward resolving their own.

Before applying the principles of hermeneutics to my denominational grouping, it is important to describe its nature and background, since that is one important first step in applying hermeneutics to a given group. In this case it is also important for non-Brethren readers, since the Brethren are very loose organizationally and tend to avoid the development of theological training institutions and a professional ministry. Hence, they may sometimes seem to be the "invisible sector" in modern evangelicalism. I will attempt to make these sectors visible. Remember to do the same for your own group.

A SHORT HISTORICAL SURVEY OF THE BRETHREN[8]

What I refer to as the Christian Brethren began, in part, as a reactionary movement to certain sectarian attitudes dividing the churches in England and Ireland in the 1820s and '30s. It was an attempt to find a new ground for unity among genuine believers, one based on the sincerity of faith in Christ alone, regardless of theological preference or ecclesiastical background on subsidiary matters. The young men and women who played a part in the founding were a mixture of Anglicans and "dissenters" looking for some way to recapture the unity of the church of Christ and the freedom of the authority of the Word of God in their lives. They were not content with the prevalent notion that to choose membership in one church was only to be excluded from fellowship in another. Edward Cronin, one former "dissenter" who joined in the earliest days in Dublin, stated, "Special membership, as it is called among dissenters, was the primary and most offensive condition of things to our minds, so that our first assembling was really marked as a small company of evangelical malcontents."[9] The spawning of the Brethren Movement was in itself a response to this sort of sectarianism and a move toward a more catholic understanding of the church.

Among the influences of the Brethren tradition toward the larger church are the development of the classical "dispensationalist" mode of interpretation (contributed in large part by the prolific Brethren writer, John Nelson Darby),[10] the strong emphasis on "lay ministry," and the development of "faith" missions on the pattern of the lesser known Anthony Norris Groves and his brother-in-law, the better known George Müller of Bristol.[11]

The Brethren today are of two major types, as a result of a major split that occurred in 1848, soon after the movement began: the *Open* Brethren and the *Exclusive* Brethren.

In the twenty-year period prior to the 1848 split, there was a developing spirit of catholicity apparent within the movement, especially in the heart of prime mover Anthony Norris Groves (1795–1853). Groves was a highly successful Anglican dentist living in Plymouth, England. After an acute family crisis, and a period of intense Bible study, Groves and his wife Mary became discontent with their wealth. They agreed that Mary should distribute to the poor first a tenth, then a fourth, then virtually all of their income. The care of God experienced in this process of obedience had such a profound impact on the couple that Groves wrote a booklet on the Christian and wealth in 1825 entitled *Christian Devotedness.* This book served as a challenge to all to return to a more biblical attitude toward wealth and living by faith. He claimed in that booklet, "The Christian motto should be, labor hard, consume little, give much, and all to Christ."[12] This focus on a genuine, personal spirituality, as first exemplified by Groves, has long been a crucial concern for the Brethren.

As an extension of their sacrificial living, the Groves concluded God would have them go to the mission field. So Groves began to travel periodically to Trinity College, Dublin, to take his examinations in preparation for ordination with the Anglican *Church Missionary Society.* While on his trips to Dublin in 1826–27, Groves came into contact with a small group of devoted nonconformists meeting for Bible study and prayer, among whom was a lawyer named J.G. Bellett. In the religious context of Ireland, where denominational ties meant much less than in England, there developed a healthy tendency for all Protestants to find ways to encourage and support each other in the face of a robust Irish Roman Catholicism. Groves began to see in this unusual but refreshing cross-denominational fellowship a key to Christian unity. He later recorded in his diary about this time:

> I was almost forgetting, till a letter from Mr. Bellett of Dublin reminded me, that I was the first to propose that simple principle of union, the love of Jesus, instead of *oneness* of judgment in minor things, things that may consist with a true love of Jesus.[13]

Here are the earliest glimmerings of a catholic spirit among the Brethren. Unity is connected, in a highly sectarian context, to the simple principle of the love for Jesus rather than a uniform agreement on secondary issues. In addition, Groves came to some convictions regarding ministry within the Christian community. He concluded, despite his own educational process, that formal ordination was *not* a requirement of Scripture for serving God in a missionary (or other) capacity; nor was a clergyman needed in order for sincere Christians to participate in communion. In the spring of 1827, Bellett told another person what Groves had passed on to him:

> Groves has just been telling me, that it appeared to him from Scripture, that believers, meeting together as disciples of Christ, were free to break bread together, as their Lord admonished them; and that, in as far as the apostles could be a guide, every Lord's day should be set apart for thus remembering the Lord's death, and obeying his parting command.[14]

Groves did not believe that it was wrong, or in error, to practice ordination. Groves felt, rather, that ordination was *unnecessary*. Ultimately, this lack of biblical necessity prompted Groves to abandon his own plans for ordination and to leave the Anglican communion in early 1828 to connect more fully with these like-minded nonconformists.

The spirit of catholicity toward his former Anglican friends can be seen in the letter Groves wrote back from the mission field to a good friend of his who was also an Anglican priest, Mr. Caldecott, on December 16, 1828. Groves responded to Caldecott's dismay at his departure from Anglicanism in these words:

> You say I quitted *your* communion; if you mean by that, that I do not now break bread with the Church of England, this is not true; but if you mean that I do not *exclusively* join you, it is quite true, feeling this spirit of exclusiveness to be the very essence of schism, which the apostle so strongly reproves in the Corinthians. I therefore know no distinction, but am ready to break the bread and drink the cup of holy joy with all who love the Lord and will not lightly speak evil of His name. I feel every saint to be a holy person, because Christ dwells in him, and manifests Himself where he worships; and though his faults be as many as the hairs

of his head, my duty still is, with my Lord, to join him as a member of the mystical body, and to hold communion and fellowship with him in any work of the Lord in which he may be engaged. . . . As bodies, I know none of the sects and parties that wound and disfigure Christ; as individuals, I desire to love all that love Him. Oh! when will the day come when the love of Christ will have more power to unite than our foolish regulations have to divide the family of God?[15] (original emphasis)

The letter to Caldecott came to him from Baghdad, where Groves and his family had already begun to serve as independent missionaries. They left England on June 12, 1828. Groves' large-hearted spirit of catholicity allowed within the Brethren Movement in its earliest years a healthy latitude of diversity around a shared love for the person of Christ. One of his long-remembered sayings from these years was, "Talk of loving me while I agree with them! Give me men that will love me when I differ from them and contradict them: those will be the men to build up a true Church."[16] That is unity in diversity. That is catholicity.

But there was another man who began to meet with the small group in Dublin in those early days. He was an Anglican clergyman with prodigious intellectual acumen, John Nelson Darby, another friend of J.G. Bellett, who was troubled in 1827 by the interference of the state in his successful ministry among the Irish poor. That year, Archbishop Magee of Dublin decreed all Roman Catholic converts must swear allegiance to the English crown, and the droves of converts to Christ in the counties where Darby ministered abruptly came to an end. With this political interference with the work of Christ, Darby began to radically rethink his understanding of the church.[17] In 1828 (the year Groves left for Baghdad), Darby publicly responded and issued his *Considerations on the Nature and Unity of the Church of Christ*. In this work, we can almost see inklings of a broader catholicity in Darby's mind, but there are troubling differences as well. He said, in that work:

No meeting, which is not framed to embrace all the children of God in the full basis of the kingdom of the Son, can find the fullness of blessing, because it does not contemplate it—because its faith does not embrace it.[18]

Yet, there is no professed unity among you at all. So far as men pride themselves on being Established, Presbyterian, Baptist, Independent, or anything else, they are antichristian. How then are they to be united? I answer, it must be the work of the Spirit of God.[19]

But at the same time something more subtle appears in Darby's writing, namely, that there is intrinsic wrong in the denominational approach.

> From all this has flowed an anomalous and trying consequence; namely, that the true Church of God has no avowed communion at all. There are, I suppose, none of its members who would not acknowledge, that individuals of the children of God are to be found in all the different denominations, who profess the same pure faith; but where is that bond of union? It is not that unbelieving professors are mixed with the people of God in their communion, but that the bond of communion is not the *unity* of the people of God, but really (in point of fact) their *differences.*[20]

> Let believers remove the hindrances to the Lord's glory, which their own inconsistencies present, and by which they are joined to the world, and their judgments perverted. Let them commune one with another, seeking His will from the word, and see if a blessing does not attend it; at any rate it will attend themselves; they will meet the Lord as those that have waited for Him, and can rejoice unfeignedly in His salvation.[21]

To Darby, some sort of federation or broad mutual acceptance of existing denominations would not do. That would not show forth the genuine spiritual unity of all who believe. The need is to gather *out from* the denominations to find unity in gathering to Christ alone. Denominationalism, to him, was simply a matter of self-interest, not the Lord's glory. Ultimately, Darby was to pronounce the entire institutional church of any shape or form "in ruins" at the end of the church dispensation.[22]

This subtle but critical difference between Groves and Darby led Darby to a stricter assessment of the professing churches than Groves. In fact, it forced Darby into a stronger focus on the *purity* over the *unity* of the church in Christ. And Groves caught Darby at this subtle shift from original principles. In 1836, while on brief furlough from his missionary work, Groves wrote Darby to warn him of these tendencies. He already detected in Darby a principle operating that was significantly *different* from the original principles of catholicity that motivated the Dublin Brethren:

I ever understood our principle of union to be the possession of the common life or common blood of the family of God (for the life is in the blood); these were our early thoughts, and are my most matured ones. The transition your little bodies have undergone, in no longer standing forth the witnesses for the glorious and simple truth, so much as standing forth witnesses against all that they judge error, have lowered them in my apprehension from heaven to earth in their position of witnesses.[23]

Groves continued:

The moment the witnessing for the common life as our *bond* gives place to a witnessing *against* errors by separation of persons and preaching (errors allowably compatible with the common life), every individual, or society of individuals, first comes before the mind as those who might need witnessing against, and all their conduct and principles have first to be examined and approved before they can be received; and the position which this occupying the seat of judgment will place you in will be this: the most narrow-minded and bigoted will rule, because his conscience cannot and will not give way, and therefore the more enlarged heart must yield. It is into this position, dear D[arby], I feel some little flocks are fast tending, if they have not already attained it, making *light*, not *life* the measure of communion.[24]

And, in a key section contrasting the Brethren's original attitude toward catholicity with the growing sectarian attitude of Darby, Groves summarized the changes that had overcome him:

As any system is in its provision narrower or wider than the truth, I either stop short, or go beyond its provisions, but I would INFINITELY RATHER BEAR *with all their evils,* than SEPARATE from THEIR GOOD. These were the *then* principles of our separation and intercommunion; we had resolved never to try to *get men to act* in UNIFORMITY *further than* they FELT IN UNIFORMITY; neither by frowns, nor smiles; and this for one simple reason, that we saw no authority given us from God thus to act.[25]

Unfortunately for the future of this movement, Groves went back to finish his life out on the mission field, and his letter to Darby went unheeded. Darby became more and more insistent on conformity to his system of thinking about the church and on expecting genuine believers to separate out from the corrupt systems and gather in "twos and threes" to express unity around the person of Christ alone.[26]

So, with Darby energetically forging ahead and establishing many new groups along his principles, a confrontation between his supporters and those who followed the original ideal embodied in Groves' statements was inevitable. That confrontation came with a sudden and frightening finality.

Its first doleful glimmers took place in December of 1845, when Darby withdrew from the thriving assembly at Plymouth due to a conflict with Benjamin Wills Newton, who had become the principle teacher there during Darby's absence on the continent. Darby soon set up a rival meeting for disenchanted Brethren at another location in Plymouth. Watching Newton carefully for several years afterward, Darby and his supporters snatched onto a clearly heretical statement he made about the person of Christ in the spring of 1847 and, despite his written retraction of the error,[27] he was driven from the movement by Darby and his supporters.[28]

But that was just the beginning of the tragedy. When some of the former members of the Newton's assembly in Plymouth went to Bristol the following spring to join at Bethesda Chapel (where George Müller and Henry Craik ministered), Darby put the elders at Bethesda on notice: to receive these people was to entertain heresy, for they had sat under Newton's teaching. The elders at Bethesda duly examined these men. They pronounced them free from Newton's heresy[29] and said so in a public document in late June of 1848, indicating further that the assembly at Bethesda had proper authority to evaluate heresy without outside interference.[30]

Darby was unmoveable. He suspected some sort of malevolent force at work in this blatant challenge to his own convictions. Since Bethesda refused to put these men out, he issued a letter in August of 1848 for all those who sided with him to remove Bethesda from their fellowship, or to see *themselves* rejected for participating in their "evil."[31] From that point on the Brethren Movement formally diverged into two separate paths, one following Darby in his exclusivism, and one following Groves, Müller and Craik in their model of catholicity. Judging this "Bethesda Question" thus separated them into the *Open* and *Exclusive* Brethren ever since.[32]

The Exclusives disavow the Opens over this issue of church discipline and local autonomy and were led by the strong hand of

John Nelson Darby and his successors. Their focus has been on the doctrinal purity of the church: "separation from evil is God's principle for unity,"[33] and they have had numerous separations as doctrinal purity became more and more narrowly defined.[34]

The Open Brethren, ostracized by the Exclusives, feel that the others departed from the original spirit of the movement, which was really focused on the catholicity and unity of the body of Christ around the love and worship of Christ alone. The Open Brethren have thus been far more ready to recognize the great breadth of the body of Christ outside their circles. They had leaders like Müller and Craik, who followed the more open-minded model of Groves, rather than Darby.[35] George Müller himself expressed this spirit of Open Brethren catholicity in 1863:

Yet while we hold fast the truth, all the truth which we consider we have been instructed in from the Holy Scriptures, we must ever remember, that it is not the degree of knowledge to which believers have attained which should unite them, but the common spiritual life they have in Jesus; that they are purchased by the blood of Jesus; members of the same family; going to the Father's house—soon to be all there: and by reason of the common life they have, brethren should dwell together in unity. It is the will of the Father, and of that blessed One who laid down His life for us, that we should love one another.[36]

Similarly, an anonymous Open Brethren writer spoke in the early part of this century within this same spirit of catholicity:

We amongst Open Brethren . . . rejoice to unite in Christian work with all who are truly converted, whose lives are upright and who hold the fundamentals of the faith. We love them and honor them, and although we may think that in some respects we have found, by grace, a more excellent way, yet we recognize to the praise of God that there are amongst them many holy and devoted souls, evangelists of power and earnestness, teachers and hymn writers to whom we and the world owe a deep debt. When they care to join us at the Lord's Table, they are most sincerely welcome.[37]

The preceding survey has not been a happy one to review, but these two streams, the more sectarian Exclusives and the more catholic Opens, ironically flow from the same headwaters. Such, in distilled fashion, the noble and ignoble origin of the Christian (Plymouth) Brethren Movement.[38]

How to Recognize the Brethren

Earlier I mentioned the relative invisibility of the Brethren today as a sort of "hidden" evangelicalism. That leaves one just learning about this movement, in a bit of quandary. Just how could one recognize the Brethren? Following are a few essential clues.[39]

(1) Brethren tend to name their meeting places "Chapels" (among the Opens) or "Halls" and "Meeting Rooms" (among the Closed-Open/Tights[40] and Exclusives), and, more often than not, name these buildings in connection with a geographical feature: "Raleigh Street Bible Chapel," "Southampton Gospel Hall," "87th Avenue Bible Chapel."

(2) Brethren tend to call the Christians who meet with them "the assembly" more frequently than "the church," and often refer to "going to meeting" rather than "going to church." The church, to Brethren, is the *people* — not the building.

(3) Brethren historically have a *distinct* meeting for the assembly each week called "breaking of bread" or "remembrance" meeting, where the assembly gathers at the Lord's Table. That meeting is normally unguided, and open for any male to participate in by suggesting a hymn, leading in prayer, or giving some spiritual encouragement from Scripture. Women are traditionally expected to remain silent and to wear some sort of head covering. Genuine believers who visit from other churches or assemblies are allowed to participate in the Lord's Table immediately on a clear assertion of faith only among the Open Brethren.[41]

(4) Brethren (at least the Open and the Tights [Closed/ Open]) are normally led by a group of men whom they refer to as "elders" or (less frequently) "overseers." These men are selected from the congregation by existing leaders rather than by popular vote, primarily on the basis of spiritual maturity rather than on theological training. Exclusives do not formally recognize elders, but have a monthly "Brothers Meeting" or "Care Meeting" where all men are invited to conduct the business of the assembly.

(5) When Brethren have a supported pastoral staff person (only among the Opens), they tend to avoid the term "pastor," since he is mostly under the supervision of the elders, or at most

he will be viewed as a co-elder. The term most often used for this person is a "full-time worker." The worker is "commended" to this work and not ordained (based on the terminology of Acts 14:26). But the bulk of ministry in a typical Brethren assembly is carried on by what is most frequently known in other circles as a "lay ministry." They are strongly opposed to whatever may be constituted as "clericalism" to them, that is, the concentrating of the ministry in the hands of a few privileged people. Exclusives have only itinerant workers, not resident local workers.

(6) The Open Brethren in the United States[42] have a communication network in *Interest Ministries* of Carol Stream, Illinois which publishes their *Interest* magazine. They also have a school in Dubuque, Iowa called *Emmaus Bible College.*[43] Their missionary service organization located in Spring Lake, New Jersey is *Christian Missions in Many Lands,* although in recent years short-term missions and some long-term missions have been serviced by *International Teams* of Prospect Heights, Illinois.

They have two service organizations, *Stewards Foundation,* which funds low-interest loans to qualifying Brethren assemblies for building purposes and provides health insurance for workers and missionaries and *Stewards Ministries,* which grants funds to ministries connected to Brethren assemblies. None of these support organizations constitute the Brethren as a "denomination" in their thinking, since there is no external authority recognized outside or above the local congregation, nor are any dues or fees ever paid to these agencies. In fact, denominationalism continues to be deemed by the Brethren in a rather negative light, as a defacing of the unity of the body of Christ.

A further word about the Exclusive Brethren is necessary.[44] Although you would find similar characteristics to those above, Exclusives have what they call "circles of fellowship" into which one enters upon clearing their strict standards of moral and doctrinal purity. Unity is understood to be gathering only "to the name of the Lord" (the way these Brethren do it) and to do so is to get onto a special and hallowed "divine ground." Many Exclusives practice household or infant baptism (the Opens practice believer baptism only).

A non-Brethren visitor attending a Breaking of Bread service at an Exclusive meeting would normally be required to not take part until a period of observation ensued, unless he or she came with a letter from an approved assembly. Exclusive publications in North America come most often from a group known as *Bible Truth Publishers* in Addison, Illinois and the King James Version predominates in these assemblies, as does a small words-only hymnbook produced by Darby called *Hymns for the Little Flock.*[45]

How Many of Them Are There?
Considering the Open and Closed/Open (Tight) Brethren only, there are approximately 820 Brethren assemblies in the United States, and 467 in Canada, for a total of 1,287 in North America. These figures yield some 79,545 adults in fellowship.[46] The Exclusive assemblies are now more difficult to calculate, since they keep few records and refuse to have contact with the Opens (or any other Christian group for that matter). Meade estimated some 300 total Exclusive meetings in North America with something less than 10,000 in fellowship.[47] The largest bodies of Exclusives in North America are the Tunbridge-Wells Exclusives and the Kelly-Lowe Exclusives: the two sides of a 1909 division.

The Brethren Interpretive Background

The broader interpretive background. A few comments must first be made about the broader interpretive tradition within which the Brethren fit. The characteristics here are shared with other groups that have a common derivation and hence are not Brethren distinctives per se. But they will help the reader to identify more clearly the kind of group about which we are speaking.

(1) The Brethren are a Protestant group. As such they share a common heritage with emphases on the doctrines of judicial justification by faith alone, as distinct from the growth process of sanctification; *sola Scriptura*; the priesthood of all believers; and (as typical Protestants) a strong suspicion of things Roman Catholic.

(2) The Brethren are a free church group. As such, they emphasize the doctrines of separation of church and state, and, for the most part, the doctrine of the autonomy of the local church (although, in practice, the Exclusives deny autonomy and have been known to remove whole assemblies and groups of assemblies from fellowship).[48]

(3) The Brethren are non-sacramentalist in their soteriology. As

such, although they break bread as a central function of their worship and remembrance, they do not recognize any soteriological value in the Eucharist: the bread and wine are merely reminders of a spiritual reality. Baptism does not have a soteriological function, but is an act of obedience.

Although other broader brushstrokes could be suggested,[49] these form a broad framework into which the unique distinctives of the Brethren may be set and evaluated in terms of their traditional nature.

Brethren distinctive characteristics. In one sense, it is difficult to capture adequate documentation for the unique characteristics of the Brethren since their doctrine is not often passed on in written form. Further, there is often an aversion to biblical and theological scholarship and a propensity to publish practical and devotional works. They sustain their practices in an informal social network, but if one is among the Brethren for long, one learns of the interconnectedness and the accepted practice, despite the claim to nondenominational or nonsectarian status.[50] In fact, most of their distinctives focus in the areas of ecclesiology and eschatology.

Although the latter yields a variety of Brethren viewpoints, it must be admitted at least in North America, that even among the Opens, John Nelson Darby's dispensational premillennialism has tended to dominate. But even so, the Brethren fit comfortably into the mainstream of dispensational premillennialism that has dominated in North American circles since the latter quarter of the nineteenth century and is found at non-Brethren schools like *Moody Bible Institute, Dallas Theological Seminary,* and *Multnomah School of the Bible.* Thus, apart from the issues of eschatology, the most *uniquely* Brethren principles, in the context of North America, tend to congregate around issues of ecclesiology. It is around the doctrine of the church that all distinctively Brethren characteristics center.

CONCLUSION

One of the first tasks toward the recovery of a spirit of catholicity in any group is to know the history and practices of the denomination or group well. This chapter has tried to show how I apply that principle to my own group; others will need to repeat this exercise in their particular context. The next step is to identify and assess the distinctives of one's denominational grouping and their biblical basis, applying principles of hermeneutics so as to detect the presence of the traditional.

In the next chapter our task will be to look closely at these Brethren "denominational distinctives" that center around their understanding of the nature and function of the church. Our point will be, as we have laid out earlier, to apply the principles of hermeneutics to the texts and arguments appealed to by the Brethren to see if their unique characteristics are in fact New Testament principles or mandates which should be followed by all, or whether they are not sustainable at that level. If so, they must be understood as merely part of the Brethren tradition.

Eight

DETECTING DENOMINATIONAL TRADITIONS, PART 2: A HERMENEUTICAL FIELD TRIP THROUGH BRETHREN DISTINCTIVES

Indeed, in some more enclosed traditions the authority of Scripture will be identified with the authority of the accepted interpretation and application, because it has never occurred to those inside the enclosure that Scripture could be interpreted or applied otherwise. . . .
— F.F. Bruce

 I remember listening to a lecture given by a Baptist seminary professor in which he argued for the congregational election of leaders. A key passage he offered to support his argument was Acts 14:23: "Paul and Barnabas *appointed* elders for them in each church." He asserted that the Greek word employed for "appointed" means, etymologically, "to stretch out one's hand, to vote."[1] Therefore, he concluded, congregational voting is God's means of selecting elders or other officers of the church.[2]

Of course, we non-Baptists tend to smile at such interpretive naiveté. We can see the "root" fallacy operating here.[3] Further, we know that even *if* the meaning here is "vote" (itself quite doubtful), it is obvious from the context that the *congregation* did not do the "voting" for its leaders, but *existing church leaders* did, that is, Barnabas and Paul. They are the subjects of the verb. Even if the passage were didactic rather than descriptive in nature, it simply does *not* support the concept of congregational determination of its own leadership by the voting process.[4]

But I do not want to be too harsh on the Baptists. They are not alone in having specialized interpretive foibles. If God would grant all of us honesty and sincerity, we could all humbly admit similar interpretive errors on our part, be we Brethren, Presbyterian, Methodist, or Reformed. In the last chapter, I introduced my own denominational background, one that has—not unlike others—a rather checkered history. I gave an overview of some of the unique distinctives necessary to understanding the Brethren as they focus uniquely on matters of ecclesiology and eschatology. It was noted that the *central* uniqueness today still remains in areas of ecclesiology (particularly church polity), since their eschatology has been more broadly accepted in dispensational circles.

In this chapter, many of the ecclesiastical distinctives of the Brethren will be assessed in terms of their hermeneutical appropriateness. I hope to show that very little that is unique to the Christian Brethren Movement has direct biblical mandate. I assume the same could be said about the denominational distinctives of others. Brethren distinctives, like those of other traditions, therefore would need to fall into the category of (micro-) tradition.

This self-analysis is not an easy step to take, but a necessary one for recovering a broader sense of the church catholic. Avery Dulles has observed:

> Each participant in the [interdenominational] discussion must be seriously critical of its own traditions and genuinely anxious to receive enrichment from the heritage of other Churches. Through this process of mutual teaching and learning we can progressively rediscover one another—and deserve to be rediscovered by one another—in Christ. As we do so, we shall undoubtedly find Christ Himself in a new and richer way. For He wills to be found not simply as the head of various separate sects and denominations, but as the bond of mutual union among all who have life in His name.[5]

Gordon Fee echoes these same thoughts:

> The first and most difficult task is for any one of us to be able to discover our own traditions, and how in many different ways they affect our exegesis and hermeneutics. . . . [There is need for] a willingness on the part of all of us to be open to one another—to reexamine how we perceive our tradition as affecting us, especially in light of how others perceive it. This of course, can be terribly threatening, because most of us take considerable comfort—and rightly so—in the stability and security that tradition affords.[6]

This is so true. I gain nothing but respect for brothers and sisters of other traditions who face up squarely and honestly to the failures of their distinctives biblically. Their mistakes I can see all too easily; mine I miss as simply being the "only way" to read the text of Scripture. So, I must allow others to help me in my self-analysis of the distinctives to which Brethren lay claim. Again, this does not mean that any of the Brethren distinctives (if understood as tradition) are automatically wrong or fall under the condemnation of our Lord. It simply means they cannot be used as something to bludgeon the rest of the body of Christ with, as if others were seriously lacking the truth.

It also means we must go on to assess each particular distinctive further to see whether they are worth maintaining as traditions which *enhance* the Word of God, or whether they are traditions which *violate* it. This self-critical chapter will conclude with what I consider to be a way to *positively* state Brethren traditions (the reader may do a similar sort of thing with his or her own denominational traditions), without using them as tests of orthodoxy for other believers.

OVERVIEW OF BRETHREN DISTINCTIVES
The following are Brethren distinctives that are a part of their understanding of "New Testament church truth" which will be discussed in this chapter.[7]

Regarding the *worship* of the church:
(1) There is to be a weekly Breaking of Bread to remember the Lord.
(2) That weekly Breaking of Bread experience is to be a distinct meeting from the other meetings of the church.
(3) That weekly Breaking of Bread meeting is not to be planned, but is to be directed by the Spirit of God (as individual men sense His leading).
(4) (Many contexts). Singing during the Breaking of Bread is to be without instrumental accompaniment.
(5) The women are to remain silent during the Breaking of Bread meeting and are to keep their heads covered.
(6) The prayer for the elements, and their distribution, may be done by any man within the congregation.

Regarding the *leadership* of the church:
(1) There is to be a plurality of male elders leading the local congregation.

(2) The elders are to be selected from the congregation by existing leadership on the basis of spiritual maturity, rather than by popular vote.

(3) The elders are to serve as long as they are qualified and do not therefore have terms.

(4) The elders make their decisions on the basis of unanimity rather than by a vote.

Regarding the *mission* of the church:

(1) The local congregation is autonomous, and recognizes no ultimate authority but Christ operating in the midst of the congregation.

(2) The local congregation serves as the sending agency of the missionary.

(3) The local congregation is expected to stay at a relatively small size.

I think this would be a fair summation of Brethren distinctives as they pertain to the church. There are a number of other characteristics, but these should serve us in our investigation. But please bear in mind that the degree to which individual Brethren assemblies adhere to each of these distinctives varies greatly. As in any denomination, time, culture, and experience tend to alter practices within individual congregations. So, with this in mind join me as we address these general distinctives one by one in the pages that follow.

BRETHREN DISTINCTIVES REGARDING THE WORSHIP OF THE CHURCH

There is to be a weekly Breaking of Bread to remember the Lord. One of the most cherished Brethren "principles" is the weekly Breaking of Bread. The Brethren have emphasized the centrality of the Lord's Table as the visible symbol of the unity of all believers in Christ. It is a style that has been much appreciated by others outside the Brethren Movement who have visited their meetings and much misunderstood by those who have not. But the Brethren are not the only group that breaks bread weekly.[8] And many Christians who celebrate the Lord's Supper do not do so weekly, in some instances because they are afraid that too frequent practice will cause it to be mundane, losing its precious-ness, rather than from some deliberate disobedience of Scripture.

And that is what brings up the hermeneutical question. Is the *weekly* celebration of the Lord's Supper mandated by the New Testament? The appeal most often heard in Brethren circles is to two texts, Acts 20:7 and (as illustrated earlier) 1 Corinthians 11:26.[9] The first text, Acts 20:7 describes an event in which Paul and a contingent from a number of churches, along with Luke, were at Troas: "On the first day of the week we came together to break bread."

The hermeneutical factor to observe here is that this is a *de-scriptive* statement rather than a mandate. It is an "is" statement and not an "ought." We do not know if this was the norm for each week, nor whether (even if it was such a regular practice for them), it is to be the norm for us. We are mandated elsewhere to remember the Lord (e.g., Matt. 26:26-29), but here we are not given any kind of frequency mandate.

The 1 Corinthians passage states, "For as *often* as you eat this bread and drink the cup, you proclaim the Lord's death until He comes" (NRSV). As observed earlier, this does not teach a given frequency. It only communicates *what* goes on *when* the Lord is remembered (His death is proclaimed).[10] In view of these factors, it would appear that, as much as the Brethren enjoy a weekly Breaking of Bread, they cannot strictly claim that it has a biblical mandate attached to it. This distinctive therefore must be classed as a Brethren tradition.

The weekly Breaking of Bread experience is to be a distinct meeting from the other meetings of the church. I am completely unaware of any biblical basis appealed to for this practice among the Brethren. It is, however, a very important factor for Brethren in view of the need to maintain several other worship distinctives, listed below. But, strictly speaking, this idea of a distinct meeting (apart from the preaching/teaching meeting) is clearly a Brethren tradition, since it derives directly from no specific Scripture.

The weekly Breaking of Bread meeting is not to be planned, but is to be directed by the Spirit of God. It is primarily the central, distinct Breaking of Bread meeting that is opened up to the spontaneous leading (within parameters) of the Spirit of God. The Brethren have a somewhat deep-seated belief that the use of planning, structure, or format in the remembrance meeting is not found in the New Testament.[11] It is assumed that such things are prohibited by the New Testament and contrary to the Holy Spirit's direction in the meeting.[12] At other times, 1 Corinthians 14:26 is appealed to: "What then shall we say, brothers? When you come together, everyone has a hymn, or a word of instruction, a revelation, a tongue or an interpretation. All of these must be done for the strengthening of the church."

Brethren often argue that this meeting, if no other, is a meeting where there is no human leadership—where Christ can exercise His lordship directly over the assembly in worship, since "where two or three come together in my name, there am I with them" (Matt. 18:20).[13] Exclusive writer C.H. Mackintosh describes this kind of spontaneous worship meeting and its value to Brethren, despite its tendency at times toward "dryness."

> We have but little conception of what an assembly would be were each one distinctly led by the Holy Ghost, and gathered only to Jesus. We should not then have to complain of dull, heavy, unprofitable, trying meetings. We should have no fear of unhallowed intrusion of mere nature and its restless doings—no making of prayer—no talking for talking's sake—no hymnbook seized to fill a gap. Each one would know his place in the Lord's immediate presence—each gifted vessel would be filled, fitted, and used by the Master's hand—each eye would be directed to Jesus—each heart occupied with Him. If a chapter were read, it would be the very voice of God. If a word were spoken, it would tell with power upon the heart. If prayer were offered, it would lead the soul into the very presence of God. If a hymn were sung, it would lift the spirit up to God, and be like sweeping the strings of the heavenly harp. We should feel ourselves in the very sanctuary of God, and enjoy a foretaste of that time when we shall worship in the courts above and go no more out.[14]

First off, although this idyllic presentation of the Brethren worship meeting may sound magnificent, we should resist assuming it is biblically taught. We do not even possess a clear description of an early Christian worship format in the New Testament—much less a mandated form.[15] What we glean from 1 Corinthians 14 is simply a description of what went on at Corinth, a rather wild and notorious church in which Paul was attempting to bring some order.[16] In view of that, we should be extremely reticent to normalize or standardize his attempt to bring order to Corinthian excess into a precedent for worshiping the Lord as if it were a "New Testament pattern." And the appeal to the Lord's special presence when two or three are together in His Name, coming as it does in the context of church discipline (Matt. 18:15-20), cannot serve as a mandate in terms of a worship style or pattern.[17]

Secondly, there is an underlying assumption that whatever is planned and organized is not of the Spirit of God, while whatever is spontaneous and unplanned is of the Spirit of God. The implications of that idea in relation to the eternal plan and counsel of God, who determined the intricate details of creation and redemption before the foundation of the world, are mind boggling! Furthermore, it is rather odd that many Brethren who have come to appreciate the unplanned creativity that is possible in such a service are unaware of the fact that a refusal to plan *is, in fact, a formal plan*—one that does not allow for creative alternatives![18]

In addition, it is interesting to note that, traditionally, many Brethren assemblies followed this principle to a rather odd conclusion: the Spirit of God must not only lead the worship experience without prior planning, but He must by direct, unplanned impulse lead those who would minister in their midst.[19] That has led to the practice in some segments of the movement that it is contrary to the work of the Spirit of God for an assembly to designate ahead of time who is to speak to the assembly. As noble a philosophy as that may be, it has left too many Brethren starving for a careful, studied exposition of God's Word.

Many Brethren elders have come to realize that the presence of the Spirit of God does not necessarily override the presence of the human flesh with all its failings, nor does careful planning preclude (but in fact often enhances) the Spirit's ministry. If this is so in the pulpit ministry, then why are the Brethren so slow to see that the same thing may apply in terms of the form of the Breaking of Bread? The New Testament has simply not given direct mandates on this matter. Hence, the Brethren may *prefer* their way of doing worship, but to call this the only biblical way falls wide of the mark.[20] This would therefore also need to be classed as a Brethren tradition, and not as a New Testament mandate.

Singing during the Breaking of Bread is to be without instrumental accompaniment. The Brethren often restrict the Breaking of Bread meeting—but not their other meetings—against the use of musical instruments.[21] I learned more about the biblical warrant for this from a brother within the movement who commented that this Brethren practice was based on Israel's having no musical instruments during their forty years wandering in the desert awaiting the Promised Land. I might have asked how we knew that was true for one, and what that had to do with the New Testament church for another, but I was given an answer: we are pilgrims and wanderers just as they were, in this world of sin.

Granted, the above example is an extreme use of typology. However, it is not the most common reason given for the lack of instruments in the Breaking of Bread service. The most common reason I've heard is simply this: "You don't find musical instruments mentioned in New Testament worship. The only mention of instruments is under the Old Testament—a bygone dispensation."[22]

But here we have come up against an application of the "negative hermeneutic." Simply because instruments are not mentioned does not mean that they were not used. It may simply not have been in the mind of a New Testament writer to mention any during his discussion of related topics. And, further, even if we could prove that they did not use musical instruments in the New Testament, what would that demonstrate since they are not in fact prohibited? All it would prove is that they *did* not use them, not that they *should* not have used them. If they did not use them, there may have been any number of reasons for such: lack of availability, lack of time for musical creativity due to persecution, or lack of permanent meeting locations. We simply do not know.

But the bottom line is this, the Brethren, or any other groups for that matter, are simply wrong to prohibit (if you are a leader responsible for such things) or decry (if you are not) the use of instruments in worship if the reason is "I don't find them being used in the New Testament." Once again, the "negative hermeneutic" leads to a gross interpretive error. This, then, is simply another aspect of the Brethren tradition and not a biblical mandate.

The women are to remain silent during the Breaking of Bread meeting and are to keep their heads covered. As a seminary student, I brought my Baptist roommate to church with me one Sunday. I forgot to forewarn him about the head attire of the women; I had grown so accustomed to it. But he was flabbergasted at what he saw—he could not at all understand its value in our culture. If you were to visit a Brethren Breaking of Bread, you too might find the fact that women are veiled to be a rather odd, countercultural custom. However, the Brethren are sincere in putting into practice what they believe to be the teaching of the New Testament. But what does the New Testament teach on these matters?

Few Brethren realize that in 1 Corinthians 11 and 14, we are in fact dealing with a serious *crux interpretum* (a notoriously difficult passage to interpret).[23] If we superficially gloss over the issue, or blithely assume that we are the only Christians who read these texts properly, we are not exerting interpretive care over a passage that many in the church have struggled with for centuries.[24]

I do not bring this up with a view to solving the intricacies of Paul's thought. I mention it to point out a bit of interpretive inconsistency which the Brethren have inherited in their accepted handling of these passages. The Brethren interpretive approach argues that we are to take 1 Corinthians 11 literally and expect some sort of veil (or head covering) on the heads of the women. And so the Brethren do in their assemblies, for the most part. In the previous generation they insisted on the women wearing hats; in the current it is often some kind of lace mantilla.

But that is not all, Brethren also argue that 1 Corinthians 14 is to be taken literally when it says that women are "to keep silent in the churches." And so, when open participation is offered during the Breaking of Bread meeting, women are expected to remain silent. This is where the Brethren have developed their inconsistency. In chapter 11, Paul says that women are to have their head covered "when they pray or prophesy." These are, in the context of the New Testament, two forms of oral, public communication within the community of believers.[25] We can have it no other way. But, based on the inherited Brethren interpretation of chapter 14, they do not allow the women to even "pray or prophesy"—since that would be a forbidden form of speaking.

That is where the inconsistency comes up. Either the Brethren must allow women to pray and prophesy publicly and maintain the expectation of a head covering and therefore assume that Paul's restriction of chapter 14 is not a universal prohibition of all *forms* of feminine speech in the congregation,[26] or they must maintain that it is a universal prohibition and enforce it and thus forget about requiring a head covering, since Paul only requires that when women "pray or prophesy" in public. The Brethren cannot have it both ways.[27]

This interpretive selectivity again indicates a distinctive among the Brethren that must be treated as an interpretive tradition. Therefore, it cannot be treated as a biblical mandate. The very difficulty of interpreting the issue can only mean that we cannot detect here any genuine biblical mandates to be universally practiced by Christians.

The prayer for the elements, and their distribution, may be done by any man within the congregation. This practice is based on the Brethren extension of the priesthood of all believers, as expressed in a non-clerical system.[28] Even if there is a full-time pastoral worker in a given assembly, "he will not be identified as clergy or given control over the Communion services."[29] The Brethren understand *clericalism* as the development of a clergy-laity distinction in which there are special functions and ministries of the church that are restricted to one who has special training and ordination. This is often popularly referred to as "one-man ministry." Anglican clergyman John Stott himself identifies the problems with clericalism and its impact on the self-perception of the church:

> What clericalism always does, by concentrating power and privilege in the hands of the clergy, is at least to obscure and at worst to annul the essential oneness of the people of God. Extreme forms of clericalism dare to reintroduce the notion of privilege into the only human community in which it has been abolished. Where Christ has made out of the two one, the clerical mind makes two again, the one higher and the other lower, the one active and the other passive, the one really important because it is vital to the life of the Church, the other not vital and therefore less important.[30]

There are dangers in such a system, no doubt, as Stott wisely points out. But the basic issue here is the degree to which clericalism is commended, condemned, or even identified in the New Testament. One reason often used by Brethren in support of the non-clerical system is simply, "you don't find clergy in the New Testament."[31] Beyond that, the clerical system is said to: (1) violate the principle of the priesthood of all believers; (2) prohibit the free exercise of gifts in the church; (3) confine the administration of the ordinances to a priestly class; (4) promote a salaried ministry, which implies control of one's ministry; (5) cater to the potential of gathering to a man instead of the Lord; (6) obscure in practice or theory the headship of Christ; and (7) miss the importance of checks and balances on ministry.[32]

But Stott is also aware of something the Brethren are not, that is the danger of anti-clericalism, the extreme toward which the Brethren tend:

> The spirit of clericalism is to despise the laity, and behave as if they did not exist. The spirit of *anticlericalism is to despise the clergy and to behave as if they did not exist, or rather, since they do exist, to wish they didn't.* Anticlericalism is a natural and understandably vigorous reaction to clericalism. Historically, it was current clerical abuses which led both Quakers and Christian Brethren to dispense with an ordained ministry altogether. . . .[33]

Stott hits the nail on the head. The danger among the Brethren is one of reactionism on this issue, which causes them to overlook other important dimensions of ministry in the church community. For example, there is a tendency to downplay or squelch certain spiritual gifts in the assembly, particularly leadership type gifts, since overt leadership expressed by any specific individual is suspiciously eyed as the rise of clericalism, a one-man ministry.[34]

But Stott's description of anticlericalism as "behave as if clergy did not exist" is a rather unhelpful phrase for Brethren. For "clergy" is a negative term for the Brethren, with a parallel in one-man ministry. I would prefer the Brethren (and Stott) substituted instead the phrase "gifted" ministry, since spiritual gifting is a clear biblical concept (e.g., Rom. 12; 1 Cor. 12–14; Eph. 4). I argue that Brethren tend to behave as if "gifted" ministry did not exist in their fear of clericalism.

And the issue of "gifted ministry" would better describe the concerns I have with this issue. Since spiritual gifts should be

allowed to function in the church as they are sovereignly be-
stowed by the Spirit (1 Cor. 12:4-11), the *leadership* gift must be
given its rightful place in a Brethren assembly.[35] This is not violat-
ing the priesthood of all believers, since not all believers are
gifted at teaching, or leading, and should learn to defer to those
who are so gifted. We do the same thing when we send a pasto-
rally gifted person to help a strained relationship. And one man
who is gifted does not necessarily stand between the congregation and God so as to mediate in some way.[36]

The real problem is not simply that one man provides (gifted)
leadership to the congregation, but rather "that one man in the
holy brotherhood has been elevated to a sacred, unscriptural
status."[37] But, as Strauch points out in his more balanced
approach:

> Most people don't realize that biblical eldership actually combines
> the best of both leadership structures; an exceptionally gifted
> leader can lead and teach with all his zeal and might, yet he is
> subject to his fellow leaders and brothers who jointly lead and
> guide the congregation. . . . So the gifted leader or teacher is the
> person who can greatly profit from the checks and balances bibli-
> cal eldership provides.[38]

Further, the Brethren denial of the leadership gift is in fact a
prohibition of the free exercise of gifts that they so earnestly
defend by resisting one-man ministry as clericalism. In this context the leadership gift is restricted from fully functioning.

The confining of the administration of the ordinances to a
priestly class is not *necessarily* connected with one-man ministry,
that is, gifted ministry. But we must acknowledge that precisely
who distributes the elements in the New Testament is not mentioned. Restricting it *to* a gifted person, or keeping it *from* a
gifted person has no direct biblical basis at all either way. Either
practice must be supported elsewhere, namely, by external
tradition.

And what of the concern over the control implied by a salaried
ministry? Is this an evil of control over a pastoral worker?[39]

I received a recent edition of *A.D. 40,* a flier in the "Bible
Believer's Lessons" series, produced by a Brethren publisher.[40]
Entitled "Who Paid the New Testament Preacher?" it argues
precisely that New Testament Christianity does not set salaries

for its teachers. The author articulates the traditional Brethren argument well, but there are several problems with his arguments. From a hermeneutical standpoint they cause me to be a bit more cautious in defining this position as solely characteristic of "New Testament Christianity"—which means, of course, that it is God's mandate for us all.

First of all, the author never defines his terms. His discussion is on the New Testament "Preacher," but one is never entirely sure as to what he means by that (Is that the equivalent of a missionary, or an evangelist, or an elder?). Nevertheless, he goes on to use our Lord and several of the apostles as examples of those who did not receive salaries, arguing that we are to imitate both our Lord and the apostles (especially Paul, based on his comment in 1 Cor. 11:1).

I do not dispute greatly the practical advantages of such a system, apart from the fact that it tends on occasion to substitute *form* for *spirit*. I have known some "full-time workers" among the Brethren as well, who too easily tailor their message to what their audience wants to hear because they know that to teach otherwise would spell doom for their acceptance (and financial "fellowship").[41]

Also, I am acquainted with many salaried denominational Christians who are not in any sense of the term "hirelings,"[42] but come closer to "living by faith" than some Brethren I have known—even to the point of leaving one ministry for another at half the salary because they were convinced God wanted them to do so. Such people are sent from God every bit as much as some of the Brethren workers. God, in my opinion, looks at the heart, not the form, for New Testament Christianity on these issues.[43]

These matters aside, the basic question is the flier author's hermeneutics in using Scripture to support his case. He believes Paul to be the pattern for biblical support, for example, because he calls on the believers to imitate him not just in matters of salvation, but in his service for God.

But what did Paul mean when he wrote, "Be imitators of me, as I am of Christ" (1 Cor. 11:1, NRSV). If we are to follow through on the writer's opinion, then Paul is requiring *all* of the Corinthians to imitate him in "going out on faith" (since that is to whom he wrote it!).[44] Of course that is preposterous. Paul did not mean that all the Corinthians were to follow him in all that he did.

But then *which* of Paul's many actions were to be imitated by the Corinthians? The absolute *most* that can be said is that Paul's practice may be a precedent for potential evangelists or any modern church planter parallels. But even then we must ask how Paul could be understood as implying two separate patterns in such a statement. Were all the Corinthians to follow Paul as he followed Christ, and were some—the evangelistically gifted—to follow Paul in specific ways he followed Christ? As for resident pastoral workers ("preachers"), we have no example, apart from the fact that New Testament elders were paid for their ministry, contrary to accepted Brethren practice.[45]

Does one-man ministry (meaning gifted ministry) cater to the idea of gathering to a *man* instead of to *Christ,* or does it obscure the headship of Christ in the congregation? It certainly *could,* since high-profile communicators produce an exodus of some of their devoted followers when they leave a given congregation. But that is not always the fault of the leader. I know of Brethren assemblies that went into decline and lost people after the death of a beloved elder. People simply have to be taught that their loyalty is not to a *person,* but to *Christ.* The profile of a person is not entirely to blame for this. And people with leadership gifts will inevitably have a higher profile than others, although that does not at all mean they are intrinsically more spiritual or important.

And, finally, it was objected that this approach leads to a lack of accountability. Again, it can, but not necessarily. There are high-profile, gifted persons in the church who are aware of the danger of nonaccountability, and develop accountability mechanisms to protect themselves from this danger. And gifted leaders in Brethren assemblies *by definition* do not have any functionality above that of an elder (since elder is the highest office in the congregation).[46] By definition, the most a gifted leader could be is a co-elder, who is allowed to function and set the leadership tenor of the rest of the eldership. After all, that is what his gift is.

So, when it comes down to it, the issue of non-clericalism among the Christian Brethren is really a shibboleth that often prevents them from heeding a balanced view of leadership gifting within the church. It must be used carefully and in a well-balanced way or it will lead the Brethren into error in practice. As long as clericalism is rightly understood as an *attitude* rather than a *system*, it can be successfully combated. That is why I would define clericalism as *the attitude of superiority or special privilege conveyed by formal or gifted leadership to those within the greater Christian community.* This attitude is sometimes also found in other groups which have a recognized and functioning "gift ministry."

Is the Brethren *worship* tradition a good or bad one? I have concluded that the distinctives surrounding Brethren worship: the weekly Breaking of Bread, in a distinct meeting, which is unplanned, without instrumental accompaniment, where women are to remain silent and keep their heads covered, and where any man may pray for or be appointed to distribute the elements, are all a part of the Brethren interpretive tradition and are therefore not legitimately biblical mandates, or New Testament principles.

The next step is to assess whether these traditions, like the synagogue, actually enhance a biblical teaching, or whether they detract from one. If the former, they are *good* traditions, if the latter, they are *bad* ones.

Quite frankly, weekly celebration of the Lord's Supper tremendously enhances my understanding of the signficance of the atoning work of Christ. Further, the fact that worship is unguided and therefore much more *reflective* and *participatory* provides the context in which it can easily become owned and practiced by more within the Brethren community. The non-clerical emphasis has a further value in prompting all the believers in a given assembly to take ownership of their responsibility to do the ministry, and "every-member involvement" becomes an ideal among the Brethren that is often near to fulfillment. This non-clerical approach to ministry also provokes a more general desire to study out the Scriptures for oneself, since the congregation does not expect another to feed them.

However, I must demur on several items within the Brethren tradition that have questionable value, and in fact must be faced as potentially damaging. First is the avoidance of musical instrumentation. I have no great quarrel here, apart from the fact that worship, in my experience, has been enhanced by a sensitive use of instrumentation.

Of greater concern in terms of traditions which may conflict with the Word of God is the role of women (which among the Brethren often becomes, contrary to their claims, a priesthood of all male believers). More study must be done on the areas of the distinction between *gift* (given without gender restrictions) and *office* (given with gender restrictions) for the Brethren to find a more satisfying, and biblical approach to the place of women in worship.

Other concerns in the tradition are the dangerous tendency toward an anti-clericalism in the form of opposition to "gifted" (read one-man) ministry. Although no one man can be allowed to assume that he has all the spiritual gifts, those with leadership and teaching gifts must be set free to function according to their gift in the local church. And those who would restrict it must be careful not to "quench the Spirit" in the life of the community.[47]

BRETHREN DISTINCTIVES REGARDING THE LEADERSHIP OF THE CHURCH

There is to be a plurality of elders leading the local congregation. Were the congregations of the New Testament plural in their eldership? Of course. There is abundant evidence for that.[48] But the question is whether this *pattern* is to be a *precept* for all congregations at all times in the church of Christ.[49] Quite simply, although there is abundant evidence for a plural pattern, there is no evidence that this is a divine precept.[50]

Furthermore, we must bear in mind the New Testament sociology of the church, mentioned in the first chapter. The house churches made up the local (city) church, and, based on sociological and archaeological research into ancient house size, it does not appear likely that each house church would have a plurality of elders so much as the city-church did. The local (city) church was likely made up of all the elders of the house churches of an area. And, as has been noted, the local church of today is not the equivalent of the local (city) church, but rather the house church.

With these factors in mind, the descriptive nature of the plural eldership model, and the house/city church functionality behind it, we must conclude that the Brethren are wrong if they set forth this model as a normative pattern or mandate for the church. These are simply part of the Brethren interpretive tradition.

And there is danger in encouraging that tradition for others as if it were a mandate. In the last ten to fifteen years I have been observing the phenomenon of churches and movements outside

Brethren circles developing a similar form of church government, but separate from direct Brethren influence. One such movement is the *Bible Fellowship Church* which began in Dallas, Texas under the guidance of Gene Getz and others.[51] These groups select elders from within the congregations based on character rather than strictly on theological training, and insist on the biblical expression of a multiple number (as do the Brethren). And this model is beginning to look appealing to groups that traditionally operate under a single pastor model, sometimes with devastating results.

Recently, within at least one denominational fellowship of Baptist churches, the same phenomenon has been occurring. Due at times to the influence of zealous young seminarians with a Brethren ecclesiology, future pastors who were their classmates became convinced about the actual data of the New Testament on plural eldership. I have talked to individual leaders within these groups and with those who are thinking of transitioning toward a plural, elder-rule system. Their zeal for and delight in this "new" system is astonishing.

As much as I value the plural eldership model, I must grieve over what is happening in certain places outside the Brethren tradition. Here's why. I am aware of a large, traditional Baptist church in a well-known community in Oregon that took on a new pastor who was enthusiastic over elder rule. That church is now a large, elder-ruled congregation. It is, in fact, flourishing. But not without casualties to the work of God and the fellowship of the saints.

That church was in the process of planting a daughter church across town when they took on the new young pastor. When the pastor was successful in establishing his new leadership agenda, a large section of the older people in the congregation left for the daughter church. The daughter church had become perhaps the most traditional of Baptistic churches I had seen. They wanted nothing to do with elder rule. The congregation had by choice made itself staunchly Baptistic with solid congregational vote and order of service. Great bitterness toward the mother congregation resulted.

Besides the hermeneutical issues involved, the above incident is one of the reasons I am reluctant to suggest the Brethren model as a biblical norm for all churches to follow. It seems that there are more fundamental issues at stake. And that is why I do not wholeheartedly encourage all churches to shift to this system. The work of God can well go on—perhaps even better—without such a transition in their own traditions.

Why do I say this? Because I do not think that plurality of leadership is important? No, I think it is very important and very wise. But I do not believe that it is *absolutely necessary* before a congregation can receive God's blessing.

That being said, I must still ask if this is a *good* or *bad* tradition among the Brethren. I firmly believe that it is a good one, and it is proper for the Brethren to continue in their plurality of eldership mode. It is no worse, nor necessarily any better, than any other form of polity. And it does have its advantages.

It offers a good check and balance on decision-making. It allows for a healthy diversity of spiritual gifts within the leadership structure. It easily develops a sense of divine wisdom in the council of the many. A context is offered for a shared leadership load. It provides for healthy mutual accountability. And it allows for any mature man to develop into leadership within the congregation.[52]

But the plurality mode is not God's only way of working. The Brethren can have this form and be devoid of the heart of God on many other important matters. Others may not have this form and be far closer to the Lord. So the Brethren need to learn to be flexible and tolerant in spite of their own preferences. They have no biblical mandate, only a biblical interpretive tradition, to fall back on.

The elders are to be selected from the congregation by existing leadership on the basis of spiritual maturity (rather than by popular vote). For years among the more traditional denominational churches, the primary qualifications for calling a pastor included a strong emphasis on theological training. More recently, especially since the late sixties and early seventies, and the publication of Ray Stedman's influential *Body Life*,[53] the pastor's spiritual giftedness became an important issue. The Brethren tend to look at this approach as verging on the theologically naive. A careful reading of those passages which describe the qualifications of an elder show that the focus of the New Testament period was in fact on spiritual *character*—not on the theological training of the elder nor even the spiritual gift.[54]

The Brethren expect elders to perpetuate themselves as mature men, and do not expect the congregation to vote them in and out, even though a wise eldership must take into account significant input from the congregation in the process.[55] But the important factor here is the basis for their selection.

It is not my purpose here to go through the list of character qualities in detail.[56] And I do not question that these qualifications serve as clearly mandated guidelines for spiritual leadership in the church.[57] That, after all, was Paul's intent. But there are some implications drawn from these spiritual qualifications which the Brethren develop without adequate biblical justification.

The first is the observation that there is no theological-educational requirement in any of the listings. To some, since formal theological training is not stated, it is therefore a sort of "disqualification" to have had some.[58] The "self taught" man (better, "Spirit taught") is idealized instead. But all that has led to in too many Brethren assemblies is a shallow passing on of unreflected tradition which cannot sustain itself in the face of a more and more educated populace.[59]

Perhaps a better attitude is to remember that sound theological training does not automatically *qualify*, nor does it automatically *disqualify* a young man for eldership or other leadership in the assembly.[60] He must prove himself based on *character* just like anyone else who has not had the privilege of such training, but his training must not be perceived as any sort of disqualification.

Another unwritten qualification for elders not found on the list is that of *age*. I recently heard a young faculty colleague try to explain the age of elders in the New Testament. His reasoning was simple: elder means simply "older one"; hence, those who are the elders in the congregation must fit the definition of "older one" as it was understood in New Testament times. He proceeded to explain the historical background for the term, and concluded that it implied an age of about forty to fifty. That, then, is the minimum age for an elder.

Knowing that this young man had spent time in parish ministry prior to joining our faculty, I asked how he justified taking a pastorate while at a significantly lower age than he had given as the minimum. Straight-faced, he replied that he was a "pastor" not an "elder." My fellow colleagues grinned along with me at such naïveté, for they knew that such a distinction does not fit the New Testament data from a historical standpoint. What they called "elders" are those who did the "pastoring" of the local churches. The qualifications of a "pastor" are therefore those of an elder: a pastor is an elder.[61]

But his other conclusion should also undergo a bit of scrutiny, for the Brethren have a similar unwritten principle as well. The tendency among existing Brethren elders in searching for others to share the eldership is to look for middle-aged (or older) men rather than younger men. And especially to avoid those younger men who may "desire" the work of an elder.[62] No matter how qualified or mature they may otherwise be, these younger men are often quickly bypassed in discussions of leadership due to an unwritten age requirement.

But does the New Testament have an age requirement? The requirements of 1 Timothy 3 and Titus 1 offer the important warning not to lay hands too suddenly on a recent believer, but no *age* qualification is listed.[63] If one appeals to the term *elder* or attempts to draw implications from it as my colleague did, then he or she is guilty of an etymological error, since the term is used in two senses: the first in context of a person's age and the second in reference to an office in the church.[64] Elder requirement lists point to the latter.

The Brethren Movement's early history even runs counter to its current extension of elder qualification to include age. When the movement began about 1827 in Dublin, the earliest elders and leaders were quite young. In fact, the movement was a movement of young radicals. In that year George Müller and Henry Craik, who would develop the work at Bethesda and later become the object of Darby's judgment, were both twenty-two years old. Benjamin Wills Newton, who would serve alongside Darby and others at Plymouth until he and Darby went at odds with each other, was a mere twenty years old that year. John Nelson Darby himself was one of the older ones at age twenty-seven. The real old men that year would have been J.G. Bellett and Anthony Norris Groves, who were each the ripe old age of thirty-two years!

No wonder there was such energy, vibrancy, and high commitment in those early years. The energy of the movement was carried by young men. Yet Brethren today are fearful of their own younger generation. By insular practices, sectarian attitudes, and pietistic aversion to biblical scholarship, they sometimes drive away the younger, educated generation. How ironic to think that the very group which harbors these attitudes was itself begun as a movement of "young" elders, hungry for genuine biblical scholarship and spirituality.

Leadership qualifications are explicit in the New Testament: they are demonstrable character qualities. These cannot be changed. They are a biblical mandate that can be expected of all spiritual leaders everywhere. But the Brethren variations on that theme, downplaying of theological education and implying an age requirement, are going beyond the biblical mandate. That is a part of the Brethren tradition and an unhealthy one at that. Brethren *must* rethink those dimensions of their tradition.

The other dimension is the avoidance of a congregational vote on these matters. Voting on congregational matters (especially on leaders) is something the Brethren simply do not do. This rather horrifies my Baptistic friends, for whom every member has a vote at many levels on how the church goes, since Baptists view voting as an expression of the priesthood of all believers.[65] What reason do the Brethren give for not voting in the congregation on such matters as choosing their leadership? Again, a paltry "you don't find voting in the New Testament" is too often the response.[66] This is, therefore, another example of the negative hermeneutic and cannot be sustained as a biblical mandate.

In fact, if we are to be honest with the text, there is some evidence that congregational involvement was apparent in at least some instances of church decision-making. One example we find pertains particularly to the selection of some of its leaders.[67] So the bottom line is this: Brethren cannot expect congregational involvement in the selection of their leaders to be considered a wrong procedure.[68] Their preference against it is simply without biblical warrant.

Again, this is part of the Brethren tradition. Is it a bad tradition? I would argue not. There are good reasons why, in a healthy assembly, existing leaders should (with sensitivity to the congregation) select more leaders. First, shepherds certainly would be expected to know the sheep better than the sheep know each other. They should be able to assess the spiritual maturity of people over the long haul better than peers, who often do not know much about names set before them on a ballot. Secondly, a *team* of mature leaders can easily assess given individuals in a congregation and therefore make selections more wisely. In view of these factors, I would argue that the eldership selection process among the Brethren, although not a biblical mandate, is a tradition well worth maintaining.

The elders are to serve as long as they are qualified and do not therefore have terms of service. In the United States we are used to terms of service for our leaders. A president can serve for four years, and then might be reelected for another four. But even if that is the case, our national leader cannot serve over two terms. As Americans, most of us find this a useful system. We know that a poor president will be out in less than four years. And, we can reelect a good one for an extra four. Most of us have lived through the tenures of numerous presidents in our lifetimes. We much prefer this to a monarchical or dictatorial system in which a leader, good or bad, rules as long as he or she lives or until deposed.

But there is something we miss out on with such a system. Continuity and consistency. The ebb and flow of the economy and taxes depends in many ways on the policies of a given president and, of course, the Congress. It is this continuity and consistency which Brethren appreciate about their elders. Perhaps that is why it is rare for the issue of the terms of service for an elder to come up. Brethren enjoy the stability; the continuity reminds them of the continuity and stability of God Himself.

We are constrained to ask the basis for such a practice among the Brethren. Biblically, the only stated grounds for exclusion from the office of elder are that one no longer is qualified, since terms are not at all mentioned in the New Testament.[69] This, by itself, would be an argument from silence, and therefore unsustainable as but another instance of the negative hermeneutic. It is a Brethren tradition, plain and simple.

Although this Brethren tradition may have sustaining value of continuity attached to it, I am concerned there are some side effects that are the downside of this issue. Brethren elders who take their pastoral responsibility seriously, and who are employed full-time in some other work (as most are), are candidates for spiritual burnout. And there is an unwritten sort of self-perpetuating guilt among elders that they cannot step down or step aside for rest and or recuperation. The idea of not having terms—since it does not have clear biblical warrant—should be either reconsidered or modified. An elder group with whom I served, for example, concluded that a rotating, required three-month sabbatical would do them all good—and it has. But some assemblies would resist this based on the Brethren tradition of not having terms for elders since they must serve until they die or are disqualified. This is an unhelpful tradition. Regardless of one's tradition, we must beware of burned-out elders. Simply put, arguing for no terms or breaks is not arguing from Scripture.

The elders make their decisions on the basis of unanimity rather than by a vote. The concept of elder unanimity in decision-making is founded on a basic principle: spiritual men should be expected to come to a meeting of the mind when the lordship of Christ is sought, without resorting to majority votes.[70] Fine and good, but is this a complete theological picture of the nature of people, even redeemed people?[71] Even godly leaders carry with them a sinful nature which can show itself at the worst of times. Witness the split of Paul and Barnabas in Acts 15. Or recall, as described in the last chapter, the terrible showdown between John Nelson Darby and Benjamin Wills Newton—and later with George Müller—which led to the severing of the Brethren Movement in 1848.

In fact, more than one assembly has been led to decline and death because one elder has refused to agree to a positive action. That one man, by withholding his consent, has hindered the assembly from going forward for the Lord—all in the name of "biblical" unanimity. But where do we find a clear teaching of absolute unanimity in the New Testament, for that matter? Nowhere. The *manner* in which elders make decisions is simply not addressed in the New Testament at all.[72] The Brethren style is, simply put, a Brethren tradition. And, though it may have a good side, there is a downside that must carefully be guarded against.

BRETHREN DISTINCTIVES REGARDING THE MISSION OF THE CHURCH

The local congregation is autonomous, and recognizes no ultimate authority but Christ operating in the midst of the congregation. This, as noted, is a distinctive that is followed by the Open Brethren only. Autonomy refers to the belief that a local assembly is accountable only to the Lord Himself for its own life and ministry—not to any denominational center or even to any collective authority among the Brethren. This element of church polity is not unique to the Brethren, but is shared with Baptist and other congregations of the free church movement.

But there is quite a bit of confusion and abuse on this matter. Autonomy has been used as an excuse to not seek advice outside the assembly when such counsel may be sorely needed. It has even been used as an excuse to avoid any form of inter-assembly cooperative work, or to avoid a needed merger.[73] But autonomy actually backfires on the Brethren from a New Testament perspective. For, although this has been held as a cardinal doctrine and, I believe, a critically important one in our day and age,[74] it unfortunately is undemonstrable even as a *practice* of the New Testament churches.

Looking carefully at the Book of Acts, we find a critical juncture in the life of the church reached in the fifteenth chapter. Teachers from Judea had gone to the Gentile center of Christian life in Antioch of Syria and had attempted to require circumcision as a condition for eternal salvation (15:1). The interesting thing at this point is what the local leadership at Antioch did *not* do.

The church at Antioch did not expel these teachers as heterodox and go about its own autonomous way. It appointed Paul, Barnabas, and some other believers to go to the church at Jerusalem to investigate this question (15:2). The dispute prompted a meeting of the apostles and elders at Jerusalem to consider the question. Acts 15:6-29 shows the process of their deliberation, and the victory won for justification by faith as a result.

But notice very carefully, the council issued a letter from the apostles and elders in Jerusalem containing certain requirements that the Gentile churches *were to obey* (see 15:23b-29). This is made clear by Luke's statement in 16:4-5, as Paul took along Timothy with him and traveled from town to town, where "they delivered the decisions reached by the apostles and elders in Jerusalem *for the people to obey.* So the churches were strengthened in the faith and grew daily in numbers."

Note well, what was decided *at Jerusalem* was enforced in the churches elsewhere.[75] This is not supportive of the notion of autonomy at all.

Now I am not advocating a return to some sort of centralized authority structure over all of the local churches or assemblies. I am simply saying that if the Brethren (or any one else for that matter) are to claim to follow a New Testament pattern, then they must be consistent. The practice in the Book of Acts was a hierarchy of authority over the churches. True, one may say, but they also had apostles then. We have no apostles now. Hence, we either substitute some other form of intermediate authority over the churches, or we have autonomy. But that's my point, the situation has changed so that the New Testament pattern does not fit the nature of the non-apostolic church, and hence we cannot follow it here. So let's be careful about being too strong on our claim to following the "New Testament pattern!" We are admitting that it does not apply, at least in some instances, today. Autonomy for the Brethren is a tradition, as well as for those other groups who practice it.

But is it a good tradition? In the absence of live apostles, I would argue that it is. It protects the pastoral care and instruction of God's people from outside manipulation, by entrusting it to the elders of each congregation. And it helps keep the danger of state interference at arm's length. Thus, I'm in favor of practicing and insisting on autonomy, but for practical reasons and not clear biblical ones. It is a good tradition in many ways, as long as it is not forced to an extreme of independence that hinders catholicity.

The local congregation serves as the sending agency of the missionary. When I first aligned myself with the Brethren, I was delighted to learn that their missionary endeavors were more in line with the "New Testament pattern" as it was called. Missionaries were sent out by the local church rather than through some sending agency; there was no formal "deputation" on the part of the missionary to gain funds; missionaries were not ordained, but were "commended" (Acts 13:1-3; 14:26). It all sounded so downright biblical to me.

But as the years went on I became aware of what denominations were really doing in terms of sending missionaries, and I began to see some of the personal strengths of some of their missionaries who had gone through that "unbiblical" process of ordination and deputation. I began to wonder just how important or proper our Brethren emphases had been. And then it struck me again, we have another example of both the negative hermeneutic and patternism.

Of course it is right to say that there are no examples of missionary organizations in the New Testament. And, in this case it is likely that there *were* none in existence at that stage of the church's history. But are they *prohibited?* Hardly. Can they be a hindrance to the mission of the church? Of course, if they usurp prerogatives that rightfully belong to the local congregation. Are they always a hindrance to the mission of the church? Of course not; often they can do a great service in terms of testing and training that cannot always be done satisfactorily by the local congregation.

And despite what many Brethren like to think, their own *Christian Missions in Many Lands*[76] (CMML) organization does some of the kinds of things (certainly not all) that a missionary society or organization does anyway. Some Brethren assembly elders recognize that they are often simply not qualified enough to handle the international complexities associated with today's missionary endeavor. The Brethren therefore often depend on what they call a "service group," like CMML, to help with such things as handling of funds, representations and guarantees to various governments, and advice and counsel as necessary. If they are strictly "autonomous," the Brethren should not need even this. But Brethren must acknowledge this is a useful service to busy elders and minimally informed assemblies. Further, where is the Brethren tolerance of other missionary agencies, some of which add several other services as well?

There are weaknesses in the Brethren system too. It is hard for busy elders of a local assembly to understand international monetary exchange and some international political matters (hence the place for an organization like CMML). Admittedly, it is also difficult for elders to give advice on sensitive cultural, linguistic, and social issues from a biblical perspective when they have no personal experience with such concerns. In that sense, veteran missionaries—such as those found in missionary sending agencies—are many times a great help for field missionaries.

The strengths and weaknesses of the Brethren approach are not my point here. It is the issue of which is the *biblical* way to do missions, that is, what squares with a fair interpretive treatment of the Bible's teachings. And in this case, biblical support is wrongly claimed. This is therefore, again, a Brethren tradition. But is it a bad one?

I would not call this a bad tradition. There are tremendous practical values in seeing the local assembly as the primary sending and accountability agency for mission work. I would never want to give this up. With this approach the Brethren may send fewer missionaries (per individual assembly),[77] but there is a tendency for the financial support to be proportionally higher than in traditional "deputational" models. Also, the accountability/support relationship between the missionary and one local church is often much stronger than in other models due to the widespread geographical nature of other types of missionary support. Finally, missionaries end up having a better "home base" for nourishment and support on furlough, rather than needing to contact dozens of supporting churches.

So, the Brethren approach to missions is a tradition too. It is not a mandate, and the biblical course is for Brethren to be honest and patient with those who choose a different approach than they, since the Scriptures do not teach directly on the matter. Ultimately, it is a *good* tradition when rightly handled.

The local congregation is expected to stay at a relatively small size. Brethren historically have argued for small companies of believers, from the time of Darby's "little flocks" of gathered "twos and threes" down to the present day.[78] Consequently, many Brethren assemblies have less than 100 persons in fellowship, and even from that some often "hive off" to form a new group.[79]

One brother told me he was taught that the optimum size of the local assembly was 100 believers, because Jesus had the multitudes sit down in groups of hundreds and fifties (Mark 6:40)! An article in the Open Brethren organ *Interest* posited what the author called the "plateau hypothesis," by which he meant when an assembly reaches a certain size, no matter how many new people join them, an equal number will leave—thus leaving the assembly at the same size. He compared it to adding new grains of salt to a pile of salt which had already reached to the edge of the table—some always drop off.[80]

But with all the Open Brethren tendency toward patternism, they have truly missed a clear biblical example in these areas.

Small gatherings are not the only "pattern" of the early church. The church at Jerusalem, for example, numbered in the *thousands*,[81] and almost every new church mentioned in the New Testament was started as a result of missionary *strategy*—which has come to be called "church planting" today, and not a simple "hive off."

Yet in Brethren circles these two areas are all too often overlooked. I tend to think that this desire for smaller assemblies, apart from the good that such intimacy can achieve, has several dangers with it. First, it tends to stifle vision in terms of the Lord's plan to *build* His church (Matt. 16:18).[82] Secondly, if it is made out to be the biblical pattern, then the Brethren are really inconsistent with the testimony of the New Testament itself—where we find both small "house churches" as well as larger city-churches. Thirdly, it is inconsistent with the history of the Brethren Movement itself. Certainly, John Nelson Darby was a vigorous church planter who set up small assemblies, but there was also enough diversity in the movement to accommodate larger assemblies as well.

At Plymouth, for example, there were over 1,200 people in fellowship at its peak.[83] At the assembly at Bethesda, before the terrible split, there were over 500 people sitting under the ministry of Müller, Craik, and others, with about 75 people being added to the fellowship annually.[84] And in 1863 the massive Merrion Hall was built in Dublin to house the 3,000 believers who met there and for years supported a healthy Open Brethren assembly. All I am saying is that Brethren diversity should allow thinking in terms of larger assemblies (especially in urban areas) and not just in terms of smaller groups. And that is not to mention the many practical benefits that come from such a philosophy.[85]

There has not been much thought given to the *philosophy* of starting new churches among the Brethren. Often they will start a new assembly in a community or even neighborhood where there is already an evangelical church, often with the simple claim "but there is not as yet a New Testament testimony there"—meaning, of course, that there is no Brethren assembly there yet.

And the motive? In my experience, too often the reason for a hive off has been so that certain members of the assemblies simply would not have to drive as far to meeting. That is why I have tended to use the rather (admittedly) derogatory term "convenience cluster" for such hive offs. The reason for starting the new assembly was really more a matter of *convenience* than it was strategy and vision. What has happened to the desire to proclaim the Gospel to the unreached? Has it been in these instances replaced with a desire to promote uniquely Brethren teachings in an area where other churches already exist—to promote "separation truth"?

So, biblical justification is lacking for these Brethren distinctives that pertain to the local congregation. They too must fall under the title of "Brethren tradition" and not "New Testament principles." They are not necessarily *bad* traditions if handled correctly, but they can never be used as a sort of divine mandate that other groups have missed out on.

AFFIRMING THE GOOD TRADITIONS OF THE BRETHREN WITHOUT OFFENSE TO OTHERS IN THE BODY OF CHRIST

I have laid out some of the core Brethren distinctives in this chapter, and I have concluded that each of them is, with few exceptions, part of a Brethren interpretive tradition. And, for the most part, these traditions are neutral or positive ones—that is, they do not "nullify" the Word of God and therefore do not come under our Lord's condemnation as *bad* tradition. Instead, for the most part, they are like the synagogue which went uncondemned by our Lord, and which was certainly serviceable for His use.

One last step is needed. Since denominational distinctives like these are good, there is need for a way to express these to others as traditions or values, without communicating that others are in some way missing "truth" or "core orthodoxy" by not practicing them. There is a way to show how a group's traditional distinctives may be communicated in a rather nonoffensive form by showing their *value* and *secondary nature* within the church. That is by constructing a doctrinal statement which displays these distinctives in connection with the actual biblical values they express for a given group.

After the core orthodox teachings are displayed, a secondary, value statement may then be appended, linking the group with its denominational heritage. Here is an example of one that has been used by one Brethren assembly:[86]

Distinctives of Bethesda Bible Chapel

The following are values we have developed from the rich heritage of the (Plymouth) Brethren Movement, from which we have descended. We are committed to maintaining those values which we find to be biblical, yet we are open to changing the way those values are expressed if such expressions are found to be unbiblical or extrabiblical in fulfilling our God-given mandate in this generation.

(1) Because of the way we value the centrality of the cross of Christ,
> we will remember Him weekly in the Breaking of Bread.

(2) Because of the way we value the unity of all true believers in Christ,
> our worship will be open to all true believers
> our service will be open to cooperative ventures
> our fellowship will stress the fundamentals of the faith.

(3) Because of the way we value the priesthood and ministry of every believer among us,
> we will avoid the concentration of ministry in a clerical class
> we will stress the development and deployment of spiritual gifts among all believers, both men and women
> we will expect every member to take on a regular ministry responsibility.

(4) Because of the way we value the wisdom of council,
> we will maintain a plurality of leadership among the elders
> we will encourage team ministries at home and abroad.

(5) Because of the way we value male leadership,
> we will constantly develop mature men to be elders and leaders
> we will train our married men to be loving leaders in the home.

(6) Because of the way we value genuine devotion and godly living,

we will foster a life of personal, family, and corporate discipleship and spirituality.

(7) Because of the way we value the centrality of the Word of God,

we will focus our preaching on expositing its meaning, formulating its doctrines and principles, and submitting to its mandates both in the congregation, in the home, and in the workplace.

(8) Because of the way we value the lordship of Christ over the congregation,

we will yield to His direction as a congregation

we will seek His guidance through prayer.

(9) Because of the way we value a true sense of community

we will encourage an atmosphere of family burden-sharing

we will encourage full family participation in our activities.

(10) Because of the way we value the place of the family,

we will resist the temptation to make heavy, regular time expectations for church service

we will honor the loving leadership of husbands

we will honor the deferential submission of wives

we will honor the place of children in our congregation.

Each of these distinctives is connected with a core biblical value and therefore gives it legitimacy as a way of expressing it. And each communicates that it is practiced "because of the way we value a biblical truth." It is therefore nonjudgmental toward other Christian groups who may express that same value in other ways.

I should hope that such a statement does not alienate those from outside the Brethren tradition, but rather communicates that the Brethren are simply trying to express their own style of doing things. It does not mean that this is the only "biblical way" to do these things, yet it connects it with the unique Brethren manner of valuing these things. Other denominations may value many of these very same things, but the *way* they express their values may differ from the way the Brethren express theirs. That is fine, so long as we all respect one another and allow for that diversity within the body of Christ.

Every denominational grouping has traditions which uniquely *enhance* biblical truths for them, and such traditions are therefore to be appreciated as such, and embraced as useful. This will be valuable as long as each of us remembers the proper place of tradition, based on a healthy application of biblical hermeneutics. As long as the Brethren can do this, they will be able to resume their appropriate place as but one of the denominational expressions of the one church catholic and as exemplars of the renewed spirit of catholicity.[87]

CONCLUSIONS

The Brethren story is rather localized and personal, but it is not entirely unique. Baptists will have a similar trail of interpretive issues to work through, as will Pentecostals, and Presbyterians too. The same is true for any group with which we align ourselves. Again, the process is to identify the traditions by applying a careful set of hermeneutical principles to the distinctive teachings of the group, and then to assess the traditions on the basis of their ability to enhance or detract from the Word of God. Those that enhance the Word of God can rightfully and honestly be shared as distinctive values with any and all who are interested. And those value-expressions, when shared with others in the body of Christ, have a greater opportunity to interpenetrate and enrich the entire body rather than being sheltered away in a sectarian manner.

Now as we turn to the final chapter, I plan to bring everything together to give some "shoe leather" to developing a catholic spirit today. Join me, will you?

Nine

DEVELOPING A PERSONAL CATHOLICITY TODAY

I believe in one holy, catholic, and apostolic Church.

—The Nicene Creed

 One evening, in a family discussion around the dinner table, the topic of a friend who was a member of a different denomination came up. Suddenly, one of our children popped a question, "But Daddy, is that church bad?" A bit shocked at such a sudden, negative connotation, we tried to give some balance to the situation. "No, they're not bad," we tried to assure our child, "they teach and preach the Gospel there just like we do. They are brothers and sisters in Christ. They simply understand certain parts of the Bible differently than we do. And we could be just as wrong on those little areas as they could." Our answer was not entirely satisfying to our child, but it would have to do for now. Different is too easily connected in their minds with bad or wrong. Sameness perhaps offers too much security.

Isn't my child's question, though, a picture of our own inherent tendency to label those with whom we differ as bad? Such a tendency is the almost innate negative element that prods us into sectarian thinking. But our journey in this book has been a quest for an *alternative* to these terrible sectarian tendencies.

The journey began with a review of the early church's self-understanding, both in the New Testament teachings on the church (house, local/city, and universal) as well as the earliest uses of the term *catholic* for the one universal church spread abroad, with its diversity around a core of unity in the faith. We

261

looked further at the way in which this catholic understanding of the faith was increasingly obscured as the church began to understand itself more and more *structurally*. That structure was built around a class of specially-endowed persons who supplied the means of salvation for humanity—outside of which none could be saved.

This organizational entity, especially when connected with the political systems of the state, tended too easily to lose sight of its core spirit of catholicity. Yet the catholic spirit arose at several points in this historical survey: beginning with the silenced voices of the Middle Ages, finding force in the Reformational recovery of the doctrine of the church, continuing in the reflections of the seventeenth century Westminster divines and the great revivalistic movements of the eighteenth and nineteenth centuries, and developing more fully into a healthy denominational theory of the church catholic.

The denominational theory of the church was next addressed as a description of healthy catholicity and the opposite of sectarianism. The denominational theory of the church sees each Christian denomination that subscribes to a core of historic orthodoxy as simply one of many expressions of the body of Christ, the church catholic. To avoid the dangers of sectarian thinking within denominations, the issue of tradition (micro-tradition) as the expression of denominational distinctives was addressed. A use of healthy common-sense hermeneutics was presented as the mechanism by which those traditional distinctives may be discovered and placed in their proper perspective.

Next, the core of orthodoxy around which all denominational expressions of the body of Christ may rightly center themselves was discussed. The core of orthodoxy was understood to be the saving orthodoxy of the Gospel and its New Testament implications and presuppositions. This was distinguished from the sustaining orthodoxy found in the later formulations of the ancient and Reformational churches, but which, in the long run, are important statements of the extended implications of saving orthodoxy.

We then took a somewhat extended "field-trip" to understand how the use of hermeneutics from a broader church catholic context can help us to detect our own micro-traditions, those distinctives which sometimes serve as sectarian dividers within the body of Christ. My own Christian Brethren tradition was reviewed in terms of its quest for catholicity and its traditional distinctives—which make it important for that group to recognize its denominational status, lest it slip into a sectarian mode.

But it remains still to flesh out these ideas in terms of gaining a better sense of catholicity overall. I will therefore, in this chapter, begin by suggesting several ways people conceptualize catholicity today (most of which are harmful to the reality of the term), offer what I think is a better approach, and then give some practical suggestions to help develop a catholic spirit for you the reader, in the context of both denominations and local congregations.

CONCEPTUALIZING CATHOLICITY TODAY

Both the New Testament and early believers placed a high value on the unity and catholicity of the church. The New Testament depicts but one interrelated fellowship of believers, despite their diversity. Over them all was a leadership structure of apostles, who served as an organizational link between all groups, despite the fact that believers in, say Macedonia, likely would never meet and worship with believers in Cyprus. But today the apostles are gone, and the church has moved on through many centuries of triumph as well as strife. The church of today is significantly different in its outward look. In fact it is very fragmented. So, in view of the foregoing, how may we conceptualize the church today so that catholicity is best expressed? I would like to suggest four basic options.

Option 1: The church which has the clearest claims to historical continuity with the ancient church is the church catholic. One could adopt the ancient solution that the location of genuine unity and catholicity today is found within the boundaries of the "all-embracing," historic faith of the ancient church. Today, for example, if someone calls herself "Catholic," she is typically understood to mean Roman Catholic. The Roman Catholic Church makes historical claim to being a primary expression of the ancient catholic faith (Vatican II has tempered stronger statements), but similar assertions are made by churches claiming an historic episcopate, such as Eastern Orthodoxy, or Anglicanism/Episcopalianism. To many in those groups, one be-

comes "catholic" only by joining with that historic, episcopal organizational structure. They say it is the Protestant sects who
have destroyed the catholicity of the church by their organizational departure. The only way to restore the catholicity of the
church is for the "separated brethren" to rejoin with the historic
church and thus become subsumed under historic episcopal authority once more.

The Eastern Orthodox Church, using this same model, argues
that both Roman Catholics and Protestants must return to the
ancient faith by joining their structures. Peter Gillquist, an evangelical who has adopted Orthodoxy, now claims this model. This organizational expectation is expressed in his comments in that regard:

> What is it that we who are Orthodox Christians want? What is our
> vision, our desire? Simply this: We want to be the Church for all
> seriously committed Christian people in the English speaking world.
> . . . Very few have been given the chance to decide if they would like
> to be Orthodox. We wish to make that choice available and to urge
> people to become part of this original Church of Jesus Christ.[1]

Catholicity in this model is understood as organizational con-
nectivity; it is a universality available only within one organizational unit.

This structural/organizational approach to catholicity may be
diagrammed as in figure 9.1, on page 265.[2]

The problem here, as noted in our discussion of catholicity in
history, is that any representative claiming their group *alone* is
the authentic catholic church is practicing one of the most dangerous forms of sectarianism. In view of the realities of Christian
faith in the world today, it "unchurches" vast numbers of genuine believers and, in effect, invalidates the successful efforts of,
say, the Protestant missionary endeavors that have proliferated
from the eighteenth century to this day—after the ground-
breaking work of William Carey.[3] It is a unity without allowing
for genuine diversity. It is unity *organizationally* defined, with
catholicity appropriated to itself.

Further, although individual Protestants may become Roman
Catholics or Episcopalians or Orthodox, it is highly doubtful that
there will ever be a massive rejoining of all of the churches.
Convictions run too deeply on matters of the biblical claim to the
legitimacy of an episcopate[4] and the obscuring of some key ele-

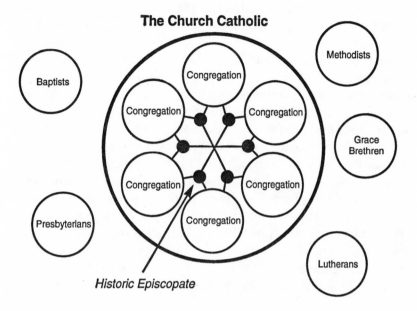

Figure 9.1.
The Historic Model of Church Catholicity

ments of the saving orthodoxy of the Gospel. Webber is right to observe regarding this structural model:

> The significant issue we must face is this: is there any one church which is catholic? Is there any one body which meets all the above requirements and has within it the whole catholic faith? There is a tendency among orthodox, Roman Catholic, and some evangelicals alike to regard their church and only their church as being the true catholic church of Jesus Christ. Such a claim is a denial of the present earthly, sinful condition of the ONE HOLY church. The full church is not seen in any one denomination or body. Rather, every branch of the church should be seen as part of the whole. The church catholic therefore needs every branch of the church to be complete.[5]

To focus on organizational unity and historical continuity as a badge of catholicity simply will not do. A broader view must certainly be had, a view (to the chagrin especially of Roman Catholics and Eastern Orthodox) that must class these groups as but denominational expressions of the whole church.

Option 2: The church which has the clearest claims to doctrinal and moral purity is the church catholic. This has been the perception of several "reform" movements in church history, including the Novatian and Donatist churches in the third and fourth centuries. Similar to those movements, however, it tends toward exclusivism: other groups are never pure *enough* to be a part of the church catholic (read true, pure church). So, the Novatianists and Donatists anathematized the traditional church.

In today's terms, fundamentalist independent churches and denominations all too often fall prey to this tendency.[6] Yet it is, in fact, a tendency *toward* sectarianism and *away* from catholicity. This principle of operation always leads to more and more separations, for nobody is ever as "pure" as I and my group. That is why fundamentalists (just like Exclusive Brethren or their kin) will quickly find fault with today's acceptable groups and split again, and again, and yet again. This purist or separatist model of the church catholic may be portrayed as in figure 9.2 below:

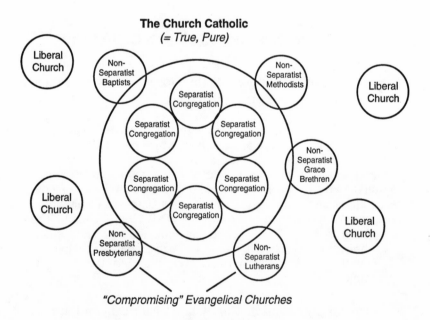

Figure 9.2.

The Separatist Model of the Church Catholic[7]

But this is a failure to apply to the church (which is the collective community of believers) that which is necessarily true of each individual believer this side of glory: he or she is, as the Reformers insisted, *simul justus et peccator*—at the same time righteous and sinner. Although God instantaneously pronounces the believer righteous due to the righteousness of Christ, he or she is not *made* righteous instantaneously. And therefore we must deal with imperfection (both intellectual and moral) in ourselves. Donald Bloesch observes:

> A sectarian mentality is evident in modern fundamentalism which is adamantly opposed to fellowship with persons and churches whose theologies are suspect. . . . The community of faith includes a vast array of people who still hold to the core of the faith but whose theological understanding is deficient or unbalanced. We should remember that Jesus himself continued to attend the temple and the synagogue even after he announced the message of the kingdom.[8]

This is the very tolerance that is called for in the concept of catholicity. The ground for our working with each other (core orthodoxy) must be less than our expectations for ourselves.

Option 3: The church which disregards denominational distinctives and gathers and receives all on the basis of faith in Christ is the church catholic. Another understanding of the return to catholicity is to simply ignore any organizational elements of the church, and to focus instead on the person of Christ as the only true ground of unity. One is thus open to accept any believer and fellowship with anyone on the basis of their love for Christ. Since unity exists in Christ alone, one must take leave of one's denominational background. The villain of catholicity and unity is understood to be the diversity of denominationalism (diversity marked by separate bodies).

On this model, the true church is often misconstrued to be a spiritual entity, with little or no organizational aspects. As discussed earlier, this is the classic position of certain renewal or restorationist movements, including a number among the Christian Brethren and some branches of the Stone-Campbell Restoration Movement. If we would simply refuse denominational labels and own Christ alone, we would be free of sectarianism and return to historic unity and catholicity. A diagram of this model would be as follows in figure 9.3 below:

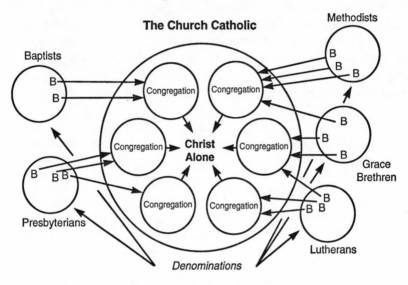

Figure 9.3.
The Restorationist Model of the Church Catholic

The problem here is that this model of catholicity can simply lead to a more subtle form of the sectarianism claimed to exist in the denominational churches. One cannot simply deny the legitimacy of hundreds of separate denominational groups with their traditional distinctives, and expect them to individually repudiate those distinctives and cling to a new "undenominational" set. To leave the denominations and gather only to Christ as a badge of catholicity is one of the most subtle forms of sectarianism ever. There is little difference in the New Testament between the sectarianism of "I follow Paul," "I follow Apollos," and "I follow Christ" (cf. 1 Cor. 1:12). In fact, the latter is even worse in the smugness it can engender. These nondenominational attempts at catholicity either empty out into clear denominationalism (as in the case of the Christian Church/Disciples wing of the Stone-Campbell Movement), or wither into raw sectarianism (as in the case of some of the Brethren).[9] Simply put, those who gather out of the denominations to Christ alone cannot constitute the only genuine expression of the church catholic in the world today.

Option 4: Wherever Christians of genuine, sincere, historic faith are found, there is the church catholic. The final understanding of the presence of the church catholic is one that squares best with the biblical and historical materials we have observed. It rests on the assertion that the church itself is fundamentally a community of converted, believing *people* (Matt. 16). That is, the focus is on the church as a community of *faith*. And the faith community has faith as its highlight, not community structures. And again, the faith community is not primarily a community which identifies itself with "the faith," that is, with a doctrinal formulation that is uniquely Christian (though it does that). Rather, the faith community is one into whose entrance regenerating faith is expected.

In this sense, the church catholic is sometimes more, sometimes less visible in those communities which call themselves Christian. A denomination is more or less a part of the church catholic—it all depends on the degree to which the Gospel message is communicated and responded to within the community. The church catholic, in this sense, "straddles" and transcends visible communities. It is seen most in those communities which have a Gospel-response requirement, but it is not totally absent in others which acknowledge a core Christian orthodoxy. Pannenberg rightly noted in this regard:

> The unity of the church is not primarily a unity of doctrine. It rests on a common confession of Jesus Christ. Differences and even contradictions in the way that Christians understand the faith do not necessarily negate the fact that we share a common confession of faith. Such contradiction could be regarded as contrasting expressions of what is basically the intention to hold the same faith, expressions that correct and supplement each other.[10]

Long ago, when my own Brethren heritage had already suffered its terrible split, Henry Craik, a colleague of George Müller, wrote the following:

> All who are born of God are essentially one. That oneness may never be fully manifested on earth, but we may be always approximating to its manifestation. . . . Meanwhile let us watch against a self-conceited and superficial dogmatism, and let us ever firmly protest against the assumption of those who, by reason of what they regard as a more Scriptural mode of meeting than that

adopted by other Christians, are disposed to arrogate to themselves the high prerogative of being the only true Church upon earth. Let us rather cherish the far more comforting and exhilarating conviction that *all who truly love the Saviour compose His church, and that all such, being united to Him now, shall continue to be united to Him, and to each other, throughout all the ages of eternity.*[11]

And this does not mean that those who genuinely know the Savior will in fact have complete conformity in doctrinal matters. Genuine Christians are not located in one denomination, but may be found throughout all groups that share a core of orthodoxy.[12] They may have serious divergences from each other's views in such matters as church government, the sacraments, worship forms, and eschatology. But what matters most in terms of identifying their companionship with us in the church catholic is the genuineness of their personal faith in Jesus Christ.

A model which captures this notion that the church catholic is found wherever true believers in Christ are found, may be seen in the chart, figure 9.4 on page 271.

This model acknowledges that each denominational church and congregation will doubtless have a mixture of the believer and the professing nonbeliever within their congregation. Some congregations are likely to have more genuine believers than others due to the clarity and consistency with which the Gospel message is communicated. The model also recognizes that there may well be genuine believers not affiliated with any local congregation, although this is an anomaly that should be remedied. It also communicates that there are religious organizations which will have no genuine believers within them (most often these groups have moved from orthodoxy into heresy, or have simply adopted the name *church* since it has become used for any gathering religious organization).

This last model is the most inclusive (catholic) of all, since it allows for all believers to genuinely be considered a part of the body of Christ based on their faith alone, through the saving core of orthodoxy, the Gospel. It also acknowledges that all legitimate, historic Christian denominations and congregations which affirm the Gospel have a part in the body of Christ. And it also indicates that there are likely unbelievers in any congregation, since not all who are a formal part of a Christian denominational

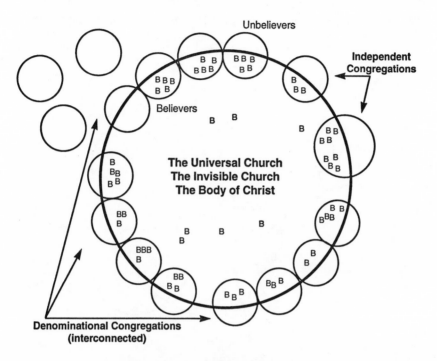

Figure 9.4.
The Pistic Model of the Church Catholic[13]

organization have necessarily come to genuine saving faith. This alone suffices for an adequate understanding of catholicity today and as a significant grounds for cooperative and relational unity in Christ.

CATHOLICITY AND SECTARIANISM: CENTRIPETAL AND
CENTRIFUGAL FORCES IN THE CHURCH
But there is a further step. Since the notion of catholicity implies a diversity in the church, it is too easy to forget the fact that there is the notion of *unity* in that diversity. The core of Gospel orthodoxy, enhanced by a healthy dose of catholicity draws believers together in fellowship and mission. In this sense, a proper view of catholicity has a *centripetal* force to it: unity in Christ *draws together* all toward certain ends. In contrast, sectarianism

has a certain *centrifugal* force to it: it forces and *separates* Christians from one another on inappropriate grounds. The centripetal element of catholicity may be portrayed as in figure 9.5 below:

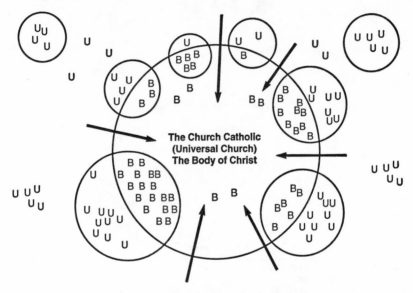

Centripetal Forces of Catholicity

Bases for Catholicity
•Recognition of a common
 core orthodoxy
•Understanding of tradition
 and its place

Results of Catholicity
•Cooperation in evangelism
 and mission
•Cooperation in discipline
•Mutual prayer and support
•Respectable and humble
 theological dialogue
•Organizational coordination

Figure 9.5.
The Centripetal Forces of Catholicity

This centripetal force of catholicity must be portrayed against its opposite extreme, the centrifugal forces of sectarianism. Whereas catholicity draws diverse churches together by an intrinsic Spirit-fed unity found in Christ, sectarianism pushes them apart on the assumption that they are in some way fundamentally superior to other expressions of Christianity. This difference may be shown in the chart, figure 9.6 on page 273.

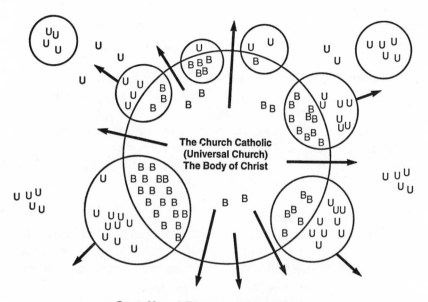

Centrifugal Forces of Sectarianism

Bases for Sectarianism
•Emphasis on greater appropriation of truth
•Ignorance of the role of tradition

Results of Sectarianism
•Independence in evangelism and mission
•Loss of effective discipline
•No mutual prayer and support
•No theological dialogue
•Organizational independence

Figure 9.6.
The Centrifugal Forces of Sectarianism

SUMMARY

Catholicity and unity go together. Catholicity is an aspect of unity. Catholicity focuses on unity *in diversity,* around a central core of Gospel orthodoxy. Historically, catholicity has often fallen prey to a narrower demand for unity. But real catholicity is much more all-embracing. It sees the presence of Christ and His Spirit wherever the Gospel is preached and faith is spawned. It accepts the diversity of others who truly believe, out of love for the Savior.

There is yet one last, practical path we must develop so as to think—and act—with genuine catholicity. In the next section I will outline that path. This last step is a methodology for thinking and acting with catholicity precisely in the ecclesiastical climate in which we find ourselves and our congregations.

DEVELOPING A PERSONAL STAKE IN GENUINE CATHOLICITY

The first priority in becoming truly catholic is to determine the degree to which sectarian attitudes have invaded us as individuals. Sectarian attitudes are often one individual's opinions transmitted to others. And often we have been corrupted in our thinking by others—and have even passed these attitudes on ourselves.

Gain a fresh perspective on ancient history. To develop a healthier understanding of the church catholic, it is imperative to understand how diverse and broad the body of Christ really is. Fundamentalists need to warmly receive evangelicals as beloved brothers and sisters in Christ. Baptists need to accept and welcome historic Presbyterian, Lutheran, and Episcopalian fellow believers. And all Protestants need to realize that there have been, and will continue to be, genuine believers in the Roman Catholic and the Eastern Orthodox confessions. We Protestants may not agree with the biblical legitimacy of their claims, but genuine believers have successfully lived and given their lives for Christ in both of those entities. There are many surviving works of theology and spirituality produced by those brothers and sisters in Christ. We simply must know church history, with its warts as well as its beauty spots, recognizing it as the corporate diary of believers, with all their saintly as well as sinful acts.

It is helpful to understand the reasons behind the ancient conflicts and divisions which led to the current denominational diversity within the church. This has several values for us. First, it helps us see whether the reasons which led to denominational splits are any longer valid. Churches and individuals change, and issues may be easily overstated. The seventeenth (or even the nineteenth) century Roman Catholic Church is significantly different than the post-Vatican II version. And although real differences remain between Roman Catholicism and Protestantism, we need to ascertain that the issues we are concerned with are still the current matters for concern, or whether subsequent modifications have changed things. In addition to understanding ancient church history, we need to gain a perspective on our own national experience of the Christian church.

Develop a fresh perspective on North American church history. As noted earlier, North America, in particular, helped proliferate the notion of a denominational model of the church. Denominationalism is a theory of the church which promotes a delicate balance between sectarianism and latitudinarianism. It seeks to embody the catholic notion of the church by arguing for a unity around a central orthodoxy only, without demanding conformity in details. And yet it honors the convictions of each group in favor of those details.

By gaining a better perspective on denominationalism as an aspect of North American church history, we can learn the distinctives of denominations different from our own; debate and/or interact with those distinctives, while respecting their right to differ from us; and receive them as family members in the kingdom of God.

Suggestions here that may enhance our thinking include: (1) reading or rereading some good books on North American church history (my notes in Phase IV of chapter 2 can give you some starters) and (2) asking for and reading denominational history and/or literature which may be available through the other denominational pastors in one's area.

But perhaps the greatest need for developing a greater spirit of catholicity comes in relationship to working with other Christians in one's own local area. So, in addition to broadening our thinking about catholicity by these preceding steps, we need a fresh, practical look at the city-church.

Develop a new perception of the local city-church. As noted in chapter 1, perhaps the most fundamental change needed in Christianity today is a new understanding of the nature of the New Testament church, one that sees the local church as far broader than any single local congregation — including all the believing congregations within an entire city or locality. Thus, all the local congregations of a city are seen as parallel to the house churches that made up the local city-church of New Testament times. As such, the leadership of those congregations (regardless of polity or denomination) make up the leadership of the church in that city, even though they collectively exercise little or no oversight beyond their specific congregation. We urgently need to realign our thinking here.

One writer, mentioned earlier, who has been especially good in developing this idea is the British evangelical H.L. Ellison who in 1963 wrote *The Household Church,* a fascinatingly practical book that has been largely unavailable in the United States.[15] After analyzing the New Testament data and developing the house church model in connection with the local or city church, he applies his conclusions:

> There can be very few cases in Great Britain, where an assembly can claim to be the Church of God in that place, the only company there that may have any expectation of Christ's presence and blessing, the only group of people meeting in the name of Christ to worship the Father through Jesus Christ, its Saviour and Lord. In other words, though it will normally meet in some building set aside as a place of worship, its status in New Testament language is far more that of a household church than that of "the church that is in X." I am personally convinced that there is probably no place in England where we can find a local church in the New Testament sense, but that everything that claims to be one is no more than a bigger or smaller household church.[16]

There are several advantages practically for returning to this model, not to mention it certainly follows the biblical practice more successfully. First, it allows us to gain a perspective on the "entire church" in our area. It makes us think catholicity not in any vague, conceptual way, but in real, day-to-day terms. It makes us face diversity and strive for acceptance of others around a core of Gospel orthodoxy in a very real way. Although we may not be affiliated in direct, ongoing fellowship with any other congregations in our area, believers at other churches in our hometown are our brothers and sisters in Christ, regardless of denominational labels. I am firmly convinced that the first step to thinking catholicity is to think *locally* (within natural geographical boundaries such as a metropolitan area) and not simply congregationally or denominationally.

Secondly, it enables us to be more assured of evangelizing our communities with the Gospel. If we see that the community of believers in mission to our towns and cities is larger than our congregation, or even congregations—within denominational groups—and that we can all coordinate together and support each other, our goals are not impossible.

Third, it puts a practical focus on issues of ecumenicity. Most ecumenical discussions are carried on by denominational representatives on a national or international level. The "trickle-down" effect is slow and filled with all sorts of suspicion, and it could take years for any practical value to arise from larger ecumenical discussions. But real, practical ecumenism can begin at a local level far more effectively. In some cases, denominational congregations drop or change their affiliations due to greater affinities among local congregations than with others afar off. At other times, there will at least be practical discussions of differences in view of real problems and differences.

Fourth, it places our denominational loyalties in proper perspective as secondary. Our primary loyalties as congregations are to our brothers and sisters in our local area or city. And our joint task as congregations is not to *compete* with each other but to *cooperate* with each other to reach our city. Although our convictions will differ from each other on many traditional interpretations, this must not hinder us from gathering and working with each other on the basis of the core of orthodoxy we share: the powerful Gospel of Jesus Christ.

Fifth, this places the full spectrum of the spiritual giftedness at the disposal of the entire church. One of the objections to denominationalism is the very fact that denominations tend to cloister specific kinds of spiritual gifts within them and thus keep these gifts to themselves rather than sharing them with the entire body of Christ. A focus on the city-church can retain the nurturing of certain kinds of gifts within certain kinds of congregations while allowing them to be shared within the church of a given city for the benefit of the entire body.

We need to conceive of the church in its local expression as more closely linked with each other than with outside loyalties. This may be demonstrated in figure 9.7 on page 278.

Here are some practical suggestions for developing a local city-church outlook. *First,* participating (by financial or personnel support) in the ministries of parachurch organizations, such as *Campus Crusade for Christ, Youth for Christ, The Navigators,* and others can serve as an effective catalyst to smooth the connec-

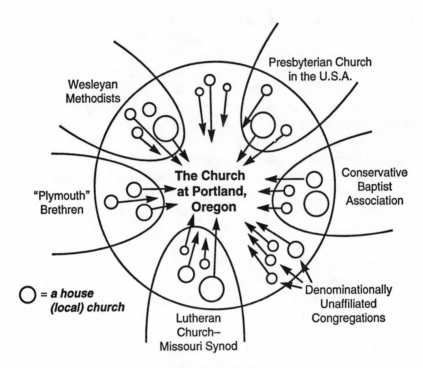

Wesleyan
Methodists

Presbyterian Church
in the U.S.A.

The Church
at Portland,
Oregon

Conservative
Baptist
Association

"Plymouth"
Brethren

O = *a house
(local) church*

Denominationally
Unaffiliated
Congregations

Lutheran
Church–
Missouri Synod

Figure 9.7.
Mission Commitments of the Local City-Church

tions of otherwise independent and non-networked congregations. Not only can such ministries be a tremendous tool for
developing a broader, catholic spirit in any of our people we may
encourage to serve in them, but they can also serve as ministries
that can link together our churches in accomplishing our local
mission more effectively.

In my own city, for example, God has graciously enabled the
leadership of the college where I teach (Multnomah School of
the Bible, a nondenominational Bible college) to serve as a liaison for a number of churchwide activities (e.g., Pastors Conferences, Northwest Renewal Conferences, Elder-Deacon Conferences, Regional Prayer Retreats, Women-in-Ministry Seminars),
bringing divergent denominational Christians and leaders together for mutual support and ministry. Similarly, our college has
been privileged to form a partnership with *The Navigators,* the
highly respected parachurch group, to help network churches

and paraministries in the greater Portland/Vancouver metroplex to work together as teams. Sponsoring such ambitious and all-encompassing tasks through a denominationally sponsored Bible college would be much more difficult, since certain competitive agendas may be understood to be in operation. Parachurch organizations, especially if they can work well with each other, can provide a valuable service for the local city-church. Check out the options in your local area.

Second, it is necessary to bring people together. The first priority in developing a sense of the city-church is to foster a spirit of unity and cooperation among church leaders. The development of interdenominational pastors' prayer summits is an excellent and necessary element for developing this aspect of catholicity.

One dimension of the Northwest Renewal movement in our region is the development of just such retreats.[17] Under the leadership of our school, groups of 20 to as many as 160 pastoral staff from diverse denominational backgrounds in select cities in our region are invited to four-day prayer retreats at various conference centers. There is no agenda—only guidelines for sensitivity. Hours upon hours are spent exclusively in prayer—for personal spiritual needs, in repentance, and in worship. Pastors from across the theological spectrum are finding a bond of kinship with diverse denominational groups that were formerly antagonistic toward each other. One pastor wrote back after participating in one of these in the fall of 1991:

I have been reflecting on my participation with the Clark County pastors in the prayer summit at Cannon Beach. I cannot adequately express the impact it has had on my life. A creeping paralysis of prayerlessness had invaded my life. I went, not to pray for revival for our community, but to cry out for revival in my own life. Thankfully a work of renewal was begun at the beach.

It was hard for me to imagine praying for so many hours when my personal prayers had been so brief, but the group prayers drew me in. I grew to appreciate this diverse group. I remember a prayer of one of our Nazarene brothers who asked the Lord that he could "take the best of all our backgrounds . . . learn to enjoy the security that my Calvinist brothers enjoy, learn to worship as my charismatic brothers do, and still keep the emphasis of holiness from my background." These kinds of expressions helped open me up to God's further work in my life.[18]

Another pastor wrote, in the early summer of 1990:

> For months, a number of pastors and Christian leaders in our area
> have been anticipating a "Pastors' Prayer Summit" together. On
> Memorial Day, we all loaded in our vans—about sixty men in all—
> from the towns of Kitsap County to go up to Warm Beach for the
> much-anticipated happening. And a caravan it was indeed.
> Charismatics and Baptists, Church of Christ, and Episcopalians
> were all headed in the same direction!
>
> On Monday afternoon, we began four days of prayer together.
> Not one message was given (that in itself is a miracle among sixty
> preachers!). . . .
>
> During this time, an Assembly of God minister stood to confess
> his sin of judgment toward a Conservative Baptist minister. With
> tears in his eyes he said, "I was told in Bible school that you
> believed all the wrong things. I thought that you were elitist. Now
> I see that I was wrong. You love the same Jesus. You believe the
> same things. Please forgive me."
>
> The Baptist pastor then blurted out, "I thought the same things
> about you. But I was wrong. Would you forgive me?" The two of
> them then crossed the room and hugged each other as the tears
> flowed freely. They didn't just fall from their eyes. All of us in the
> room were being instructed and forever changed.[19]

Things are changing. Regional and city pastors are beginning
to support each other, hold area wide worship meetings—even
sharing pulpits and developing long-range prayer strategies.
These sorts of things are clearly bringing back a spirit of catholicity at the local levels in a unprecedented way.

In addition to getting the leaders together, Christians themselves within separated congregations need to get together. Interdenominational activities need to occur, such as fellowship times,
teaching, and worship times. One of the most exciting times in
my area was a recent citywide worship service which involved
over 13,500 Christians in a standing-room only crowd at the Portland Memorial Coliseum. Again, there was no denominational
agenda. No speaker or singers were highlighted, the entire focus
was on worshiping God as a city-church. What a context in which to
sense the great breadth of the church catholic! One pastor who was
there wrote an article describing it, which is here excerpted:

The Spirit of Portland

Intellectually I knew I was not alone in my love for Christ and my
burden for the city of Portland. There is my family, my congrega-

tion, my Thursday pastors' fellowship. But living in a city where Christians are not respected and pastors are especially ridiculed, I "felt" alone.

Until this night: January 19, 1992.

This night over 13,500 Christians from every evangelical denomination dismissed their evening services. In buses, vans, and cars they came to fill the Portland Coliseum. The opening words of this historic worship and praise service were, "This is the best family reunion Portland has ever had."

To that, cheers and applause thundered across the vast auditorium. For the next two and a half hours our spirits were one in Christ. The celebrating never let up. Together we sang and prayed and clapped for God. All of us share the burden. All of us feel the spiritual oppression in Portland and the Northwest. All of us want to have the city of Portland shaken for God and righteousness.

Never has there been in Portland a unifying force as this one was. With minimum human leadership, our focus was totally on God and His Son, Jesus Christ. In unity people freely worshiped in their own unique ways. Some stood and sang with hands raised to the heavens, while others sat quiet with heads bowed. Occasionally the whole crowd felt the same thing at the same time and unanimously burst out in applause or expressed its agreement by standing . . .

Intellectually, I knew I was not alone. But at 8:30 p.m. January 19, 1992, I saw that I was not alone. For the first time in my life, every fiber of my being FELT like I was not alone. . . .[20]

Again, there is an experience of the church catholic in the context of the city-church. Great care must be used in these times to not let a specific model of worship predominate, whether it be a charismatic or liturgical model. Elements from both can successfully be incorporated if handled with a great deal of prayer and careful planning. And care must be used to make sure that certain aspects of worship in some groups (hand raising or speaking in tongues) are kept from spoiling the experience for others who are less demonstrative and yet who are every bit as spiritual.

Such times can be greatly enriching and extremely encouraging, especially to those from smaller congregations (who see that the forces of the church are larger than they may have any awareness of) or to those in large cities (who may see the task of city evangelization as completely overwhelming).

A *third* element in developing a healthy city-church approach is to begin to identify and strategize on some of the unique problems in one's area. Of course, a key set of strategies must deal with evangelization. Sponsoring and rallying around interdenominational evangelistic crusades (e.g., Billy Graham or Luis Palau) and other forms of evangelistic training can be tremendously galvanizing for any congregation that has become introspective and ingrown.

In the planning for our September 1992 Billy Graham Crusade, some 1,280 individual churches participated, with some 93 denominations being represented. The four counties comprising the Portland metropolitan area serve as home to some 1.5 million people. However, the churches draw an estimated 3 to 17 percent on an given Sunday. At most, there are 150,000 to 300,000 believers in the metro area, this region often referred to as the "spiritual wasteland of America."[21] That leaves over 1 million unchurched people to be reached with the Gospel. Certainly there is need for cooperative strategy! But God is at work as we attempt to work together for His glory. Some 26,000 Christians turned out for five weeks of discipleship training so they could follow up on the Graham Crusade.[22] Similar statistics, concerns, and possibilities could be reproduced in other localities.

Fourth, besides the core need of evangelization, local community problems need a corporate addressing by the church in the area. In larger cities, there are social problems such as gang proliferation, political corruption, and racial prejudice. Moral problems such as homosexuality and abortion activism must be challenged. There are spiritual problems such as the proliferation of cults, spiritism, and the New Age movement. And, there are intellectual problems such as secularism and humanism.

A united city-church can pray together much more effectively and spot areas for specific prayer and corporate action. Three years ago, Mission Portland, the rallying point for the unified effort in the Portland area, envisioned a prayer army of 5,000 prayer warriors to pray for the city. The number to date is 5,368 and climbing. And 18,500 Christians in the Portland area, despite their denominational differences, united to line up along major thoroughfares, recently, to protest abortion on demand by participating in a Life Chain. The secular press, although they disagreed with the stance taken, at least took note of the amazing number of participants. Christians were clearly not a fragmented minority, but a significant voice to be heard. That is the city-church—a microcosm of the church catholic—in action.

Encourage cooperative efforts with other churches nationally. I purposely held back these last two elements of developing a catholic spirit until last, since I am convinced that once a local city-church catholic spirit has started to develop, it is much easier to cooperate on national and international levels with believers of other denominational persuasions. But once the issue of national or international cooperation comes into the discussion, issues of ecumenical concern on the part of the evangelical come back into the forefront.

The ecumenical movement historically has raised many problems for the sensitive evangelical. Many of these concerns are appropriate ones and some have been frequently addressed. Evangelicals should not go into any sort of ecumenical venture that would cause them to violate their consciences before God. For example, much of what has been coming out of the *World Council of Churches* has been viewed by many evangelicals as a theological reductionism and political pandering unworthy of the church of Jesus Christ.[23]

But could there be too many reactionary responses to ecumenism? Some evangelicals are beginning to urge things akin to the ecumenical ideal.[24] And, there is some good coming out of the ecumenical movement, even beyond the things found in evangelical cooperative groups. For example, there is inter-church discussion on theological and ecclesiastical matters among evangelicals, who tend to avoid differences to focus more on cooperative mission. And the boycotting of ecumenical groups by evangelicals does not allow the historic evangelical message much space for discussion and influence there—especially when both the *National Council of Churches* and the *World Council of Churches* have Protestant member-denominations strongly influenced by theological liberalism. Why do evangelicals boycott such meetings? If they are excluded, that is one matter, but to stay away? Is evangelical faith afraid to express itself? Or is it afraid that it is not strong enough to handle critique? Or does it not think that liberalism has modified and backed toward some conservatism through the years?[25] The time for shallow ecumenism is gone, as is the time for reactionary responses. A robust evangelical faith is alive and well, regardless of its presence or absence from such discussions.[26]

I believe there is a place for ecumenical discussion and cooper-

ation, especially when focused around the core of Gospel orthodoxy. Without a degree of ecumenical cooperation and discussion, the genuine relational unity of the church catholic cannot
realistically be displayed. While, as we have argued, true catholicity must allow for denominational diversity for the sake of
conscience, this does not mean we must live in cloistered communities.[27] At a minimum we as evangelicals need to be meeting
together, discussing seriously our traditional differences and emphases. Unless there is some sort of actual working together,
relational unity cannot be seen in reality. The *National Association of Evangelicals* (NAE) is a good place to start, as is the *World
Evangelical Fellowship* (WEF). But perhaps we need to have an
even stiffer challenge, perhaps within a local context, toward
considering certain types of mergers where historic differences
are no longer legitimate. This is not a shallow ecumenism at all,
but a trend toward genuine relational unity around the Gospel
that requires genuine repentance, forgiveness, and reception.

And, as mentioned, the place where genuine ecumenicity (and
hence catholicity) must focus its attention is not in interdenominational discussions on the national or international level, but at
the local level—the level of the city-church. There the problems of
society meet head-to-head with the reality of a divided church. As
long as ecumenical discussions are understood to be cooperative
theological dialogues that drive us back to the reality of a core
Gospel orthodoxy, around which we may work with and support
each other, then they can develop a healthy catholicity. But if the
predominant issue is organizational unity, then ecumenicity can
become a replacement for, rather than an aid to, genuine catholicity. Healthy catholicity allows for the denominational diversity that
maintains the ability to follow individual conscience before God.

As suggested earlier, one key national organization that finds
its center around the core of Gospel orthodoxy, and which
should provide little difficulty for those of evangelical faith to
cooperate with, is the *National Association of Evangelicals,* with
over 50,000 churches from seventy-seven denominations represented in their membership.[28] The NAE "fosters Christian unity
and cooperation on the basis of a clearly defined evangelical
theological consensus, offering an ecclesiastical alternative to the
theologically more inclusive *National Council of Churches.*"[29]
Their purposes as a cooperative organization are as follows:

(1) to affirm our commitment to historic biblical Christianity as summarized in our Statement of Faith, taking a distinct position from those claiming to represent Christianity but not having a loyalty to the Word of God and the gospel of our Lord Jesus Christ; (2) to provide a means of fellowship and voluntary united action without the exercise of legislative control over constituent members; (3) to furnish opportunity for more effective witness and ministry through national programs, the services of our commissions and affiliates, and the activities of our regional, state, and local organizations; and (4) to represent the evangelical cause by confronting society with the relevance of the gospel of Jesus Christ and the imperatives of the Word of God.[30]

The NAE sponsors an annual national convention for evangelical leaders, a World Day of Prayer program, and several Washington observation events. They publish *United Evangelical ACTION* on a bimonthly basis, every other year produce a *National Evangelical Directory,* and send out a monthly newsletter, *NAE Washington Insight.* They also have a dozen subsidiaries, affiliates, and commissions, such as the Evangelical Fellowship of Mission Agencies, World Relief Corporation, the National Religious Broadcasters, Evangelical Child and Family Agency, and many others.

At its annual convention, the NAE makes resolutions as directed by its constituent members on matters of current societal problems from a Christian perspective, such as abortion, AIDS, capital punishment, homosexuality, the Equal Rights amendment, pornography and obscenity, racism, and many other issues.[31] One such resolution, that on Christian Unity (Ecumencial Relations) was produced in 1966 and fits well the concerns of this book in understanding that genuine catholicity is a unity in diversity rather than fundamentally an organizational unity. It reads as follows:

In a period of our history when pressures toward organizational unity are being directed against every segment of the Christian church in a degree never before known, the National Association of Evangelicals reaffirms its conviction that Christian unity is primarily a spiritual relationship among people throughout the world who have been brought into a living relationship to God through the new birth and are thereby members of the body of Christ and who accept the authority of the Bible as their rule of faith and practice.

We believe that this unity, given by God and made real in us by the ministry of the Holy Spirit, is manifested in a love-inspired fellowship that promotes cooperative effort in our Christian witness *without the necessity of ecclesiastical union or uniformity in practice.* We recognize *our helpful diversity* in structural relationship and rejoice in our oneness in the body of which Jesus Christ is the Head. We will endeavor to maintain the unity of the Spirit in the bond of peace so that the world may believe.

We encourage and urge Evangelicals to join in fellowship with other evangelical Christians *at local and national levels* so that they might speak to the world unitedly and strongly on issues confronting our nation, conscious that our message rests upon the authority of the Word of God.

The National Association of Evangelicals is grateful to God for the formation of evangelical fellowships throughout the world and assures our evangelical brethren of prayerful support in their efforts to *resist pressures toward an unbiblical conformity and to present a pure gospel* of redeeming grace to their countrymen.[32]

This resolution expresses the kind of healthy approach to catholicity that I have been urging in this book. In addition to the focus on a broad, local support in mission at the city/local level, the NAE should be considered on the national level.[33]

Encourage cooperative efforts with other churches internationally. Perhaps the most consistent effort toward international cooperation among those of evangelical faith has been the *World Evangelical Fellowship.*[34] The WEF began in 1846 as the *World Evangelical Alliance* in England, but it became much broader in international scope after 1951. That year an International Convention of Evangelicals was held in the Netherlands, comprised of ninety-one delegates from twenty-one countries who formed a doctrinal statement and constituted themselves under the newer name. The WEF, as its name signifies, is an international coalition of evangelical groups and serves as a resource and catalyst toward helping local evangelical churches fulfill their task in terms of defending and advancing the Gospel.[35] As of 1990, there were some eighty autonomous national and regional evangelical bodies connected with the WEF, as well as over seventy agencies in associate status.[36]

Like the NAE, the focus of the WEF is on cooperative coalition rather than organizational control. Neither organization perceives itself as an organizing center for a united evangelical church, but as a cooperative aid to independent evangelical groups. The value of denominational catholicity is hereby preserved in both of these groups.

Again, the focus on developing a catholic spirit must begin at the local, city level. It must begin as individual churches in a given city find their mandate to reach their cities for Christ *together*. It means coming to deeply recognize that their loyalties must fundamentally be locally oriented rather than outwardly oriented. It means that we must respect the traditional distinctives of each and every denomination and local church not connected with our own circles of denominational fellowship, and develop an honesty about our own traditional distinctives through a more catholic, cooperative application of hermeneutics toward those distinctives.

CONCLUSION

Genuine catholicity finds a ground for cooperation in the core of orthodoxy that binds all genuine believers in Christ: the Gospel. That same Gospel becomes the tool which drives us together in a cooperative mission. And catholicity begins with an attitude check deep in the soul of every Christian. Is my heart ready to wholeheartedly accept and work with anyone who has genuinely come to faith in Christ as I have, despite significant diversity in other areas? If not, perhaps a deep-seated spirit of sectarianism is there. May God keep us from that, and restore all of us to a genuine oneness of the Spirit in Jesus Christ our Lord. That is the spirit of the church catholic, the one body of Christ spread throughout all our denominations and throughout all the world — to the ends of the earth.

Appendix A

ANCIENT CREEDS AND FORMULATIONS OF THE CHURCH

THE APOSTLE'S CREED

Traditional Text

I believe in God the Father, Almighty,
Maker of heaven and earth,
and in Jesus Christ, his only Son, our Lord

Who was conceived by the Holy Ghost,
born of the virgin Mary,
suffered under Pontius Pilate,
was crucified, dead, and buried.

He descended into hell.[1]
The third day he arose again from the dead.
He ascended into heaven.
From thence he shall come to judge the quick and the dead.

I believe in the Holy Ghost,
the holy catholic[2] Church,
the communion of saints,
the forgiveness of sins,
the resurrection of the body,
and the life everlasting. Amen.

A Contemporary Episcopal Version

I believe in God, the Father almighty,
    creator of heaven and earth.
I believe in Jesus Christ, his only Son, our Lord.
    He was conceived by the power of the Holy Spirit
    and born of the Virgin Mary.
    He suffered under Pontius Pilate,
    was crucified, died, and was buried.
    He descended to the dead.
    On the third day he rose again.

He ascended into heaven,
and is seated at the right hand of the Father.
He will come again to judge the living and dead.
I believe in the Holy Spirit,
the holy catholic Church,
the communion of saints,
the forgiveness of sins,
the resurrection of the body,
and the life everlasting. Amen.[3]

1. The Greek here is *hades.*
2. Following Martin Luther's translation, some Lutheran versions translate the Greek word "catholic" in the creed as "Christian."
3. *The Book of Common Prayer According to the Use of the Episcopal Church,* 1977 proposed revision.

The Nicene Creed (A.D. 325/381)

We believe in one God the Father Almighty, Maker of heaven and earth, and of   all things visible and invisible;
And in one Lord Jesus Christ, the only begotten Son of God, begotten of the Father before all worlds, God of God, Light of Light, Very God of Very God, begotten, not made; who for us men, and for our salvation, came down from heaven, and was incarnate by the Holy Spirit of the Virgin Mary, and was made man, and was crucified also for us under Pontius Pilate. He suffered and was buried, and the third day he rose again according to the Scriptures, and ascended into heaven, and sitteth on the right hand of the Father; and he shall come again with glory to judge both the quick and the dead, whose kingdom shall have no end.
And we believe in the Holy Spirit, the Lord and Giver of Life, who proceedeth from the Father and the Son, who with the Father and the Son together is worshiped and glorified, who spoke by the prophets.
And we believe in one holy catholic and apostolic Church. We acknowledge one baptism for the remission of sins. And we look for the resurrection of the dead, and the life of the world to come. Amen.

The Definition of Chalcedon (A.D. 451)

Therefore, following the holy Fathers, we all with one accord teach men to acknowledge one and the same Son, our Lord Jesus Christ, at once complete in Godhead and complete in manhood, truly God and truly

man, consisting also of a reasonable soul and body; of one substance
with the Father as regards his Godhead, and at the same time of one
substance with us as regards his manhood; like us in all respects, apart
from sin; as regards his Godhead, begotten of the Father before the
ages, but yet as regards his manhood begotten, for us men and for our
salvation, of Mary the Virgin, the God-bearer; one and the same Christ,
Son, Lord, Only-begotten, recognized in two natures, without confusion, without change, without division, without separation; the distinction of natures being in no way annulled by the union, but rather the
characteristics of each nature being preserved and coming together to
form one person and subsistence, not as parted or separated into two
persons, but one and the same Son and Only-begotten God the Word,
Lord Jesus Christ; even as the prophets from earliest times spoke of
him, and our Lord Jesus Christ himself taught us, and the creed of the
Fathers has handed down to us.

The Athanasian Creed/Quicunque Vult/Fides Catholica (after A.D. 381)

It is necessary, however, to eternal salvation that he should also faithfully believe in the incarnation of our Lord Jesus Christ. Now the right
faith is that we should believe and confess that our Lord Jesus Christ,
the Son of God, is equally both God and man.

He is God from the Father's substance, begotten before time; and he
is man from his mother's substance, born in time. Perfect God, perfect
man composed of a rational soul and human flesh, equal to the Father
in respect of his divinity, less than the Father in respect of his
humanity.

Who, although he is God and man, is nevertheless not two but one
Christ. He is one, however, not by the transformation of his divinity into
flesh, but by the taking up of his humanity into God; one certainly not
by confusion of substance, but by oneness of person. For just as rational
soul and flesh are a single man, so God and man are a single Christ.

Who suffered for our salvation, descended to hell, rose from the
dead, ascended to heaven, sat down at the Father's right hand, whence
he will come to judge living and dead: at whose coming all men will rise
again with their bodies, and will render an account of their deeds; and
those who have behaved well will go to eternal life, those who have
behaved badly to eternal fire.

This is the Catholic faith. Unless a man believes it faithfully and
steadfastly, he will not be able to be saved.

Appendix B

THE CHICAGO CALL

In every age the Holy Spirit calls the church to examine its faithfulness to God's revelation in Scripture. We recognize with gratitude God's blessing through the evangelical resurgence in the church. Yet at such a time of growth we need to be especially sensitive to our weaknesses. We believe that today evangelicals are hindered from achieving full maturity by a reduction of the historic faith. There is, therefore, a pressing need to reflect upon the substance of the biblical and historic faith and to recover the fullness of this heritage. Without presuming to address all our needs, we have identified eight of the themes we as evangelical Christians must give careful theological consideration.

A CALL TO HISTORIC ROOTS AND CONTINUITY
We confess that we have often lost the fullness of our Christian heritage, too readily assuming that the Scriptures and the Spirit make us independent of the past. In so doing, we have become theologically shallow, spiritually weak, blind to the work of God in others and married to our cultures.

Therefore we call for a recovery of our full Christian heritage. Throughout the church's history there has existed an evangelical impulse to proclaim the saving, unmerited grace of Christ, and to reform the church according to the Scriptures. This impulse appears in the doctrines of the ecumenical councils, the piety of the early fathers, the Augustinian theology of grace, the zeal of the monastic reformers, the devotion of the practical mystic, and the scholarly integrity of the Christian humanists. It flowers in the biblical fidelity of the Protestant Reformers and the ethical earnestness of the Radical Reformation. It continues in the efforts of the Puritans and Pietists to complete and perfect the Reformation. It is reaffirmed in the awakening movements of the 18th and 19th centuries which joined Lutheran, Reformed, Wesleyan and other evangelicals in an ecumenical effort to renew the church and to extend its mission in the proclamation and social demonstration of the Gospel. It is present at every point in the history of Christianity where the Gospel has come to expression through the operation of the Holy Spirit: in some of the strivings toward renewal in Eastern Orthodoxy and Roman Catholicism and in biblical insights in forms of Protestantism differing from our own. We dare not move beyond the biblical limits of the Gospel; but we cannot be fully evangelical without recognizing our need to learn from other times and movements concerning the whole meaning of the Gospel.

A CALL TO BIBLICAL FIDELITY

We deplore our tendency toward individualistic interpretation of Scriptures. This undercuts the objective character of biblical truth, and denies the guidance of the Holy Spirit among his people through the ages.

Therefore we affirm that the Bible is to be interpreted in keeping with the best insights of historical and literary study, under the guidance of the Holy Spirit, with respect for the historic understanding of the church.

We affirm that the Scriptures, as the infallible Word of God, are the basis of authority in the church. We acknowledge that God uses the Scriptures to judge and to purify his Body. The church, illumined and guided by the Holy Spirit, must in every age interpret, proclaim and live out the Scriptures.

A CALL TO CREEDAL IDENTITY

We deplore two opposite excesses: a creedal church that merely recites a faith inherited from the past, and a creedless church that languishes in a doctrinal vacuum. We confess that as evangelicals we are not immune from these defects.

Therefore we affirm the need in our time for a confessing church that will boldly witness to its faith before the world, even under threat of persecution. In every age the church must state its faith over against heresy and paganism. What is needed is a vibrant confession that excludes as well as includes, and thereby aims to purify faith and practice. Confessional authority is limited by and derived from the authority of Scripture, which alone remains ultimately and permanently normative. Nevertheless, as the common insight of those who have been illumined by the Holy Spirit and seek to be the voice of the "holy catholic church," a confession should serve as a guide for the interpretation of Scripture.

We affirm the abiding value of the great ecumenical creeds and the Reformation confessions. Since such statements are historically and culturally conditioned, however, the church today needs to express its faith afresh, without defecting from the truths apprehended in the past. We need to articulate our witness against the idolatries and false ideologies of our day.

A CALL TO HOLISTIC SALVATION

We deplore the tendency of evangelicals to understand salvation solely as an individual, spiritual and otherworldly matter to the neglect of the corporate, physical and this-worldly implication of God's saving activity.

Therefore we urge evangelicals to recapture a holistic view of salvation. The witness of Scripture is that because of sin our relationships with God, ourselves, others and creation are broken. Through the atoning work of Christ on the cross, healing is possible for these broken relationships.

Wherever the church has been faithful to its calling, it has proclaimed personal salvation; it has been a channel of God's healing to those in physical and emotional need; it has sought justice for the oppressed and disinherited; and it has been a good steward of the natural world.

As evangelicals we acknowledge our frequent failure to reflect this holistic view of salvation. We therefore call the church to participate fully in God's saving activity through work and prayer, and to strive for justice and liberation for the oppressed, looking forward to the culmination of salvation in the new heaven and new earth to come.

A CALL TO SACRAMENTAL INTEGRITY

We decry the poverty of sacramental understanding among evangelicals. This is largely due to the loss of our continuity with the teaching of many of the Fathers and Reformers and results in the deterioration of sacramental life in our churches. Also, the failure to appreciate the sacramental nature of God's activity in the world often leads us to disregard the sacredness of daily living.

Therefore we call evangelicals to awaken to the sacramental implication of creation and incarnation. For in these doctrines the historic church has affirmed that God's activity is manifested in a material way. We need to recognize that the grace of God is mediated through faith by the operation of the Holy Spirit in a notable way in the sacraments of baptism and the Lord's Supper. Here the church proclaims, celebrates and participates in the death and resurrection of Christ in such a way as to nourish her members throughout their lives in anticipation of the consummation of the kingdom. Also, we should remember our biblical designation as "living epistles," for here the sacramental character of the Christian's daily life is expressed.

A CALL TO SPIRITUALITY

We suffer from a neglect of authentic spirituality on the one hand, and an excess of undisciplined spirituality on the other hand. We have too often pursued a superhuman religiosity rather than the biblical model of a true humanity released from bondage to sin and renewed by the Holy Spirit.

Therefore we call for a spirituality which grasps by faith the full content of Christ's redemptive work: freedom from the guilt and power of sin, and newness of life through the indwelling and outpouring of his Spirit. We affirm the centrality of the preaching of the Word of God and a primary means by which his Spirit works to renew the church in its corporate life as well as in the individual lives of believers. A true spirituality will call for identification with the suffering of the world as well as the cultivation of personal piety.

We need to rediscover the devotional resources of the whole church, including the evangelical traditions of Pietism and Puritanism. We call for an exploration of devotional practice in all traditions within the church in order to deepen our relationship both with Christ and with other Christians. Among these resources are such spiritual disciplines as prayer, meditation, silence, fasting, Bible study and spiritual diaries.

A CALL TO CHURCH AUTHORITY

We deplore our disobedience to the Lordship of Christ as expressed through authority in his church. This has promoted a spirit of autonomy of persons and groups resulting in isolationism and competitiveness, even anarchy, within the body of Christ. We regret that in the absence of godly authority, there have risen legalistic, domineering leaders on the one hand and indifference to church discipline on the other.

Therefore we affirm that all Christians are to be in practical submission to one another and to designated leaders in a church under the Lordship of Christ. The church, as the people of God, is called to be the visible presence of Christ in the world. Every Christian is called to active priesthood in worship and service through exercising spiritual gifts and ministries. In the church we are in vital union both with Christ and with one another. This calls for community with deep involvement and mutual commitment of time, energy and possessions. Further, church discipline, biblically based and under the direction of the Holy Spirit, is essential to the well-being and ministry of God's people. Moreover, we encourage all Christian organizations to conduct their activities with genuine accountability to the whole church.

A CALL TO CHURCH UNITY

We deplore the scandalous isolation and separation of Christians from one another. We believe such division is contrary to Christ's explicit desire for unity among his people and impedes the witness of the church in the world. Evangelicalism is too frequently characterized by an ahistorical, sectarian mentality. We fail to appropriate the catholicity of historic Christianity, as well as the breadth of the biblical revelation.

Therefore we call evangelicals to return to the ecumenical concern of the Reformers and the later movements of evangelical renewal. We must humbly and critically scrutinize our respective traditions, renounce sacred shibboleths, and recognize that God works within diverse historical streams. We must resist efforts promoting church union-at-any-cost, but we must also avoid mere spiritualized concepts of church unity. We are convinced that unity in Christ requires visible and concrete expressions. In this belief, we welcome the development of encounter and cooperation within Christ's church. While we seek to avoid doctrinal indifferentism and a false irenicism, we encourage evangelicals to cultivate increased discussion and cooperation, both within and without their respective traditions, earnestly seeking common areas of agreement and understanding.

May 3, 1977[1]

1. Reprinted in Robert Webber and Donald Bloesch, eds., *The Orthodox Evangelicals* (Nashville: Nelson, 1978). Original copyright: Westchester, Ill.: Cornerstone Books, 1977.

Appendix C

"The History of Higher Criticism" *by Canon Dyson Hague*
"The Mosaic Authorship of the Pentateuch" *by George Frederick Wright*
"Fallacies of Higher Critics" *by Franklin Johnson*
"The Bible and Modern Critics" *by F. Bettex*
"The Holy Scriptures and Modern Negation" by *James Orr*
"Christ and Criticism" by *Sir Robert Anderson*
"Old Testament Criticism and New Testament Christianity" by *W.H. Griffith Thomas*
"The Tabernacle in the Wilderness: Did It Exist?" by *David Heagle*
"Internal Evidence of the Fourth Gospel" by *Canon G. Osborne Troopby*
"The Testimony of Christ to the Old Testament" by *William Caven*
"The Early Narratives of Genesis" by *James Orr*
"One Isaiah" by *George L. Robinson*
"The Book of Daniel" by *Joseph D. Wilson*
"The Doctrinal Value of the First Chapter of Genesis" by *Dyson Hague*
"Three Peculiarities of the Pentateuch which are Incompatible with the Graf-Wellhausen Theories of Composition" by *Andrew Craig Robinson*
"The Testimony of the Monuments to the Truth of the Scriptures" by *George Frederick Wright*
"The Recent Testimony of Archeology to the Scriptures" by *M.G. Kyleby*
"Science and the Christian Faith" by *James Orr*
"My Personal Experience with Higher Criticism" by *J.J. Reeve*
"The Inspiration of the Bible—Definition, Extent and Proof" by *James M. Gray*
"Inspiration" by *L.W. Munhall*
"The Moral Glory of Jesus Christ, A Proof of Inspiration" by *William G. Moorehead*
"The Testimony of the Scriptures to Themselves" by *George S. Bishop*
"Testimony of the Organic Unity of the Bible to Its Inspiration" by *Arthur T. Pierson*
"Fulfilled Prophecy a Potent Argument for the Bible" by *Arno C. Gaebelein*
"Life in the Word" by *Philip Mauro*
"Is There a God?" by *Thomas Whitelaw*
"God in Christ the Only Revelation of the Fatherhood of God" by *Robert E. Speer*

"The Deity of Christ" by *Benjamin B. Warfield*
"The Virgin Birth of Christ" by *James Orr*
"The God-Man" by *John Stock*
"The Person and Work of Jesus Christ" by *Bishop Nuelson*
"The Certainty and Importance of the Bodily Resurrection of Jesus Christ from the Dead" by *R.A. Torrey*
"The Holy Spirit and the Sons of God" by *W.J. Erdman*
"Observations on the Conversion and Apostleship of St. Paul" by *Lord Lyttelton*
"Christianity No Fable" by *Thomas Whitelaw*
"The Biblical Conception of Sin" by *Thomas Whitelaw*
"Paul's Testimony to the Doctrine of Sin" by *Charles B. Williams*
"Sin and Judgment to Come" by *Sir Robert Anderson*
"What Christ Teaches Concerning Future Retribution" by *William C. Proctor*
"The Atonement" by *Franklin Johnson*
"At-One-Ment, by Propitiation" by *Dyson Hague*
"The Grace of God" by *C.I. Scofield*
"Salvation by Grace" by *Thomas Spurgeon*
"The Nature of Regeneration" by *Thomas Boston*
"Regeneration, Conversion, Reformation" by *George W. Lasher*
"Justification by Faith" by *H.C.G. Moule*
"The Doctrines that Must Be Emphasized in Successful Evangelism" by *L.W. Marshall*
"Preach the Word" by *Howard Crosby*
"Pastoral and Personal Evangelism, or Winning Men to Christ One by One" by *John Timothy Stone*
"The Sunday School's True Evangelism" by *Charles Gallauder Trumbull*
"The Place of Prayer in Evangelism" by *R.A. Torrey*
"Foreign Missions, or World-Wide Evangelism" by *Robert E. Speer*
"A Message from Missions" by *Charles A. Bowen*
"What Missionary Motives Should Prevail?" by *Henry W. Frost*
"Consecration" by *Henry W. Frost*
"Is Romanism Christianity?" by *T.W. Medhurst*
"Rome the Antagonist of the Nation" by *J.M. Foster*
"The True Church" by *Bishop Ryle*
"The Testimony of Foreign Missions to the Superintending Providence of God" by *Arthur T. Pierson*
"The Purposes of the Incarnation" by *G. Campbell Morgan*
"Tributes to Christ and the Bible by Brainy Men Not Known as Active Christians" by *Franklin, Jefferson, et al.*
"Modern Philosophy" by *Philip Mauro*
"The Knowledge of God" by *David James Burrell*
"The Wisdom of this World" by *A.W. Pitzer*
"The Science of Conversion" by *H.M. Sydenstricker*
"The Decadence of Darwinism" by *Henry H. Beach*
"The Passing of Evolution" by *George Frederick Wright*

APPENDIX C

"Evolutionism in the Pulpit" by *An Occupant of the Pew*
"The Church and Socialism" by *Charles R. Erdman*
"Millenial Dawn: A Counterfeit of Christianity" by *William G. Moorehead*
"Mormonism: Its Origin, Characteristics and Doctrines" by *R.G. McNiece*
"Eddyism, Commonly Called 'Christian Science' " by *Maurice E. Wilson*
"Modern Spiritualism Briefly Tested by Scripture" by *Algernon J. Pollock*
"Satan and His Kingdom" by *Mrs. Jessie Penn-Lewis*
"Why Save the Lord's Day?" by *Daniel Hoffman Martin*
"Apologetic Value of Paul's Epistles" by *E.J. Stobo*
"Divine Efficacy of Prayer" by *Arthur T. Pierson*
"Our Lord's Teaching About Money" by *Arthur T. Pierson*
"The Scriptures" by *A.C. Dixon*
"What the Bible Contains for the Believer" by *George F. Pentecost*
"The Hope of the Church" by *John McNicol*
"The Coming of Christ" by *Charles R. Erdman*
"The Testimony of Christian Experience" by *E.Y. Mullins*
"A Personal Testimony" by *H.W. Webb-Peploe*
"The Personal Testimony of Charles T. Studd" by *Charles T. Studd*
"A Personal Testimony" by *Philip Mauro*

Appendix D

INTERDENOMINATIONAL EVANGELICAL STATEMENTS OF FAITH

THE STATEMENT OF FAITH OF THE NATIONAL ASSOCIATION OF EVANGELICALS (1943)

1. We believe the Bible to be the inspired, the only infallible, authoritative Word of God.

2. We believe that there is one God, eternally existent in three persons: Father, Son, and Holy Spirit.

3. We believe in the deity of our Lord Jesus Christ, in His virgin birth, in His sinless life, in His miracles, in His vicarious and atoning death through His shed blood, in His bodily resurrection, in His ascension to the right hand of the Father, and in His personal return in power and glory.

4. We believe that for the salvation of lost and sinful man, regeneration by the Holy Spirit is absolutely essential.

5. We believe in the present ministry of the Holy Spirit by whose indwelling the Christian is enabled to live a godly life.

6. We believe in the resurrection of both the saved and the lost; they that are saved unto the resurrection of life and they that are lost unto the resurrection of damnation.

7. We believe in the spiritual unity of believers in our Lord Jesus Christ.[1]

THE STATEMENT OF FAITH OF THE WORLD EVANGELICAL FELLOWSHIP (1951)

We believe in
the Holy Scriptures as originally given by God, divinely inspired, infallible, entirely trustworthy; and the supreme authority in all matters of faith and conduct . . .

One God, eternally existent in three persons, Father, Son, and Holy Spirit . . .

Our Lord Jesus Christ, God manifest in the flesh, His virgin birth, His sinless human life, His divine miracles, His vicarious and atoning death, His bodily resurrection, His ascension, His mediatorial work, and His personal return in power and glory . . .

The Salvation of lost and sinful man through the shed blood of the Lord Jesus Christ by faith apart from works, and regeneration by the Holy Spirit . . .

The Holy Spirit, by whose indwelling the believer is enabled to live a holy life, to witness and work for the Lord Jesus Christ . . .

The Unity of the Spirit of all true believers, the Church, the Body of Christ . . .

The Resurrection of both the saved and the lost; they that are saved unto the resurrection of life, they that are lost unto the resurrection of damnation.[2]

1. NAE literature.
2. David M. Howard, *The Dream That Would Not Die: The Birth and Growth of the World Evangelical Fellowship 1846–1986* (Exeter, Great Britain: Paternoster), 31.

Appendix E

BRETHREN BREAKING OF BREAD CUSTOMS AS UNDERSTOOD BY ONE ASSEMBLY[1]

As a guest or visitor to Bethesda Bible Chapel,[2] the Worship or Breaking of Bread service style we use is perhaps new to you. Please understand that these are our own customs as heirs of the Open (Plymouth) Brethren movement. Scripture does not detail the *manner* of worship and thus each local church or denomination develops its own variation of worship practice. To help you understand our own otherwise unwritten customs in this service, please read the following carefully before participating. If you belong to Jesus Christ by personal faith in Him, you are free to partake of the bread and cup regardless of your church membership elsewhere. If you have not yet personally trusted Christ as your Savior, you are welcome to observe us in worship, but we ask that you refrain from the bread and cup as they are passed before you.

1. This is "open" worship. All who love the Lord Jesus may come to join us around the Table of the Lord in fellowship as members of the Body of Christ. You need not become a formal "member" of our group, or of the Brethren Movement. We wish to receive all whom Christ has received.

2. This is "participative" worship. The worship and remembrance meeting is led by any Spirit-directed believer without detailed prior arrangement or order of service. Any believer may suggest a hymn, lead in prayer, or open up the Scriptures so as to guide the group, under the Spirit's leadership, into worship and remembrance. Sensitivity and submissiveness are important Scriptural elements for all participants in this meeting. In this regard, any believing woman who feels led to share is required by the Scriptures to demonstrate a submissive spirit toward her husband and/or the eldership of this local church in the process.

3. This is "reflective" worship. The believer who opens the meeting will suggest a theme for the body to follow for the day (i.e., the blood of Christ; the grace of God; the resurrection of Christ, etc.). Any passage suggested for consideration, hymn given out, or prayers offered, should be somehow tied in with the theme. The theme may certainly be changed by the Spirit of God in midstream, but it is preferred that the person who shifts the theme make a suitable transition to aid the others in shifting their focus.

NOTE: This is our worship and remembrance meeting and not our "body life" or even our "teaching" meeting. Personal testimonies (unless they highlight an aspect pertinent to the worship theme) are not encouraged here, nor are public exhortations or rebuke, but rather reflection on and worship of our Great God and Savior.

4. This is "musical" worship. If a believer wishes to give out a chorus or hymn, the piano will normally be used as accompaniment unless the hymn is specifically asked to be *a capella*. We prefer that songs not be selected simply because they are favorites, but because they will help others worship along the suggested theme. It may be helpful if a brief introduction be given by the one who gives out a hymn, so that all may easily see how it fits into the theme.

5. This is "considerate" worship. Personal preference is a significant consideration in the manner of worship. The raising of hands, standing, or kneeling, etc. should only be done as suggestions by the person requesting this action, rather than as some kind of requirement for the entire congregation. In this way forms of worship that are uncomfortable for some will not be forced upon them by mere social pressure.

Also, any who would share publicly should be guided by some sense by the clock, out of consideration for those with young children, and for nursery personnel. The meeting should be completely finished (bread and cup passed, offering taken, and announcements begun) one hour after it has begun. In order to accomplish this, the Bread must be prayed for no later than 45 minutes after the meeting has begun, and the Cup soon afterward.

Please do not interrupt the continuity of the Bread and Cup by sharing *after* the Bread has been prayed for. The pianist will normally play some worshipful accompaniment music while the symbols are being passed. Please feel free to partake without further leadership. After the trays have been returned, it is expected that the next person to participate will pray for the Cup, and when the cup has been passed, that the next person to participate will ask the Lord's blessing on our giving.

If you have any questions, please contact one of the elders.

1. This "Custom Sheet" is the way one Brethren Assembly perpetuates its values while honoring the distinctions between New Testament truth and Brethren tradition. One might also observe from this statement that this particular assembly has diverged from some Brethren traditions which it has determined to be unsupportable from Scripture, namely, the complete silence of women in the Breaking of Bread meeting and the non-use of musical instruments.
2. "Bethesda" is a fictitious name here, but the assembly who uses this service style is alive and well.

ABBREVIATIONS

ANF   Roberts, Alexander, and James Donaldson, eds. *The Ante-Nicene Fathers,* 9 vols. Grand Rapids: Eerdmans, 1977, reprint.

BAGD   Arndt, William F., and F. Wilbur Gingrich. *A Greek-English Lexicon of the New Testament and Other Early Christian Literature: A Translation and Adaptation of the 4th Revised and Augmented edition of Walter Bauer Griechisch-Deutsches Wörterbuch,* 2nd ed., rev. F. Wilbur Gingrich and Frederick W. Danker from Bauer's 5th ed. Chicago: Univ. of Chicago Pr., 1979.

CC   Schaff, Philip. *The Creeds of Christendom,* 3 vols. Grand Rapids: Baker, 1985, reprint.

CGNTC   *Cambridge Greek New Testament Commentary.* Cambridge.

DCA   Reid, Daniel G. et al., eds. *Dictionary of Christianity in America.* Downers Grove, Ill.: InterVarsity, 1990.

DCC   Bettenson, Henry, ed. *Documents of the Christian Church,* 2nd ed. London: Oxford Univ. Pr., 1963.

EDT   Elwell, Walter, ed. *Evangelical Dictionary of Theology.* Grand Rapids: Baker, 1984.

GNB   *Good News Bible*

ICC   *International Critical Commentary.* T & T Clark.

JB   *The Jerusalem Bible*

LN   Louw, Johannes P., and Eugene A. Nida, eds. *Greek-English Lexicon of the New Testament Based on Semantic Domains,* 2 vols. New York: United Bible Societies, 1988.

NAB   *New American Bible*

NASB   *New American Standard Bible*

NICNT   *New International Commentary on the New Testament.* Grand Rapids: Eerdmans.

NIDCC   Douglas, J.D. ed. *The New International Dictionary of the Christian Church.* Grand Rapids: Zondervan, 1974.

NIGTC   *New International Greek Testament Commentary.* Grand Rapids: Eerdmans.

NIV   *New International Version*

NPNF   *Schaff, Philip, and Henry Wace, eds. Nicene and Post-Nicene Fathers.* 2nd Series. 1890. Reprint. Grand Rapids: Eerdmans, 1979.

NTC   *New Testament Commentary.* Grand Rapids: Baker.

REB   *Revised English Bible*

TNTC   *Tyndale New Testament Commentary.* Grand Rapids: Eerdmans.

TOTC   *Tyndale Old Testament Commentary.* Downers Grove, Ill.: InterVarsity.

WBC   *Word Biblical Commentary.* Waco, Texas: Word.

E N D N O T E S

(Unless otherwise noted, all emphases in the following citations are the author's.)

PREFACE

1. The figures are adapted from Frank S. Mead, *Handbook of Denominations in the United States*, 7th ed. (Nashville: Abingdon, 1983). (I prefer the 7th edition to the 8th in some ways, since the 8th obscures the ongoing divisions among my own Christian [Plymouth] Brethren tradition by simply having one descriptive entry for the Brethren. We are not quite that clean of sectarian divisiveness.) Excluding groups included in his book which make no claim to being Christian, and groups that have diverged from historic orthodoxy and may be considered Christian cults, Meade lists the following denominations: Adventists (4 subgroups), Baptists (28 subgroups), Brethren/Dunkers (3 subgroups), Plymouth Brethren (8 subgroups), River Brethren (3 subgroups), United Brethren (2 subgroups), Church of God (8 subgroups), Eastern Orthodox Groups (14 subgroups), Episcopal Church (2 subgroups), Friends (3 subgroups), Lutherans (10 subgroups), Mennonites (13 subgroups), Methodists (19 subgroups), Moravians (2 subgroups), Old Catholic Churches (5 subgroups), Pentecostal Groups (13 subgroups), Presbyterians (10 subgroups), Reformed Churches (6 subgroups), and United Church of Christ (4 subgroups). Other sources yield somewhat different numbers.

2. The figures are Mead's. Other figures besides those listed above for the United States are given as 2,050 "organized churches and denominations" (Barrett), or 1,500 (Melton). See Moberg, "Denominationalism," in *DCA:* 350–51.

3. Robert McAfee Brown, *The Spirit of Protestantism* (New York: Oxford, 1961), 24.

4. Ibid., 217.

5. The name "Christian Brethren" is the one I will use most frequently to refer to the group. It is not in common use among them. In fact they prefer to have no label (since they ideally do not wish to divide themselves from the rest of the body of Christ by some sort of "tag"). If they must have one, they do not mind "Brethren," since they use that among themselves. But that term can be confusing to the general audience of this book, since it is used of Grace Brethren, Lutheran Brethren, Mennonite Brethren, or any number of other groups as well. "Plymouth Brethren" is another term that is often used, and it was first applied to them by outsiders, when referring to the influence of one of its earliest groups in Plymouth, England. "Christian Brethren" is a common term outside North America for this group and is used in an increasing number of reference works. I prefer it here because of that, and because of many of the negative associations connected with the Plymouth event (to be explained later). It is not used here as some sort of accepted title for the group since, as I said, the only commonly accepted term among them is "Brethren."

ONE LORD, ONE FAITH

CHAPTER 1: THE CHURCH AT THE START

1. I will be using the term "free church tradition" on occasion within this book. The phrase refers to those churches or denominations which are opposed to a close relationship of church and state. This idea will be developed historically in the next chapter. Sidney Mead's definition will suffice: "The phrase 'free churches' . . . designates those churches under the system of separation of church and state. Here the qualifying word 'free' is used in the basic sense of independent and autonomous, and in the context of long tradition thus designates those churches that are independent of the State and autonomous in relation to it" (Sidney E. Mead, "Denominationalism: The Shape of Protestantism in America," *Church History* 23 [1954]: 291).

2. Apostolic succession is the belief that the only legitimate church leadership (the episcopate) is spiritually transmitted from the apostles by means of a continuous succession of events and people. Cf. Peter A. Angeles, *Dictionary of Christian Theology* (San Francisco: Harper & Row, 1985), 19. The historic understanding is that any movement or group which begins or operates outside this succession is not part of the legitimate, visible church.

3. George F. Marsden, *Understanding Fundamentalism and Evangelicalism* (Grand Rapids: Eerdmans, 1991), 81.

4. Carson comments at this point: "Thus *ekklesia* ("church") is entirely appropriate in Matthew 16:18; 18:17, where there is no emphasis on institution, organization, form of worship, or separate synagogue. . . . Acknowledged as Messiah, Jesus responds that he will build his *ekklesia,* his people, his church — which is classic messianism" (D.A. Carson, "Matthew," in *The Expositor's Bible Commentary,* vol. 8, ed. Frank E. Gaebelein and J.D. Douglas, [Grand Rapids: Zondervan, 1984], 369).

5. The individual Christian believer must come first, then the community of those who similarly have become Christian believers. Otherwise, one does not have a community of "Christians" at all. As Schaeffer noted, "I would stress again, however, that a person does not come into relationship with God when he enters the Christian community, whether it is a local church or any other form of community. . . . The modern concept is that you enter into community; in this community there is horizontal relationship; in these small I-thou relationships you can hope that there is a big I-Thou relationship. This is not the Christian teaching. There is no such thing as a Christian community *unless it is made up of individuals who are already Christians who have come through the work of Christ.* One can talk about Christian community till one is green, but there will be no Christian community except on the basis of a personal relationship with the personal God through Christ" (Francis A. Schaeffer, *The Church at the End of the Twentieth Century* [Downers Grove, Ill.: InterVarsity, 1970], 53–54).

6. The English word *church* unfortunately suffers from religious usage over the years (derived as it is from the Greek term *kyriakon,* meaning "of the Lord, the Lord's [place]." Because of this cultural association, the term itself frequently does not convey the meaning of the Greek term it translates, which has the notion of a "gathering."

7. The term used in the New Testament is the Greek word ἐκκλησία,

(ekklesia, from which the English word "ecclesiastical" is derived) but note: the commonly understood etymological/theological notion of "called out ones" is linguistically unwarranted, since the term is commonly used of non-Christian gatherings (the same term is used, whether it refers to the totality of Christians living in one place, to the household congregations, or to the totality of all Christian congregations everywhere). See *BAGD:* 240–41 and *LN:* 1:126–27.

8. The Book of Acts portrays Paul as establishing "elders" (presbyters) in gatherings of believers during his first missionary journey in the late A.D. 40s (Acts 14:23), and also portrays the community in Jerusalem as having "elders" (presbyters) as well as apostles about the same time (Acts 11:30; 15:2, 4, 6, 22; 16:4). During the late 50s, Paul's third missionary journey yielded elders (presbyters/overseers/bishops) at Ephesus (Acts 20:17, 28). Philippians 1:1 indicates that by the early 60s, Paul could address the community at Philippi together with their overseers (bishops) and their deacons. The passage in Acts 20 suggests that "elders" (presbyters) and "bishops" (overseers) are overlapping terms in the New Testament, if not interchangeable terms.

9. Earl D. Radmacher, *The Nature of the Church* (Portland, Ore: Western Baptist Pr., 1972). See especially chapter 7: "The Doctrine of the Local Church." Radmacher's emphasis may be found in these words: "The working method of God in the world at any given time is to carry out His purpose through the members of the body of Christ who are living in the world at that time, and the New Testament always views these members of the body as banded together in groups known as local churches. Thus, the church is in the world in the form of local churches which are physical organizations with physical relationships and definite physical responsibilities. The local church is God's agency in the world transacting God's business" (p. 322). Radmacher does not discuss any subcategories of the "local church," that is, that it is really made up in the New Testament of the total of the regularly meeting house churches.

10. F.F. Bruce notes the likelihood, for example, that Peter and James belonged to different house churches in Jerusalem, based on a close reading of Acts 12:17. Peter, in his thinking, belonged to a house church that met in the home of Mary the mother of John Mark; James met in another house church. See "Some Reflection on the Primitive Church: In Memory of Cecil Howley (1907-1980)," in F.F. Bruce, *A Mind For What Matters* (Grand Rapids: Eerdmans, 1990), 236.

11. "The brothers with them [e.g., with Asyncritus, Phlegon, Hermes, Patrobas, Hermas]" (Rom. 16:14) and "all the saints with them [e.g., with Philologus, Julia, Nereus and his sister, and Olympas]" (Rom. 16:15) are both understood by commentators to refer to two other distinct house churches in Rome, besides that of Priscilla and Aquila (Rom. 16:3-4). Thus, Romans 16 indicates at least three house churches in Rome. See John Murray, *The Epistle to the Romans,* vol. 2 of *NICNT* (Grand Rapids: Eerdmans, 1965), 232; James D.G. Dunn, *Romans 9–16 WBC* 38b (Dallas: Word, 1988), 898; C.E.B. Cranfield, *A Critical and Exegetical Commentary on the Epistle to the Romans,* vol. 2 of ICC (Edinburgh, Scotland: T & T Clark, 1979), 795; William Sanday and Arthur C. Headlam, *A Critical and Exegetical Commentary on the Epistle to the Romans,* 5th ed., *ICC* (Edinburgh, Scotland: T & T Clark, 1902), 427. Grossman and Peters

see evidence in excavations and martyrologies for others, and (going beyond the commentators) also see two more house churches in Romans 16; that of Aristobulus (Rom. 16:10) and that of Narcissus (16:11). Siegfried Grossman and Peter Davids, "Church in the House" (Paper delivered at the Northwest Section of the Evangelical Theological Society, Portland, Ore., 1984), 7. This is a translation and expansion of Grossman's *Der Referrunderbrief,* 1982/3.

12. Abraham J. Malherbe, *Social Aspects of Early Christianity* (Baton Rouge: Louisiana State Univ. Pr., 1977), 70. See also Robert Banks, *Paul's Idea of Community: The Early House Churches in Their Historical Setting* (Grand Rapids: Eerdmans, 1980).

13. Watchman Nee was correct in identifying the important role of the city-church (the one church in a locality). His error was in equating the city-church (the one church of a locality) with only one house church, with all others being illegitimate. The problem is that this inevitably leads to sectarianism, since the reality is that there are many house churches (today's local churches) in a given city locality. Their need is to recognize themselves as but a part of the city-church locality, and not for one to lay claim to sole legitimacy. See Watchman Nee, *Further Talks on the Church Life* (Los Angeles: The Stream Publishers, 1969), 38, 40–41.

14. See the reference to the availability of a larger home in Corinth, from where Paul writes his comments in Romans. "Gaius, whose hospitality I and the *whole* church here enjoy, sends you his greetings" (Rom. 16:23). The NIV reading suggests the point made, but it is possible that Gaius gave hospitality to the whole church (universal) by entertaining traveling Christians passing through Corinth. See Cranfield, *Romans 2,* 807. Banks argues that the term *ekklesia* is not used by Paul in his letters addressed to given congregations unless they in fact "gather together." In this sense, he points out that the "saints" at Rome are addressed rather than the "church." They likely did not have a place where they could all meet together but were restricted to house churches, which are highlighted in the last chapter of the epistle. Banks, *Paul's Idea of Community,* 40

15. The "local congregation" at Corinth would have been the city-church. Walker observes this city-church trend from the beginning of the second century, but the house church evidence of the New Testament indicates that it was far earlier: "The Christians of a particular city had been regarded, certainly from the beginning of the second century, as constituting a single community, whether meeting in one congregation or many. As such they were [or rather, came to be] under the guidance of a single bishop. Ancient civilization was strongly urban in its political constitution" (Williston Walker, *A History of the Christian Church,* 3d ed. [New York: Scribner's, 1970], 81).

16. Banks notes this: "Not until the third century do we have evidence of special buildings being constructed for Christian gatherings and, even then, they were modeled on the room into which guests were received in the typical Roman and Greek household" (Banks, *Paul's Idea of Community,* 41). Grossman and Davids note that the end of the house church came about quickly after two centuries, and cite an archaeological example: "In Dura-Europa, a Roman garrison city on the Euphrates, one can virtually excavate the

decline of the house church. In A.D. 232/233 a dwelling house was built on old foundations. A Christian owned it. It appears that between 240 and 245 through the enlargement of the garrison the Christian church had grown so large that the space was no longer sufficient. Instead of forming other house churches, they renovated the house which they had. The owner moved out, a dividing wall was demolished, and space for about sixty to seventy participants was made. In the courtyard the latrine pit was walled up and new benches were built in the quadrangle in order to have room to spread out. In a smaller room they built a baptismal font and painted the walls with biblical motifs. There, where only a few years before a Christian family lived together with others as a house church, a formal church building had now come into being" (Grossman and Davids, "Church in the House," 17).

17. The most insightful and practical work on this subject, unfortunately, is rarely consulted and difficult to access in North America. It is H.L. Ellison, *The Household Church*, 2nd ed. (Exeter, England: Paternoster, 1979). Ellison convincingly argues that our notion of a local church today is really the equivalent of the New Testament notion of a household church in a city. The true *local* church (city-church) today would be comprised of all the individual churches (equivalent of house churches) in a city. This has fascinating implications for perceiving our own congregation in a more catholic way: as a *part* of the city-congregation with whom I should have fellowship and cooperative efforts. This in itself has rather important implications for a development, on the local level, of a more serious model of the church catholic. If I understand that I am more closely related locally to other denominationally identified Christians in a local area than I am with denominationally similar Christians at a distant locality, working for unity in mission around a core orthodoxy becomes quite practical and real. This also runs contrary to the sectarian tendency of some groups to reserve the claim to be the only true "local church" in a given city, since the New Testament only gave names of churches in relation to cities and no other names. Only the church that identifies itself as the "Church of (such and such a) city" can properly claim to be the true local church. This, of course, is sectarianism, and runs contrary to the catholicity that is implicit in the notion of a local church made up of diverse house churches in a city.

18. And, as is often pointed out, both here and in heaven (based on Hebrews 12:23). Cf. Westcott's comment on this passage: "Christian believers in Christ, alike living and dead, are united in the Body of Christ. In that Body we have fellowship with a society of 'eldest sons' of God, who share the highest glory of the divine order" (B.F. Westcott, *The Epistle to the Hebrews: The Greek Text with Notes and Essays*, 2d ed. [1892; reprint, Grand Rapids: Eerdmans, 1977], 415).

19. Banks notes the limitations on size that must come with the nature of the church as foundationally a house church: "The entertaining room in a moderately well-to-do household could hold around thirty people comfortably—perhaps half as many again in an emergency. The meeting in Troas, for example, was large enough for Eutychus to use the windowsill for a seat (Acts 29:9). But it is unlikely that a meeting of the 'whole church' [in a city] could have exceeded forty to forty-five people [that is, based on available room size], and many may well have been smaller. This would compare with the number of people

who belonged to a voluntary association. Though there could be as few as ten (also the smallest number of men required to found a synagogue) and as many as one hundred, the average membership was around thirty people. The 'house-churches' and the domestic groups as well, would have been much smaller. In any event we must not think of these various types of community as particularly large.... Even the meetings of the 'whole church' were small enough for a relatively intimate relationship to develop between the members. So long as they preserved their household setting this was bound to be the case" (Banks, *Paul's Idea of Community,* 41–42).

20. When referring to the gatherings in a region beyond the city-church, the New Testament writers use the plural: the churches of Galatia (Gal. 1:2; cf. 1 Cor. 16:1), the churches of Judea (Gal. 1:22; 1 Thes. 2:14), the Macedonian churches (2 Cor. 8:1); and the churches in the province of Asia (Rev. 1:4).

21. It should be acknowledged that there is a textual problem with this reading of "church" as singular. But, as Metzger notes, "The range and age of the witnesses which read the singular number are superior to those that read the plural. The singular can hardly be a scribal modification in the interest of expressing the idea of the unity of the church, for in that case we should have expected similar modifications in 15.41 and 16.5, where there is no doubt that the plural number ἐκκλησίαι is the original text. More probably the singular number here has been altered to the plural in order to conform to the two later passages" (Bruce M. Metzger, *A Textual Commentary on the Greek New Testament* [London: United Bible Societies, 1971], 367). The UBS committee rated the singular reading as "B." It appears that the use of the singular caught some later scribes off guard in view of the more common Lukan usage. If a fair case can be produced that "churches" *is* the correct original reading, however, then this example should be omitted without damage to my argument. The plural would simply refer to regional groups, distinguishing Judea, Galilee, and Samaria.

22. See, for example, Radmacher, *Nature of the Church,* 1972, chap. 6: "The Doctrine of the Nature of the Universal Church."

23. D. Martyn Lloyd-Jones, *The Basis of Christian Unity: An Exposition of John 17 and Ephesians 4* (Grand Rapids: Eerdmans, 1962). This idea of relational unity will be developed from these passages in greater detail later in this chapter.

24. F.F. Bruce, *Commentary on Galatians NIGTC* (Grand Rapids: Eerdmans, 1982), 90 argues that at the early date of Paul's persecuting the church, he had in mind by the use of the singular the entire Jerusalem church, looking at all of the house churches as one unit. However, from the standpoint of the original readership of this epistle, Paul's use of this term would be understood as referring to that of which they were a part as well. In that sense, the term "church" in the singular hints at Paul's broadened, universalized use. In this sense, Burton is probably more correct when he notes that the phrase denotes "not a local body but the Christian community at large [which] shows that Paul had not only formed the conception of churches as local assemblies and communities of Christians (vv. 2, 22), but had already united these local communities in his thought into one entity—the church" (Ernest De Witt Burton, *A*

Critical and Exegetical Commentary on the Epistle to the Galatians, ICC [Edinburgh, Scotland: T & T Clark, 1921], 45). This latter conclusion is supported by Paul's reference to his former persecution of the "church" in the singular in his later epistles of 1 Corinthians (15:9) and even Philippians (3:6). The readership certainly of these later letters would not have exclusively thought of the Jerusalem congregation when Paul used this terminology.

25. Fee would disallow this verse as an explicit example of the universality usage here: "It is not clear . . . that this usage 'transcends a local reference.' It may become the source of such usage (e.g., in Colossians and Ephesians), but here it probably refers first of all to the church of God in Corinth" (Gordon D. Fee, *The First Epistle to the Corinthians* [Grand Rapids: Eerdmans, 1987], 489, n. 68). Robertson and Plummer note, similarly, "In [the phrase 'or to the church of God'] . . . he is again thinking of the weak brethren who have needless scruples" (Archibald Robertson and Alfred Plummer, *A Critical and Exegetical Commentary on the First Epistle of St. Paul to the Corinthians,* 2d ed. *ICC* [Edinburgh, Scotland: T & T Clark, 1911], 224). If this interpretation is correct, then Paul is saying not to give offense to Jews, to Greeks, or to *themselves,* which, though it cannot be dismissed out of hand, seems a bit unusual: he would then be using the unqualified term "church" to refer to a *portion* of the congregation at Corinth. Those who have the greater scruples, i.e., the "weak," are the church of God.

26. Since Paul was the only "apostle" the Corinthians actually dealt with, the term *church* in the singular here is combined with the plural "apostles." This is anticipatory of the later use of the "church" in Paul. "Since this sentence is coordinate with v. 27, with its emphatic "you are," meaning the church in Corinth, there can be little question that by this phrase Paul also primarily intends the local assembly in Corinth. . . . But its use in this kind of context seems also to prepare the way for its broader use in the Prison Epistles to refer to the church universal—especially so since the first item 'God has placed in the church' are 'apostles' (plural)" (Fee, *Epistle to the Corinthians,* 618, n. 13).

27. Lincoln notes the obvious: "Here in Eph. 1:22, following Col. 1:18, 24, where ἐκκλησία is used in opposition to σῶμα as a designation for the new community in Christ, the reference is to the universal Church, the Christian community in its totality. This is also the case in the other eight uses of the term in Eph[esians]. . . ." (Andrew T. Lincoln, *Ephesians, WBC* [Dallas: Word, 1990], 67). Similarly, Bruce: "The church is here the complete or universal church—manifested visibly, no doubt, in local congregations (although local congregations scarcely come into the picture in Ephesians, as they do in all the other Pauline writings)" (F.F. Bruce, *The Epistles to the Colossians, to Philemon, and to the Ephesians NICNT* [Grand Rapids: Eerdmans, 1984], 275).

28. Bruce comments that the phrase "one body and one Spirit," which echoes 1 Cor. 12:13, "was . . . never envisaged as applicable to one local church only: wherever the people of Christ were found, there was his body, of which they were individually members" (Bruce, *Epistles to the Colossians, to Philemon, and to the Ephesians,* 336).

29. Fee points out regarding this verse that "the universal nature of the church is further emphasized by the phrase 'everywhere' (lit. 'in every

place'). . . . Thus the Corinthians are being reminded that they are not alone; rather there are those all over the world who call on the name of the Lord when they meet together. . . . The one whom the Corinthians call 'Lord' is also Lord of the whole church, and as such is finally to have his way among them as he does in the other churches" (Fee, *1 Corinthians NICNT,* 34).

30. This is not to say that the local church is a "part" of the universal church. It is, rather, an expression of the universal church. Newport comments: "The church is not a sum or composite of the individual local groups. A better statement would be that the local congregation is the church in local expression. The one church of God expresses itself locally in the fellowship of believers. The church in Ephesus is the church of God, not merely a part of the church of God" (John P. Newport, "The Purpose of the Church," in *The People of God: Essays on the Believers' Church,* ed. Paul Basden and David S. Dockery, [Nashville: Broadman, 1991], 19).

31. J.H. Bernard, *A Critical and Exegetical Commentary on the Gospel According to St. John,* vol. 2, *ICC* (Edinburgh: T & T Clark), 576–77.

32. William Hendriksen, *Exposition of the Gospel According to John, NTC* (Grand Rapids: Baker, 1953), 364. Emphases his.

33. C.K. Barrett, *The Gospel According to St. John,* 2nd ed., Philadelphia: Westminster, 1978), 512. Barrett goes on to cite Bultmann approvingly: "Such unity has the unity of Father and Son as its basis. Jesus is the Revealer by reason of this unity of Father and Son; and the oneness of the community is to be based on this fact. That means it is not founded on natural or purely historical data, nor can it be manufactured by organization, institutions or dogma; these can at best only bear witness to the real unity, as on the other hand they can also give a false impression of unity. And even if the proclamation of the word in the world requires institutions and dogmas, these cannot guarantee the unity of true proclamation. On the other hand the actual disunion of the Church, which is, in passing, precisely the result of its institutions and dogmas, does not necessarily frustrate the unity of the proclamation. The word can resound authentically, wherever the tradition is maintained."

34. Francis Schaeffer, *The Mark of the Christian.* Reprinted as an appendix in Schaeffer, *The Church at the End of the Twentieth Century.*

35. See also the same focus on the Johannine epistles: 1 John 3:10-11, 14, 16-18, 23; 4:7-21; 5:2-3; 2 John 5-6.

36. Bernard comments appropriately: "This unity . . . as appertaining to Christian discipleship, is not invisible; it is to be such as will convince the world of the Divine mission of the common Master of Christians. And He has already explained that the badge of this unity is love, the love of Christian for Christian which all men may see (13:35)" (*Gospel According to St. John ICC* 2:577).

37. Lincoln comments appropriately: "This type of ethical exhortation demonstrates that the writer's visionary conception of the Church and its role is accompanied by a realism about the problems of community life with its inevitable clashes of character, attitudes, and actions. . . . Here in Eph. 4:2 love is seen as the only means of Christian forbearance. Bearing with others means fully accepting their uniqueness, including their weaknesses and faults, and allowing them worth and space. . . . Via the mention of love, the opening ex-

hortation moves to the theme of unity that will dominate the rest of the passage. The transition is an appropriate one, for the absence of love always leads to the loss of unity" (Lincoln, *Ephesians,* 236–37).

38. Similarly, Paul had earlier stated in 1 Corinthians 8:6, "Yet for us, there is one God, the Father, from whom all things and for whom we exist; and one Lord, Jesus Christ, through whom are all things and through whom we exist" (NRSV).

39. Lincoln, *Ephesians,* 238.

40. An attempt to define a "core orthodoxy" will be found in a later chapter.

41. Achtemeier's comments, although presuming greater conflict and revisionism of New Testament writers than may have existed, still warrants reflection: "The evidence from the New Testament is clear: The church, from its beginning, faced problems of division and disunity, with the result that such unity still remains a goal to be achieved in the life of the visible body of Christ. Only a clear, hard-eyed view of the kind of problems that have beset the Christian community from its beginning will enable that community to move forward, under the guidance of God's Spirit, to that unity to which it is called" (Paul J. Achtemeier, *The Quest for Unity in the New Testament Church* [Philadelphia: Fortress, 1987], 2). The key example that comes to mind is this: cultural conflicts leading to diversity in emphasis and focus in the churches of Judea which were heavily dominated by Jewish believers (for whom Jewish customs were important) and the Gentile churches. One church under one set of apostles had to allow for that cultural diversity, which is what the "Jerusalem Council" of Acts 15 gathered to address.

42. It should be noted that "unity in diversity" has theological dimensions as well, finding its roots directly in a core sustaining theology of the church: trinitarianism. God is one, yet God eternally exists as three. To demand unity in God at the expense of His diversity is the heresy of unitarianism. To demand diversity in God at the expense of His unity is tritheism. We must learn to hold both truths in balance to maintain theological orthodoxy. And it is this theological unity in diversity that finds parallel in the expression of the body of Christ, the church.

43. "Greeks" is read by the NIV, NASB, JB, NAB, and, by implication, GNB and REB. The term "Greeks" here means, as elsewhere in the New Testament, "Gentiles" (so it is translated by GNB and REB). The NRSV and the NKJV read "Hellenists" instead of "Greeks." "Hellenists" can mean "Greek-speaking Jews" rather than Gentiles (as in Acts 6:1. See NASB and NRSV mg). This difference reflects a textual problem in that the two words Ἑλληνάς (Greeks/Hellenes) and Ἑλληνιστάς (Hellenists) are confused in the manuscript tradition. But even if "Hellenists" is the correct reading, it cannot be understood in this context to simply mean "Greek-speaking Jews" but "Greek-speaking persons," meaning the mixed population of Antioch in contrast to the "Jews" of v. 19. See Metzger, *Textual Commentary,* 389. Cf. Bruce, who notes, "The [manuscript] witnesses are fairly evenly divided between these two readings. . . . But the sense of the passage is determinant for Ἑλληνάς [Greeks/Hellenes]. Since the companions of these Cypriots and Cyrenaeans had already been preaching to Jews (who in that area would certainly be Helle-

nists), it would be pointless to say that the Cypriots and Cyrenaeans preached also to the Hellenists (see on 6:1). What is meant is that they preached to Gentiles, i.e., to Greeks. . . . " (F.F. Bruce, *The Acts of Apostles: The Greek Text with Introduction and Commentary*, 3d rev. and enlarged ed. [Grand Rapids: Eerdmans, 1990], 272).

44. An example was Paul and his use of vows (Acts 18:18).

45. The Greek term we "transliterate" as "catholic" is the adjective καθολικός *(katholikos)*, meaning "general" or "universal," *BAGD:* 390. It has a parallel in the adjective καθόλου *(katholou)*, meaning "entirely, completely." The seven non-Pauline epistles were called by the earlier Christians the *"katholikos"* epistles, in that they were addressed to the entire church rather than, like the Paulines, to a particular local gathering of Christians. Cf. Eusebius, *Ecclesiastical History*, 2.23.25.

46. Avery Dulles, S.J., *The Catholicity of the Church* (New York: Oxford Univ. Pr., 1985), 31. Avery Dulles has been a chief thinker and spokesman for the new perspective on catholicity Roman Catholics have been articulating in this era of Vatican II.

47. Ignatius' Greek reads like this: ὅπου ἂν φανῇ ὁ ἐπίσκοπος, ἐκεῖ τὸ πλῆθος ἤτω, ὥσπερ ὅπου ἂν ᾖ Ἰησοῦς Χριστός, ἐκεῖ ἡ καθολικὴ ἐκκλησία. *(he katholike ekklesia)*.

48. Moltmann comments on this passage in Ignatius: "The church is not universal, general and related to the whole in itself, but solely in and through Christ. That is why Ignatius is right (if we leave his episcopalism on the side). . . ." (Jürgen Moltmann, *The Church in the Power of the Spirit*, trans. Margaret Kohl [New York: Harper and Row, 1977], 348).

49. The phrase is πάσαις ταῖς κατὰ πάντα τόπον τῆς ἁγίας καὶ καθολικῆς ἐκκλησίας *(katholikes ekklesias)* παροικίαις. Similarly, Polycarp's martyrdom is described with this preface: "Now when he had finished his prayer, after remembering all who had ever even come his way, both small and great, high and low, and *the whole Catholic Church throughout the world* (πᾶσα ἡ κατὰ τὴν οἰκουμένην καθολικῆς ἐκκλησία), the hour came for departure . . ." *Martyrdom of Polycarp* 8.1.

50. Dulles notes, "Catholicity, as applied to the church, means the quality of being universal, complete, or all-embracing. . . . In some cases they [the early Fathers] are contrasting the whole church, as catholic, with the local or particular churches, which participate in the catholic in contrast to the heretical sects, which have broken off from it" (Avery Dulles, S.J., "Catholicity," in *The New Dictionary of Theology*, ed. Joseph A. Komonchak, Mary Collins, and Dermot A. Lane [Wilmington, Del.: Michael Glazier, 1987], 172). In another place, he writes, "In the theological tradition catholicity has come to connote the absence of barriers, unboundedness, transcendence. Whatever restricts or hems in is opposed to catholicity" (Avery Dulles, S.J., "Catholicity and Catholicism," *Concordia Theological Quarterly* 50:2 [April 1986]: 81–82).

51. Again, Dulles states: "The catholicity of the church . . . is the diversified unity enabling it to reconcile in itself the contrasting values of diverse peoples and cultures, to elevate these through the gifts of grace, and thus to achieve an unexcelled plentitude through mutual enrichment. Theologically, catholicity is

rooted in Christ, the universal reconciler" (Dulles, "Catholicity," 174). Dulles notes how this newer view of catholicity began to overtake the purely external, visible, and quantitative aspects of the church catholic due to the influence of Johann Adam Moehler. The newer idea is much more qualitative and theological, as it was understood in the first millennium of Christianity. Dulles points out how this view highly influenced the changes in Vatican II: "Thanks to this vision of catholicity, Vatican II was able to present the church as a diversified unity, made up of distinct local and regional churches, each having its own proper characteristics and gifts to contribute to the whole . . . This vision of catholicity made it possible for Vatican II to propose a more realistic and appealing concept of Christian unity than had been current in preconciliar ecumenism. The goal of ecumenical action was now seen as a 'reconciled diversity' in which the uniting churches would retain their distinct traditions and customs, enjoying a measure of autonomy within the catholic communion of churches" (Dulles, "Catholicity," 173–74).

52. At this early stage, the predominant notion of the church catholic is the visible community of believers. The need to deal with the mixture of mere professing persons and believing persons within the visible communities (that is, to address the issues of the "elect" as it pertains to the real among the professing) was rarely if at all addressed at this point in the church's history. "What these early fathers were envisaging was almost always the empirical, visible society; they had little or no inkling of the distinction which was later to become important between a visible and an invisible Church" (J.N.D. Kelly, *Early Christian Doctrines*, 2nd ed. [New York: Harper & Row, 1960], 191).

53. Cited in Richard Lovelace, *Dynamics of Spiritual Life: An Evangelical Theology of Renewal* (Downers Grove, Ill.: InterVarsity, 1979), 296. This quotation is sometimes found only in its Latin form: *In necessariis, unitas; in non necessariis, libertas; in utruisque, caritas* (in essentials, unity, in nonessentials liberty, in all things charity). According to Oden, this was a favorite quote of the Reformers. Thomas C. Oden, *After Modernity . . . What? Agenda for Theology* (Grand Rapids: Zondervan, 1990), 173. Interestingly, this quote was also picked up and popularized among Roman Catholics by Pope John XXIII (pope from 1958–1963), the convener of the Second Vatican Council (1962–65). See Dulles, *Catholicity*, 23. For the background on this writer, see John McClintock and James Strong, "Meldenius, Rupertus," in *Cyclopedia of Biblical, Theological, and Ecclesiastical Literature*, vol. 6 (Grand Rapids: Baker, 1981 reprint), 59–60.

54. Moltmann insists, appropriately in my estimation, that apostolicity includes a second focus in addition to that of doctrinal consistency: that of apostolic mission. "The historical church must be called 'apostolic' in a double sense: its gospel and its doctrine are founded on the testimony of the first apostles, the eyewitnesses of the risen Christ, and it exists in the carrying out of the apostolic proclamation, the missionary charge. The expression 'apostolic' therefore denotes both the church's foundation and its commission" (Moltmann, *The Church in the Power*, 358).

55. Denyer has appropriately commented here: "The apostolicity of the Church's belief has however been preserved, and in spite of all the errors to which human beings are liable, can continue to be preserved, because the

Church is a body of believers multifariously interconnected by an entire fabric of testimony. In short, that apostolicity is preserved by a certain catholicity" (Nicolas Denyer, "Catholic and Apostolic," *Scottish Journal of Theology* 38 [1985]: 524–25). Similarly, Lane states: "The truth is entrusted to and proclaimed by the whole church—not just one individual or one congregation or one denomination or one generation or one part of the world. There is truth entrusted to the 'catholic church' embracing all generations, all parts of the world and all denominations" (Tony Lane, "Essential and Non-Essential Doctrines and Practices," *Christian Brethren Review* 38 [1987]: 24). This issue of the central teaching of the entire church as a bellwether of apostolic core orthodoxy will be discussed in a later chapter under the discussion of macro-tradition.

56. *Commonitorium,* 434. The Latin for this "Vincentian Canon" is this memorable phrase often quoted in the literature: *Quod ubique, quod semper, quod ab omnibus creditum est.* Vincent continues: "That is truly and properly 'Catholic,' as is shown by the very force and meaning of the word, which comprehends everything almost universally. We shall hold to this rule if we follow universality, antiquity, and consent. We shall follow universality if we acknowledge that one Faith to be true which the whole Church through the world confesses; antiquity, if we in no wise depart from those interpretations which it is clear that our ancestors and fathers proclaimed; consent, if in antiquity itself we keep following the definitions and opinions of all, or certainly nearly all, bishops and doctors alike." The fuller text may be found in *DCC:* 83-85.

57. The Greek form was καὶ εἰς μίαν ἁγίαν <u>καθολικὴν ἐκκλησίαν</u> *[katholiken ekklesian]* The term "catholic" became a part of the creed later in its history (ca. 350), although the creed itself dates to some time before A.D. 250. See John Tiller, "Apostles' Creed," *NIDCC:* 58.

58. The Greek form was εἰς μίαν, ἁγίαν, <u>καθολικὴν καὶ ἀποστολικὴν</u> <u>ἐκκλησίαν</u> *[katholiken kai apostoliken ekklesian].*

59. Two Anglican theologians comment appropriately: "Any Christians who for any reasons cut themselves off from their fellow-Christians in order to form tight little groups, whether they call themselves Gospel Hall Christians or Pentecostals, or Continuing Anglican or simply Catholics, are likely to have a defective doctrine of the church and to be lacking in orthodoxy" (A.T. Hanson and R.P.C. Hanson, *The Identity of the Church: A Guide to Recognizing the Contemporary Church* [London: SCM, 1987], 81.)

60. Nathan DeLynn Smith, *Roots, Renewal and the Brethren* (Pasadena: Hope, 1986), 138. Smith refers to this problem as "parochialism."

61. Ibid., 139.

62. Ibid., 62.

63. "The progress of biblical and historical criticism has put a question mark against some of the "catholic" claims of the ancient churches. For example, when a "catholic" of any complexion claims "my church is the original body which goes back to the apostles," he can no longer justify such a claim on strictly historical grounds, since the specific sign of apostolic authority which emboldens him to make this claim, to wit episcopal succession back to the apostles, cannot be maintained. The only body that goes uninterruptedly back to the apostles is the whole body of Christians" (Hanson and Hanson, *The Identity of the Church,* 111).

64. R. Newton Flew and Rupert E. Davies, *The Catholicity of Protestantism* (Philadelphia: Muhlenberg Press, 1950), 23. They elaborate on this in their definition of catholicity in this same place: "The term 'catholicity' means, then, in the first place, the presence of the living Christ. It also means 'wholeness' or 'totality'—the 'wholeness' of the Gospel. . . . Only that Church, or communion, or tradition, is in the full sense catholic which possesses the 'wholeness' of the Gospel, and such 'wholeness' can be derived only from our Lord Jesus Christ, His message of the Kingdom of God, His work of salvation and His way of life for mankind. By common consent, no communion can lay claim to 'wholeness' which does not believe in the Word of God contained in the Holy Scriptures, the catholic Faith, the One, Holy, Catholic and Apostolic Church, the Gospel Sacraments, the Holy Scriptures, the Christian Ministry. But to a communion which does so believe the title catholic may not be denied."

65. Newport, "The Purpose of the Church," 19.

CHAPTER 2: THE CHURCH IN HISTORY

1. This is sometimes referred to as the "trail of blood" approach to church history, which argues that the true Christians always stand outside of and are often persecuted by the established church. See the classic work, in this regard, by E.H. Broadbent, *The Pilgrim Church* (1931; reprint, London: Marshall Pickering, 1989) and Gunnar Westin, *The Free Church Through the Ages,* 3rd ed. trans. Virgil A. Olson (Nashville: Broadman, 1958). Similarly, in Jerry Falwell, ed., *The Fundamentalist Phenomenon* (Garden City, N.Y.: Doubleday, 1981), the chapter on church history (chap. 2) treats modern fundamentalists as simply the current expression of Religious Nonconformity, which has recurred throughout church history, beginning with Marcionism and Montanism (heresies!). It seems that works such as these conceive of virtually any group that opposed the institutional church, regardless of theological aberration, as heroic expressions of the genuine church despite other abnormalities.

2. As an example, see the *Cunctos Populos* of Theodosius I, written in 380: "According to the apostolic teaching and the doctrine of the Gospel, let us believe the one deity of the Father, the Son and the Holy Spirit, in equal majesty and in a holy Trinity. We authorize the followers of this law to assume the title of Catholic Christians; but as for the others, since, in our judgment they are foolish madmen, we decree that they shall be branded with the ignominious name of heretics, and shall not presume to give to their conventicles the name of churches" *(DCC: 22).*

3. Kraus appropriately observes: "The apostle bore in his calling and function the essential character of the new movement. The church is in essence the apostolic mission. Now an apostle is not in essence an administrator of a religious society, but a divinely commissioned messenger to lead a movement. That is why the apostles delegated this important but nevertheless secondary organizational responsibility to helpers. Had they accepted the role of administrators of internal affairs in the community, they would have subverted the integrity of the mission" (C. Norman Kraus, *Community of the Spirit* [Grand Rapids: Eerdmans 1974], 28).

4. The apostles, selected by our Lord, were considered "laymen" by the trained leadership of Judaism—untrained and ignorant by their standards. See Acts 4:13.

5. See 1 Timothy 3; Titus 1.

6. Craik describes well these earliest periods: "In that time of genuine faith and true prosperity, the internal regulated the external. The manifested results all sprung from unseen workings in the hearts of individual believers. True faith naturally led to confession, and a common confession legitimately called forth mutual sympathy. Affection led to association. Church fellowship was not the fruit of obedience to a rule so much as the gratification of a heaven-born instinct. This manifested union must have wrought very effectually upon those by whom they were surrounded. The warmth of holy affection which knit together those who were one in Jesus, irradiated their countenances with the glow of a heavenly gladness which the men of the world had never experienced, and which earth had never witnessed before" (Henry Craik, *New Testament Church Order* [Bristol, England: W. Mack, 1863], 22–23).

7. The writer warns the Corinthians about those who rebel against the plural eldership at Corinth: "Who among you is noble, who is compassionate, who is filled with love? Let him cry:—'If sedition and strife and division have risen on my account, I will depart, I will go away withersoever you will, and I will obey the commands of the people; only let the flock of Christ have peace with the presbyters [elders] set over it'" (*1 Clement* 54:1-2, cf. 42:4, 44:4-5). Kirsopp Lake, trans., *The Apostolic Fathers, with an English Translation*, 2 vols. (Cambridge, Mass.: Harvard Univ. Pr., 1912).

8. *1 Clement* 40:1-5. This suggests bishop, elders, and deacons as the parallel offices.

9. In 6.1, Polycarp speaks to the Philippians of the duties of their elders/ presbyters: "And let the presbyters [elders; note the plural] also be compassionate, merciful to all, bringing back those that have wandered, caring for all the weak, neglecting neither widow, nor orphan nor poor, etc." Polycarp, who was a bishop at Smyrna, begins his letter with "Polycarp and the Elders [presbyters] with him to the Church of God sojourning in Philippi." This may indicate that Polycarp was a bishop/overseer in his congregation which also had its elders.

10. See, for example, *Smyrneans* 8: "See that you all follow the bishop [overseer, *episkopos*], as Jesus Christ follows the Father, and the presbytery [group of elders] as if it were the Apostles. And reverence the deacons as the command of God. Let no one do anything appertaining to the Church without the bishop [overseer, *episkopos*]. Let that be considered a valid Eucharist which is celebrated by the bishop, or by one whom he appoints. . . . It is ,not lawful either to baptize or to hold an 'agapé' without the bishop; but whatever he approve, this is also pleasing to God, that everything which you do may be secure and valid." See also the letters of Ignatius to *Ephesians* 1:3; 4:1-2; and *Philadelphians* 4.

11. Walker notes: "[In Ignatius] the monarchical bishopric [the single leading bishop] is not yet diocesan [overseeing many congregations], it is the headship of the local church, or at most of the congregations of a single city; but Ignatius does not treat it as a new institution. He accepts it as established, though it

evidently did not always command the obedience which he desired" (Williston Walker, *A History of the Christian Church,* ed. [New York: Scribner's, 1970], 42).

12. See *Against Heresies* 3.3. *ANF:* 1.

13. *On the Unity of the Church* (written A.D. 251): 5. *DCC:* 72. Similarly, "Hence you should know that the bishop is in the Church and the Church in the bishop, and that if anyone be not with the bishop he is not in the Church . . . the Church is one and may not be rent or sundered, but should assuredly be bound together and united by the glue of the priests who are in harmony one with another." *Epistle* 66.7. *DCC:* 74.

14. *Unity:* 6. *DCC:* 73.

15. *Epistle* 72.21. *ANF:* 5:384. The Latin Cyprian used, and which is often found in theological discussions of this matter, is *extra ecclesiam nulla salus.* In fairness, the Reformed writer Berkouwer comments as follows about this phrase: "Summarizing the problem of the Church's boundaries in this way has caused much annoyance and resistance, because one feels that it contains the height of ecclesiastical haughtiness. . . . Hence, the recommendation has been made that the *extra ecclesiam* might better be replaced by a testimony that directly corresponds to Scripture: *extra Christum nulla salus.* Nevertheless, it would be unjust to designate *a priori* the background of the phrase *extra ecclesiam nulla salus* as ecclesiastical haughtiness. Rather, these words contain an insight into the relatedness of Christ to the Church. . . . The original intention was certainly not to put *extra ecclesiam* in place of *extra Christum.* The intention was not to push Christ into the background for the sake of an institutional pretension, but to attract attention to the way Christ gathers His Church" (G.C. Berkouwer, *The Church,* trans. by James E. Davison [Grand Rapids: Eerdmans], 139–41).

16. Similarly, "Whoever he may be and whatever he may be, he who is not in the church of Christ is not a Christian," *Epistles* 51–55: 24.

17. Flew and Davies note the danger of this concept, developed more fully in the medieval period, that the church precedes the believer: "It is indefensible to erect a temporal sequence as though the Church came first and the Christians came after. It seems to depend on the erroneous identification of the Kingdom and the Church. The truth is that the Church is there at Pentecost because the Spirit promised for the last days has entered the lives of those who have faith in the person and promise of Christ. From henceforth there cannot be faithful individuals before there is a Church, nor a Church before there are faithful individuals" (R. Newton Flew and Rupert E. Davies, *The Catholicity of Protestantism* [Philadelphia: Muhlenberg, 1950], 22–23).

18. We should note the emphasis on faith here in relationship to the participation in the church. Here a fundamental difference between Roman Catholic and Protestant thinkers arises. This is nowhere put better than by the father of modern Protestant liberalism, Friedrich Schleiermacher. He asserts that for Protestants, the individual's relationship to the church depends upon a relationship to Jesus Christ, whereas in Catholicism the reverse is true (*The Christian Faith* [New York: Harper Torchbooks, 1963], sec. 24, 103). There is much truth to this. The Protestant notion focuses on the fact that one's faith brings one into the sphere of the co-redeemed. Hence its emphasis on the Gospel and its

proclamation. Response to the Gospel brings one into the church. The Catholic notion focuses on the fact that the church has redeeming and sanctifying structures within it. Hence its sacramental emphasis. The differences appear subtle, but it seems clear that the Protestant notion parallels what one finds occurring during the initial stages of the church's history. The question is whether God intended to develop any changes in these fundamental structures after the church grew out of the first few centuries.

19. Stott warns of the harm this clerical notion has done to the nature of the church: "What clericalism always does, by concentrating power and privilege in the hands of the clergy, is at least to obscure and at worst to annul the essential oneness of the people of God. Extreme forms of clericalism dare to reintroduce the notion of privilege into the only human community in which it has been abolished. Where Christ has made out of the two one, the clerical mind makes two again, the one higher and the other lower, the one active and the other passive, the one really important because vital to the life of the Church, the other not vital and therefore less important" (John Stott, *One People: Laymen and Clergy in God's Church* [Downers Grove, Ill.: InterVarsity, 1968], 19). But do note: as Stott points out, the spirit of clericalism is to see the laity as unnecessary to the existence and operation of the church; the spirit of anticlericalism (its opposite, of which the Brethren are often guilty) is to see gifted leadership as unnecessary to the existence and operation of the church.

20. Caecilian had been ordained in 311 at the hands of one who had been in "mortal sin" during the persecution (he had handed over Scriptures to the authorities to be burned).

21. *Catecheses* 18.23. See *NPNF*, Series 2:139-40.

22. The text of the Edict of Milan can be read in *DCC:* 15-16.

23. One should note that this negative assessment of the Constantinian era is not shared equally by all, especially those of the Eastern Orthodox faith. Ware, for example, considers the time of Constantine as "the Church's coming of age" (Timothy Ware, *The Orthodox Church* [London: Penguin, 1964], p. 28). To the Orthodox, the freedom and favoritism under Constantine and the cessation of persecution led to a period of unparalleled theological growth within the church. Granted, but the point here is that the notion of the church as an organization and its union under the structures of the state had disastrous implications that would only show themselves in time.

24. Avis notes the following: "In traditional catholic theology [in contrast to Reformational thought], the catholicity of the church was guaranteed by the apostolic succession through which the grace of holy orders was transmitted and by virtue of the power of holy orders sacramental grace was imparted" (Paul D. L. Avis, *The Church in the Theology of the Reformers* [Atlanta: John Knox, 1981], 127-28).

25. See Moltmann: "It was only in the quarrels with the heretics and schismatics in the first centuries that 'catholic' was used as a mark of the 'true church,' the sole and rightful church. The term then included its quality—fullness of truth, its unity and holiness in Christ, and its apostolic legitimation" (Jürgen Moltmann, *The Church in the Power of the Spirit*, trans. by Margaret Kohl [New York: Harper and Row, 1977], 348).

26. In the nineteenth century, Maude noted four characteristics of the Roman Catholic definition of "catholicity" as it was contemporary to him: (1) The Church was intended by God to be literally universal, i.e., diffused throughout the world; (2) As applied to the Church at any particular time, this universal extension must be understood in a moral sense, whether it be simultaneous or successive; (3) This moral catholicity is a note of the Church, that is, a quality which distinguishes it from any other body; and (4) It is a quality which is possessed only by the Roman Church. "The quality of the catholicity of the Church is almost merged in that of its unity. Even the question of orthodox doctrine enters into the conception only in a subordinate degree, and *unity of government becomes the real test of catholicity*" (J.H. Maude, "Catholicism, Catholicity," in *Encyclopedia of Religion and Ethics*, vol. 3, ed., James Hastings (New York: Charles Scribner's Sons, n.d.), 260).

27. This is contained in the famous bull known as *Unam sanctam.* It closes with the statement: "Furthermore, we declare, state, define, and pronounce that it is altogether necessary to salvation for every human creature to be subject to the Roman pontiff" (*DCC:* 115-16). See Robert G. Clouse, "Boniface VIII," in *NIDCC:* 143.

28. Vatican I, it should be noted, led to a further schism within Catholicism. A number of Roman Catholics were offended (as were Protestants and Eastern Orthodox) by the declaration of Papal Infallibility declared by this council. In German-speaking Europe, a group which came to be known as the Old Catholic Churches, withdrew and formed a new communion at Munich in September of 1871. These groups, numbering approximately 350,000, still continue in opposition to Rome.

29. *The Dogmatic Decrees of the Vatican Council,* Chapter 3. *CC* 2.262-63. See also the classic pre-Vatican II theology of Ott: "Membership of the Church is necessary for all men for salvation (De fide.). . . . As against modern religious indifferentism, [Pope] Pius IX declared: 'By Faith it is firmly held that outside the Apostolic Roman Church none can achieve salvation. This is the only ark of salvation. He who does not enter into it, will perish in the flood. . . .' " (Ludwig Ott, *Fundamentals of Catholic Dogma,* 4th ed., trans. Patrick Lynch [1960; reprint, Rockford, Ill.: Tan, 1974], 312). Do note, however, that Vatican II changed this notion considerably for modern Roman Catholics.

30. Ware, *The Orthodox Church,* 250. Ware goes on to discount the notion that there is any sort of overarching notion of the church, of which Orthodoxy is simply a "branch," such as the Roman, Anglican, and Orthodox branches of the church: "If we are going to speak in terms of 'branches,' then from the Orthodox point of view the only branches which the Catholic Church can have are the local Autocephalous Churches of the Orthodox communion" (p. 251).

31. Steven E. Ozment, ed., *The Reformation in Medieval Perspective* (Chicago: Quadrangle, 1971), 4. Some of the earlier glimmers of Reformational thought in the Medieval period are found in the following: Philip the Fair, the Spiritual Franciscans, nominalism, William of Occam, Marsilius of Padua, The Waldensians and Cathari, the Conciliarists, John Wycliffe, John Hus, and the Hussite revolt in fifteenth century Bohemia

32. John Hus, *The Church,* chapter 1. Cited in Heiko Oberman, *Forerunners*

of the Reformation: The Shape of Late Medieval Thought Illustrated by Key Documents (Philadelphia: Fortress, 1966), 218.

33. For illustrative purposes only. Of course, as indicated earlier, by the time of the Great Schism which split Rome and the East, the Novatian and Donatist Churches did not exist any longer.

34. Ibid., 234–35.

35. Ibid., 236.

36. Ironically, Hus and John Wycliffe were both condemned by the Council of Constance of 1415, which met during a period of widespread discontent with the church over the schism of the papacy (one pope had been established at Avignon and one in Rome). The Council was, in this sense, a reform movement in and of itself. The Council of Constance represented the efforts of the Conciliar Movement, who argued that the fullness of the church resided in the whole body of the faithful rather than in the pope, and that the whole body was represented only in an ecumenical council. The Council of Constance was one such council called to heal the breach, and did so. They elected a new pope and issued a decree that even the Pope himself is subject to the decree of a general council. The new pope, Martin V, accepted his nomination and then subsequently repudiated the decree by asserting that all councils were under the authority of the pope. For the decree, see *DCC:* 135.

37. In about 1375, John Brevicoxa wrote a treatise on Scripture and Tradition that indicated there were sufficient numbers of scholars who had begun to adopt the notion that "only those truths which are asserted explicitly in the canon of the Bible or which can be deduced solely from the contents of the Bible are Catholic truths and should be believed as a condition for salvation." Although Brevicoxa does not share this viewpoint, his reference to this view and his understanding of the support given for it shows that the Protestant Reformers were not the first to suggest this idea. For another example, Wessel Gansfort is accused by Jacob Hoeck in 1489 of rejecting indulgences simply because they cannot be substantiated in Scripture, and he provides a lengthy reply justifying his position. For these and many other examples of these early formations of what became known as Reformational thought, see Oberman, *Forerunners of the Reformation,* 67–119.

38. As can be noted, sometimes they stressed Word and Sacrament; sometimes Word, Sacrament, and Discipline. But the key issue is that the Word (the Gospel) creates and sustains the Church.

39. *Augsburg Confession,* Article 7. *CC:* 3:11-12.

40. *The Belgic Confession,* Article 29. *CC:* 3:419-20.

41. *The Thirty-Nine Articles of the Church of England,* Article 19. *CC:* 3:499. The translation cited is that of the American Revision of 1801.

42. *Westminster Confession,* Chapter 25. *CC:* 3:657-58.

43. Avis, *The Church,* 127–28.

44. Morrison summarizes the situation: "The Reformers had no intention of breaking with the historic church. They were out to rescue the historic church from the clutch of an alien regime which had fastened itself upon it and kept it unconscious of its true nature for a thousand years. . . . It was the high task of the Reformation to emancipate this ecumenical church from its bondage to a

sacerdotal authoritarian hierarchy which had stripped the church catholic of the very organs and functions by which it could manifest its true nature as the Church of Christ" (Charles Clayton Morrison, *The Unfinished Reformation* [New York: Harper, 1953], 22–23).

45. Lowell C. Green, "Erasmus, Luther, and Melanchthon on the *Magnus Consensus:* The Problem of the Old and the New in the Reformation and Today," *Lutheran Quarterly* 27 (November 1975): 372.

46. Donald G. Bloesch, *The Future of Evangelical Christianity: A Call for Unity amid Diversity* (Colorado Springs: Helmers & Howard, 1988), 87.

47. Alexander B. Grosell, ed., *The Complete Works of Richard Sibbes,* 7 vols. (1862-64; reprint, Edinburgh, Scotland: Banner of Truth, 1983), 2:241. Quoted in Bloesch, *The Future,* 87.

48. Other earlier expressions of nonconformity that were excluded as heretical by the established church (besides the Novatianism and Donatism of the third and fourth century) were the Albigenses, Waldensians, Lollards, and Hussites in the Medieval period. Further, as Steven Ozment argues, many of the "radical ideas" of the Protestant Reformers were expressed by others within the church structures during the late medieval period of 1250–1550. See Steven Ozment, *The Age of Reform 1250–1550* (New Haven, Conn: Yale, 1980); Steven Ozment, ed., *The Reformation in Medieval Perspective* (Chicago: Quadrangle, 1971); and Oberman, *Forerunners of the Reformation.* However, it took a series of events and individuals such as those which arose during the Reformation era to bring this all to a head.

49. But not without great struggle with the Holy Roman Emperor Charles V, who favored Roman Catholicism. At the 1526 Diet of Speyer (or Speier), in order to gain military support from Lutheran princes in Germany in his struggle against the Frankish-Ottoman alliance, Charles granted a limited toleration, despite his earlier Edict of Worms (1521) proscribing Lutheranism: "Each one [prince] is to rule and act as he hopes to answer to God and his Imperial majesty." By 1529, Charles felt he was strong enough not to need the military support of the princes and so rescinded the 1526 toleration and began to enforce the earlier Worms edict. Those who resisted filed a formal "protest," lending that name to the movement. Subsequent concessions were granted for the sake of military needs, until ultimately Lutheranism was granted full recognition with the Peace of Augsburg in 1555. For a fuller discussion, see Kenneth Scott Latourette, *Reformation to the Present,* vol. 2 of *A History of Christianity,* rev. ed. (New York: Harper & Row, 1975), 726–29. See also Howard F. Vos, "Speyer, Diets of" in *DCC:* 925.

50. For some of the theological and political pressures behind this Marburg event, see Ozment, *The Age of Reform,* 332–35.

51. Cited in A.N.S. Lane, "Scripture, Tradition and Church: An Historical Survey," *Vox Evangelica 9* (1975): 45.

52. See the distinctions in the early Anabaptist confession, the Schleitheim Confession of Faith (1527): "The sword is obtained of God *outside* the perfection of Christ" (Hans J.J. Hillerbrand, *The Protestant Reformation* [New York: Harper Torchbooks, 1968], 133).

53. J.G.G. Norman, "Territorialism," in *DCC:* 959–60. This notion was chal-

lenged by the notion of Collegialism, in which the state and church are both voluntary associations *(collegia)* rather than compulsory. The king or prince therefore is to have no official relationship with the church other than he would have with any other voluntary organization. Although territorialism predominated from the earliest days of the Reformation, it was only formulated sometime later by C. Thomasius (1644–1728) and J. Bohmer (1749). Collegialism was pressed, with little immediate success, by the Dutch statesman Hugo Grotius (1583–1645) and the German philosopher Samuel Pufendorf (1632–1694). It should be noted, as Goen points out, that "The state churches of Europe were congruent with the nation politically and geographically; they included by birthright membership all who did not deliberately opt out of the arrangement; and they were maintained by universal infant christening and state support. On the other hand, the sects were those who withdrew from the state churches to form dissenting groups based on an understanding which differed appreciably from that held in the national church. The church was inclusive, the sect was exclusive; the church had somewhat lax standards, the sect enforced strict standards for membership; the church accommodated easily to the ambient culture, the sect was often antagonistic to culture" (Clarence C. Goen, "Ecclesiocracy Without Ecclesiology: Denominational Life in America," *American Baptist Quarterly* 10:4 [December 1991]: 271). As will be pointed out later, modern "catholic" denominational theory arose from the desire for toleration on the part of those groups labeled with approbation "sects." The classical use of the term "sect," as defined, refers to any non-state-sanctioned, voluntary group of evangelical believers. The term, in European context, is used to refer to groups operating outside of the territorially sanctioned churches. In the denominational model, however, "sect" refers to any group which restricts the term "church" to itself alone, that is, to any group that exhibits sectarianism.

54. By the seventeenth century, the European ecclesiastical dust had settled this way: northern Germany, Denmark, Norway, Sweden, and portions of northeastern Europe had become *Lutheran;* Spain, Portugal, Italy, Ireland, France and portions of Switzerland remained loyal *Roman Catholic* states; and parts of Switzerland, England, Scotland, and ultimately the Netherlands went *Calvinist-Reformed.*

55. There is still the tendency for some to assess American denominations based on the European territorial model of church (state-church), sect (dissenters from the state church), and mysticism. But, as Moberg points out, since, in America, there was no established church after the Revolution, one could not define any group as a "sect" that splintered from it. See D.O. Moberg, "Denominationalism," in *DCA:* 350.

56. Blaschke noted that "we must remember above all that only the territorial State could represent the Reformation to, and protect it from, higher authorities, such as the Empire, the emperor, and the Roman Curia. The close interpenetration of ecclesiastical and secular affairs, which was the order of the day on both local and imperial levels, meant that only a strong temporal power could undertake any sort of church reform, and in Germany only the princes had such power. In the absence of such a state, the alternatives—Protestant episcopal or congregational organizations—are simply inconceivable. The Ref-

ormation of necessity depended on the territorial state" (Karlheinz Blaschke, "The Reformation and the Rise of the Territorial State," trans. Thomas A. Brady, Jr., in *Luther and the Modern State in Germany*, ed. James D. Tracy [Kirksville, Mo: Sixteenth Cent., 1986], 69). See also E. Harrison Harbison, *The Age of Reformation* (Ithaca, N.Y.: Cornell Univ. Pr., 1955), 56–57.

57. Mead notes that "inevitably the spiritual reformation and consequent institutional fragmentation of the Church developed affinities with the rising national consciousnesses—and found physical protective power in the new states to oppose the physical power controlled by Rome. Thus the one reformation of the Church found diverse expressions in the nations—Lutheranism within the realms of the German princes and the Scandinavian countries, Anglicanism in England, Reformed in Geneva and Scotland, and so on. The conflict culminated in the Thirty Years War that devastated Europe. The Westphalian settlements of 1648 marked a grudging recognition of the necessity to live-and-let-live within the several territorial areas. The basis for the churches that thus emerged was both confessional and territorial. And each of these churches in its own territory and in its own way continued to make the claims traditionally made by the one true Church. Each as a Church assumed the traditional responsibilities, and each clung to the long established principle of religious uniformity enforced by the civil power within a commonwealth" (Sidney E. Mead, "Denominationalism: The Shape of Protestantism in America," *Church History* 23 [1954]: 293).

58. Wolfhart Pannenberg, *The Church*, trans. Keith Crim (Philadelphia: Westminster, 1983), 11.

59. Both poem sections are cited in Pannenberg, *The Church*, 10–11.

60. Winthrop S. Hudson, "Denominationalism as a Basis for Ecumenicity: A Seventeenth Century Conception," *Church History* 24 (1955): 33.

61. Wesley's citation is noted as a prime example of the positive dimension of the term "denomination" by Winthrop S. Hudson, *American Protestantism* (Chicago: Univ. of Chicago Pr., 1961), 33.

62. Albert C. Outler, ed. "John Wesley," in *Sermons on Several Occasions,* III (New York: Oxford Univ. Pr., 1964), 96–97. Cited in Russell E. Richey, " 'Catholic' Protestantism and American Denominationalism," *Journal of Ecumenical Studies* 16 (1979): 215–16.

63. Cited in Hudson, *American Protestantism,* 45.

64. Ibid.

65. This ironic twist of catholicity, at least among the Brethren, will be traced out in a later chapter.

66. It may seem odd here to single out *American* denominationalism. But, as Latourette pointed out, "The Christianity which developed in the United States [after 1800] was unique. It displayed features which marked it as distinct from previous Christianity in any other land. In the nineteenth and twentieth centuries the Christianity of Canada most nearly resembled it, but even that was not precisely like it" (Kenneth Scott Latourette, *A History of the Expansion of Christianity,* vol. 4 [New York: Harper, 1941], 424).

67. There are many good histories of American Christianity. For starters, one should read the well-illustrated survey, Mark A. Noll et al., *Eerdmans' Hand-*

book to Christianity in America (Grand Rapids: Eerdmans, 1983). For further study, consult the general histories of Clifton E. Olmstead, *History of Religion in the United States* (Englewood Cliffs, N.J.: Prentice-Hall, 1960); Robert T. Handy, *A History of the Churches in the United States and Canada* (New York: Oxford Univ. Pr., 1976); or Sidney E. Ahlstrom, *A Religious History of the American People* (New Haven, Conn.: Yale, 1972).

68. The Southern Colonies tended to establish Anglicanism. *Virginia,* for example, legalized Anglicanism as the colonial established church; *Maryland* at first was a refuge for persecuted Roman Catholics in the colonies, but by 1702 the Anglican Church was established there; *South Carolina* tolerated dissenters until 1706, when the Anglican Church was established; *North Carolina* did the same until 1715; originally *Georgia* was founded as a haven for religious liberty to all (except Roman Catholics), but it established Anglicanism when it became a royal colony in 1758; *New York* likewise established Anglicanism—the only Northern colony to do so despite its loyalty toward the Dutch Reformed church until 1664. The New England colonies tended to affirm Puritanism. *Massachusetts,* beginning with the Plymouth landing in 1620, developed into a Puritan stronghold. A similar establishment of Puritanism took place in *Rhode Island, Connecticut,* and *New Hampshire.* Several of these colonies flirted with religious freedom for periods of time, but *Pennsylvania* and its Quakers under William Penn allowed religious freedom, as did *Rhode Island, Connecticut,* and *New Hampshire.* Several of these colonies flirted with religious freedom, and *Rhode Island* insisted on it later under Roger Williams and the Baptists. The Middle Colonies, such as *New Jersey* and *Delaware,* with a high degree of immigrant populations outside of England, could never form an establishment and therefore settled for a degree of religious toleration in the colonial period. Handy points out regarding this period: "There is no little irony in the fact that members of a Christian church which confidently established itself as the 'true church' whenever possible could become articulate voices for religious freedom when they lived under someone's else's establishment! So Puritans objected to Anglican establishment in Virginia, and Anglicans in New England demanded their rights as Englishmen. Members of churches which in Europe remained solidly committed to state-church patterns on the American scene could find themselves in minority status, resisting establishment as defined by others" (Robert T. Handy, *A Christian America: Protestant Hopes and Historical Realities,* 2nd ed. [New York: Oxford Univ. Pr., 1984], 13).

69. The disestablishment of the church by the Federal Constitution did not mean necessarily that a given state could not have an established religion. Several New England states, as well as Virginia, struggled hardest with state disestablishment. See Robert T. Handy, *A History of the Churches in the United States and Canada,* 142–45. One should further note that separation meant separation from state sponsorship of any *particular* denomination. It did not originally mean separation *from* religion, that is, that religion was to be kept out of politics so that America would become a "secular" state. See, e.g., Francis Schaeffer, *The Christian Manifesto* (Westchester, Ill.: Crossway, 1981).

70. To adopt the title of Robert Handy's 1984 work.

71. Lefferts A. Loetscher, "The Problem of Christian Unity in Early Nine-

teenth Century America," *Church History* 32 (March 1963): 5.

72. Russell E. Richey, "Catholic Protestantism and American Denomination-alism," *Journal of Ecumenical Studies* 16 (1979): 229.

73. See, e.g., the classic work by H. Richard Niebuhr, *The Social Sources of Denominationalism* (1929; reprint, New York: Meridian, 1957). Niebuhr's ideas may be summarized in this statement from his book: "Denominationalism in the Christian church is such an unacknowledged hypocrisy. It is a compromise, made far too lightly, between Christianity and the world. Yet it often regards itself as a Christian achievement and glorifies its martyrs as bearers of the cross. It represents the accommodation of Christianity to the caste-system of human society. It carries over into the organization of the Christian principle of broth-erhood the prides and prejudices, the privilege and prestige, as well as the humiliations and abasements, the injustices and inequalities of that specious order of high and low wherein men find the satisfaction of their craving for vainglory. The division of the churches closely follows the division of men into the castes of national, racial, and economic groups. It draws the color line in the church of God; it fosters the misunderstandings, the self-exaltations, the hatreds of jingoistic nationalism by continuing in the body of Christ the spuri-ous differences of provincial loyalties; it seats the rich and poor apart at the table of the Lord, where the fortunate may enjoy the bounty they have provided while the others feed upon the crusts their poverty affords" (p. 6).

Although Niebuhr's striking sociological assessment has some merit to it (once radical new movements are formed, they before long succumb to "accept-ability" and the conservativism of the middle class, thus spawning the need for new radical movements of Christianity), there is a tendency to overplay the sociological and underplay the theological in the development of new denomi-national groupings. As Hanson and Hanson point out, "It is perfectly true that the doctrine of the church has been much influenced by the social conditions in which the church exists in any age or place. But we say 'conditioned' not determined. We would be so wholly determined by our environment that we could not get sufficiently far away from it to criticize it. The very fact that we can put forward a theory about the social conditioning of the church shows that we are not wholly determined by our social situation. It is inevitable that the church will take its colouring from the society in which it exists. Our task must be to become aware of this and to be constantly on the alert to judge the church's being and life by the standard of the gospel" (A.T. Hanson and R.P.C. Hanson, *The Identity of the Church: A Guide to Recognizing the Contemporary Church* [London: SCM, 1987], 64–65).

74. Hudson, *American Protestantism*, 33–34.

75. Richey's observations here are well put: "There is a curious irony to denominationalism and to the history of many denominations. Denominational-ism has become a synonym for division, schism, even ethical failure, a scandal to the church, as H. Richard Niebuhr observed. Never has Christianity been so fragmented. On the other hand, despite the diversity there are unitive features to denominations and denominationalism. Many of the denominations were by origin and at points along the way actually movements committed to Christian unity" (Richey, " 'Catholic' Protestantism," 213–31).

76. Hudson, "Denominationalism," 32. Again, in his later work on American Protestantism, he writes: "A 'sect' claims the authority of Christ for itself alone. By definition a sect is exclusive—separate. The word 'denomination,' on the other hand, is an inclusive term—an ecumenical term. It implies that the group referred to is but one member, called or denominated by a particular name, of a larger group—the Church—to which all denominations belong. The basic contention of the denominational theory of the Church is that the true Church is not to be identified exclusively with any single ecclesiastical structure. No denomination claims to represent the whole Church of Christ. No denomination claims that all other churches are false churches. Each denomination is regarded as constituting a different 'mode' of expressing in the outward forms of worship and organization that larger life of the Church in which they all share" (Hudson, *American Protestantism,* 34). A contrary opinion is that often given in sociological rather than theological terms, following Ernst Troeltsch's sociological study (1912/1931). In this conception, a denomination is a universal body into which all people are born. To him a sect is a group which renounces the world, has a voluntary membership, insists that its members experience a new birth and practice holiness, and are dominated by lay leadership. See D.O. Moberg, "Denominationalism," in *DCC,* 350. This model, however, confuses sociological phenomena with theological and historical definition. The denomination in this model really is defined in territorial European terms only rather than organizational or theological terms, and contrary to the intent of the real architects of denominational theory as noted above. And the sect, with its negative connotations, is (on this definition) an appropriate definition of highly interdenominational and catholic groups of genuine believers. It is unfortunate, in this sense, that Elmer Towns argues (following Troeltsch and Moberg's lead) that denominationalism is a negative factor and that sects are positive factors. Fundamentalists, he argues, are appropriately labeled "sects" in the sociological sense, and the true basis for the growth of the church in their independent megachurches. This is sad to see, since it runs against the biblical and historical model of the church catholic by deriding the historic understanding of denominationalism. It follows an older European definition of "sect" and "denomination" that is unfamiliar with historic denominational theory, particularly as it applies to the American scene. See Elmer L. Towns, *Is the Day of the Denomination Dead?* (Nashville: Nelson, 1973). Far better to follow Hudson: Denomination historically means a subset of the church catholic; sect is a denial of the church catholic.

77. This will be discussed in more detail in the next chapter. Hanson and Hanson are surely right when they note the following: "Any Christians who for any reasons cut themselves off from their fellow-Christians in order to form tight little groups, whether they call themselves Gospel Hall Christians or Pentecostals, or Continuing Anglican or simply Catholics, are likely to have a defective doctrine of the church and be lacking in orthodoxy" (Hanson and Hanson, *The Identity of the Church,* 81).

78. Earle E. Cairns, *Christianity in the United States* (Chicago: Moody, 1964), 70.

79. Loetscher, "The Problem of Christian Unity," 6, notes three types: (1)

the proposal for federative action, in which each denomination would unite federatively and confirm a twelve-point creed of essential doctrines, while retaining their own denominational doctrine, polity, and worship; (2) organic union, in which all the denominations unite organizationally on the basis of a minimum of core doctrines; and (3) cooperative interdenominational unity on the basis of voluntary societies made up of individual Christians. The final model won out and allowed denominations to retain their structures and distinctives, and allow for support and cooperation between them.

80. Ibid., 7.

81. The Southern Baptist Convention formed over the slavery issue in 1845. That same year saw the formation among the Methodists of the Methodist Episcopal Church, South. In 1843, the Wesleyan Methodist Church was formed in New York in opposition to slavery. The Presbyterians underwent several splits and schisms over these issues, until in 1864 the Presbyterian Church in the Confederate States merged with the Southern Presbyterian groups that had split earlier.

82. A contemporary critic, Presbyterian J. Gresham Machen, wrote *Christianity and Liberalism* in 1923 to argue that liberalism and historic evangelical Christianity were two entirely different religions.

83. The "social gospel" is often connected with Walter Rauschenbush (1861-1918), a Baptist pastor who became deeply concerned for the socially and economically disadvantaged in New York. He wrote *Prayers of the Social Awakening* (1910), *Christianizing the Social Order* (1912), and *A Theology for the Social Gospel* (1917).

84. Liberalism was something completely new, a philosophical shift to a sort of existentialism that used Christian terminology. It is interesting at this point to note Webber's comment about the paradigm shift in liberalism: "I can affirm the evangelical nature of any one of the many different sociological groupings of twentieth-century evangelicals, the evangelical nature of the Reformers, and the evangelical basis of Catholic or Orthodox theology. The only groups within Christian history that are not evangelical at bottom are those who deny apostolic Christianity or those who so thoroughly reinterpret it through their conceptual grid (i.e., Gnostics, anti-supernatural liberals) that it ceases to retain integrity with apostolic intent" (Robert E. Webber, "An Evangelical and Catholic Methodology," in *The Use of the Bible in Theology: Evangelical Options*, ed. Robert K. Johnston [Atlanta: John Knox, 1985], 152).

85. The term *neo-evangelicalism* was coined by Harold J. Ockenga in 1947 in view of the fact that "evangelical" was being misused to describe fundamentalists, with whom he did not want to identify. But it should be noted that the term is only used today in a pejorative sense by fundamentalists to imply a theological laxness on the part of evangelicals who do not follow their separatistic ideals. Non-fundamentalist evangelicals tend to prefer simply to be referred to as "evangelicals." See Harold J. Ockenga, "From Fundamentalism, Through New Evangelicalism, to Evangelicalism," in *Evangelical Roots*, ed. Kenneth Kantzer (New York: Nelson, 1978).

86. Because the term has shifted in meaning from Ockenga's original intent, what he termed "neo-evangelicalism" will simply be referred to henceforth in

this book as "evangelicalism" as distinct from the more separatistic "fundamentalism."

87. Fundamentalists maintain an extensive list of the failures of Graham in this and subsequent crusades. See a "partial" list of his offenses in Ernest Pickering, *Biblical Separation: The Struggles for a Pure Church* (Schaumburg, Ill: Regular Baptist, 1979), 143–44.

88. Marsden's comments fit the picture: "During the 1950s and 1960s the simplest, though very loose, definition of an evangelical in the broad sense was 'anyone who likes Billy Graham' " (George M. Marsden, *Understanding Fundamentalism and Evangelicalism* [Grand Rapids: Eerdmans, 1991], 6).

89. See Robert Webber and Donald Bloesch, eds., *The Orthodox Evangelicals: Who They Are and What They Are Saying?* (Nashville: Nelson, 1978). For the text of the Chicago Call, see Appendix B.

90. The term "ecumenical" is derived from the Greek word οἰκουμένη *(oikoumene)*, which means "the inhabited world." The historic church has held numerous "ecumenical" councils, meaning by that the bishops of the church "in the whole world" were present. But in the twentieth century, it has been used to refer to the "uniting" movements of the church, which seek to bring together churches of various denominations for discussions on their differences with various proposals for union, merger, or cooperation. The term "ecumenical" has often been suggested as the modern equivalent of "catholic," but the modern idea differs in the degree to which an alien liberal theology is tolerated and the degree to which structural unity is expected.

91. Subsequent meetings were held in Evanston, Illinois in 1954, New Delhi, India in 1961, Uppsala, Sweden in 1968, Nairobi, Kenya in 1975, Vancouver, Canada in 1983, and in Canberra, Australia in 1991.

92. For an early evangelical appraisal of the WCC and the NCC, and ecumenism in general, see the classic work by J. Marcellus Kik, *Ecumenism and the Evangelical* (Grand Rapids: Baker, 1957). See also Addison H. Leitch "The National Council and the World Council," 6–8; and "The Ecumenical Movement Today," 3–4, *Christianity Today*, 29 January 1965. Further, see G.C. Berkouwer, "What Conservative Evangelicals Can Learn From the Ecumenical Movement," and John A. Mackay, "What the Ecumenical Movement Can Learn from Conservative Evangelicals," in *Christianity Today,* 27 May 1966, 17–23; Henry A. Buchanan and Bob W. Brown, "The Ecumenical Movement Threatens Protestantism," *Christianity Today*, 20 November 1964, 21–23.

93. The current nine are the African Methodist Episcopal Church, African Methodist Episcopal Zion Church, Christian Church (Disciples of Christ), Christian Methodist Episcopal Church, Episcopal Church, International Council of Community Churches, Presbyterian Church (USA), United Church of Christ, and United Methodist Church. See "What is the Consultation on Church Union?" flier produced by COCU, 151 Wall Street, Princeton, NJ 0540-1514.

94. See P.A. Crow, "Consultation on Church Union," in *DCA*: 316. For evangelical reservations on COCU, see Howard Conn, "There's a Better Way than COCU," *Christianity Today*, 5 July 1968, 16–17.

95. The new phrasing, adopted at Vatican II, is this: "This is the sole Church

of Christ which in the Creed we profess to be one, holy, catholic and apostolic. . . . This Church, constituted and organized as a society in the present world, subsists in the Catholic Church, which is governed by the successor of Peter and by the bishops in communion with him." *Dogmatic Constitution of the Church* 1.8. Some of the later language tries to preserve a degree of the exclusivity of the earlier traditions: "[Christ] affirmed at the same time the necessity of the Church which men enter through baptism as through a door. Hence they could not be saved who, knowing that the Catholic Church was founded as necessary by God through Christ, would refuse either to enter it, or to remain in it." [2.14]. But it appears that there is here an attempt to understand the Church a bit more broadly than has traditionally been understood.

Writing in the *American Catholic Catechism,* Richard P. McBrien, Roman Catholic professor of Theology at Boston College, and President of the Catholic Theological Society of America (1973-74), comments on the Vatican II implications: "[Question 8] *Our understanding of the Church thus far doesn't seem to make room for the special place of the Catholic Church within the Body of Christ. Do we no longer affirm that the Catholic Church alone is the one, true Church of Christ?*

[Answer] The expression 'one, true Church of Christ' is misleading and it should be avoided. It implies that Catholics are the only real members of the body of Christ. . . .

On first reading the eighth article of the Second Vatican Council's Dogmatic Constitution on the Church, it seems that the council is simply reaffirming the teaching of those earlier encyclicals. The text of the constitution reads: 'This (one) Church (of Christ), constituted and organized in the world as a society *subsists in* the Catholic Church' [italics mine].

As a matter of fact, however, the phrase 'subsists in' was not in the original draft of the document. Rather it was selected as a more accurate and suitable replacement for the 'is' that appeared in the first draft. The reason offered for this change was that *de facto* there do exist outside the visible boundaries of the Catholic Church genuine elements of sanctification (see, e.g., the *Decree on Ecumenism*, n. 3). Vatican II was saying, therefore, that the means of Christian holiness are not confined to the Catholic Church, and that *the Body of Christ is larger in scope and extent than the Catholic Church by itself* [italics mine].

One can conclude that the Body of Christ 'subsists' in the [Roman] Catholic Church, but one cannot say, without serious qualification, that the Body of Christ and the [Roman] Catholic Church are simply 'one and the same thing.' Other Christians, who do not belong to the [Roman] Catholic Church, share in the life of Christ's Body, even though the degree of such participation may differ from one Christian community to another, or from individual to individual" (George J. Dyer, ed., *An American Catholic Catechism* [San Francisco: Harper and Row, 1975], 18–19).

96. See the important article by Tony Lane, "Evangelicalism and Roman Catholicism," in *Evangelical Quarterly* 61 (1989): 351–64.

97. See J. Oliver Buswell, Jr. "The American and International Councils of Christian Churches," *Christianity Today*, 29 January 1965, 9–11.

98. See Everett L. Cattell, "National Association of Evangelicals and World

Evangelical Fellowship," *Christianity Today*, 29 January 1965, 12–14.
99. "Principles of Christian Unity," *Christianity Today*, 29 January 1965, 29.

CHAPTER 3: DENOMINATIONALISM AND CATHOLICITY

1. That is its historic definitional limitation. More recent attempts at the sociological analysis of the American religious scene have tended to use the term *denomination* of religious groupings in general rather than of a sub-category of Christian religion and therefore avoided the nuanced terms "sect" and "cult" in favor of "new religious movements." See, e.g., Frank S. Mead, *Handbook of Denominations in the United States,* 7th ed. (Nashville: Abingdon, 1980), who includes as "denominations" such groups as Buddhist Churches of America, Muslims, Bahai, Jewish congregations, and other groups not typically classed as Christian denominations.

2. D.O. Moberg defines a denomination similarly: as "an association or fellowship of congregations within a religion that have the same beliefs or creed, engage in similar practices and cooperation with each other to develop and maintain shared enterprises" (D.O. Moberg, "Denominationalism," *DCA:* 350). Similarly, Tinder defines a denomination as "associations of congregations—though sometimes it might be said that congregations are localized subdivisions of denominations—that have a common heritage" (D.G. Tinder, "Denominationalism," in *EDT:* 310). These fairly uniform definitions differ significantly from the perception of Frame, who would define denominationalism as "sometimes (1) the very fact that the Christian church is split into many denominations and sometimes (2) the sinful attitudes and mentalities that lead to such splits and perpetuate them" (John M. Frame, *Evangelical Reunion: Denominations and the One Body of Christ* [Grand Rapids: Baker, 1991], 11). As noted, this is more appropriately the understanding of sectarianism, not denominationalism. A similar negative judgment is implied in the definition of Morrison: "A denomination is a part of the Church of Christ existing in a structure of its own and exercising by itself and for itself those functions which belong to the unity of the whole Church of Christ" (Charles Clayton Morrison, *The Unfinished Reformation* [New York: Harper, 1956], 56). Morrison's statement presumes that the "whole Church" visible should have a visible, unified organizational structure. Towns' definition of a denomination is somewhat skewed: "A denomination is a group of churches with similar doctrinal beliefs, who have similar traditions and background, who share the same goals in ministry, who desire fellowship to encourage one another, and *have organically bound themselves together* to establish corporately what they feel cannot be wrought separately" (Elmer Towns, *Is the Day of the Denomination Dead?* [Nashville: Nelson, 1973], 49). The italicized portion restricts his definition to what is in fact a "tight" or "structured" denomination. This is not as inclusive as it needs to be, since there are far less structured groups which would qualify.

3. Tinder, "Denominationalism," 311.

4. The term "denominational family" is borrowed from Moberg, "Denominationalism," 350.

5. Goen, "Ecclesiocracy Without Ecclesiology," 272.

6. Robert Webber, *Common Roots: A Call to Evangelical Maturity* (Grand Rapids: Zondervan, 1978), 64.

7. "The ecumenical movement is the movement among the Christian churches for the recovery of their visible and institutional unity" (Barry Till, *The Churches Search for Unity* [Middlesex, England: Penguin, 1972], 15).

8. How that organizational unity is to be expressed differs among ecumenists. E.g., Cullmann argues for "an ultimate goal of all our strivings toward unity . . . a union of all Christian churches within which each would preserve its valuable elements, including structure. Lacking a better expression ('alliance'?), I have called this a 'federation' (in contrast to merger), despite the fact that the word in its secular sense is not adequate" (Oscar Cullmann, *Unity Through Diversity* [Philadelphia: Fortress, 1986], 15). Cullman's model would be much more amenable to a denominational understanding of catholicity, since he does not see the value of an organizational superstructure in terms of preserving diversity: "I resist the idea of merger not primarily because I consider it unrealistic and utopian—which it is, of course—but because it appears to me that this goal contradicts the nature of a true unity. What I propose is a real community of completely independent churches that remain Catholic, Protestant, and Orthodox, that preserve their spiritual gifts, not for the purpose of excluding each other, but for the purpose of forming *a community of all those churches that call on the name of our Lord Jesus Christ*" (p. 33). He prefers a description of ecumenical unity that is a "community of (harmoniously separated) churches" (p. 35). He states, "What we have in common should be emphasized when possible, but really only when possible: that means only as far as the border beyond which there is homogenizing merger and disregard of confessional identity. This border may not be violated" (p. 38).

9. A listing of the North American denominations that are a part of the World Council of Churches includes several large denominations that allow for theological liberalism, such as the American Baptist Churches in the USA, the Evangelical Lutheran Church in America, the Presbyterian Church (USA), the United Church of Christ, and the United Methodist Church. Most North American evangelical denominations have opted out of the WCC due to this. There are also a number of evangelical charismatic churches in the WCC, especially from third world countries.

10. For a classic treatment of the arguments for ecumenism, see Charles Clayton Morrison, *The Unfinished Reformation* (New York: Harper, 1953). Morrison considers American denominationalism a "decadent survival of an era that is past." (p. 13). Although many of his arguments are outdated (being pre-Vatican II), his case is built during the earliest days and fervor of the World Council of Churches and demonstrates the antidenominational bias that helped motivate ecumenists from the earliest days. Morrison's arguments against denominationalism are: (1) they are wasteful of the resources of Protestantism; (2) they are an embarrassment to the missionary expansion of Christianity; (3) they frustrate the efforts and responsibilities of the social work of the church; (4) they rob Protestantism of its strength against a formidable and aggressive Roman Catholicism; (5) they provincialize Protestant mentality by setting up

barriers against the free flow of Christian thought; (6) they breed a subtle moral insincerity among Protestants; (7) they deny to the local church the breadth of status which is its birthright as a part of the catholic church; (8) they condemn the local pastor to adopt methods and appeals which stultify his self-respect and the dignity of his vocation; and (9) they glorify in a false freedom while denying a genuine freedom that is in Christ. For a more recent treatment, Marlin Van Elderen, *Introducing the World Council of Churches,* rev. ed. (Geneva: WCC Publications, 1992).

11. John M. Frame, *Evangelical Reunion: Denominations and the One Body of Christ* (Grand Rapids: Baker), 1991.

12. Ibid., 11.

13. The practical problems he lists are as follows: (1) it weakens church discipline; (2) it leads to church membership meaning very little today; (3) it leads in the church to an imbalance of spiritual gifts; (4) it leads to a lack of common courts to resolve ecclesiastical disputes; (5) it hardens existing divisions; (6) it makes reconciliation more difficult; (7) it creates unholy alliances by promoting loyalty in the face of denominational liberalism; (8) it compromises the church's witness in the world; (9) it leads to creedal stagnation since truly ecumenical creeds cannot be made; (10) it leads to distorted priorities and focus on secondary matters; (11) it leads to superficiality by a focus on receiving nurture from only part of the body of Christ; (12) it leads to nationalistic parochialism; (13) it leads to a weakening of worldwide Christian solidarity; (14) it provides unhealthy competition among denominational groups; and (15) it leads to ungodly pride and snobbery. I would agree that most, if not all, of these problems have arisen in connection with denominationalism. But I would argue that the problem is not the fact of denominationalism, but rather the implicit human tendency toward *sectarianism* (especially in numbers 3, 5, 8, and 10–15). It is sectarianism that is the true culprit, not historic denominational theory. Denominationalism is the delicate balancing means by which catholicity—the opposite of sectarianism—is achieved. Denying denominationalism in favor of organizational unity does not achieve genuine catholicity—only an uglier form of intolerant sectarianism. The other problems listed in denominationalism may be solved in other ways than simply in ridding ourselves of denominations.

14. "It is clear . . . that all denominational division has been due to sin somewhere—either among the founders of the new denomination, or in the previous denomination, or both. The difference between the church and the denominations is indicated by this fact: that the birth of a denomination is always attended by sin, but the birth of the church was attended by rejoicing among the angels of heaven" (Frame, *Evangelical Reunion,* 38).

15. Ibid., 45.

16. I find Frame's comments at this point most puzzling. Although he (rightly) argues that Christ gave His church a government (citing apostles, prophets, evangelists, pastors, teachers, elders, and deacons), he then surprisingly states, "This is Christ's church, Christ's church government. If we do not like it, we dare not set up our own government to rival his. Thus, Christ's intention was to unite all his people under his officers. One Lord, one church, one church

government" (Frame, *Evangelical Reunion*, 27). But Frame, as a Presbyterian, must acknowledge that all churches today must set up their government differently from that established from our Lord, since there are no apostles serving today (or prophets) in the strict sense in which our Lord gave them. Denominations (and independent local churches) make conscientious attempts to recognize our Lord's establishment of church government in view of the changes that have occurred after the first century.

17. I use the term "ambiguous" with careful intent. As noted earlier, the New Testament itself does not make clear a normative form of church government. Hence, conscientious interpreters yield congregational, presbyterian, and episcopal models from the same New Testament data, as Frame himself observes.

18. The body of Christ is not coterminous with even the ancient Catholic Church as an organization. The body of Christ is made up of the elect, the believing, many of whom are within the external structures mixed with those who merely profess or feign a profession, and some are even outside those structures.

19. Cullmann, *Unity Through Diversity*, 29.

20. See the classic evangelical response to the historic ecumenical argument that denominationalism is the result of sin by J. Marcellus Kik, *Ecumenism and the Evangelical* (Philadelphia: Presbyterian and Reformed, 1957). His third chapter, "Is Denominationalism Sinful?" is insightful in this regard.

21. See Towns, *Is the Day of the Denomination Dead?* (Nashville: Nelson), 1973.

22. Ibid., 63.

23. Ibid., 73. Towns lists the following "dangers" of denominationalism: (1) Christians give more loyalty to the denomination than to Christ (p. 73), but this same criticism can be applied to the megachurch; (2) the Christian's loyalty is shifted away from the local church to the denomination (p. 74), but this depends in large part on the type of denominational structure and the kinds of people in its leadership; (3) the control of local churches shifts from the congregation to the denomination (pp. 74-75); (4) Christians in denominations are candidates for compromise (with liberalism) (p. 76), but any Christian is a candidate for this (besides, some sorts of compromise are necessary for catholicity, just so those compromises are not on essential doctrine); (5) denominationalism leads to the apostate church (he argues from Rev. 17–18 against one world church) (p. 77), but a worldwide church is not necessarily an apostate church (cf. the pre-Constantinian church). And a church does not need to be worldwide or nationwide to become apostate.

24. Strictly speaking, many Brethren (especially the "Exclusives," and those influenced by John Nelson Darby's style of Dispensationalism) are not restorationist in the sense of returning to a pristine unity of the New Testament church. Darby's dispensational model convinced him that the New Testament church dispensation had failed and that it was therefore impossible to try to recapture it at this "end" of the dispensation. Instead, he encouraged believers to "come out" of the corrupt denominations and simply gather in "twos and threes" so as to await the imminent return of Jesus. It is therefore more

appropriate to speak only of the Open Brethren as being "restorationist" (in its truest sense) in their thinking.

25. Martin E. Marty, in his foreword to Mark G. Toulouse, *Joined in Discipleship: The Maturing of an American Religious Movement* (St. Louis: Chalice Press, 1992), xi. Similarly, "There are few ecological niches and crannies in the environment that some new denomination cannot be designed to meet. No space exists between denominations in our sociological forms. Start a movement, be anti-institutional, work for 'emerging viable structures of ministry,' try to unite all the churches, and you soon find yourself designated a denomination in the yearbook of American and Canadian Churches. That process gives no sign of diminishing or being ended in the immediate future" (Martin E. Marty, "Denominations: Surviving the 70's," *The Christian Century* 94:42 [December 21, 1977]: 1187).

26. Toulouse, *Joined in Discipleship*, 207–8. It should be noted that not all of those descended from the Stone-Campbellite movement affirmed this development, especially when they saw a theological liberalism seeping in around the fundamentalist era. Around 1906, the more conservative Christian Churches/Churches of Christ (Independent) split off, as did the Churches of Christ (Non-Instrumental). See also Richey's comments regarding this kind of movement: "Many of the denominations were by origin and at points along the way actually movements committed to Christian unity. The Christian movements of the nineteenth century, the most prominent of which were the Disciples—movements dedicated to the overthrow of denominations and the unification of all Christians upon a creed of fundamentals—are the obvious illustrations. Their folly in founding what would become denominations with loud proclamations of the end of denominations is in actuality the folly of denominationalism itself" (Russell E. Richey, " 'Catholic' Protestantism and American Denominationalism," *Journal of Ecumenical Studies* 16 [1979]: 215).

27. Winthrop S. Hudson, "Denominationalism as a Basis for Ecumenicity: A Seventeenth Century Conception," *Church History* 24 (1955): 32–50. See also his *American Protestantism* (Chicago: University of Chicago Press, 1961).

28. Hudson, *American Protestantism*, 41.

29. Cited in Hudson, "Denominationalism," 38.

30. Ibid.

31. Clarence C. Goen, "Ecclesiocracy without Ecclesiology: Denominational Life in America," *American Baptist Quarterly* 10:4 (December 1991): 268.

32. Hudson, *American Protestantism*, 41.

33. Hudson, "Denominationalism," 38.

34. Hudson, *American Protestantism*, 41.

35. Hudson, "Denominationalism," 40.

36. Hudson, *American Protestantism*, 41.

37. Hudson, "Denominationalism," 47.

38. Hudson, *American Protestantism*, 42.

39. Hudson, "Denominationalism," 45.

40. Ibid.

41. Hudson, *American Protestantism*, 42.

42. Hudson, "Denominationalism," 42.

43. For one important collection of studies on this subject, see Ross P. Scherer, ed. *American Denominational Organization: A Sociological View* (Pasadena, Calif.: William Carey Library, 1980).

44. Mormons and Jehovah's Witnesses certainly class themselves as Christian, but distinguish their doctrines from the historic tenets of the church. The tendency to emphasize secondary elements and de-emphasize primary elements and to diverge from historic orthodoxy may be seen in groups like *The Way, International* and the *United Pentecostal Church*, both of which emphasize certain charismatic elements while denying historic, trinitarian teachings. See R. Enroth, "Way International, Inc., The" and E.L. Blumhofer, "United Pentecostal Church, International" in *DCA*: 1237–38, 1203.

45. Wolfhart Pannenberg, *The Church*, trans. Keith Crim (Philadelphia: Westminster, 1983), 65.

46. Thomas N. Finger, *Christian Theology: An Eschatological Approach* (Nashville: Nelson, 1985), 242–43.

47. H. Ray Dunning, *Grace, Faith and Holiness: A Wesleyan Systematic Theology* (Kansas City, Mo: Beacon Hill, 1988), 82.

48. Clark H. Pinnock, "How I Use Tradition in Doing Theology," *TSF Bulletin* 6:1 (1982): 3.

49. Tradition and its inevitability will be discussed more fully in the next chapter.

50. Richey notes that "the denomination is one of the most familiar, enduring, and important aspects of American religion. It is, however, less understood and more maligned than almost any other religious institution. Slurs on the denomination and on denominationalism recur throughout religious literature, made as though they were so self-evident as to require no elaboration" (Russell E. Richey, ed., *Denominationalism* [Nashville: Abingdon, 1977], 9).

51. See 2 John for these fundamental emphases for the Christian life. See also my brief article on this subject, "Initial Theological Input for a Neophyte Believer," *Interest* 41:3 (March 1976): 12–13.

52. I think Frame is absolutely correct here. See Frame, *Evangelical Reunion*, 44.

53. This lack of a bureaucratic center beyond the local church, combined with the tendency to not have a "trained" ministry and its concomitant need for specialized theological schools indicates why the fundamentalist controversy never really hit the (Plymouth) Brethren Movement. There are to this day no "liberal" Brethren congregations: only those more or less favorable to traditional distinctives and the adequacy of their biblical support.

54. Hudson, *American Protestantism*, 47.

55. It could also begin its new congregation if there are not *enough* churches to accommodate the needs (evangelistic or ecclesiastical) in the area.

56. I cannot accept Morrison's argument that "there is scarcely a town or village in the United States that is not scandalously overchurched" (Morrison, *The Unfinished Reformation*, 30). This depends on one's perspective. If one is looking at the number of seats in each congregation and comparing that to the number of current Christians, then perhaps this kind of statement has merit. But if one looks at the number of churches in a given city compared to the

number of unchurched in a given city, the figures would yield otherwise. There is plenty of work for all the churches in any given city, if they will all work together to reach that city for the kingdom of God. For example, in my own city, this would simply not be the case. See some statistical considerations in the final chapter.

57. More will be said of this later in terms of practical assessment of the recovering of catholicity.

58. On the church and parachurch among evangelicals, see for starters, J. Alan Youngren, "Parachurch Proliferation: The Frontier Spirit Caught in Traffic," *Christianity Today*, 6 November 1982, 38–41; Stephen Board, "The Great Evangelical Power Shift," *Eternity*, June 1979, 17–21.

59. Note how even the strongly hierarchical Roman Catholic Church [denomination] since Vatican II has begun to emphasize the value of the local congregation once again. See the *Dogmatic Constitution of the Church.*

60. See the fascinating study of Timothy L. Smith, "Religious Denominations as Ethnic Communities: A Regional Case Study" *Church History* 35 (1966): 207–26.

61. Even today several denominations sponsor ethnic congregations in high immigration areas. On the West Coast, for example, where Asian immigration is at its highest, one can find Chinese Baptist, Christian Missionary Alliance, or Evangelical Free churches, as well as similar denominations reaching out to the Japanese or Korean immigrants.

62. Both elements of the risk of independency are related in some ways. Of the ten largest megachurches in North America, six are denominationally unaffiliated.

63. Although the megachurch is not limited to North America (Korea has perhaps the largest in the world), there are a number of them in the United States alone. The ten largest include: First Baptist Church of Hammond, Indiana, with pastor Jack Hyles (15,000–30,000 members seasonally); Willow Creek Community Church of South Barrington, Illinois with pastor Bill Hybels (14,000 members); Calvary Chapel of Costa Mesa of Santa Ana, California with pastor Chuck Smith (12,000 members); Thomas Road Baptist Church of Lynchburg, Viginia with pastor Jerry Falwell (11,000 members); First Assembly of God of Phoenix, Arizona with pastor Tommy Barnett (10,500 members); North Phoenix Baptist Church of Phoenix, Arizona with pastor Richard Jackson (9,500 members); Second Baptist Church of Houston, Texas with pastor Edwin Young (8,500 members); Grace Community Church of Sun Valley, California with pastor John MacArthur, Jr. (8,000 members); Mount Paran Church of God of Atlanta, Georgia with pastor Paul Walker (8,000 members); and Chapel Hill Harvester Church of Decatur, Georgia with pastor Karl Paulk (7,500 members). See Lyle E. Schaller, "MegaChurch," *Christianity Today*, 5 March 1990, 22.

64. One can detect this sort of potential in statements like these, from megachurch proponents: "The large church has the community acceptance to conduct special evangelistic rallies that attract multitudes. The Thomas Road Baptist Church will attract more to its evangelistic meetings than all of the other churches in its city could gather in a city-wide cooperative program" (Towns, *Is the Day of Denominationalism Dead?* 137).

65. "Voluntaryism is the necessary corollary of religious freedom which, resting on the principle of free, uncoerced consent made the several religious groups voluntary associations, equal before but independent of the civil power and of each other. What the churches actually gave up with religious freedom was coercive power—the revolution in Christian thinking which they accepted was dependence upon persuasion alone" (Sidney E. Mead, "Denominationalism: The Shape of Protestantism in America," *Church History* 23 [1954]: 299).

66. Goen notes that there is much truth in the statement that "the close parallel between laissez-faire economics (capitalism) and laissez-faire religion (denominationalism) means that church life in America can no longer be understood in biblical categories but only in terms of marketplace imagery" (Goen, "Ecclesiocracy Without Ecclesiology," 277).

67. The term is from Goen, "Ecclesiocracy Without Ecclesiology," 273.

68. Ibid.

69. For a helpful treatment of the positive role of the laity in the church, see Robert Banks, *Redeeming the Routines: Bringing Theology to Life* (Wheaton, Ill.: BridgePoint/Victor, 1993).

70. Gillquist is right when he says, "I believe the old Baptist premise that authority can corrupt, and that absolute authority corrupts absolutely. . . . But the opposite is true: Independence corrupts, and absolute independence corrupts absolutely. For such independence promotes absolute authority—absolute authority in the hands of each individual" (Peter E. Gillquist, *Becoming Orthodox: A Journey to the Ancient Christian Faith* [Brentwood, Tenn.: Wolgemuth & Hyatt, 1989], 44).

71. Pannenberg, *The Church*, 69–70. Robert McAfee Brown similarly comments, "In the providence of God denominations have not been merely divisive. They have also conserved things essential to the full ordering of the gospel, and the proclamation of that gospel would have been weakened, if not destroyed apart from their witness. The ecumenical cause will best be served today as each denomination holds up for public inspection, discussion, and possible amendment, its own particular gifts to 'the coming great church.' In this way, the claims, counter-claims, gifts, and shortcomings can be looked at openly and honestly" (Robert McAfee Brown, *The Spirit of Protestantism* [New York: Oxford, 1961], 217–18). And, finally, Cullman states, "Every Christian confession has a permanent spiritual gift, a charisma, which it should preserve, nurture, purify, and deepen, and which should not be given up for the sake of homogenization" (Cullman, *Unity Through Diversity*, 9).

CHAPTER 4: CATHOLICITY AND TRADITION

1. Alfred Kuen, *I Will Build My Church* (Chicago: Moody, 1970), 40.

2. Saul K. Padover, ed., *The Complete Jefferson* (New York: Duell, Sloan & Pearce, 1943), 23. Cited in Mead, "Denominationalism," 293.

3. Marsden, *Understanding Fundamentalism and Evangelicalism*, 81.

4. See, e.g., the intriguing article by Les Parrott III and Robin D. Perrin, "The New Denominations," *Christianity Today*, 11 March 1991, 29–33.

5. Lane states it well: "If we are to avoid an unthinking conservativism opposed to all change, we must also beware of the opposite danger. There are many churches today in which 'old' and 'traditional' are automatically words of condemnation while 'new' and 'change' are automatically words of approval. We must not be carried away by the spirit of the age to the extent of abandoning all that is good from the past, jettisoning the riches of our tradition. Christian freedom towards such traditional practices means being free to change them—and to keep them if that is appropriate" (Tony Lane, "Essential and Non-Essential Doctrines and Practices," *Christian Brethren Review* 38 [1987]: 19–34).

6. Do note at this point that I wish to make a distinction between what I call *macro*-tradition and *micro*-tradition. Macro-tradition is tradition broadly defined, that is, the interpretive tradition of the church *as a whole*, taking into account its full breadth and history. This will be discussed more thoroughly in chapter 6 when dealing with the nature of core orthodoxy. But what is being referred to here is micro-tradition, that is, those traditions which make up the unique interpretive distinctives of a congregation, denomination, or stream within the whole church. Micro-traditions are roughly the equivalent to what James B. Torrance called "traditions" (small "t" and in the plural), while macro-tradition would equate roughly to what he calls "Tradition" (capital "T" and in the singular). See James B. Torrance, "Authority, Scripture, and Tradition," *Evangelical Quarterly* 87 (1987): 245–51.

7. Similarly, the more popular *Webster's Seventh New Collegiate Dictionary* proposes the following definition: "The handing down of information, beliefs, and customs by word of mouth or by example from one generation to another without written instruction." Again, the classic and monumental *Oxford English Dictionary* captures these same ideas involved in the term: "[Tradition is] the action of transmitting or handing down, or fact of being handed down, from generation to generation; transmission of statements, beliefs, rules, customs, or the like, especially by word of mouth or by practice without writing."

8. See Matthew 27:15 (using the term εἰώθα) and John 18:39 (using the term συνήθεια). The two distinct words are from the word group used for "tradition" in the New Testament. For nuances between them, see especially *LN:* 33.226, 240; 41.25–28.

9. For discussions of the relationship between unwritten and written religious authority from a broader religious perspective, see F.F. Bruce and E.G. Rupp, eds., *Holy Book and Holy Tradition* (Grand Rapids: Eerdmans, 1968).

10. John Karmiris, *A Synopsis of the Dogmatic Theology of the Orthodox Catholic Church,* trans. George Dimopoulos (Scranton, Pa.: Christian Orthodox Edition, 1973), 5. See also how tradition rises above the Scripture in this further statement by the same writer: "Sacred Tradition is both *older and richer* than the Scriptures, which latter were written later" (p. 6). Timothy Ware, a well-known Orthodox writer, argues that it is strictly incorrect for the Orthodox to even speak of *two* sources of the Christian faith (Scripture and Tradition), since the Bible is simply a part of, or within, Tradition, and it is Tradition which is the ultimate source of the genuine Christian Faith: "Note, that the Bible forms a part of Tradition. Sometimes Tradition is defined as 'the oral teaching of

Christ, not recorded in writing by his immediate disciples' (Oxford Dictionary). Not only non-Orthodox but many Orthodox writers have adopted this way of speaking, treating Scripture and Tradition as two different things, two distinct sources of the Christian faith. But in reality there is only one source, since Scripture exists *within* Tradition. To separate and contrast the two is to impoverish the idea of both alike" (Timothy Ware, *The Orthodox Church* [London: Penguin, 1964], 204–5). See especially chapter 10. If Timothy Ware's model were viewed as normative here, then the illustration in figure 4.1 would place Scripture in a smaller circle within the larger circle of Tradition, rather than as an element parallel to Tradition. Of course, this is the logical extension of placing the Bible in any role other than the *ultimate* authority in the church.

11. *Council of Trent, Fourth Session, April 8, 1546.* This was reaffirmed by the First Vatican Council of 1870 as well, where the Tridentine statements are clearly echoed: "Further, this supernatural revelation, according to the universal belief of the Church, declared by the sacred Synod of Trent, is *contained in the written books and unwritten traditions which have come down to us,* having been received by the Apostles from the mouth of Christ himself, or from the Apostles themselves, by the dictation of the Holy Spirit, have been transmitted, as it were, from hand to hand" (*Dogmatic Constitution of the Catholic Faith [April 24, 1870], Chapter II of Revelation. CC*: 2:77ff).

12. *Documents of Vatican II,* 58:2.8–9. It should be noted that there has been considerable divergence within Roman Catholic interpretation of the meaning of the statements at Trent since Vatican I in 1870. The substance of this interpretive dispute lingers around the meaning of the original draft of the decree of Trent (April 8, 1546). Records indicate that it originally read that the divine revelation was *"partly* in written books, *partly* in unwritten traditions," but to appease a minority in the council who objected, it was modified to read that it was "in written books *and* in the unwritten traditions." The dispute was whether Roman Catholic theologians at Trent affirmed one or two sources of divine revelation. For a discussion, see S.A. Matczak, "Tradition (in Theology)," in *The New Catholic Encyclopedia,* ed. William J. McDonald (New York: McGraw-Hill, 1967), 15:225–28. The discussion does not materially affect the model I have constructed other than that some traditional Roman Catholic teaching would see not a two-part voice of God, but two separate voices of God. There would be two circles rather than one circle divided into two parts. In Vatican II the single-source model won out. Neither model is acceptable to Protestants.

13. Jacob Neusner, *The Way of Torah: An Introduction to Judaism,* 2nd ed. (Encino, Calif.: Dickenson, 1974), 43. See also Eckstein: "In summary, the oral tradition, one of the principal Pharisaic contributions to the survival of Jewish life after the destruction of the temple, revolves around the written tradition, or Tanakh [abbreviation for what Christians call the O.T.]. . . . The traditional belief dating back at least as far as the time of the Pharisees in that the principles, and perhaps even the content of this oral tradition, while written down in the first few centuries of the Common Era [what Christians call A.D.], were actually imparted by God at Sinai. Accordingly, *the oral tradition is treated as constituting the word of God just as the written Tanakh does"* (Rabbi Yechiel

Eckstein, *What Christians Should Know About Jews and Judaism* [Waco, Texas: Word, 1984], 39). For a discussion about the variations in use of this tradition in modern Judaism, see Leon J. Yagod, "Tradition," in *Encyclopaedia Judaica*, ed. Cecil Roth (Jerusalem: Keter, 1971): 15:1308–1311. For historical evidence that this was the case in the centuries surrounding our Lord's ministry, see especially The Mishnah tractate *Aboth*.

14. One should note that the idea of "unwritten" as associated with tradition tends to lose its strength somewhat as the "unwritten" traditions of these religious groups came to be written down. The notion is useful however, in this discussion as well. The traditions are still "unwritten" in the sense that they are not written *in Scripture*. That is, they are not found in Scripture but *elsewhere* in their current expression.

15. Because much of the tradition is formulated long after the apostolic era, one ends up with what amounts to eisegesis of the text for the sake of maintaining justification for its "implications." Wells noted well this tendency: "What this understanding of tradition really does, however, is to force the vagaries of later religious experience back into Scripture on the grounds that what is experienced religiously later must have been implicit in Scripture in the first place" (David F. Wells, "The Role of Tradition for Pinnock and Dulles: A Response." *TSF Bulletin* 6:5 [1983]: 6). From an exegetical standpoint, the New Testament does display the presence of tradition in the apostolic teaching (cf. 1 Cor. 11:2; 15:1; Col. 2:6; 2 Thes. 2:15), but it is not found in oral statements that were distinct from the apostolic message found in the epistles; it is simply a term for the apostolic message which was handed on. And, since the apostles passed away, the deposit of the apostolic tradition (NIV: "teachings") must find its enduring focus in the New Testament alone. In this sense, apostolic tradition now comprises the Scriptures. Bruce's comments on the 2 Thessalonians passage are appropriate here: "In New Testament times, however, the apostolic teaching was equally valid whether it was delivered by word of mouth or in written form. . . . But when face-to-face communication was not convenient, the teaching was imparted in a written letter. We in our day must be thankful that the latter course was so often necessary; the spoken words have gone beyond recall, but the letters remain, preserving the traditions for our instruction and obedience" (F.F. Bruce, *1 & 2 Thessalonians*, *WBC:* 45 [Waco, Texas: Word, 1982], 194). Similarly, Wells comments in another place: "In the biblical context what was handed on was the deposit of teaching concerning the facts of Christ's life, their theological importance and their ethical significance. Once committed to writing, apostolic teaching itself came to be viewed as tradition, that which was to be transmitted in its purity to succeeding generations" (David F. Wells, "Tradition: A Meeting Place for Catholic and Evangelical Theology?" *Christian Scholars Review* 5 [1975]: 50–61).

16. The "tradition" of the elders here is one of the other terms in the "tradition" group in the New Testament, παράδοσις (the term used throughout this particular passage for "tradition"). The second clause contains one of the terms for "receiving as a tradition," παραλαμβάνω. The parallel passage in Matthew 15:1-20, incidentally, does not include this Markan explanation of the Pharisaic traditional practices, although Jesus' critique of them is equally portrayed.

17. *Corban* (found only in Mark 7:11) is a Greek transliteration of a Hebrew term for "offering" or "oblation." In rabbinic thought, to declare something as *Corban* was to establish it as an offering dedicated to God and thus no longer available for ordinary use. The thing so declared did not necessarily need to be given to God as a sacrifice in actuality, but only in principle. Either way, the item was not available for normal use. See C.E.B. Cranfield, *The Gospel According to St. Mark*, CGNTC (London: Cambridge, 1959), 237. In the example cited by the Lord, it is money that could have been used to care for aging parents that is so designated.

18. The Greek term here is ἀκυρόω, which has the idea of "making void," *BAGD*: 34a, or "to invalidate the authority of, to reject, to disregard," *LN*: 76.25. It is precisely this problem of tradition usurping or invalidating the authority of the written Word of God which goes to the heart of the matter of this particular critique.

19. Lane comments, "The Reformers coined the slogan *sola Scriptura:* Scripture alone. What does this mean? It does not mean that we should use nothing but the Bible—that there is no place for dictionaries of theology and the like. It does not mean that we should learn Christian doctrine only directly from the Bible, which would make sermons and other books redundant. It does not even mean that we should recognize no other authority than the Bible in our Christianity. Tradition and church inevitably and properly function as authorities in some sense. But the Bible remains the decisive and final authority, the norm by which all the teaching of tradition and church is to be tested" (A.N.S. Lane, "Scripture and Tradition," in *New Dictionary of Theology*, ed. Sinclair B. Ferguson and David F. Wright [Downers Grove, Ill.: InterVarsity, 1988], 633).

20. A more formal statement may be found in the Lutheran Formula of Concord, written in 1576. From Epitome 1–2, we note the following: *"But other writings, whether of the fathers or of the moderns, with whatever name they come, are in nowise to be equaled to the Holy Scriptures, but are all to be esteemed inferior to them*. . . . In this way a clear distinction is retained between the sacred Scriptures of the Old and New Testaments, and all other writings; and *Holy Scripture alone* [the Latin here is *sola Sacra Scriptura] is acknowledged as the only judge, norm, and rule,* according to which, as by the only touchstone, all doctrines are to be examined and judged, as to whether they be godly or ungodly, true or false."

21. *DCC:* 201.

22. See, for another example of Reformational thinking on the matter, Article 7 of the Protestant *Belgic Confession* of 1561: "We believe that these Holy Scriptures *fully contain the will of God,* and that whatsoever man ought to believe unto salvation, is *sufficiently taught therein.* For since the whole manner of worship which God requires of us is written in them at large, it is unlawful for any one, though an Apostle, to teach otherwise than we are now taught in the Holy Scriptures: nay, though it were an angel from heaven [Gal. 1:8-9], as the Apostle Paul saith. For since it is forbidden to add unto or take away anything from the Word of God [Deut. 12:32], it doth thereby evidently appear that the doctrine thereof is most perfect and complete in all respects. *Neither may we compare any writings of men, though ever so holy, with those divine*

Scriptures; nor ought we to compare custom, or the great multitude, or antiquity, or succession of times or persons, or councils, decrees, or statutes, with the truth of God, for the truth is above all: for all men are of themselves liars, and more vain than vanity itself. *Therefore we reject with all our hearts whatsoever doth not agree with this infallible rule. . . ." CC:* 3:387–89.

23. This idea will be developed later. As noted earlier, the Reformers' appeal here was to macro-tradition rather than to the micro-tradition of contemporary Roman Catholicism. Lane notes this in the following words, "The Catholic Church claimed that its teaching was *semper eadem* [always the same] and this was an extremely vulnerable position as well as a powerful polemical point. Calvin and his fellow Protestant scholars sought to demonstrate the falsity of the claim. They also sought to show the harmony of their own teaching with that of the early church. Thus, although tradition was not normative, there was constant appeal to the consensus of the early fathers" (A.N.S. Lane, "Scripture, Tradition and Church: An Historical Survey," *Vox Evangelica* 9 [1975]; 44).

24. Cf. Calvin's assessment of the practical implications of the elevation of tradition as an equal authority to Scripture, as it found expression in his day — obedience to the tradition tended inevitably to override obedience to the Scriptures: "Moreover, this evil thing is added, that when religion once begins to be defined in such vain fictions, such perversity is always followed by another hateful depravity, for which Christ rebuked the Pharisees. It is that they nullify God's commandment for the sake of the traditions of men. . . . But how could they excuse themselves, since among them it is far more wicked to have skipped auricular confession at the turn of the year than to have led an utterly wicked life the whole year through? to have infected their tongue with a slight taste of meat on Friday than to have fouled the whole body with fornication every day? to have moved the hand to honest work on a day consecrated to some saintlet or other than religiously to have exercised all the bodily members in the worst crimes? for a priest to be bound in one lawful marriage than to be entangled in a thousand adulteries?" (John Calvin, *Institutes of the Christian Religion*, ed. John T. McNeill, trans. Lewis Ford Battles [Philadelphia: Westminster, 1960], 4.10.10).

25. Note Calvin's title to chapter 10 of book 4 of his *Institutes:* "The Power of Making Laws, in Which the Pope, with His Supporters, Has Exercised Upon Souls the Most Savage Tyranny and Butchery."

26. This will be developed in more detail in our discussion of hermeneutics in the next chapter.

27. The Reformers protected from this danger by the hermeneutical principle of "Scripture interprets Scripture." See, for example, the *Westminster Confession of Faith* 1.9: "The infallible rule of interpretation of Scripture is the Scripture itself; and therefore, when there is a question about the true and full sense of any Scripture (which is not manifold, but one), it must be searched and known by other places that speak more clearly" (*CC:* 3:605).

28. Craik, *New Testament Order*, 3–4.

29. For some works arguing that there is a normative pattern in the New Testament, see Gene Getz, *Sharpening the Focus on the Church* (Chicago: Moody, 1970) and the more recent Kenneth A. Daughters, *New Testament*

Church Government: The Normative Church Government Structure of the New Testament (Kansas City, Kansas: Walterick, 1989). I shall argue more fully the weakness of this position in a discussion of the problems within my own tradition in a subsequent chapter.

30. Robert Webber, *Common Roots: A Call to Evangelical Maturity* (Grand Rapids: Zondervan, 1978), 133.

31. This was an implication drawn by them from Deuteronomy 29:29.

32. For an insightful and honest treatment of this subject as applied to the Christian Reformed Church, see John Van Engen, "The Problem of Tradition in the Christian Reformed Church," *Calvin Theological Journal* 20 (1985): 69–89. Van Engen's comments can readily be applied to other evangelical Protestant groups. Interestingly, Dulles (as a Roman Catholic) makes similar poignant comments regarding the biblical "clarity" of certain distinctive beliefs of Clark Pinnock (a Baptist): "As an outsider to the Baptist tradition, I would have questions about how Baptists find compelling biblical evidence for many of their cherished beliefs, such as the sufficiency of Scripture, the separation of Church and State, and the autonomy of the local church" (Avery F. Dulles, S.J. "Tradition and Theology: A Roman Catholic Response to Clark Pinnock," *TSF Bulletin* 6:3 [1983]: 7).

33. Webber identifies four levels of tradition, which he describes as concentric circles: "the central apostolic tradition, surrounded by those traditions universally accepted and practiced by all Christians, surrounded by those traditions practiced by a particular grouping or denomination, and surrounded in an outer ring by those traditions peculiar to a specific congregation" (Webber, "An Evangelical and Catholic Methodology," 146–47).

34. F.F. Bruce, *Tradition: Old and New* (Grand Rapids: Zondervan, 1970), 13–14. Newport writes, "Oftentimes, sometimes in an unconscious way, *groups are influenced by the founder of their particular group, or by some of the historic creeds. . . . After all, although most conservative groups claim to be under the Bible . . . do they not often times judge what their teachers and leaders say on the basis of traditional and popular views or interpretations of the Scriptures?* A neutral outsider — assuming that there can be such a thing as a neutral outsider — might be excused for concluding that, in fact, *many denominational and confessional groups appear to feel that the view of the Bible and the interpretations expressed by their founders or early leaders are to be exalted (and in some cases almost deified).* A group may fail to note that its creeds and historical confessions of faith are themselves historically conditioned. Of course, the founder or early leaders could have been absolutely right, not only for his own time, but, theoretically even for the future. But should such a sweeping assumption be made?" (John P. Newport, *Why Christians Fight Over the Bible* [Nashville: Nelson, 1974], 14).

35. One of the early Brethren who came under the strong influence of Darby, and who was later to defect from the movement was F.W. Newman. His comments are well put regarding Darby: "He *only* wanted men 'to submit their understandings *to God,*' that is, to the Bible, that is, to his interpretation!" (Francis W. Newman, *Phases of Faith*, [n.p., 1850], 34; cited in F. Roy Coad, *A History of the Brethren Movement,* 2nd ed. [Exeter, England: Paternoster, 1976], 26). Emphases his.

36. Kuen, *I Will Build My Church*, 39–40.

37. That is not to say that these traditions are to be abandoned, but only that they are not to be used as a wedge of orthodoxy to divide other genuine believers from us. Often these interpretive traditions arise from a failure or distortion that had developed in its source-group. Theological dialogue is a key means for working back toward a mean that was lost. When the interpretive traditions at variance with one another do not engage in renewed dialogue, distortion to the other end of the continuum can easily happen, and heterodoxy can slip in.

38. Bruce Shelley, *By What Authority? The Standards of Authority in the Early Church* (Grand Rapids: Eerdmans, 1965), 149. On the same page he goes on to state, "Any religious movement that operates within human affairs and is not concerned solely with individualist mysticism will develop its own *didaskalia* [here = accretion, enlargement, and confirmation of the faith, viz., tradition]. What of Sunday Schools, missionary societies, Easter, and instrumental music in worship services of our own day? Must these be jettisoned as 'unbiblical'?"

39. Webber, *Common Roots*, 125–26. Similarly, see Osborne: "It is common to relegate the concept of 'tradition' to the Roman Catholic 'magisterium,' but this is too simplistic. Every Protestant denomination also has its own magisterial 'tradition,' and in many ways these traditions are just as binding as Roman Catholic dogma" (Grant R. Osborne, *The Hermeneutical Spiral* [Downers Grove, Ill: InterVarsity, 1991], 290–91).

40. Berkouwer comments: "In choosing one source [of revelation = Scripture] instead of two . . . one must also be concerned with the problem of tradition. Otherwise, one would fail to realize that the church, in its relationship to God's Word, has *always been informed by traditions. We never deal with a blank sheet of paper*" (G.C. Berkouwer, *Holy Scripture* [Grand Rapids: Eerdmans, 1975], 304–5). Brown concludes ". . . the issue can no longer be stated as 'Scripture vs. tradition.' This is a wrong way of posing the problem that can only produce wrong answers. The real problem is to discover a proper relationship between Scripture and tradition. This means that the question for Protestants is not, 'How can we get rid of tradition?' or 'How can we set Scripture against tradition?' It is rather, 'How can we employ tradition creatively within a Protestant context?' This is a very different question. To busy ourselves with it does not mean that we have already become crypto-Catholics. It means rather that we have acknowledged that there may be more fruitful ways of understanding the fullness of our Protestant heritage than we have yet explored" (Robert McAfee Brown, "Tradition as a Protestant Problem," *Theology Today* 17 [1961]: 443).

41. Clark H. Pinnock, "How I Use Tradition in Doing Theology," *TSF Bulletin* 6:1 (1982): 3.

42. Van Engen points this out: "We twentieth-century North Americans have on the whole been still less reflective on the relationship between Scripture and tradition. We *inevitably* read Scripture through the eyes of our tradition and find in it largely what we expect: no women in office, strict Sabbath observance, supralapsarian predestination, infrequent communion, and so on. In method and effect this is no different from the Roman Catholic inclination to read the entire papacy back into the Matthean text on Peter and the keys or transubstan-

tiation into Christ's reference to the bread as his body. Like Catholics, we are never so self-righteous as when we are beating some poor opponent over the head with the supposed 'plain meaning of the text' " (Van Engen, "Tradition in the Christian Reformed Church," 72).

43. He goes on to illustrate: "a. *No one approaches the Bible free of denominational or theological presuppositions.* Lutherans tend to read the Bible in the light of the interpretive principle of justification by faith, Presbyterians in terms of the sovereignty of God. The sect groups read it from the perspective of their own practices, which may range from snake handling to speaking in tongues. Liberal Protestants find the Bible a handbook for social justice, while conservatives find it depicting an everlasting hell fire designed for liberals. . . . b. *But our contemporary situation also conditions the way we read the Bible.* Americans in East Lansing hear Romans 13 in a different way from Germans in East Berlin. When Mississippi Senators and Afrikaner nationalists read Paul's speech on Mars Hill, they draw different conclusions about racial discrimination than do natives of Indonesia or Ghana who read the same passage. . . . No one is trying to be dishonest. Everyone claims to be hearing the Word of God. But the indisputable fact of the matter is that Lutherans, Presbyterians, sectarians, liberals, conservatives, Lansingites, East Berliners, southern Americans, southern Afrikaners, Indonesians, and Ghanaians, all read the same Scriptures and hear different things. . . .

"Much of this may be due to faulty reading and faulty listening. But it cannot all be explained so simply. It can be explained only by recognizing honestly that Protestants do not rely on sola Scriptura in quite the pure way that Reformation Sunday sermons would suggest" (Brown, *Spirit of Protestantism,* 215–16). Emphases his.

44. Once again, Lane hits it on the head: *"Our teaching today is not, cannot be, a simple summary of the Scripture.* Twentieth-century theology, even when most firmly based on Scripture, is clearly the outcome of nineteen centuries of Christian thought. But this awareness does not mean that Protestants have to abandon the *sola Scriptura* in the sense that Scripture is the sole norm, the *norma normans non normata* [the rule that rules, but is not ruled]. Development there may be, but *this development is neither normative nor irreformable"* (Lane, "Scripture, Tradition, and Church," 48).

45. Fee states that "coming to the text with our tradition(s) in hand is not in itself a bad thing. Indeed, it is impossible to do otherwise. . . . To the contrary, the ability to hear texts through the ears of other traditions may serve as one of the best exegetical or hermeneutical correctives we can bring to the task" (Gordon D. Fee, *Gospel and Spirit: Issues in New Testament Hermeneutics* [Peabody, Mass.: Hendrickson, 1991], 78–79).

46. Van Engen, "Tradition," 1106. In another place Van Engen had made this clear statement of the Protestant conundrum: "The fact is that we confessional Protestants are helplessly caught in a mighty contradiction: in principle we have repudiated tradition since the Reformation and have no real theological place for it in our self-understanding, but in practice we have been largely, sometimes wholly, molded by it" (Van Engen, "Tradition in the Christian Reformed Church," 69–89).

47. Webber, *Common Roots*, 140.

48. John Jefferson Davis, *Foundations of Evangelical Theology* (Grand Rapids: Baker, 1984), 223. See also Fee, *Gospel and Spirit*, 68–69.

49. Kuen, *I Will Build My Church*, 40. Bloesch notes this tendency well, and suggests that, since tradition is unavoidable, the key is to gain a proper attitude of humility toward our traditions: "Until the church attains visible unity, we need to keep alive the distinctive hallmarks of our respective traditions, but this must be done in a spirit of self-criticism and humility. We should always remember that our foremost loyalty is to Jesus Christ and that when anything in our tradition becomes more of an obstacle than an aid to the proclamation of the gospel of Christ, we must then be willing to give up what had been previously cherished" (Bloesch, *The Future of Evangelical Christianity*, 88).

50. Webber, *Common Roots*, 140.

51. The model of denominational or interpretive traditions is presented for illustrative purposes only and is not meant to be exhaustive.

52. The phrase is κατὰ τὸ εἰωθός. This latter term is, as noted earlier, one of the terms found in the collection of New Testament words for "custom" or "tradition."

53. See Matthew 12:9; 13:54; Mark 1:21-29; 3:1ff; 6:2; Luke 6:6; and John 6:59.

54. See, e.g., the extensive article by W.S. LaSor and T.C. Eskenazi, "Synagogue" in *The International Standard Bible Encyclopedia*, rev. ed., ed. Geoffrey W. Bromiley (Grand Rapids: Eerdmans, 1988), 4:676-84.

55. Cf. Wells, "Tradition," 51.

56. I owe this further example to Mark Porter, "Tradition: Friend or Foe," *Interest* 58:3 (March 1992): 20–21.

57. Read the thrilling account of this event in the intertestamental work 1 Maccabees, chapters 1–4. See especially, for the beginning of this festival, the remarks in 4:52-59: "Early in the morning on the twenty-fifth day of the ninth month, which is the month of Chislev [roughly December], in the one hundred and forty-eighth year [164 B.C.], they rose and offered sacrifice, as the law directs, on the new altar of burnt offering which they had built. At the very season and on the very day that the Gentiles had profaned it, it was dedicated with songs and harps and lutes and cymbals. All the people fell on their faces and worshiped and blessed Heaven, who had prospered them. So they celebrated the dedication of the altar for eight days, and offered burnt offerings with gladness; they offered a sacrifice of deliverance and praise. . . . Then Judas and his brothers and all the assembly of Israel determined that every year at that season the days of the dedication of the altar should be observed with gladness and joy for eight days, beginning with the twenty-fifth day of the month Chislev." See also Josephus' secondary account of the beginnings of this festival in his *Antiquities* 12.7.7.

58. Beasley-Murray suggests the significance of John's record of this particular event: "[In the Feast of Dedication] a great deliverance from an Antichrist and the triumph of true religion was being celebrated, but the frosty temperature without corresponded to the frozen spirits of 'the Jews.' For them there was no sign of the Deliverer, but among them stood Jesus, whom many of the

populace regarded as the Messiah. . . ." (G.R. Beasley-Murray, *John*, *WBC*: 36 [Waco, Texas: Word, 1987], 173).

59. One author argues, "[Paul] implacably set his face against any move to circumcise Gentile believers like Titus (Gal. 2:3-5), but Timothy was in a different situation. For Paul, circumcision in itself was *a matter of indifference* (Gal. 5:6; 6:15); only when it was regarded as a condition of acceptance with God did it involve a lapse from grace and the obligation to keep the whole law of Moses (Gal. 5:3-4)" (F.F. Bruce, *The Book of Acts*, rev. ed., *NICNT* [Grand Rapids: Eerdmans, 1988], 304).

60. Haenchen summarizes the nature of these purification rites which Paul freely participated in: "The period of their [the four poor Nazarites in the Jerusalem Christian community] Nazarite vow had already elapsed. The expense, which they could not afford, was to be assumed by Paul (the assumption of such expense counted as a pious deed); he had only to report this to the priest concerned and agree upon the time of absolution. Since Paul had come from abroad, he was however considered as levitically unclean. He had therefore first to regain levitical purity by a purification ritual. This consisted of being sprinkled with the water of atonement on the third and seventh day after reporting to the priest. Only when he was levitically clean could Paul be present at the absolution ceremony of the four, which took place in the 'holy place' " (Ernst Haenchen, *The Acts of the Apostles: A Commentary* [Oxford: Basil Blackwell], 612).

61. Bruce's comment here is to the point: "Paul's position in such matters is fairly clear from his letters. The circumcising of Gentile converts as a kind of insurance policy, lest faith in Christ should be insufficient in itself, he denounced as a departure from the purity of the gospel (Gal. 5:2-4). *But in itself circumcision was a matter of indifference; it made no difference to one's status in God's sight* (Gal. 5:6; 6:15). If a Jewish father, after he became a follower of Jesus, wished to have his son circumcised in accordance with ancestral custom, Paul had no objection" (F.F. Bruce, *Acts*, 405–6).

62. A parallel situation today exists in the various messianic Jewish congregations, where numerous Jewish customs continue to be practiced and enjoyed *as customs* and not as part of the Gospel requirement.

63. Cranfield concludes regarding Romans 14–15, that "the weakness of the weak consisted in a continuing concern with literal obedience of the ceremonial part of the Old Testament law, though one that was very different from that of the Judaizers of Galatians. The Judaizers of Galatians were legalists who imagined that they could put God under obligation by their obedience and insisted on the literal fulfillment of the ceremonial part of the law as necessary for salvation. With such legalism Paul could not compromise. But the possibility which we have in mind here is that the weak, while neither thinking they were putting God in their debt by their obedience nor yet deliberately trying to force all other Christians to conform to their pattern, felt that, as far as they themselves were concerned, they could not with a clear conscience give up the observance of such requirements of the law as the distinction between clean and unclean foods, the avoidance of blood, the keeping of the Sabbath and other special days" (C.E.B. Cranfield, *A Critical and Exegetical Commentary on*

The Epistle to the Romans, vol. 2, *ICC* [Edinburgh: T & T Clark, 1979], 694–95).

64. It should be noted that the radical reformers (Anabaptists) and Zwingli differed from Luther on these matters. For them, all that pertained to doctrine and practice that was not directly ordered by Scripture was to be rejected. To Luther, only doctrine and practices directly *condemned* by Scripture were to be rejected. Cf. Kuen, *I Will Build My Church,* 228; Wells, "Tradition," 56.

65. The term is Greek: ἀδιάφορα (the plural form of ἀδιάφορον), which means "indifferent things," or "things neither good nor bad." See Henry George Liddell and Robert Scott, *A Greek-English Lexicon,* 9th ed. (Oxford: Clarendon, 1940): 226-23a.

66. *Augsburg Confession,* Article VII. *CC:* 3:12. See also Melanchthon's distinction: "There are some traditions that can be kept without doing any sin, such as those that have been instituted about vestments or foods or similar minor matters. It is enough to feel about them as the Gospel says—when kept, they do not justify. Nor do they do any harm when neglected. . . . There are, indeed, other traditions which cannot be kept without sin. And of this kind is that unclean celibacy so cruelly and wickedly demanded by the pope. But Christ denies that celibacy is given to all. And Paul has written that it is better to marry than to burn. . . . For no human tradition can be instituted *against* the Word of God" (Philip Melanchthon, *Summary of Doctrine,* trans. Charles Leander Hill in Elmer E. Flack and Lowell Satre, eds., *Melanchthon: Selected Writings* [Minneapolis: Augsburg, 1962], 99).

67. See, e.g., Luther's retention of so many elements of the mass which were not contrary to the Word of God in "Concerning the Order of Public Worship" (Spring 1523) and "An Order of Mass and Communion for the Church at Wittenberg" (late 1523). Timothy F. Lull, ed., *Martin Luther's Basic Theological Writings* (Minneapolis: Fortress, 1989), 445–70. See also in this regard Paul D.L. Avis, *The Church in the Theology of the Reformers* (Atlanta: John Knox, 1981). Some Protestant groups are beginning to (or historically have) stress(ed) the value of tradition as a means of appropriating or mediating the authoritative Word. Modern Lutheran theology utilizes what they call the "Lutheran Trilateral" with Scripture as the primary source for doing theology, and with reason and experience (subdivided as Personal and Corporate [=tradition]) the two other points, but secondary in function. See Duane W.H. Arnold and C. George Fry, *The Way, the Truth, and the Life: An Introduction to Lutheran Christianity* (Grand Rapids: Baker, 1982), 48. Traditional Wesleyan Methodism (and its historical derivatives) added to the Anglican notion of Scripture/ Reason/ Tradition the notion of Experience to form what is known as the "Wesleyan Quadrilateral," a diamond shaped model with Scripture at the apex, flanked by reason and experience, and leading to tradition. See, in this regard, H. Ray Dunning, *Grace, Faith and Holiness: A Wesleyan Systematic Theology* (Kansas City, Mo.: Beacon Hill, 1988), 77ff. See also Donald A.D. Thorsen, *The Wesleyan Quadrilateral* (Grand Rapids: Zondervan, 1990).

68. Lane, "Scripture, Tradition and Church: An Historical Survey," 42. He later comments: "Tradition had in a sense been desacralized [by the Reformers]. . . . *But in practice he was very concerned with tradition.* His greatest need was to establish his pedigree: had the whole church erred for more than a

thousand years? Calvin and his fellow Protestant scholars sought to demonstrate the falsity of the claim. They also sought to show the harmony of their own teaching with that of the early church. *Thus, although tradition was not normative, there was constant appeal to the consensus of the early fathers"* (pp. 44–45). This is what I have called earlier an appeal to macro-tradition.

69. Cf. the Lutheran *Formula of Concord,* Epitome 2. "And inasmuch as immediately after the times of the Apostles, nay, even while they were yet alive, false teachers and heretics arose, against whom in the primitive Church symbols were composed, that is to say, brief and explicit confessions, which contained the unanimous consent of the Catholic Christian faith, and the confession of the orthodox and true Church (such as are the Apostles', the Nicene, and the Athanasian Creeds): we publicly profess that we embrace them, and reject all heresies and all dogmas which have ever been brought into the Church of God contrary to their decision" (*CC:* 3:94-95).

70. See Pinnock, "How I Use Tradition," for a clear discussion on these distinctions. See also Lane, "Scripture, Tradition and Church," 48. Silva makes a good point here: "The Reformers opposed the authority of tradition and of the church, but *only insofar as this authority usurped the authority of Scripture.* They never rejected the value of the church's exegetical tradition when it was used in submission to the Scriptures. . . . It is clear, then, that the Reformation marked a break with the *abuse of* tradition but not with tradition itself" (Moisés Silva, *Has the Church Misread the Bible? The History of Interpretation in the Light of Current Issues* [Grand Rapids: Zondervan, 1987], 95–96).

71. Brown observes: "Recognition of this fact [of our having traditions] will be the beginning of its cure. For once it is acknowledged that our approach to Scripture is conditioned by the tradition and situation in which we stand, then we can listen with new attentiveness to Scripture to see in what ways it may challenge that tradition and situation. In the very risky process of being exposed to Scripture, our own tradition can be made more conformable to it. The mark of Protestant courage is precisely this willingness to subject not simply tradition, but our own tradition, to the destructive and healing power of Scripture" (Brown, *Spirit of Protestantism,* 216).

72. A short clarification is in order here. One should be careful to distinguish between the *value* of tradition and the *management* of tradition. That is, the way a given tradition is handled may cause polar opposite reactions depending on how it is managed (transmitted). The very same tradition can be perceived as what I would call a "hallowed' tradition, or a "hollow" tradition. A *hallowed* one is a tradition or custom in which the rationale is clearly understood. The tradition is acknowledged as such and thereby *enjoyed* for the function it serves. A *hollow* one is a tradition which is transmitted rotely, without the benefit of the rationale. It is followed out of a blind faith and loyalty to the source of the tradition.

Any tradition can be hollow if the rationale and flexibility of the tradition is not understood. And that often is the kind of tradition that is reacted to by intended links in the line of tradition, rather than hallowed tradition. This is true at all levels of tradition, religious or not. The same may be said of doctrine. It is a shame when a good tradition (or doctrine) is rejected because it is handled without explanation and becomes all too hollow. The lesson is clear: one must not use the mismanagement of tradition as a reason for a rejection of that tradition. If the rationale for a tradition is not communicated adequately, then it is the recipient's responsibility to investigate the grounds for that tradition so that it may be assessed in terms of enhancing or detracting from the Word of God. Knee-jerk rejection of tradition, without investigation, is no better than authoritarian enforcement of tradition.

73. Shelley, *By What Authority,* 149.

74. Van Engen, "Tradition in the Christian Reformed Church," 70.

75. A classic statement of these two dimensions of tradition, favored by the Eastern Orthodox, is found in the writings of Basil the Great (ca. 329–379). In his work *De Spiritu Sancto (On the Holy Spirit),* chapter 27, we find these statements: "Of the beliefs and practices whether generally accepted or publicly enjoined which are preserved in the Church some we possess derived from written teaching [Scripture]; others we have received delivered to us 'in a mystery' by the tradition of the apostles; *and both of these in relation to true religion have the same force.* And these no one will gainsay;—no one, at all events, who is even moderately versed in the institutions of the Church. For were we to attempt to reject such customs as have no written authority, on the ground that the importance they possess is small, we should unintentionally injure the Gospel in its very vitals; or, rather, should make our public definition a mere phrase and nothing more. For instance, to take the first and most general example, who is there who has taught us in writing to sign with the sign of the cross those who have trusted in the name of our Lord Jesus Christ? What writing has taught us to turn to the East at the prayer? Which of the saints has left us in writing the words of the invocation at the displaying of the bread of the Eucharist and the cup of blessing? For we are not, as is well known, content with what the apostle or the Gospel has recorded, but both in preface and conclusion we add other words as being of great importance to the validity of the ministry, and these we derive from unwritten teaching. Moreover we bless the water of baptism and the oil of the chrism, and besides this the catechumen who is being baptized. On what written authority do we do this? Is not our authority silent and mystical tradition? Nay, by what written word is the anointing oil itself taught? And whence comes the custom of baptizing thrice? And as to the other customs of baptism from what Scripture do we derive the renunciation of Satan and his angels? Does not this come from that unpublished and secret teaching which our fathers guarded in a silence out of the reach of curious and meddling and inquisitive investigation?" (*NPNF,* 2nd series 8:41) He goes on to give the meaning for these "level 2" traditions. Protestants can acknowledge a place for these two levels, but not their authority.

76. Bowman comments, "The Protestant principle does not mean that all traditions are based on falsehood. Traditions that cannot be found in the Bible are not thereby proved false. To prove a tradition false, it must be shown to *contradict* the Bible" (Robert M. Bowman, Jr., *Orthodoxy and Heresy: A Biblical Guide to Doctrinal Discernment* [Grand Rapids: Baker, 1992], 61–62).

77. On the difficulty of authentic apostolic tradition surviving unscathed outside the canonical Scriptures, see R.P.C. Hanson, *Tradition in the Early Church* (London: SCM, 1962).

1. The discussion of the interpretational legitimacy of other elements of the Christian Brethren tradition will be reviewed following the pattern outlined here in a subsequent chapter.

2. And that is sometimes the case. See, for example, J. Barton Payne, "Hermeneutics as a Cloak for the Denial of Scripture," *Bulletin of the Evangelical Theological Society* 3 (1960): 93-108. But see the interesting example of some who express concern over hermeneutics by I. Howard Marshall on this count in "Are Evangelicals Fundamentalists?" *Vox Evangelica* 22 (April 1992): 18–19.

3. Fee notes, "Human speech, by its very nature (i.e., the use of symbols [words] to convey meaning), requires hermeneutics. When we speak we tend to think it rather straightforward: *my* thoughts, expressed in words common to both of us, heard by *your* ears, and recorded and deciphered by *your* mind. . . . The problem, of course, is that between the mind of the speaker and that of the hearer are symbols—chiefly words, sometimes inflections or body language" (Fee, *Gospel and Spirit*, 25–26). Emphases his.

4. Do note: sectarian (hyper-denominational) attitudes can be found in organizationally independent local churches as well as groups. These attitudes are found anywhere the notion of "I have a corner on the truth" is found, wherever independence is taken over by the notion that I am better because I am independent. See Ken McGarvey, "The Independent Church Myth," *Christianity Today*, 22 July 1991, 8.

5. In many ways, the difficult task of determining what the author meant is "one-upped" by the even more difficult interpretive task of determining what the text, once interpreted historically, means *today*, that is, its application. Here the interpreter's presuppositions all too easily can interfere. Fee rightly states, "The other side of the task, however, and for the interpretation of Scripture the urgent one, is that of relevance. How do these ancient texts have meaning for us today, or do they? At this point nearly *everything* depends on the presuppositions of the interpreter. . . . What the text *means*—that is, *how* it is a word for *us*—that is the crucial hermeneutical question" (Fee, *Gospel and Spirit*, 27). Emphases his.

6. A comment is important here. When we face diversity in interpreting the Bible, several options present themselves in terms of handling this diversity: (1) we could practice hermeneutical agnosticism: the diversity of interpretation indicates we cannot really know what the Bible is saying, so why try to find out; or (2) we could practice hermeneutical over-optimism: the problem is simply one of hermeneutics. If we all believed and practiced the same interpretive principles, then we would have far more uniformity of interpretation and thus practice. The problem in the former approach is the failure to recognize that there is a degree of uniformity in terms of understanding what the Bible is saying on certain core issues (what will be considered later under the discussion of "core orthodoxy"), even though there may be diversity in other areas. Furthermore, the diversity of interpretation in other areas may be explained by other reasons: difference of preunderstanding or training and not necessarily lack of clarity of the text, although the latter may be true in certain areas. The problem with the latter approach is a failure to recognize that other factors

come into play in interpreting the Bible which extend beyond the principles involved: ecclesiastical, social, and political concerns. A better approach is what I would call cooperative hermeneutical humility: There are certain common sense interpretational principles that we could all agree to (e.g., those outlined in this chapter), but at the same time, we must adopt the posture that we can learn from any who differ from our conclusions, as we diligently seek conclusions rather than throwing up our hands in uncertainty.

7. *The Fourth Session of the Council of Trent* (8 April 1546), *CC:* 2:83.

8. Charles Clayton Morrison, *The Unfinished Reformation* (New York: Harper, 1953), 7.

9. For an excellent review of this issue, see Peter Toon, *The Right of Private Judgment: The Study and Interpretation of Scripture in Today's Church* (Portland, Ore: Western Conservative Baptist Seminary, 1975).

10. Fackre appropriately says, "Perspicuity refers to the accessibility of Scripture. The plain meaning of the text is its controlling significance. As such, its understanding is not confined to a privileged few, i.e., ecclesiastical or academic *cognoscenti.* We have noted that both the ecclesial and critical communities do make their contributions, but they do not hold the keys that unlock the mysteries. The Bible is an open book. Here the priesthood of all believers (and thus the availability of the Scriptures to all with the will, mind, and heart to encounter them) is a crucial hermeneutical presupposition" (Gabriel Fackre, "The Use of Scripture in My Work in Systematics," in *The Use of the Bible in Theology,* 211).

11. Protestants often refer to an underlying principle of the *perspicuity,* or *clarity* of Scriptures. This does not mean that the Bible is equally clear in all its parts, but that it is sufficiently clear in its central message to not require a priestly class (the Roman Catholic magisterium) to interpret it for us. See, in brief, Bernard Ramm, *Protestant Biblical Interpretation,* 3rd ed. (Grand Rapids: Baker, 1970), 97–99. Further, their hermeneutical principle connected with this was "Scripture interprets Scripture," the obscure must yield to the clear.

12. Fackre describes the traditional Protestant understanding of perspicuity as "the clarity and accessibility of Scripture to the common sense *(sensus literalis)* of the whole people of God, and thus without dependence on a teaching office, ecclesial or academic, or deferral to the claims of mystical cognoscenti" (Gabriel Fackre, "Evangelical Hermeneutics: Commonality and Diversity," *Interpretation* 43:2 [1988]: 123).

13. Two works which are most helpful as an introduction to the subject are Henry A. Virkler, *Hermeneutics: Principles and Processes of Biblical Interpretation* (Grand Rapids: Baker, 1981) and Gordon D. Fee and Douglas Stuart, *How To Read the Bible For All Its Worth* (Grand Rapids: Zondervan, 1982). The two supplement each other and should be used together. Still of use are Bernard Ramm's classic text *Protestant Biblical Interpretation,* A. Berkeley Mickelsen, *Interpreting the Bible* (Grand Rapids: Eerdmans, 1963), and the long-time classic Milton R. Terry, *Biblical Hermeneutics* (Grand Rapids: Zondervan, 1974, reprint), written in the nineteenth century and still of enduring worth. Some useful, and thorough, recent works are Walter Kaiser, *Toward an Exegetical Theology* (Grand Rapids: Baker, 1981); Elliott E. Johnson, *Expository*

Hermeneutics: An Introduction (Grand Rapids: Zondervan, 1990); and Grant R. Osborne, *The Hermeneutical Spiral* (Downers Grove, Ill.: InterVarsity, 1991). In a more popular vein, the following books may provide a motivational introduction to the subject for you: Roy B. Zuck, *Basic Bible Interpretation* (Wheaton, Ill.: Victor, 1991); R.C. Sproul, *Knowing Scripture* (Downers Grove, Ill.: InterVarsity, 1977); J. Robertson McQuilkin, *Understanding and Applying the Bible* (Chicago: Moody, 1983); T. Norton Sterrett, *How to Understand Your Bible* (Downers Grove, Ill.: InterVarsity, 1974); and the informative book by James W. Sire, *Scripture Twisting: 20 Ways the Cults Misread the Bible* (Downers Grove, Ill.: InterVarsity, 1980). There are other works which address some of the philosophical and linguistic issues associated with the idea of meaning, but these books are more useful for the beginner. Also, some of the newer methodologies which arise in higher critical circles (who do not grant the theological presupposition that the Bible is an authoritative book from God) will not be addressed.

14. Much of what is passed today as a lack of clarity is produced from the historical-cultural-linguistic gap rather than to any extensive lack of clarity to the original readers of the Bible. This will be discussed later in this chapter. In modern discussions what is often called Special Hermeneutics, in terms of biblical interpretation, has often been subsumed under the discussion of Bible *genre*.

15. I recognize that there are other factors that keep us from interpreting the Bible fairly. Political pressure within denominational structures or theological institutions often keeps people from honestly investigating certain passages for fear of reprisal if they come up with an unacceptable alternative interpretation. Social pressures also have a similar impact. But at some point individuals must face the question of whether they, before the Lord, have a responsibility and desire to really find out what Scripture is saying, regardless of the economic and political consequences. This does not necessarily mean that those who have lost their positions or reputation for the sake of a different conclusion on Scripture have come to the right conclusion (the correct interpretation), but at least it may indicate an openness to the truth. It could also simply indicate that one has a propensity for having an iconoclastic temperament. See, in this regard, Cedric B. Johnson, *The Psychology of Biblical Interpretation* (Grand Rapids: Zondervan, 1983).

16. Morgan and Barton's comment is certainly appropriate: "The rules for interpreting all texts, which is where biblical interpretation begins, are 'simply' an extension and formalization of what happens unconsciously in ordinary conversation and reading the newspapers" (Robert Morgan and John Barton, *Biblical Interpretation* [New York: Oxford Univ. Pr., 1988], 5). See also Fee, "Hermeneutics and Common Sense," *Gospel and Spirit,* chapter 1.

17. Wells is entirely right when he says: "If we do not assert the right of Scripture to stand in authoritative relationship to every presupposition, custom, and tradition, every teaching, practice, and ecclesiastical organization, then that authority will be co-opted either by an ecclesiastical magisterium or by a scholarly one. Magisterii of this type may imagine that they are invested with some form of infallibility but time will reveal how mistaken this assumption is. The

word of God must be freed to form our doctrine for us without the interference of these pseudo-authorities. It was for this that the Reformers argued and it is for this that we must argue. It is this contention that is heralded by *sola scriptura,* and without the *sola scriptura* principle an evangelical theology is no longer evangelical" (David F. Wells, "The Nature and Function of Theology," in *The Use of the Bible in Theology,* 187).

18. This is like the Jewish Masoretic scribal tradition. At the end of each book the number of letters, the middle letter, and other arithmetical checks pertaining to that book were copied. Once the scribe completed a manuscript, he checked to see if the appropriate number of items were there. If they were, he felt comfortable that he had done a proper scribal job. If they were not, he had to redo his work to see where he went wrong. Such numeric checks did not guide his work, but helped him assess his work. One could surmise that the numerics could be proven wrong at some point. Similarly, the macro-tradition should not influence the process of interpretation, but they should be used in assessing an interpretation. But at the same time, a sound interpretation may call a given tradition into question.

19. Pinnock states, "Tradition is a defense in the church against individualism in interpretation. It is needed in order to protect God's people from private misinterpretations of the Bible. . . . Tradition cannot and should not prevent insight from edifying the church, but it can and should have a voice in evaluating its reliability. The authority of tradition is one of counsel, not of command" (Clark H. Pinnock, *The Scripture Principle* [San Francisco: Harper & Row, 1984], 217). Osborne discusses this as the control on novel interpretation produced by the history of dogma (which I call macro-tradition). See Osborne, *The Hermeneutical Spiral,* 313.

20. As much as I appreciate the Chicago Call and its tremendous affirmations, I must express reservations about the Call to Creedal Identity section, when it reads: "Confessional authority is limited by and derived from the authority of Scripture, which alone remains ultimately and permanently normative. Nevertheless, as the common insight of those who have been illumined by the Holy Spirit and seek to be the voice of the 'holy catholic church,' a confession should serve as *a guide for the interpretation of Scripture.*" If the Creeds (or anything else for that matter) serve as a "guide," then we are not allowing the Scriptures the implicit authority they deserve. Better to see them as a "check." See the entire Chicago Call in the appendix.

21. This assumption derives directly from the doctrine of *revelation:* in the Bible God is communicating and not involved in a passing on of divine riddles.

22. This development is what led to the fundamentalist reaction in North America. Evangelical groups (such as my own Christian Brethren) which did not rely on formal theological training institutions did not undergo the drift into theological liberalism and hence cannot be classed as fundamentalist, since they had no part in the controversy. Fundamentalist authors who tend to classify all non-fundamentalist evangelicals merely as compromising fundamentalists certainly do not understand the full stream of evangelicalism that bypassed the liberal-fundamentalist controversy. See this tendency in Edward Dobson, *In Search of Unity: An Appeal to Fundamentalists and Evangelicals* (Nashville: Nelson, 1985).

23. I remember hearing a series on the tabernacle done in an extremely typological manner, not uncommon in Brethren circles. The refrain "this speaks to us of" this or that aspect of Christ was frequent in the series. But I must honestly admit, it was hard for me to have a great deal of confidence in the validity of such interpretation. I wondered often whether Moses, or Yahweh the designer of the tabernacle, meant us to understand all the details in His choice of this or that element. The larger view, the purpose and theology of the tabernacle, was lost in the interpretive morass. The Song of Songs is another favorite Brethren typology. Thanks be to God that more sane historical interpretive methods have recovered the chief value of the book for us today: the divine sanction on the human body and romantic love between a husband and his wife. See especially S. Craig Glickman, *A Song for Lovers* (Downers Grove, Ill.: InterVarsity, 1976), and G. Lloyd Carr, *The Song of Solomon: An Introduction and Commentary, TOTC* (Downers Grove, Ill.: InterVarsity, 1984).

24. See the discussion of the psychology of the dogmatic type of person in Johnson, *Psychology of Biblical Interpretation,* 58–61.

25. There is debate over this issue under the terminology of whether the Bible may have a *sensus plenior* (fuller meaning) than what was intended by the biblical writer. This develops out of one's understanding of the New Testament writers' use of the Old Testament. Did they see something more in the Old Testament than those writers meant? If they did, then God could have meant something other than what the human writer of Scripture meant. This idea can be found, e.g., in Wenham, when he states the following: "The Holy Spirit knew beforehand the course of history with its consummation in Christ, and so in guiding the writers he intended a deeper meaning than they understood" (*Christ and the Bible* [Downers Grove, Ill.: InterVarsity, 1972], 103). Similarly, the Roman Catholic scholar Brown defined it thus, "The *sensus plenior* is that additional, deeper meaning, intended by God but not clearly intended by the human author, which is seen to exist in the words of a Biblical text (or group of texts, or even a whole book) when they are studied in the light of further revelation or development in the understanding of revelation" (Raymond E. Brown, *The "Sensus Plenior" of Sacred Scripture* [Baltimore: St. Mary's, 1955], 92). The literature is very full on this subject. From a Roman Catholic perspective, see Raymond E. Brown, "The 'Sensus Plenior' in the Last Ten Years," *Catholic Biblical Quarterly* 25 (1963): 262–85; Rudolf Bieberg, "Does Sacred Scripture Have a 'Sensus Plenior'?" *Catholic Biblical Quarterly* 10 (1948): 195; John J. O'Rourke, "Marginal Notes on the 'Sensus Plenior,' " *Catholic Biblical Quarterly* 21 (1959): 65–66. For Protestant treatments, see Douglas J. Moo, "The Problem of *Sensus Plenior,*" in *Hermeneutics, Authority, and Canon,* ed. D.A. Carson and John Woodbridge (Grand Rapids: Zondervan, 1986): 179–211; or William Sanford LaSor, "The *Sensus Plenior* and Biblical Interpretation," in *Scripture, Tradition, and Interpretation,* ed. W. Ward Gasque and William Sanford LaSor (Grand Rapids: Eerdmans, 1978), 260–77. Vawter is one Roman Catholic who had problems with this notion of *sensus plenior,* on whether a sense not connected to the writer's understanding can be called a scriptural sense at all. See Bruce Vawter, *Biblical Inspiration* (Philadelphia: Westminster, 1972), 115. Kaiser has been a Protestant writer who has steadfast-

ly opposed the notion of a *sensus plenior* as well. See Walter Kaiser, "The Fallacy of Equating Meaning with the Reader's Understanding," *Trinity Journal* 6 (1977): 190–93, and "The Single Meaning of Scripture," in *Evangelical Roots in Memoriam of Wilbur Smith*, ed. Kenneth S. Kantzer (Nashville, Nelson, 1978). The debate can go on, but my point is that *at a minimum*, the author's intended meaning must be our base, a fundamental working platform for validating our interpretation.

26. For a good treatment of these two tensions as the evangelical must balance them, see Fee, "The Evangelical Dilemma: Hermeneutics and the Nature of Scripture," in Fee, *Gospel and Spirit*.

27. Fee states rightly, regarding the epistolary form in particular, "It must be a hermeneutical axiom for the straight prose of a letter that the 'meaning' of the text cannot possibly be something neither the author nor his readers could have understood" (Fee, "Normativeness and Authorial Intent," in *Gospel and Spirit*, 43).

28. One is exegesis; the other is eisegesis. *Exegesis* means drawing meaning *out of* the text (the author determines meaning); *eisegesis* means imposing meaning *into* the text from the outside (I determine meaning).

29. Morgan and Barton are correct when they say the following, "Only the presence of human intentionality, or something analogous to that, makes interpretation an appropriate activity" (*Biblical Interpretation*, 2). Without human intent to *mean* something, we have no basis to look for meaning. Certainly we cannot attribute an alternate meaning for one placed there by an author, nor can we create a meaning for one that was never there. The latter is like looking for some special meaning in a person's name which was never intended by the parents of the individual who assigned it. Their intent in giving the name should be the only intent. For another interesting example of the same sort of phenomenon, see Elliott Johnson's treatment of the variety of interpretations of the nursery rhyme, "Little Jack Horner," in *Expository Hermeneutics*, 7–8.

30. Some would argue that seeking an author's original meaning in the words he or she chose to use is only appropriate when dealing with a *living* communicator. To them once an author dies, meaning is, in some sense, "set free," and the moral obligation to return to his or her intent is unnecessary. See Morgan and Barton, *Biblical Hermeneutics*, 6–13. But, as Hirsch appropriately warned (in speaking of literature in general, not biblical interpretation specifically), "To banish the original author as the determiner of meaning [is] to reject the only compelling normative principle that could lend validity to an interpretation" (E.D. Hirsch, *Validity in Interpretation* [New Haven, Conn: Yale Univ. Pr., 1967], 4–5). See also Fackre, "The Use of Scripture," 211.

31. David Masson, an elder over me at my Brethren assembly in Portland until his death some years ago, used to tell me that unless we are willing to "sweat over a passage," we haven't done our homework. I still pass that sound advice on to my students. Sound interpretation takes work.

32. Occasionally this phenomenon comes up in the Bible itself, just as we find many other typically human language phenomena in the Bible. For example, does John mean "born again" or "born from above" in John 3, or does he mean to imply both by using a deliberately ambiguous Greek word?

33. Some argue that seeking meaning in the biblical writer's intention is a logical fallacy known as the "intentional fallacy," namely, that one can get behind the text somehow to reach the dead author's intention. Obviously, this is impossible, so seeking meaning in the intention of the author is a fruitless task. See Philip B. Payne, "The Fallacy of Equating Meaning with the Human Author's Intention," *Journal of the Evangelical Theological Society* 20 (1977): 243–52. But those who argue for the necessity of finding meaning in the human writer's intention do so *only as that intention is expressed in the text*. See the extensive treatment of this older understanding of authorial intention in Johnson, *Expository Hermeneutics*, chapter 2, and his "Author's Intention and Biblical Interpretation," in *Hermeneutics, Inerrancy, and the Bible*, ed. Earl D. Radmacher and Robert D. Preus (Grand Rapids: Zondervan, 1984): 409–29.

34. The idea of "normal" as the meaning of "literal" was suggested by Craven's editorial footnote comment in John Peter Lange, *Commentary on the Holy Scriptures*, 12 vols., trans. Philip Schaff (Grand Rapids: Zondervan, 1960 reprint), 12:98. This is the intent of the Reformer's emphasis against allegory as a method of interpretation as opposed to seeking the author's language in its normal sense: "After 1517, when Luther definitely broke with the Roman church, he ceased to make use of allegorization, and insisted on the necessity of 'one simple solid sense' for the arming of theologians against Satan. He admits the existence of allegories in Scripture, but they are to be found only where the various authors intended them" (Robert Grant, with David Tracy, *A Short History of the Interpretation of the Bible*, 2nd ed. [Philadelphia: Fortress, 1984], 94). Also, see Ramm, *Protestant Biblical Interpretation*, 121ff. For this original literary understanding of the *sensus literalis* see also Grant R. Osborne and Elliott E. Johnson.

35. The technical terminology for the author's use of common language forms of his day is *usus loquendi*, a phrase often found in hermeneutics books.

36. These are just common samplings. For some fascinating further examples of the richness of English figures of speech, see Robert Clairborne, *Our Marvelous Native Tongue: The Life and Times of the English Language* (New York: Times Books, 1983), chapter 11 "Not Everybody's English: Some Remarkable Vocabularies."

37. There is a timeworn classic of biblical figures of speech that is still in print, and still serves a useful purpose as an exhaustive encyclopedia, despite its sporadic pagination: E.W. Bullinger, *Figures of Speech Used in the Bible* (1898; reprint, Grand Rapids: Baker, 1968).

38. See Francis Schaeffer, *The Christian Manifesto* (Westchester, Ill.: Crossway, 1981) for some illuminating remarks in this regard.

39. See Colson's interesting comments in this regard in the conflict between Attorney General Edwin Meese and Supreme Court Justice William Brennan. Meese championed "jurisprudence of the original intention," similarly the ill-fated Judge Bork. Charles Colson, "Is the Constitution Out of Date?" *Christianity Today*, 6 August 1986, 48.

40. See D.A. Carson, *Exegetical Fallacies* (Grand Rapids: Baker, 1984), 20–22.

41. Silva, *Has the Church Misread the Bible?* 89.

42. They *are* found in the symbolic language in Daniel 11. But (granted the exilic production of the Book of Daniel), none of the canonical Old Testament books were produced during the Greek or Hasmonean regimes.

43. One of the best treatments of biblical cultural practices, at least for the Old Testament, is Roland de Vaux, *Ancient Israel: Volume I Social Institutions* (New York: McGraw-Hill, 1965). For material culture, there are many good works of late on biblical archaeology. For good introductions, you may wish to consult K.A. Kitchen, *The Bible in its World: The Bible and Archaeology Today* (Downers Grove, Ill.: InterVarsity, 1977), and Jack P. Lewis, *Archaeological Backgrounds to Bible People* (Grand Rapids: Baker, 1971).

44. How often does the "armor of God" in Ephesians 6 first represent in a new reader's perception the Western conception of medieval armor, rather than what Paul had in mind? Another example of this phenomenon of transposing the meaning of modern material culture backward is in medieval art on biblical themes. The material culture of the period (clothing, tables and chairs, buildings, weapons, etc.), is regularly depicted in contemporary medieval terms rather than historical terms. And I do not think it was deliberate stylization. It more likely was simply a lack of familiarity with archaeological knowledge of the material remains of those ancient cultures and their differences.

45. English poetry has a penchant for rhyme, e.g., "There are strange things done in the midnight sun" (Robert Service). Hebrew poetry has a penchant for parallel ideas: "Lord, who may dwell in your sanctuary?//Who may live on your holy hill?" (Ps. 15:1) For popular introductory works on Hebrew poetry, see Tremper Longman III, *How to Read the Psalms* (Downers Grove, Ill.: InterVarsity, 1988). Similarly, for the poetry in Proverbs, see William E. Mouser, Jr., *Walking in Wisdom: Studying the Proverbs of Solomon* (Downers Grove, Ill.: InterVarsity, 1983).

46. Two of the best introductory treatments on the subject are Fee and Stuart, *How to Read the Bible for All Its Worth,* and Leland Ryken, *How to Read the Bible as Literature* (Grand Rapids: Zondervan, 1984).

47. For a fascinating treatment on this overall subject, see Carson, *Exegetical Fallacies.*

48. What I have called the "negative hermeneutic" is akin to what has traditionally been called in logic the "argument from silence," or the fallacy of proving something from the lack of evidence. This, of course, is no way to prove something. This is, in fact, an extension of the Reformation debate on the issue of "adiaphora" (indifferent things) as discussed in chapter 4. Rather than accepting the Lutheran notion that traditional practices not explicitly found taught in the Scriptures are matters of indifference or choice, too many groups have tended to follow the more Anabaptistic model: if a thing is not explicitly found in the Scriptures it is wrong. This is what I have labeled the "negative hermeneutic."

49. Schaeffer hit on this note extremely well. He writes, "It is my thesis that we cannot bind men morally except with that which the Scripture clearly commands (beyond that we can only give advice), similarly, *anything the New Testament does not command in regard to church form is a freedom to be exercised under the leadership of the Holy Spirit for that particular time and place*"

(Schaeffer, *The Church at the End of the Twentieth Century*, 67, emphases his). His chapter on "Form and Freedom in the Church" will repay careful reading.

50. That is not to say that there is no didactic element in the narrative sections of the Bible. It is simply to say that what is being taught in those sections must be determined from the clearly didactic portions, of which the narratives are often illustrative in negative or positive ways. Furthermore, one might even argue that in those positive sections of narrative (which are not prefaced or indicated to be negative samples in anyway, and which are not clearly supported by other didactic sections), there may be a precedent being set. For example, in the New Testament one cannot find that the local church is taught directly as being the primary sending unit for the missionary. But one does find the description of the Holy Spirit using the local church as the primary sending agency in Acts 13. This is narrative literature. And it is not supported elsewhere in didactic literature. But at least we can conclude that the Holy Spirit *does* work (at least occasionally) through this means. So we may use this as an example for doing such a practice ourselves, as long as we do not limit the Holy Spirit to the means He chose to use then when He has not taught us that this is His *only* means of working. For this notion on the hermeneutical place of "precedent" in narrative literature, see especially Fee, "Hermeneutics and Historical Precedent—A Major Issue in Pentecostal Hermeneutics," in *Gospel and Spirit*, chapter 6. See also chapter 3.

51. Missionary martyr Jim Elliot certainly came to understand this notion in relation to his father's simple, but untrained, faith. He wrote the following to Elisabeth Howard (his future wife) in January of 1948, while a junior at Wheaton College: "I blush to think of things I have said, as if I know something about what Scripture teaches. I know nothing. My father's religion is of a sort which I have seen nowhere else. His theology is wholly undeveloped, both so real and practical a thing that it shatters every 'system' of doctrine I have seen. He cannot define theism, but he knows God. We've had some happy times together, and I cannot estimate what enrichment a few months' working with him might do for me, practically and spiritually" (Elisabeth Elliot, *Shadow of the Almighty* [New York: Harper, 1958], 90).

52. Brown, *Spirit of Protestantism*, 216.

53. I must agree with Hatch: "Whatever our strengths in seizing the moment in God's name, we evangelicals are inexperienced in practicing fellowship across the centuries. . . . By its instruction, history can . . . deliver us from the tyranny of our own times, the conceit that we are necessarily wiser than our fathers and mothers—what C.S. Lewis called chronological snobbery. . . . Exploring the length and breadth of historic Christendom can . . . broaden our thinking in the best sense. It removes the blinders of our own limited backgrounds—whether Arminian, Calvinist, fundamentalist, Catholic, Lutheran, Church of Christ, Pentecostal, or whatever—and opens us to the riches of God's work in other traditions" (Nathan O. Hatch, "Yesterday: The Key that Unlocks Today," *Christianity Today*, 5 August 1983, 18).

54. See, e.g., the "Call to Biblical Fidelity" in the *Chicago Call*: "We deplore our tendency toward individualistic interpretation of Scripture. This undercuts the objective character of biblical truth, and denies the guidance of the Holy

Spirit *among his people through the ages.* Therefore we affirm that the Bible is to be interpreted in keeping with the best insights of historical and literary study, under the guidance of the Holy Spirit, *with respect for the historic understanding of the church."* To their credit, the Christian Church (Disciples of Christ) has traditionally kept the interpretation of the *entire* church in mind: "Disciples resist any tendency toward a sectarian emphasis. Our intention is to read the biblical message in the light of the common judgment of the whole Christian community and for the sake of the whole church. We Disciples did not decide which books belong in the Bible. The ancient catholic church decided that. In their judgment at that point we concur. So we must give heed, insofar as we are able, to the judgment of the best minds in all the churches across the centuries in regard to the meaning of Scripture. . . . The Bible is an ecumenical book. To read it rightly, we must read it ecumenically. When we read it rightly, it will make us ecumenical" (Ronald E. Osborn, *The Faith We Affirm: Basic Beliefs of Disciples of Christ* [St. Louis: CBP Press, 1979], 21).

CHAPTER 6: THE SEARCH FOR A CORE ORTHODOXY

1. C.S. Lewis, *Mere Christianity* (New York: Macmillan, 1952), 6. This definition echoes the catholic notion of Vincent of Lérins, mentioned earlier. Lewis acknowledges his picking up the phrase "mere" Christian from the Puritan writer Richard Baxter (1615-91), who wrote to a critic: "You know not of what Party I am of, nor what to call me; I am sorrier for you in this than for myself; if you know not, I will tell you, I am a Christian, a MEER CHRISTIAN, of no other Religion; and the Church that I am of is the Christian Church, and hath been visible where ever the Christian Religion and Church hath been visible: But must you know what Sect or Party I am of? I am against all Sects and dividing Parties; But if any will call *Meer Christians* by the name of a *Party,* because they take up with *meer Christianity, Creed,* and *Scripture,* and will not be of any dividing or contentious Sect, I am of that Party which is so against Parties: If the Name CHRISTIAN be not enough, call me a CATHOLICK CHRISTIAN; not as that word signifieth an hereticating majority of Bishops, but as it signifieth one that hath no Religion, but that which by Christ and the Apostles was left to the Catholick Church, or the Body of Jesus Christ on Earth" (Cited in N.H. Keeble, *Richard Baxter: Puritan Man of Letters* [Oxford: Clarendon, 1982], 23-24). Emphases original.

2. Thomas Ryan, "Ecumenism and Compassion," *Mid-Stream* 25 (1986): 84, as cited in Cornelius Plantinga, Jr., "Response to Thomas C. Oden, the Long Journey Home," *Journal of the Evangelical Theological Society* 34 (March 1991): 93.

3. Andrew Walker, "We Believe: The Theological Mainstream that Issues from the Church's Early Centuries Provides the Only Hope of Christian Unity in a Postmodern World," *Christianity Today,* 29 April 1991, 26.

4. Doctrinal pluralism is reducing the core of orthodoxy to such a minimal content to accommodate doctrinal diversity, that it can no longer be recognized as the apostolic faith of Scripture. See Jerry L. Walls, *The Problem of Pluralism,*

rev. ed. (Wilmore, Ky.: Bristol, 1988), for an excellent discussion of this matter, especially within the United Methodist Church, where pluralism has been an accepted principle for some time.

5. There is in this statement an important term: shared *belief*. There is, in some extreme charismatic circles, the tendency to look at a shared *experience* as more basic than a shared belief: such as the Pentecostal experience of speaking in tongues. That will not be taken up here in a discussion of "core orthodoxy" simply because that is not a suggestion of shared belief. It bypasses or downplays *belief* in favor of an *experience*. I do not wish here to argue that there is not a *biblical* version of speaking in tongues (there may be). But I want to point out that such an experience can be viewed as transcending and downplaying the necessity for any form of apostolic orthodoxy. This ecstatic experience has been found not just among charismatic Christians, but also among Mormons, Buddhists, and some non-Christian spiritualists. Would anyone want to suggest a core of orthodoxy among all these? See, for a discussion of some of these matters, P. Kildahl, *The Psychology of Speaking in Tongues* (New York: Harper, 1972), and H. Newton Malony and A. Adams Lovekin, *Glossolalia: Behavioral Science Perspectives on Speaking in Tongues* (New York: Oxford Univ. Pr., 1985).

6. *The Works of W. Chillingworth, M.A.*, 12th ed. (London: Printed for B. Blake, 1836), 19, as cited in Richey, " 'Catholic' Protestantism," 223.

7. Ibid., 224.

8. Ibid.

9. For a history of the society and its struggles over the meaning of this statement, see John Wiseman, "The Evangelical Theological Society: Yesterday and Today," *Journal ofthe Evangelical Theological Society* 28 (1985): 5–24.

10. Clifton E. Olmstead, *History of Religion in the United States* (Englewood Cliffs, N.J.: Prentice-Hall, 1960), 552.

11. Of course the next question will arise whether trinitarian addition will be adequate to maintain the evangelical intent of the original founders of the society. What if Roman Catholics who believe they could subscribe to inerrancy begin to participate? This is unlikely, but so was the JW concern. Certainly the ETS is historically a Protestant evangelical group, but even the new statement does not identify the core issues held by the entire society, among which are justification by faith and a Protestant canon. One suspects that the core doctrinal statement would once again need to be expanded to include what the group understands the Bible to mean on these matters.

12. Green, "Erasmus, Luther, and Melanchthon," 378–79.

13. Green further notes: "He held that not external organization or ties but continuity in doctrine and practice with the ancient church constituted true catholicity. Tradition was not the norm for Scripture, but Scripture was the norm for tradition. The *magnus consensus* was seen by Luther as a unanimity in agreement with Scripture; faithfulness to biblical teaching was what constituted authentic tradition" (Green, "Erasmus, Luther, and Melancthon," 371–72).

14. *The Augsburg Confession*, Part First, Article 1, and Article 3. *CC:* 3:7–10. See, in this regard, Herwig Wagner, "On the Catholicity of the Augsburg Confession," *Theology and Life* 3 (December 1980), 8–15.

15. Hanson and Hanson, *The Identity of the Church*, 74.

16. The Christian Church (Disciples of Christ) are another group which attempted to implement the "no creed but Christ!" model. Campbell commented: "The Bible alone is the Bible only, in word and deed, in profession and practice; and this alone can reform the world and save the church" (Cited in Lester G. McAllister, ed., *An Alexander Campbell Reader* [St. Louis: CBP Press, 1988], 77). The failure to define what they understand the Bible means had a serious impact on those who shared the faith of the founders in subsequent generations as opposed to those enthralled by the newer liberal theologies. The result was the exodus of many conservatives to form the Church of Christ between 1917 and 1968.

17. R.A. Torrey, ed., *The Fundamentals: A Testimony to the Truth.* (Los Angeles: The Bible Institute of Los Angeles, 1917). For a listing of the article titles for this four volume edition, see the appendix.

18. These five are those enumerated as basic in Jerry Falwell, ed., *The Fundamentalist Phenomenon* (Garden City, N.Y.: Doubleday, 1981), 7.

19. Jerry Falwell has gone on record as defining a fundamentalist as "an evangelical who is angry about something." Marsden accepts this as fairly accurate, but says "a more precise statement . . . is that an American fundamentalist is an evangelical who is militant in opposition to liberal theology in the churches or to changes in cultural values or mores, such as those associated with 'secular humanism' " (Marsden, *Understanding Fundamentalism and Evangelicalism*, 1).

20. An exception to the fundamentalist tension against catholic cooperation appears in the rare, irenic treatment of Edward Dobson, *In Search of Unity: An Appeal to Fundamentalists and Evangelicals* (Nashville: Nelson, 1985).

21. These are the *Council of Nicaea* of 325 (which asserted that Christ was fully human in opposition to Apollinarianism); the *Council of Ephesus* of 431 (which asserted that Christ was a united Person in opposition to Nestorianism); the *Council of Chalcedon* of 451 (which asserted that Christ is Human and Divine in One Person in opposition to Eutychianism); the *Second Council of Constantinople* of 553 (which reiterated Chalcedon's decision that Christ had two natures in opposition to Monophysitism); the *Third Council of Constantinople* of 680 (which asserted that Christ possessed two wills in opposition to Monothelytism); and the *Second Council of Nicea* of 787 (which allowed the kissing of images in opposition to the Iconoclasts). Orthodox scholar Ware states, "These Seven Councils are of immense importance to Orthodoxy. . . . Orthodox often call themselves 'the Church of the Seven Councils.' By this they do not mean that the Orthodox Church has ceased to think creatively since 787. But they see in the period of the Councils the great age of theology; and, next to the Bible, it is the Seven Councils which the Orthodox Church takes as its standard and guide in seeking solutions to the new problems which arise in every generation" (Ware, *The Orthodox Church*, 43).

22. Article 8 of *The Thirty-nine Articles* reads: "The Three Creeds, Nicene Creed, Athanasius' Creed, and that which is commonly called the Apostle's Creed, ought thoroughly to be received and believed: for they may be proved by most certain warrants of Holy Scripture." These three creeds were the result essentially of the first *four* ecumenical councils, noted earlier. Thus, the Angli-

can Church focuses on the consensus of these first *five* centuries rather than the first *eight*. Early Anglican writer Gilbert Burnet (1689–1715) demonstrates the Protestant reasoning behind these ideas: "For the four general councils, which this Church declares she receives, they are received only because we are persuaded from the Scriptures that their decisions were made according to them . . . we reverence those councils for the sake of their doctrine; but we do not believe the doctrine for the authority of the councils" (Cited in G.R. Evans and J. Robert Wright, eds., *The Anglican Tradition: A Handbook of Sources* [Minneapolis: Fortress, 1991], 277). Similarly, King James I declared his allegiance to Anglican understanding by affirming these four councils.

23. Lutherans also adopt the Apostles' Creed, the Nicene Creed, and the Athanasian Creed in their liturgical formulas as those which express best the thinking of the great Christological Councils, which ended with the Council at Chalcedon in 451. Arnold and Fry state, "It would be wrong to assume that the teaching about the identity of Christ was established by councils, bishops, and decrees. The creedal formulas of the conciliar age only confirmed that which was already believed by the majority of Christians. Luther felt that the councils 'established nothing new . . . but defended the old faith.' Lutherans, as a whole, agree with this. If not established, then, by bishops and councils, how was the doctrine of the identity and nature of Christ arrived at? For this answer we have to turn back to the source and norm of all Christian teaching—the sacred Scriptures" (Duane W.H. Arnold and C. George Fry, *The Way, the Truth, and the Life: An Introduction to Lutheran Christianity* [Grand Rapids: Baker, 1982], 86). Luther's own words on the matter may be found in his 1539 work "On the Councils and the Church" in Helmut T. Lehmann, gen. ed., *Luther's Words,* vol. 41 (Philadelphia: Fortress, n.d.), 121.

24. "Thus councils would come to have the majesty that is their due; yet in the meantime Scripture would stand out in the higher place, with everything subject to its standard. In this way, we willingly embrace and reverence as holy the early councils, such as those of Nicaea, Constantinople, Ephesus I, Chalcedon, and the like, which were concerned with refuting errors—in so far as they relate to the teachings of faith. For they contain nothing but the pure and genuine exposition of Scripture, which the holy fathers applied with spiritual prudence to crush the enemies of religion who had then arisen. In some of the later councils also we see shining forth the true zeal for piety, and clear tokens of insight, doctrine, and prudence. But as affairs usually tend to get worse, it is to be seen from the more recent councils how much the church has degenerated from the purity of that golden age" (John Calvin, *Institutes of the Christian Religion* 4.9.8. in 2:1171–1172).

25. This is not to say that the principle behind *sola Scriptura* never existed in the church prior to the sixteenth century. The issue was debated earlier when questions arose over what to do when apostolic tradition (Scripture) came into conflict with church tradition. See Alan F. Johnson and Robert E. Webber, *What Christians Believe: A Biblical & Historical Summary* (Grand Rapids: Zondervan, 1989), 41–43.

26. Hypostatic union is the technical term for the mystery of the union of the human and divine natures in the one person (Greek *hypostasis*) of Christ.

27. Hermann Sasse, " 'The Future Reunited Church' and 'The Ancient Undivided Church,' " *Springfielder* 27 (Summer 1963): 14.

28. The fuller text may be found in *DCC:* 83–85.

29. Now published as *Agenda for Theology: After Modernity . . . What?* (Grand Rapids: Zondervan, 1990).

30. Thomas C. Oden, "The Long Journey Home," *Journal of the Evangelical Theological Society* 34 (1991): 85.

31. The first volume is entitled *The Living God: Systematic Theology* (New York: Harper, 1987). The second volume is entitled *The Word of Life: Systematic Theology* (New York: Harper, 1989). The third and final volume is entitled *Life in the Spirit: Systematic Theology* (New York: Harper, 1991).

32. Oden, "Long Journey Home," 79–80.

33. Ibid., 82.

34. Plantinga, "Response," 95.

35. For an Orthodox critique of this canon, using many similar arguments as mine, see George Florovsky, *Bible, Church, Tradition: An Eastern Orthodox View* (Vaduz, Europa: Büchervertriebanstalt, 1987), 51–54.

36. Avis, *The Church in the Theology,* 127–28.

37. See Webber, *Common Roots.*

38. Alan K. Scholes and Stephen M. Clinton, "Levels of Belief in the Pauline Epistles: A Paradigm for Evangelical Unity," *Bulletin of the Evangelical Philosophical Society* 14:2 (1991): 75.

39. Frame, *Evangelical Reunion,* 96.

40. See also Joel R. Parkinson, *Orthodoxy and Heresy: Where to Draw the Line* (Shippensburg, Pa: Companion Press, 1991). Parkinson writes, "Orthodoxy is that system of beliefs or truths all of which (nothing more and nothing less) is necessary to scripturally, systematically and consistently maintain the basis and content of the true Gospel and way of salvation" (p. 4). I agree with Parkinson's definition, but would organize and handle his "system of truths" somewhat differently. Some are presuppositions to the Gospel, and some are implications of the Gospel. In his work on the same subject, Bowman classes the Gospel as one of several principles, but does include it in his definition of orthodoxy as the Evangelical Principle: " . . . whatever is contrary to the Gospel of Jesus Christ is to be rejected as heresy" (Robert M. Bowman, Jr. *Orthodoxy and Heresy: A Biblical Guide to Doctrinal Discernment* [Grand Rapids: Baker, 1992], 63). His other principles are the Protestant Principle (the priority of Scripture), the Orthodox Principle (the creeds of the undivided church), and the Catholic Principle (the importance of that which the church as a whole believes). In my discussion, I will argue that the Protestant Principle is an undergirding apostolicity to the Gospel, and the Orthodox Principle is really a developed, "sustaining" orthodoxy rather than a "saving," core orthodoxy. I have discussed the weakness of the Catholic Principle under the Vincentian canon.

41. Similar descriptions of evangelical faith may be found in others. Bloesch, for example, states, "The key to evangelical unity lies in a common commitment to Jesus Christ as the divine Savior from sin, a common purpose to fulfill the great commission and a common acknowledgement of the absolute normativeness of Holy Scripture" (Bloesch, *The Future of Evangelical Christianity,* 5–6).

Smith similarly observes, "From that day to this, these three characteristics have defined evangelicalism in the English speaking world: the Bible is its authority, the new birth its hallmark, and evangelism its mission" (Timothy L. Smith, "The Evangelical Kaleidoscope and the Call to Christian Unity," *Christian Scholars Review* 15 [1986]: 127). Others argue for the evangelical faith containing corollaries besides these, and would tighten some of these up. Montgomery, for example, argues this way, "To my way of thinking, 'evangelicals' are bound together not by virtue of being members of the same confessional stream, but by their firm adherence to certain common theological tenets and emphases. These latter would summarize as follows: (1) Conviction that the Bible alone is God's objectively inerrant revelation to man; (2) Subscription to the Ecumenical creeds as expressing the Trinitarian heart of biblical religion; (3) Belief that the Reformation confessions adequately convey the soteriological essence of the scriptural message, namely, salvation by grace alone through faith in the atoning death and resurrection of the God-man Jesus Christ; (4) Stress upon personal, dynamic, living commitment to Christ and resultant prophetic witness for Him to the unbelieving world; and (5) A strong eschatological perspective" (John Warwick Montgomery, "Evangelical Unity in the Light of Contemporary Orthodox Eastern–Roman Catholic–Protestant Ecumenicity," *The Springfielder* 29 [Autumn 1965]: 9). Marsden argues: "One could regard evangelicalism as a unity only in a very broad sense. Evangelicals might agree in a general way on the essentials of evangelicalism: 'that the sole authority in religion is the Bible and the sole means of salvation is a life-transforming experience wrought by the Holy Spirit through faith in Jesus Christ' [citing approvingly Grant Wacker]. Other than that, they represent largely independent, even if related, traditions" (Marsden, *Understanding Fundamentalism and Evangelicalism*, 65).

42. Bruce comments, "It is the message, not the messenger, that ultimately matters. The Gospel preached by Paul is not the true Gospel because it is Paul who preaches it; it is the true Gospel because the risen Christ gave it to Paul to preach." Bruce also cites Luther: "That which does not teach Christ is not apostolic, even if Peter and Paul be the teachers. On the other hand, that which does teach Christ is apostolic, even if Judas, Annas, Pilate or Herod should propound it" (F.F. Bruce, *The Epistle to the Galatians: A Commentary on the Greek Text*, NIGNT [Grand Rapids: Eerdmans, 1982], 83). For parallel expressions of the centrality and exclusivity of Gospel orthodoxy, see John 14:6, 2 John, 1 Cor. 16:22.

43. Howard, in recalling his free-church evangelical faith, indicates this as well, "At bottom, though, one cannot distinguish evangelical teaching from traditional Christian orthodoxy. We could be counted on to embrace wholeheartedly all that is spelled out in the ancient creeds of the Church. There is nothing in the Apostles', Nicene, Chalcedonian, or Athanasian creeds that we would have jibbed at. We were stoutly among those who with Athanasius, 'hold the Catholic Faith . . . whole and undefiled.' In this sense we would have been more at home in the company of apostles, fathers, doctors, confessors, and the ancient tradition of catholic orthodoxy than among modern church men who look on the Gospel as being shot through with legendary matter. But there is

something peculiar in this way of talking about evangelicalism. Our imagination did not run to creeds, fathers, doctors, tradition, or catholic orthodoxy. When it came to anchoring our faith, we cited texts from the New Testament and nothing else. We never said, 'The Church teaches so and so.' We were not thinking of the ancient Faith or of a long lineage of the faithful when we spoke of our beliefs. Yet there is perhaps nowhere in the world where ancient Christian belief is professed more candidly and vigorously than in evangelicalism" (Howard, *Evangelical is Not Enough,* [Nashville: Nelson, 1984], 3).

44. Evangelicals have moved out of the mainstream evangelical free-church tradition into an amazing number of more liturgical, historic churches not always in keeping with the formal principles of the Reformation. For an account of a man who found evangelical faith outside of the Roman Catholic Church, but who returned to help develop an evangelical renewal within, see Keith A. Fournier, *Evangelical Catholics* (Nashville: Thomas Nelson, 1990). The story of a number of former Campus Crusade for Christ members who moved into Eastern Orthodoxy is found in Peter E. Gillquist, *Becoming Orthodox: A Journey to the Ancient Christian Faith* (Brentwood, Tenn: Wolgemuth & Hyatt, 1989). An account of former free-church evangelicals who moved into Anglican/Episcopalianism may be found in Robert E. Webber, *Evangelicals on the Canterbury Trail: Why Evangelicals Are Attracted to the Liturgical Church* (Waco, Texas: Word/Jarrell, 1985). See also Howard, *Evangelical is Not Enough.* Howard moved first to Episcopalianism and then to Roman Catholicism. One must make it perfectly clear that in each instance evangelical faith was found by the individuals involved *outside* of the non-evangelical churches. Now, as evangelical faith is brought into these more traditional structures, it remains to be seen whether evangelical faith can be sustained by those structures in the long run.

45. Bloesch points out that "evangelicals of all stripes confess to an underlying affinity with their fellow believers no matter what their ethnic, denominational or confessional background. Evangelicalism may indeed be the ecumenical movement of the future because of this capacity to transcend age-old denominational and creedal barriers" (Bloesch, *The Future of Evangelical Christianity,* 6). Snyder agrees, "Evangelical Christianity today is more than a group of theologically conservative churches. It is decreasingly a specific branch of Western Protestantism and increasingly a transconfessional movement for biblical Christianity within the worldwide Church of Jesus Christ. It could become a worldwide movement providing hope for transcending Western evangelicalism's bondage to American and European 'culture Christianity' " (Howard A. Snyder, *The Community of the King* [Downers Grove, Ill.: InterVarsity, 1977], 180–81).

46. "This is how God showed His love among us: he *sent* his Son" (1 John 4:9-10; cf. 1 John 4:14; John 3:16-19; Gal. 4:4).

47. Mark 10:45: "The Son of Man did not come to be served, but to serve, and *to give his life as a ransom for many.*" 1 John 4:10: "He loved us and sent his Son as an *atoning sacrifice for our sins.*" Cf. Matt. 1:21; Luke 19:10; 1 Tim. 1:15; Matt. 26:28; Rom. 3:24-25; 8:3; 1 Cor. 5:7; Eph. 5:2; Heb. 2:17; 9:28; John 1:28; Rev. 5:6; 1 Peter 1:18-19; 1 John 2:2.

48. See the evangelistic proclamations in the Book of Acts: 2:24, 3:15, 4:10, 4:33, 10:40-41, 17:3. See also 1 Corinthians 15:1-8: "Now, brothers, I want to remind you of the Gospel I preached to you, . . . that Christ died for our sins according to the Scriptures that he was buried, *that he was raised on the third day* according to the Scriptures." Cf. v. 14, where Paul can say, "And if Christ has not been raised, our preaching is useless and so is your faith." Cf. Rom. 1:4; 4:25; 10:9; Eph. 1:20; 1 Thes. 4:14; 1 Peter 1:3.

49. "For God so loved the world that he gave his one and only Son, that *whoever believes in him* shall not perish but have eternal life. For God did not send his Son into the world to condemn the world, but to save the world through him" (John 3:16-17). Cf. 1 John 2:2; 4:14; 1 Tim. 2:5-6; 4:10. The message of salvation is open to all who will, regardless of how one works out the divine involvement and human enablement.

50. "I write these things to you who believe in the name of the Son of God so that you may *know that you have* eternal life" (1 John 5:13). Cf. Col. 1:13-14, "For he has rescued us from the dominion of darkness and brought us into the kingdom of the Son he loves, in whom *we have redemption, the forgiveness of sins.*" See also Eph. 2:8-10 and Rom. 3:24 (NRSV).

51. Certainly one must today address the issue of who God is in this "post-Christian" culture. In the New Testament era, particularly in the context of the synagogue or other Jewish influence, one could simply use the term *God* and it would be understood to refer to the infinite and holy Creator and Sustainer of all else that exists, the personal and redeeming God of Abraham, Isaac, and Jacob. But in modern pluralistic cultures a Christian must spend time explaining what "God" means when referring to the term even before saying that God sent a "Son." Note how Paul must fill in the content of the term *God* when he communicates the Gospel to a pagan audience (Acts 14:15-17; 17:22-31).

52. See especially the Johannine literature: John the Baptist, e.g., although older than Jesus, is portrayed there as saying, "He who comes after me has surpassed me because *he was before me*" (John 1:15, 30). Similarly, Jesus there says, "I have *come down from heaven* not to do my will but to do the will of him who sent me" (John 6:38). See also John 3:13, 31; 17:4.

53. See especially John 8:58, where Jesus says, "Before Abraham was born, *I am!*" Similarly Paul refers to Jesus when he writes, "He *is* [= exists] before all things." The writer to the Hebrews as well applies Psalm 102:25-27 directly to Jesus and states, "They [the heavens and earth] will perish, but *you remain . . . you remain the same, and your years will never end*" (Heb. 1:11; cf. 1:1-2; 7:3).

54. John 1:1: "and the Word was God." See also Titus 2:13, Hebrews 1:8, and 2 Peter 2:1. Other New Testament passages parallel to this would be those from the Old Testament where Lord is used as a title for Yahweh, but which are nonetheless applied directly to Jesus in the New Testament. See Heb. 1:10 as but one example of this pattern.

55. John 1:4: "The Word *became flesh* and made his dwelling among us." Cf. 1 John 1:1-3; 2 John 7.

56. See Matthew 1:18-25 and Luke 1:26-35, cf. also Galatians 4:4-5. The connection of the virgin birth to the incarnation was a natural one, serving as the mechanism by which the eternal Son became flesh. The ancient creeds take

this for granted, though today some writers do try to affirm the incarnation while choking at the virgin birth.

57. The Jews took up stones against Jesus because 'he was even calling God his own Father, making himself equal with God" (John 5:18). John records these words stated directly to Jesus later in their attempt to stone Him again: "because you, a mere man, claim to be God" (John 10:33). Of course, John 1:1 prepares the readership for these kinds of statements (the Word was God) as does the culminational confession given to Jesus in the Gospel by Thomas: "My Lord and my God" (John 20:28).

58. Calvinists and Arminians look at this point somewhat differently. Calvinists argue that sin has so infected human nature that there is no ability left in humans at all to even express faith, that is, faith must be granted a person by an electing God or that person would not even be able to believe. Arminians grant that, but question whether there can be any genuine accountability for a lack of faith if this is pressed. They therefore argue that there is a form of prevenient grace available to all men from God which enables men, if they will, to believe.

The Gospel addresses the need-dimension of humanity. It does not primarily address the full biblical data on humanity, which would include issues of human dignity as well as these issues of "depravity." The former must include the biblical data that humanity was created in the image of God (Gen. 1:26-27) and therefore has intrinsic worth, value, and capacities that are unique. The Gospel addresses sin and the need for humanity to be restored to the Creator, so issues pertinent to human *need* tend to be stressed in its communication.

59. The sacrificial practices of historic Yahwism (e.g., Leviticus) form the context from which the New Testament writers understand the death of Messiah (see also Isa. 53). The requirement of a spotless sacrifice brought their emphasis on the sinlessness of Christ. See 2 Cor. 5:21: "God made him who had no sin to be sin for us." Cf. 1 John 3:5; 1 Peter 1:18-19; 2:22; Heb. 4:15.

60. "[He] was declared to be Son of God with power according to the spirit of holiness by resurrection from the dead, Jesus Christ our Lord" (Rom. 1:4, NRSV). See also the confession of Thomas in the upper room on seeing the resurrected Jesus for the first time, John 20:28-29.

61. Cf. Rom. 10:9: "If you confess with your mouth, 'Jesus is Lord,' and believe in your heart that God raised him from the dead, you will be saved."

62. Cf. 1 Cor. 15:20-28, especially vv. 20 and 23, "But Christ has indeed been raised from the dead, the firstfruits of those who have fallen asleep. . . . But each in his own turn: Christ, the firstfruits, then, when he comes, those who belong to him." (See also 1 Thes. 4:13-18.)

63. Cf. Gal. 3:28: "There is neither Jew nor Greek, slave nor free, male nor female, for you are all one in Christ Jesus." This is the result of the Gospel message being offered to all and making them a part of the community of faith. See also Luke 24:46-47 and Matt. 28:18-20.

64. Calvinist John Frame comments on this with excellent balance, "My own conclusion, then, is that Arminian preaching is far better than Arminian theology, better even than some of the worst forms of Calvinistic preaching. If now and then more serious errors enter Arminian sermons, I must be honest and recognize that serious errors often enter Calvinistic sermons as well. . . .

While I would certainly prefer for myself and family to hear Calvinistic preaching (not at its worst, but at its average or better) as our steady diet, I have no hesitation in admitting that Arminian preachers, on the average, do preach the biblical Gospel" (Frame, *Evangelical Reunion*, 135).

65. It is important to note that the atonement was not well articulated in the early creedal statements, with their emphasis on Jesus' identity as the God-man over His work as the Savior (e.g., in the Apostle's Creed it reads Jesus "was crucified, dead, and buried," but omits the critical New Testament datum crucified "for our sins"). But, as Bray points out, "The person and work of Christ depend on each other for their full meaning, and the one could not be grasped without the other. In seeking to explain and transmit this record, the theologians of the Early Church undoubtedly gave priority to the former, and have been accused of minimizing the work of Christ, particularly when compared with the writings of the sixteenth-century Reformers. There is a certain element of truth in this, but two points must be borne in mind. The Reformers would never have thought and written the way they did, had they not been imbued with the theology of the Early Church. They never repudiated their inheritance, but rather saw it as the indispensible foundation for their own work. If there is an imbalance in ancient theology, it was corrected, not rejected, by subsequent generations. The second point is that the Person of Christ is logically prior to his work, and this truth of the Gospel is reflected in the progress of theological construction. The Christology of the creeds and councils of the Early Church is a necessary preliminary to further thinking, just as the teaching of the earthly Jesus about himself created the conceptual framework for what he later did. There is an order in the plan of salvation which is faithfully reflected in the progress of creedal development" (Gerald Bray, *Creeds, Councils, and Christ* [Downers Grove, Ill.: InterVarsity, 1984], 71–72). In either case, the early creeds do not demonstrate thoroughly much interaction with the nature of the atonement. For the centrality of this other dimension to the apostolic Gospel, see especially John R.W. Stott, *The Cross of Christ* (Downers Grove, Ill.: InterVarsity, 1986); Leon Morris, *The Apostolic Preaching of the Cross*, 3rd ed. (Grand Rapids: Eerdmans, 1965), or his *The Atonement: Its Meaning and Significance* (Downers Grove, Ill.: InterVarsity, 1983); and Alister E. McGrath, *The Mystery of the Cross* (Grand Rapids: Zondervan, 1988).

66. The apostolic preaching focused, in part, on the forgiveness of sins available in Christ: in Peter's Pentecost message, he stated, "Repent and be baptized, every one of you, in the name of Jesus Christ *for the forgiveness of your sins*. And you will receive the gift of the Holy Spirit" (Acts 2:38; cf. 5:41; 10:43; 13:48; 26:18). See especially Eph. 1:7 and Col. 1:14.

67. Justification by faith as opposed to works is, of course, a major Pauline theme in Romans and Galatians, and the renewed appreciation of this doctrine spawned the Protestant Reformation, as well as the Evangelical Revivals of the eighteenth century.

68. See John 3:3: "No one can see the kingdom of God unless he is born again" and 1 John 5:1: "Everyone who believes that Jesus is the Christ is born of God." Cf. Titus 1:5 and 1 Peter 1:23.

69. Cf. Peter at Pentecost, "Repent . . . and you will receive the gift of the

Holy Spirit" (Acts 2:38). See also Titus 3:5: "He saved us through the washing of rebirth and renewal by the Holy Spirit (cf. Rom. 5:5; 1 Cor. 6:19; Eph. 1:13; 1 Thes. 4:8; 2 Tim. 1:14).

70. Acts 5:3-4: "You have lied to the Holy Spirit . . . you have not lied to men but to God."

71. The Reformers tended to refer to this element as "sanctification," an ongoing, linear process, as distinguished from justification, a one-time, punctiliar event. Several passages in the New Testament appear to use the terminology of salvation as a process, a linear, ongoing event. See 1 Cor. 1:18 and 2 Cor. 2:15.

72. That is why several key passages in the New Testament refer to salvation as something that has already occurred for the believer. See, e.g., Rom. 8:24 "For in this hope *we were saved*" (cf. Eph. 2:5, 8-10; Titus 3:5; 2 Tim. 1:9).

73. Note the summons to conversion in the appeal to faith in the New Testament. In Acts 16:31, Paul and Silas respond to a trembling jailer at Philippi: "Believe in the Lord Jesus, and you will be saved—you and your household" (cf. Rom. 10:9-10).

74. The Latin phrase means that, unless there is some hindering factor in the life of the recipient, as long as the sacrament is administered by the church it is effective in and of itself—*regardless* of the faith response of the individual.

75. The Reformers made a distinction between several elements of faith found in the New Testament, and drew on distinct Latin terms to identify them: *notitia* (the cognitive element of faith, "belief that"); *assensus* (the emotional element of faith, "conviction that"), and *fiducia* (the volitional element of faith, "trust in"). Saving faith expects all three elements to be there. *Notitia* acknowledges the facts of the Gospel as true; *assensus* brings them down to a deep conviction that affects the life; and *fiducia* is the entrusting of the life to the truth of the Gospel so acknowledged. See L. Berkhof, *Systematic Theology*, 4th ed. (Grand Rapids: Eerdmans, 1941), 503ff. The trust element is what is referred to here, the "belief (trust, Greek πιστεύω) *in*" of John 3:36: "Whoever believes *in* the Son has eternal life, but whoever rejects the Son will not see life, for God's wrath remains on Him." Cf. John 3:15-16, 18, 36; 6:35, 40; 7:38; 11:25-26; 12:44, 46; Acts 10:43; 1 John 5:10. The necessary cognitive aspect of this saving trust can be seen in those passages which refer to "belief *that*," such as 1 John 5:1, "Everyone who believes *that* Jesus is the Christ is born of God" (cf. 1 John 5:5).

76. The phrase of Martin Luther maintains the Reformation balance: "Works are not taken into consideration when the question respects justification. But true faith will no more fail to produce them than the sun can cease to give light." The Latin phrase favored by the Reformers was *Sola fides justificat, sed non fides quae est sola,* "Faith alone justifies, but not faith which is alone," or, more popularly, "It is faith alone that saves, but the faith that saves is never alone." I will not enter into the current Lordship salvation debate; I find too much imbalance in both positions. I would agree with the assessment of the debate by S. Lewis Johnson, Jr., "How Faith Works," *Christianity Today* 22 September 1989, 21–25.

77. This would also square with missions experience, in which the Gospel is communicated and responded to by individuals in cultures without any written

Scriptures, not to mention written language forms. Missionaries know that for long-term sustaining of the church in that type of culture, the Scriptures must be made available (hence the work of groups like Wycliffe Bible Translators). But saving faith can *occur* with the Gospel message alone, without the Bible yet present (much like in the pre-New Testament apostolic times).

78. It is this fundamental issue of final authority which actually is understood by Flew and Davies as the real *sine qua non* dividing Protestantism, Roman Catholicism, and Eastern Orthodoxy: "We suggest that the underlying cause of our differences lies in the doctrine of the Nature of Authority, and in the attitude of the separated communions to tradition, especially as this question affects the structure of the Church. There are vast divergences here. . . . It would be impossible to state simply any doctrine of authority which would be accepted alike by the Roman Catholics, Old Catholics, Orthodox, and Anglo-Catholics" (Flew and Davies, *Catholicity of Protestantism*, 132–33). This is the precise reason why the longevity of evangelical faith in these communions is questionable without a radical shift in these basic categories.

79. One way to look at the objective and subjective elements of the Gospel (including the presuppositions of the objective content) is to consider it as four parts, two presuppositions indicating human need, with the Gospel's objective and subjective elements providing the solution and application to that need. Consider this: the Need: who God is (infinite, holy, and just), and who we are (sinful and under divine judgment). The Solution: what God has done (the objective content of the Gospel: incarnation, atonement, resurrection), and what we must do (repentance and faith).

80. These are included in the appendix for your perusal if you come from a non-creedal background. It should also be noted that some historic branches of the church (e.g., the Coptic Church) demure from the Chalcedonian definition, while affirming the earlier creeds.

81. The "descent to hell" of Christ in the creed causes most consternation. See the interesting interchange of Wayne Grudem, "He Did Not Descend to Hell: A Plea for Following Scripture Instead of the Apostles' Creed," *Journal of the Evangelical Theological Society* 34:1 (1991): 103–13, and David P. Scaer, "He Did Descend to Hell: In Defense of the Apostles' Creed," *Journal of the Evangelical Theological Society* 35:1 (1992): 91–99.

82. Calvin says, "What then? You ask, will the councils have no determining authority? Yes, indeed; for I am not arguing here either that all councils are to be condemned or the acts of all rescinded, and (as the saying goes) to be canceled at one stroke. But, you will say, you degrade everything, so that every man has the right to accept or reject what the councils decide. Not at all! But whenever a decree of any council is brought forward, I should like men first of all diligently to ponder at what time it was held, on what issue, and with what intention, what sort of men were present; then to examine by the standard of Scripture what it dealt with—and to do this in such a way that the definition of the council may have its weight and be like a provisional judgment, yet not hinder the examination which I mentioned. . . . Thus councils would come to have the majesty that is their due; yet in the meantime Scripture would stand out in the higher sense, with everything subject to its standard. In this way, we

willingly embrace and reverence as holy the early councils, such as those of Nicaea, Constantinople, Ephesus I, Chalcedon, and the like, which were concerned with refuting errors—in so far as they relate to the teachings of faith. For they contain nothing but the pure and genuine exposition of Scripture, which the holy fathers applied with spiritual prudence to crush the enemies of religion who had then arisen. In some of the later councils also we see shining forth the true zeal for piety, and clear tokens of insight, doctrine, and prudence. But as affairs usually tend to get worse, it is to be seen from the more recent councils how much the church has degenerated from the purity of that golden age" (Calvin, *Institutes*, 4.9.8).

83. The citations on the atonement are found mainly in Reformational statements regarding the Lord's Supper, since that was, in most instances, where the issue of the nature of the atoning work of Christ was discussed.

84. *CC:* 3:328–29.

85. *CC:* 3:334–36.

86. *CC:* 3:507.

87. *CC:* 3:664.

88. *CC:* 3:494.

89. Part 1, Article 4, *CC:* 3:10.

90. *Westminster Shorter Catechism*, question 33, *CC:* 3:683.

91. *Westminster Confession of Faith*, 11.1. *CC:* 3:626.

92. Epitome 1, 2, *CC:* 3:93–95.

93. Article 7, *CC:* 3:387–88.

94. Article 6, *CC:* 3:489.

95. Chapter 1.4, 10, *CC:* 3:602–6.

96. But even here, Protestant liberalism has been infecting the traditional Roman Catholic understanding of Scripture as authoritative revelation.

97. But the evangelical/charismatic renewal segments are bringing some of these elements back into the Roman Catholic Church. It remains to be seen how long this can be sustained in view of some of the formal statements and traditions of that church.

98. Bowman notes two important factors to bear in mind that apply here. First, a system of beliefs (such as Roman Catholic dogma) can include many doctrines which are orthodox, as well as many which are unorthodox. The belief system may be unorthodox, even though individual beliefs may be orthodox. Secondly, people are often inconsistent with the implications of their belief system. They may, therefore, act (beneficially sometimes) contrary to that belief system (Bowman, *Orthodoxy and Heresy*, 52–53).

99. The statement of the World Council of Churches as stated comes across as too broad and undefined a starting point for those of evangelical faith: "The World Council of Churches is a fellowship of churches which confess the Lord Jesus Christ as God and Saviour according to the Scriptures and therefore seek to fulfill together their common calling to the glory of the one God, Father, Son, and Holy Spirit" (Martin Van Elderen, *Introducing the World Council of Churches*, 2nd ed. [Geneva: WCC Publications, 1992], 4).

100. The statements of the *National Association of Evangelicals* or the *World Evangelical Fellowship* (found in the appendices) could serve as working models

of this kind of broad, evangelical statement of sustaining orthodoxy formulation that has the Gospel as its center.

101. It is interesting to note the goals of the *World Evangelical Fellowship* in this regard: (a) The furtherance of the Gospel (Phil. 1:11); (b) the defense of and confirmation of the Gospel (Phil. 1:7); and (c) fellowship in the Gospel (Phil. 1:5) (David M. Howard, *The Dream that Would Not Die: The Birth and Growth of the World Evangelical Fellowship 1846–1986* [Exeter, Great Britain: Paternoster, 1986], 31).

1. See the Preface for an explanation of this terminology.

2. See E. Schuyler English, *Ordained of the Lord: H.A. Ironside,* rev. ed. (Neptune, N.J.: Loizeaux, 1976).

3. See the biography by his widow Elisabeth Elliot, *Shadow of the Almighty: The Life and Testament of Jim Elliot* (New York: Harper, 1958).

4. See his autobiography *In Retrospect: Remembrance of Things Past* (Grand Rapids: Eerdmans, 1980).

5. Keillor satirizes his growing-up experience among the Exclusive Brethren in his *Lake Wobegon Days* (New York: Viking, 1985); see his chapter entitled "Protestant." See also the interview with him entitled "The Wobegon Preacher," *Leadership* (Fall 1991): 52-59, and Gordon MacDonald, "Lake Wobegon's Prodigal Son," *Christianity Today,* 18 May 1992, 32-34.

6. Brethren historian Rowdon observes, "To pretend that the Brethren do not form a recognizable feature of the ecclesiastical landscape is to fly in the face of the facts. Ostrich-like, we may persuade ourselves that we do not exist, but outside observers have no difficulty in discerning us! Though we have no denominational structures as such, we nevertheless possess powerful infrastructures which bestow a kind of corporate identity upon us, whether we like it or not" (Harold H. Rowdon, *Who Are the Brethren and Does it Matter?* [Exeter, Great Britain: Paternoster, 1986], 41).

7. This risk is shared by any who yearn for a broader expression of catholicity. Richey points out "the passion of a [Richard] Baxter or a [Cotton] Mather for uniting the separate parties in Christendom made him seem less than fully committed to his own party. His openness to truths in other parties and to new truths made him ever suspect of heresy" (Russell E. Richey, " 'Catholic' Protestantism and American Denominationalism," *Journal of Ecumenical Studies* 16 [1979]: 225).

8. The standard scholarly works on the history of the Brethren are the following: F. Roy Coad, *A History of the Brethren Movement,* 2nd ed. (Exeter, Great Britain: Paternoster, 1976), and H.H. Rowdon, *The Origins of the Brethren 1825–1850* (London: Pickering and Inglis, 1967). A historical treatment with a practical and self-analytical focus is Nathan DeLynn Smith, *Roots, Renewal and the Brethren* (Pasadena: Hope, 1986). H.A. Ironside, *A Historical Sketch of the Brethren Movement,* rev. ed. (Neptune, N.J.: Loizeaux, 1985) has been recently reprinted, but does show an emphasis on the Exclusive Brethren (this division

will be explained later), since Ironside was among the Grant Exclusives before he became pastor of Chicago's Moody Memorial Church. A brief, but classic Exclusive portrayal, is Andrew Miller, *"The Brethren" (Commonly So-Called): A Brief Sketch*, rev. G.C. Willis (Addison, Ill.: Bible Truth, 1963). The latter two books should be supplemented by Coad and Rowdon.

9. Quoted in Ironside, *Historical Sketch*, 18.

10. For Darby's influence on modern American premillennialism, see Timothy P. Weber, *Living in the Shadow of the Second Coming: American Premillennialism 1875–1982* (Grand Rapids: Zondervan, 1983).

11. George Müller started several highly successful orphanages "by faith" with no direct appeal for money. See H. Lincoln Wayland, ed. *Autobiography of George Müller: The Life of Trust* (1861; reprint, Grand Rapids: Baker, 1981). Müller's life of faith heavily influenced J. Hudson Taylor and his *China Inland Mission* (now *Overseas Missionary Fellowship*): "All this extensive work [of Müller], carried on by a penniless man through faith in God alone, with no appeals for help or guarantee of stated income, was a wonderful testimony to the power of 'effectual, fervent prayer.' As such it made a profound impression upon Hudson Taylor, and encouraged him more than anything else could have in the pathway he was about to enter" (Dr. and Mrs. Howard Taylor, *J. Hudson Taylor: A Biography* [Chicago: Moody, 1965], 22). Müller at one point heard of Taylor's work "by faith" in China and became an active supporter of his. An excellent recent biography of Müller is Roger Steer, *George Müller: Delighted in God!* (Wheaton, Ill.: Harold Shaw, 1975). This particular biography weaves into the narrative Müller's involvement in the fateful early split of the Brethren into Exclusives and Opens.

12. Anthony Norris Groves, *Christian Devotedness*, 2nd ed. (Kansas City: Walterick, n.d.), 35, n. 1.

13. Cited in Coad, *History of the Brethren*, 24. Emphases original.

14. Ibid., 20.

15. Ibid., 49–50. Emphases original.

16. Remembered by F.W. Newman, long after his brief sojourn among the Brethren had ended, in his *Phases of Faith*, cited in Coad, *History of the Brethren*, 15.

17. Darby penned an unpublished letter to the archbishop, now available under the title: *Considerations Addressed to the Archbishop of Dublin and the Clergy Who Signed the Petition to the House of Commons for Protection*, in William Kelly, ed., *The Collected Writings of J.N. Darby*, vol. 1 (n.d.; reprint, Oak Park, Ill.: Bible Truth, 1971), 1–19. Darby said, ". . . instead of bringing them to graft them into the vine, the liberty and security of Christ, to pledge their souls to that which (if the civil Sovereign should choose wrong) would be Popery, and is in fact a denial of union with Christ being the vital principle and bond of the true Church, that general assembly and Church of the first-born whose names are written in heaven, which *is* the true Church, the fullness of Him, that filleth all in all. Here is true catholicity, and to affirm it of anything else is Popery, however, modified: and Protestantism is the manifestation of faith in the word, when Satan has hidden the true Church, the assembly of believers, in a system of this world; and such a system, in a modified shape, is that maintained in the

Charge" (p. 19). This source will be afterward abbreviated as *CW*.

18. Darby, *Considerations on the Nature and Unity of the Church of Christ*, in *CW*: 1:25.

19. Ibid., 31.

20. Ibid., 22.

21. Ibid., 32.

22. See, e.g., his *The Apostasy of the Successive Dispensations*, in *CW*: 1:123–30 and *On the Formation of Churches*, in *CW*: 1:138–55. "The church is in a state of ruin, immersed and buried in the world—*invisible*, if you will have it so." (p. 143).

23. The entire letter is cited in Coad, *History of the Brethren*, appendix A, 287–91.

24. Ibid., 288. Emphases original.

25. Ibid., 289. Emphases original. In another place, Groves wrote, "Yet as to our liberty in Christ to worship with any congregation under heaven where He manifests Himself to bless and to save, can there be in any Christian mind a doubt? . . . To the question, Are we not countenancing error by this plan? our answer is, that if we must appear to countenance error, or discountenance brotherly love, and the visible union of the Church of God, we prefer the former, hoping that our lives and our tongues may be allowed by the Lord so intelligibly to speak as at last our righteousness shall be allowed to appear . . ." (Cited by John Allan, "A New Shape, Though Unformed," in *Must Brethren Churches Die?* ed. Kevin Dyer and John Allan [Exeter, Great Britain: Partnership Pubs., 1991], 13).

26. Darby went on to write, among his voluminous and still influential titles, works such as these, which are expressive of his uncatholic direction: *The Notion of a Clergyman Dispensationally the Sin Against the Holy Ghost* (to Groves, ordination was unnecessary; to Darby, it was downright wrong), *The Apostasy of the Successive Dispensations*, (he argued that the Dispensation of the church is itself apostate and the churches must be departed from), and *Separation from Evil God's Principles of Unity*.

27. On November 26, 1847, Newton wrote a tract entitled, "A Statement and Acknowledgment Respecting Certain Doctrinal Errors." The text is found in Coad, *History of the Brethren*, appendix B. Exclusives (following Darby) argue that this statement was a sham and that he really still taught what he disowned.

28. Coad notes, "The result of Darby's campaign in Plymouth had been to destroy one of the most flourishing churches of the movement, and to drive into the wilderness one of its most brilliant teachers" (Coad, *History of the Brethren*, 151). It is ironic that Darby was later (1858) to promote a virtually identical heresy as Newton's, which led to some significant disenchantment on the part of his followers (p. 161).

29. In fact, when some of Darby's supporters in Bethesda raised some objections, they were invited by the elders to examine these newcomers themselves. They did, and concluded they were free from the heresy. See Coad, *History of the Brethren*, 156.

30. Their findings were reported in a public document known as "The Letter of the Ten." This may be found in Coad, *History of the Brethren*, appendix C.

31. This "Leeds Circular" is found in Darby's *CW:* 15:164–67. For a current Exclusive statement of the evil of Bethesda, as capsulated in the Open practice of reception and independency, see H.S. [Hamilton Smith], *Open Brethren: Their Origin, Principles and Practice* (n.p., 1948).

32. It is important to note at this point that the influence of Darby cross-pollinated into the Open Brethren in North America due to several things: the personal influence of Darby in his visits here during the Civil War era, as well as the Scottish and Irish Brethren Open evangelists in North America who imbibed some of his teachings, and the realignments of many of the Exclusives in North America with the Opens. As a result, even the Open Brethren in North America have lost many of the original catholic notions of Groves due to the influence of Darby's thinking. See Ross McLaren, "The Triple Tradition: The Origin and Development of the Open Brethren in North America" (M.A. thesis, Vanderbilt University, 1982).

33. Darby, *Separation from Evil God's Principle of Unity* in *CW:* 1:353–65. Later, in a letter entitled "Grace, the Power of Unity and of Gathering," in *CW:* 1:366–77), he attempted to modify the extremes of this position with little observable success. See also William W. Conrad, *Family Matters* (Wheaton, Ill.: Interest, 1992).

34. The Exclusive Brethren stayed united during the lifetime of Darby. But once Darby came to the point of dying, the prophetic warning against narrow minds given by Groves in 1836 began to come true. A division took place in 1881 over proper associations known as the Kelly, or Ramsgate Division; in 1885, the Exclusives divided again in the Montreal, or Grant Division; that same year another one took place known as the Reading, or Stuart Division; in 1890 the Bexhill (or Raven) Division took place; in 1908 the Glanton Division took place; and in 1909 the Tunbridge-Wells Division took place among them. These were just the major divisions. Many minor ones were interwoven. None of the Exclusive groups have fellowship with each other, and each one claims that *its* fellowship in a given city is the only legitimate expression of the body of Christ, to which all genuine believers in that city must leave their denominations to join. They are strongly averse to attempts at reunion based on their reading of Ecclesiastes 3:15, KJV: "God requireth that which is past." To them, this means that separations from evil in the past are acts of God, who expects them to be maintained out of concern for the holiness of His people.

35. The term "Open Brethren" is a derogatory term when used by the Exclusives, meaning "open to entertain doctrinal/moral evil in their midst." But the Open Brethren do not reject the terminology and view it in a positive nuance: "open to receive all whom Christ has received," that is, with a notion of oneness in Christ that was originally held by the movement before the development of exclusivism.

36. From an address given to a conference of Christians at Clifton in October 1863. Reproduced in *Jehovah Magnified* (1876), cited in Coad, *History of the Brethren*, 275.

37. A Younger Brother, *The Principles of Christians Called "Open Brethren"* (Glasgow: Pickering & Inglis, 1913), 131. Note: Brethren often prefer anonymity to avoid diverting praise from God and so that the validity of their writing

should stand on its own merit. That's why you may see older Brethren works under pure initials: e.g., JND; CHM.

38. My assessment of Darby's negative influence on the movement may come across as mere "Darby bashing" (I have been accused of such). But I should hope that it is a bit more realistic than that. Most Brethren today (even among the Opens) have more positive assessments of Darby than he really deserves in view of the separatistic attitudes he enjoined upon his followers, and in view of the tragic historical consequences he has endowed on our movement. Part of this is due to the ready availability of his works, and the inaccessibility of the works of Groves, Müller, Craik, and the early Opens.

39. The following list represents characteristics of the mainstream of the movement. There are a number of newer assemblies who would not fit some of these characteristics, although they would share the historic values, discussed in the next chapter.

40. The "Closed/Open" Brethren, or the "Tights" are a closely connected family of Brethren assemblies who do not support the Bethesda decision as did the Exclusives, yet who do not associate with the Open assemblies. Since they are not within the circles of fellowship of the Exclusives and retain the autonomy of the local assembly, then they are in fact "Open Brethren." But they call themselves "Closed." Hence, my terminology of "Closed/Open." Actually this is a sort of division that took place among the "Opens" in the early decades of this century. The Closed are much more separatistic in their thinking than most Open assemblies.

41. See a classic statement on the catholic centrality of the Lord's Table among the Opens in the "Tottenham Statement" of 1849. Found in Coad, *History of the Brethren*, appendix D.

42. The Canadian Open Brethren have similar organizations, although there is overlap in circulation on the periodicals.

43. *Regent College* in Vancouver, B.C., was begun by a number of people among the Open Brethren in that area. It is broadly evangelical and catholic in outlook, but the strong Brethren influence has significantly waned in recent years.

44. Be alert to the fact that, due to the extensive separations among the Exclusives, as mentioned earlier, there are many mutually exclusive varieties of Exclusives today. Some (not all) have passed from the sectarian and separational toward the cultic. One group has such control over its members that its leaders test their spiritual "freedom" by drunkenness, sexual immorality, and enforce divorces of members from spouses who question their teachings. All this while claiming to be the only legitimate expression of the church of Christ on earth!

45. The full title is *A Few Hymns and Some Spiritual Songs Selected 1856 for the Little Flock,* rev. (Addison, Ill.: Bible Truth, 1881).

46. These figures from January 1991 are only fair approximations due to the tendency of Brethren to avoid membership rolls as unbiblical. These figures reflect those "in fellowship," which often means those who are committed members of the congregations and are regularly at the Lord's Table. If the number of persons at the largest meeting of the congregation are followed, then

the number in fellowship in the United States and Canada is 128,722, over a 50 percent increase in the figures. The figures were obtained through a series of surveys sent to the various assemblies. *Stewards Foundation,* e.g., must keep track of these figures to know who can be serviced by their ministry. Worldwide statistics for the Brethren Movement are even harder to figure out. In 1970 there were an estimated 9,720 congregations with 534,000 adults in fellowship. See David B. Barrett, *World Christian Encyclopedia* (Oxford: Oxford Univ. Pr., 1982), 14.

47. Mead, *Handbook of Denominations,* 7th ed., 67. The new 8th edition (1985) suggests 250 Exclusive assemblies with estimates of between 20,000 and 80,000 persons in fellowship. I am inclined to think the 7th edition is more correct, knowing the generally smaller size of Exclusive meetings.

48. With an interesting twist. Among the Exclusives, the act of any local assembly is an act of the body of Christ with the authority of the Lord in their midst. Therefore any decision of a given local body is bound to be followed by all the other assemblies of which it is apart, regardless of whether they know or can assess the facts of a case!

49. A dispensational and pretribulational theology has been suggested, although this model is not uniform among the Brethren worldwide. It is predominant only where Darby's teaching has had the ascendancy (among the Exclusives, and among the Opens in North America, e.g., where a number of Darby's teachings were mixed into other elements). For discussions of the connection with Darby's hermeneutical model of dispensationalism and modern dispensationalism, see Charles C. Ryrie, *Dispensationalism Today* (Chicago: Moody, 1965); Daniel P. Fuller, *Gospel and Law: Contrast or Continuum? The Hermeneutics of Dispenationalism and Covenant Theology* (Grand Rapids: Eerdmans, 1980); and Vern S. Poythress, *Understanding Dispenationalists* (Grand Rapids: Zondervan, 1987).

50. I heard of one woman who had joined with a Brethren assembly for a number of years under the impression that they were an independent Bible Church. When a major item of Brethren distinctives came under dispute she innocently commented in exasperation, "All these years I thought we were just taking the Bible for what it said, and now I find out that we are a denomination with a set of denominational rules!" Harry Ironside similarly commented, "And each fellowship of Brethren is as truly a system as any other body of believers. If any one doubts it let him venture to act on his own initiative, or as he believes the Spirit leads, contrary to custom, and he will soon find out how sectarian an unsectarian company of Christians can be" (Ironside, *Historical Sketch,* 174).

CHAPTER 8: DENOMINATIONAL TRADITIONS, PART 2

1. χειροτονέω/cheirotoneo. From the Greek term χείρ/cheir, "hand." The older Greek lexica are vague about the definition but still see the dominant idea as that of voting. See, e.g., the outdated, but still popular work by Joseph Henry Thayer, *Greek-English Lexicon of the New Testament* (1889; reprint, Grand Rapids: Zondervan, 1972). Thayer's work was an English translation and enlarge-

ment of a Greek-Latin lexicon originally produced in 1862. But Thayer has been superseded as an authoritative Greek lexicon in the English speaking world by a new standard for some thirty-five years now. That new work is the translation of Walter Bauer's Greek-German lexicon adapted by William F. Arndt and F. Wilbur Gingrich, trans., *A Greek-English Lexicon of the New Testament and Other Early Christian Literature.* 2d ed. rev. and aug. by F. Wilbur Gingrich and Frederick W. Danker (Chicago: Univ. of Chicago Pr., 1979). Unfortunately, there are still too many who do not know this fact and rely on Thayer as their best Greek lexical authority.

2. Baptists are not alone in appealing to this passage in support of congregational voting. Personally, I am not opposed to congregational participation in the decision-making process of the local church. I am simply pointing out that appealing to *this* text to show it is biblically warranted is unjustifiable.

3. The "root fallacy" is a linguistic error in which an etymological root in a word is supposed to be a part of the meaning of a person who uses it long after that etymological sense has been lost. "Good-bye" is a good example in English. Atheists use that term of farewell just as religious people do, but it would be wrong to suppose that they somehow secretly believe in God, since its etymological root is the Old English "God be with you."

4. The latest edition of the current authoritative lexicon of New Testament Greek captures this distinction nicely: "This does not involve a choice by the group; here the word means *appoint, install,* w. the apostles as subj[ect]." *BAGD:* 881a.

5. Avery Dulles, "Dogma as an Ecumenical Problem," *Theological Studies* (Spring 1968): 416.

6. Fee, *Gospel and Spirit,* 81–82.

7. I will restrict my assessment to the Open Brethren (which I style the Christian Brethren), since they are the ones with which I am most familiar. Some of these Open Brethren ecclesiastical principles can be gleaned from popular Brethren works on the church, which have not had much circulation outside the movement. See, e.g., J.R. Littleproud, *The Christian Assembly,* 4th ed. (Orange, Calif.: Ralph E. Welch Foundation, n.d.); William MacDonald, *"Christ Loved the Church" An Outline of New Testament Church Principles* (Kansas City, Mo: Walterick, 1956); G. Fred Hamilton, *Why? Why Practice New Testament Principles Today?* (Spring Lake, N.J.: Christian Missions in Many Lands, 1985); Kenneth A. Daughters, *New Testament Church Government: The Normative Church Government Structure of the New Testament* (Kansas City, Mo.: Walterick, 1989); and Alexander Strauch, *Biblical Eldership: An Urgent Call to Restore Biblical Church Leadership,* 2nd ed. (Littleton, Colo.: Lewis and Roth, 1988). Of the lot, the books by Daughters and Strauch reflect a new generation of biblical scholarship among the Brethren, for they are certainly more conversant with issues in contemporary ecclesiological scholarship. The others are more popular in orientation. All of the principles I will discuss, whether actually noted in these works or not, do have currency within the movement to a larger or lesser degree, as anyone within can easily attest. Bear in mind that these works are from an Open Brethren perspective, and therefore tend to be more "patternistic" in terms of their use of the New Testament. The

Exclusives do not tend to produce newer works on the church, having imbibed deeply of Darby's philosophy that the New Testament church is in ruins and cannot be revived or copied. They therefore tend to simply reprint earlier works of Darby and his supporters. For an example of their reprints, see William Kelly, *Lectures on the Church of God* (Orange, Calif.: The Ralph E. Welch Foundation, n.d.).

8. Many do not realize that the Anglicans/Episcopalians, from among whom many of the early Brethren leaders came, take the "Eucharist" (break bread), at least weekly. In this they are like the Roman Catholics, from which they themselves developed. Further, the Stone-Campbellite groups do so weekly as well (e.g., Christian Churches [Disciples of Christ]; Churches of Christ).

9. MacDonald, *Christ Loved the Church*, 71–72; cf. Littleproud, *The Christian Assembly*, 128–29.

10. The NIV helps to make this clearer by translating thus: "For *whenever* you eat this bread. . . ." To his credit, MacDonald notes about this verse: "The moment a person says it must be observed every week, or month, or quarter, he has gone beyond what the Bible says" (MacDonald, *Christ Loved the Church*, 72).

11. MacDonald notes, "The assembly, then, should never fetter the Holy Spirit, either with unscriptural rules, stereotyped program, rituals, or liturgies. How grieved He must often be by rigid understandings that a meeting must end at a certain time, that a service must always follow a certain routine, that ministry at certain stages of a worship meeting is quite unacceptable! Such regulations can only lead to a loss of spiritual power" (MacDonald, *Christ Loved the Church*, 37).

12. "The local church should ever recognize the sovereignty of the Spirit. By this we mean that He can do as He pleases, and that He will not always choose to do things in exactly the same way. . . . Thus, wise Christians will be sufficiently elastic to allow Him this divine prerogative. It was so in the early church, but soon people became uneasy with meetings that were 'free and social, with a minimum of form.' Thus controls were added and formalism and ritualism took over. The Holy Spirit was quenched, and the church lost its power" (MacDonald, *Christ Loved the Church*, 33–34; cf. Hamilton, *Why?* 89).

13. See Hamilton, *Why?* 16.

14. C.H. Mackintosh, "The Assembly of God," in *Miscellaneous Writings* (N.Y.: Loizeaux, n.d.), 3:36; cited in MacDonald, *Christ Loved the Church*, 38.

15. The earliest clear description of a Christian worship service comes to us from a second century document. See Justin Martyr, *The First Apology: 67*. Earlier than this the *Didache* (c. A.D. 100, less than a decade after John completed the book of Revelation) shows clear marks of a more formal approach to worship with standard prayers of thanksgiving for the bread and the wine. The writer of this piece is an orthodox believer familiar with apostolic teaching.

16. See especially his regulations regarding tongues speaking (vv. 27-28), regarding the expression of the prophetic gift of divine revelation (vv. 29-33), and regarding women participating (vv. 33b-36). His key statements in this section are "For God is not a God of disorder but of peace" (v. 33a) and "But everything should be done in a fitting and orderly way" (v. 40).

17. If the sinning brother is not won over by personal confrontation (v. 15), one or two others are to be brought along that "two or three witnesses" may be present at this attempt at reconciliation. It is in this context that our Lord promises His presence "where two or three come together in my name," not specifically a worship context. According to Carson, "Here as elsewhere, Jesus takes God's place: Jesus will be with the judges" (Carson, "Matthew," 404).

18. It is rather ironic that the *form* of "pure spontaneity" as the *only* creative mode for the Spirit of God to work within should in fact stifle the work of the Spirit of God in terms of the form itself. In view of the paucity of New Testament data, one would expect that many different creative forms of worship should be practiced in our assemblies rather than one form alone (Ironically, this becomes a sort of unchangeable sacred liturgy, does it not?). Of course, I would not omit the traditional Brethren form from being used (it definitely has its place), but the issue is whether we should really restrict our practice to that form based on available teaching (or lack thereof) from the New Testament. Why can we not see the creativity and variety of worship in the entire church catholic as indicative of the *full* creativity of the Spirit of God?

19. It is interesting to note that G.H. Lang used his "biography" of Anthony Norris Groves as a platform from which to lament the passing away of this "spontaneous pulpit" among even the Open Brethren. See G.H. Lang, *Anthony Norris Groves*, 2nd ed. (Exeter, Great Britain: Paternoster, 1949).

20. Hanson and Hanson make the following comments on the Quaker model of worship, which is quite similar to that of the Brethren, "This represents a courageous and almost heaven-storming attempt to rely wholly upon the guidance of the Holy Spirit. The company sits in silence unless and until some person present is moved to make a contribution, whether by prayer or by singing or by exhortation. Consequently this form of service can be deeply moving or appallingly banal. It is a form best suited to spiritual athletes who know the value of silence and can use it. It probably works better with a relatively small group. As an ingredient of Christian worship it is much to be desired. As the weekly diet of ordinary Christians it is precarious" (Hanson and Hanson, *The Identity of the Church*, 244). On the connections between the early Brethren and the Quakers, see Timothy C.F. Stunt, *Early Brethren and the Society of Friends* CBRF Occasional Paper Number 3 (Middlesex, Great Britain: CBRF Pubs., 1970).

21. This characteristic is not restricted to the Christian Brethren. There are other groups which prohibit musical instruments in worship as well (e.g., some segments of the Churches of Christ).

22. Some other justifications I have heard also connect the use of instruments as providing a form of leadership in the meeting that restricts the Holy Spirit, or that (practically) the use of piano or other instruments means that the person using them is not able to participate in worship.

23. We Brethren ought not pretend to be experts on interpreting the passages of 1 Corinthians 11 and 14 before we have adequately researched the issues involved. Here is a *partial* list of important articles that have sought to interpret these two passages adequately in the light of Paul's intention: E. Earle Ellis, "The Silenced Wives of Corinth (1 Cor. 14:34-5)," in *New Testament*

Textual Criticism: Its Significance for Exegesis. Essays in Honour of Bruce M. Metzger. ed. E.J. Epp and G.D. Fee (Oxford, Great Britain: Clarendon, 1981); N.J. Hommes, "Let Women Be Silent in Church," *Calvin Theological Journal* 4 (1969): 5–22; M.D. Hooker, "Authority on Her Head: An Examination of 1 Corinthians 11:10," *New Testament Studies* 10 (1963–64): 410–16; H. Wayne House, "Paul, Women, and Contemporary Evangelical Feminism," *Bibliotheca Sacra* 136 (January-March 1979): 40–53; J.B. Hurley, "Did Paul Require Veils or the Silence of Women?" *Westminster Theological Journal* 35 (1975): 190–220; David K. Lowery, "The Head Covering and Lord's Supper in 1 Corinthians 11:2-34," *Bibliotheca Sacra* 143 (April-June 1986): 155–63; William J. Martin, "1 Corinthians 11:2-16: An Interpretation," in *Apostolic History and the Gospel*, ed. W. Ward Gasque and Ralph P. Martin (Grand Rapids: Eerdmans, 1970), 231–41; William O. Walker, Jr. "1 Corinthians 11:2-16 and Paul's View Regarding Women," *Journal of Biblical Literature* 94 (1975): 94–110; Bruce K. Waltke, "1 Corinthians 11:2-16: An Interpretation," *Bibliotheca Sacra* 135 (January/March 1978): 46–57; and Noel Weeks, "Of Silence and Head Covering," *Westminster Theological Journal* 35:1 (Fall 1972): 21–27. These scholarly articles are not consistent on the interpretation or contemporary implications of these matters.

24. Tertullian, in the late second/early third century himself had to write to try to interpret the meaning of 1 Cor. 11, in view of conflicting interpretations. See his *On the Veiling of Virgins, ANF:* 4:27–37.

25. The practice of some assemblies, of having women cover their heads even in private prayer (or silent prayer) does not do justice to Paul's argument in 1 Cor. 11. For one thing prayer is coupled with prophesying, a form of oral and public activity. When a man prophesied with head covered (or a woman with head uncovered?), it is easy for the leadership or other members of the congregation to observe due to the public nature of the oral activity. Prayer is to be understood, when coupled with prophesying, as a second type of oral, public activity. Secondly, if prayer were not oral and public (in the congregational meeting), how could the leadership judge if a woman was in violation of the Pauline mandate? After all, Hannah could only be accosted by Eli for drinking when he mistook her audible, public prayer (1 Sam. 1–2). If she only prayed in her heart, how would Eli have known?

26. That is, it is restricted, e.g., to prophetic speech, or the judging of the prophets, or speaking in tongues, or similar specific types of speaking. See the literature listed earlier.

27. I am not here stating my preference in terms of the proper interpretation of these passages. All I am saying is that we must face up to our inconsistency and look at the interpretive issue anew with honesty and candor.

28. See MacDonald, *Christ Loved the Church*, 15G; 59 #6.

29. This is from the entry under "Plymouth Brethren" (which is an accurate description of Brethren practice, written by a well-known Brethren representative), in Frank S. Mead and Samuel S. Hill, *Handbook of Denominations in the United States*, 8th ed. (Nashville: Abingdon, 1985), 201.

30. John R.W. Stott, *One People: Laymen and Clergy in God's Church* (Downers Grove, Ill.: InterVarsity, 1968), 19.

31. Cf. Hamilton, *Why?* 9–10. See also MacDonald, "But we must face honestly and squarely the fact that the idea of a clergyman is not found in the New Testament. Nowhere does one find one man in charge of a church" (MacDonald, *Christ Loved the Church,* 52).

32. MacDonald, *Christ Loved the Church,* 52–55.

33. Ibid., 34.

34. See my "The Forgotten Gift," *Interest* 55:1 (January 1989): 6–7.

35. The leadership gift is referred to, for example, in Rom. 12:8. But teaching (Rom. 12:7) is also a kind of leadership gift as well. See Kevin Dyer, *Unity Leadership Change & Vision* (Prospect Heights, Ill.: International Teams, n.d.), 24ff.

36. Strauch does an excellent job of developing the idea of an elder gifted in shepherding or leadership serving as leader on the ancient analogy of *primus inter pares,* "first among equals" (Strauch, *Biblical Eldership,* 248–51).

37. Strauch, *Biblical Eldership,* 21.

38. Ibid., 22.

39. Even Daughters suggests that "a professional pastor is more likely to be amenable to the will of man because he is dependent on men to receive his paycheck" (Daughters, *New Testament Church Government,* 79).

40. The flier is subtitled "A Call to NEW TESTAMENT Christianity" (emphasis theirs). It is produced by Walterick Publishers in Kansas City, Kansas. This one was written by Donald L. Norbie, a well-known Brethren worker from Colorado.

41. I know of one worker who was honest enough to speak his mind on some Brethren traditions at a conference. Not only did he not receive the normal financial "fellowship," he was not even reimbursed for the gasoline expenses it took to travel to the conference. It was only many months afterward that he found out that what he had said had offended his audience so that this occurred, and it was able to be corrected. But this kind of "withholding of fellowship" can all too easily influence a hungry Brethren worker to simply speak the party line! Who has control over the preacher?

42. A term sometimes used by Brethren to derogatorily refer to a salaried preacher.

43. In fact, sometimes a set salary today for a ministry can even *keep* a worker from becoming attached to the love of money. Contrast Billy Graham's fixed salary (which has always stopped cold any unbelieving criticism of his financial affairs) with the televangelist financial scandals of late.

44. "Going out in faith" is the Brethren jargon for becoming a full-time worker in the Lord's work without a set salary. As noted in the historical section, it follows the pattern of Groves and Müller.

45. See 1 Tim. 5:17-18 in context.

46. See Strauch, *Biblical Eldership,* 22.

47. For an example of how one Brethren assembly has described their Breaking of Bread meeting in terms of "customs" (traditions) rather than "New Testament principles" so that it is more sensitive to the truth (not to mention the entire church catholic), see appendix E.

48. See especially Phil. 1:1, which notes that the congregation at Philippi had

multiple elders and multiple deacons. Acts 14:23 indicates that Paul and Barnabas selected elders (plural) for each congregation after their first missionary journey into Asia Minor. In Acts 20:17, Paul sent to Ephesus for the elders (plural) of the church there. First Timothy 5:17 refers to elders (plural) who direct the affairs of the church (singular, and in context of this epistle, the church at Ephesus) well are to receive double compensation. Titus 1:5 admonishes Titus to appoint elders (plural) in every town (singular). The examples of what was done are fairly clear in the New Testament.

49. For an intelligent presentation of the argument that it *is,* see Kenneth Daughters, *New Testament Church Government.* This otherwise excellent book unfortunately suffers from the common tendency to confuse the *house* church (which may not have had a plurality of elders) with the *city*-church (which undoubtedly did have a plurality of elders). See my discussion in chapter 1. Daughters thus states "There is no Biblical warrant for having only one elder in a local [house? city?] church, nor for having a president among the elders." (p. 24). Apart from this employment of the negative hermeneutic, he bypasses the hermeneutical principle of authorial intent when he admits that there is no direct biblical injunction, but nevertheless, "a direct Scriptural command is not necessary to establish a pattern to be followed. . . . In the prescriptive manner in which it has been faithfully recorded for our instruction, it seems that we need rather strong evidence to overthrow their example" (p. 43). The latter phrase unfortunately begs the question, since the faithful recording of an example does not equal a "prescriptive" record "for our instruction." Based on the basic hermeneutical issue of authorial intent, unless it can be demonstrated that a biblical author intentionally recorded his examples for the purpose of setting a precedent, we have no right to assume that God intended to set a precedent. See my discussion of these hermeneutical issues in chapter 5.

50. Strauch offers a balanced statement, and even allows for the potential that there may be instances where only one elder exists in a congregation, "There are sufficient New Testament examples and instructions to fully justify insistence on spiritual oversight by a plurality of elders, yet there is no command from the Lord, 'Thou shalt have a plurality of elders.' (Although Titus 1:5ff and possibly a few other passages come close to that.) [The reasons he gives are that the New Testament is not a book of law and that there may not be more than one qualified man in a congregation.] So the freedom allowed in the New Testament permits a local congregation to function without disobedience if no body of elders is available" (Alexander Strauch, *Biblical Eldership,* 11).

51. See Gene A. Getz, *Sharpening the Focus of the Church* (Chicago: Moody, 1974).

52. See Strauch, *Biblical Eldership,* 137–39; and Daughters, *New Testament Church Government,* 73ff. for other advantages.

53. Ray Stedman, *Body Life* (Glendale, Calif.: Regal, 1972).

54. The two primary passages are, of course, 1 Tim. 3 and Titus 1. Neither passage has anything to say about formal theological training, nor about spiritual giftedness despite the enumeration of many other qualifications. Even "able to teach" does not speak to giftedness. There is ability to teach (expected of all elders) and giftedness to teach, just as there is the presence of faith (expected

of all believers by definition) and the gift of faith.

55. Cf. Strauch, *Biblical Eldership*, 75; Daughters, *New Testament Church Government*, 49.

56. See a good discussion of these in Gene Getz, *The Measure of a Man* (Glendale, Calif.: Regal, 1974).

57. I would include the factor here that the list of qualifications given in the pastorals includes "husband of one wife." That means that it is expected that elders should be male. Normative leadership is envisioned in the local assembly as men, much like the normative leadership in the Old Testament (the priesthood) was. That is distinct from special, or gift-leadership, which is not gender specific.

58. What makes me grieve is this: too many leaders of the Brethren assemblies are still suspicious of formal theological training. But Brethren young men, often starved for clear hermeneutics, biblical languages, and sound theological thinking, have gone off to conservative theological institutions. They have not been welcomed back into their assemblies. And they have left the movement. Why? Because they are not self-taught (or not "taught of God" if you prefer) to some and theologically suspect to others. Also a factor is that with an emphasis on "lay" ministry, there is no place for them to minister based on their training where they can receive financial support in so doing. So Brethren young men have left to lead influential churches who will receive them without suspicion or have gone off to take leadership posts in parachurch organizations—while their own assemblies would consign them to nothing more than a secondary role or back seat.

59. See Nathan DeLynn Smith, *Roots, Renewal and the Brethren* (Pasadena: Hope, 1986), 135–36 for the impact this has had on more educated people among the Brethren and why so many have left.

60. It is ironic to observe that Bellett, Darby, Groves, Craik, and Müller, and many other early Brethren leaders provided a depth to the early movement by virtue of the very fact that they had received college—and in many instances theological—education. How ironic that subsequent generations of the Brethren should have lost out on valuable theological insight that could have been gained by encouraging such training as these men had.

61. See especially Acts 20 where Paul called for the "elders" of the church at Ephesus (v. 17), referred to them as "overseers" (v. 28a) and told them to "be shepherds" (be pastors, or "pastor") of the church of God (v. 28b), where the people are referred to under the metaphor of "sheep" (v. 29).

62. One young man I know poured out his heart and soul in service to a small assembly, improved significantly the quality of teaching, and attracted several other young couples, breathing new life and vitality into what had been a dormant group. He told me that before long he was warned by an elder that he was "too ambitious." It wasn't long before the elders of that congregation had squelched all signs of life and creativity and prodded the departure of every last one of the young couples. The assembly now consists almost totally of older people and is greatly decreased in numbers and effectiveness. It doesn't take a prophet to predict their eventual demise as a congregation.

63. The closest thing you come to this is only by implication. Titus 1 states

that he must be a man "whose children believe" (v. 6). But what does that mean? Either (1) he must be old enough to be married and have had children who genuinely believe (At what age is that for children?) or (2) he must be old enough to have had children who have grown up and demonstrated that they truly believe, or (3) this passage says nothing whatever regarding a requirement for elders needing to have children at all—only that if they have them they must be believers. One must ask whether those who are unable to have children are prohibited by this statement from becoming an elder, regardless of other quali-fications. To me, it seems that the latter is the only way to go in this passage. This is a list of characteristics which characterize a "mature Christian man," rather than a "minimum list" of requirements to be held to by the letter.

64. See *BAGD:* 699–700. They define it in our sense as "designation of an official (cf. Latin, senator) elder, presbyter."

65. In my state several Baptist churches have followed the Brethren in terms of moving to plurality of eldership and elder rule rather than congregational rule. Unfortunately the results in terms of congregational harmony has not always been good. Reactionary former members have been known to establish new Baptist churches with strict congregational rule. This is quite the polar opposite of elder rule among the Brethren, where any thought of congregation-al vote brings horrific thoughts to the fellowshiping believer.

66. Strauch follows this reasoning, "In addition to saying nothing about every member having one vote, Scripture says nothing about absolute majority rule or total unanimity" (Strauch, *Biblical Eldership,* 120).

67. The sample I have in mind is, of course, Acts 6. There the apostles came to an understanding of the need to resolve a structural/social/cultural problem within the early church. They summoned "all the disciples together," (v. 2) and said to them, "Brothers, choose seven men from among you" (v. 3). When they were chosen *by the congregation* according to the spiritual criteria, then the apostles prayed for them and laid their hands on them (Acts 6:1-6). This is a clear sample of congregational selection of its leadership. We do not know that this was normative, nor do we know that this functioned at other levels of leadership, but we must at least confess that this is an example of congregation-al participation in decision-making, and *that* in regard to the selection of leadership.

68. Strauch is correct in arguing that "the congregation's recognition and counsel regarding the candidate's labor and character is absolutely essential. That which affects everyone in God's household ought to concern everyone. The entire assembly is responsible to see that *its leaders are scripturally qualified for the office*" (Strauch, *Biblical Eldership,* 76). Emphases his.

69. This is commonly held, but difficult to pinpoint in any literature.

70. See Strauch, *Biblical Eldership,* 123. Strauch believes in elder unanimity in major decisions, but (apparently) majority vote in minor decisions.

71. Sometimes the emphasis is on the fact that God's voice in a group may reside with the few or even the one rather than the many or the majority. The Old Testament prophet is given as an example. I shudder when I think of every dissenting voice as a potential prophet, especially when the dissenting voice is one "spiritual voice" among many "spiritual voices." There are other reasons

besides spiritual ones which cause people to disagree.

72. Recognizing this problem, while realizing that there is a certain value in unanimity, the elders in my local assembly have gone to a form of "modified" unanimity. This means that if only one man objects to a course of action, he is given a set period of time to pray, reflect, and put his case together. If he can convince at least one other elder, they will not proceed with the proposed course of action. If he cannot find at least one other elder to agree with him, then he must agree to see the voice of the Spirit of God in the rest of the elders.

73. Dyer gives good balance here. He states that "each individual church has its own authority and should not be subjected to a higher authority of control apart from Christ Himself. There certainly should be fellowship of churches to encourage and strengthen each other because autonomy is not the same as independence. We must maintain autonomy, but we do not have to be independent. Legislation and control from outside sources should be repudiated and resisted. But we do need challenge, encouragement, assistance, and practical help. We are in serious danger today of becoming cultic about independence. Our heritage has given us an unbalanced position that isolates, and results in weak churches trying to survive on their own" (Kevin Dyer, *Unity*, 24–25).

74. The principle of autonomy can protect a church from any doctrinal or conscience contamination that may be imposed upon it from a "higher" ecclesiastical authority. This is important for maintaining a clear testimony of conscience in a fallen world.

75. Marshall comments, "As the journey continued, Paul and his companions communicated to the churches the decisions which had been arrived at by the apostles and elders in Jerusalem. The authority of the apostolic council was regarded as binding on churches outside Jerusalem" (I. Howard Marshall, *The Acts of the Apostles: An Introduction and Commentary*, *TNTC* [Grand Rapids: Eerdmans, 1980], 260).

76. *Christian Missions in Many Lands* is a Brethren missionary service organization but not, they insist, a "sending agency." That is the prerogative of the local congregation. CMML will be the designation used for this organization hereafter.

77. I am referring to the larger number of missionaries that may be supported by denominational churches who promise a smaller fixed amount to many missionaries on the deputational model. A visit to the foyer of almost any denominational (or community) church that follows this other approach will show numerous photographs and form letters from their "supported" missionaries. But the percentage of money sent in support to each one as a church may often be far smaller than a given Brethren assembly will send to its smaller number of personally known and commended missionaries.

78. See this emphasis on smallness in MacDonald, *Christ Loved the Church*, 114–19.

79. A "hive off" is Brethren jargon for the amicable departure of a few families to begin Breaking Bread as a new group.

80. See Jim Stahr, "The Plateau Hypothesis," *Interest* 48:3 (March 1983): 2–3. Stahr is not to be criticized for observing this fact. It is a matter of simple

observation. The problem is with any who would assume from this that to try to "break the barrier" of the plateau would be fruitless. So why expend the effort? Several early Brethren assemblies surged right past that plateau. If the table cannot sustain the salt, then they figured to get a bigger table!

81. Read especially Acts 2:41 and 4:4.

82. It could be argued that Jesus referred to building spiritual growth and maturity. That may be included, but the Book of Acts certainly shows evangelistic (numerical) growth as a thematic emphasis.

83. See the primary document known as the W.H. Cole letter. Mr. Cole was present in the early years of Plymouth and saw the terrible split that took place there on Darby's return. It is found in G.H. Lang, *Anthony Norris Groves*, 327–28.

84. Keith and Alan Linton, *"I Will Build My Church": 150 Years of Church Work in Bristol* (Bristol, Great Britain: C. Hadler, n.d.), 25.

85. Larger assemblies can tend to have a greater diversity of gift and depth of leadership that is often absent from the smaller meetings. Further, pooling of larger resources means that often more missionaries can be sent and supported from larger assemblies than smaller ones. In many ways, especially in urban settings, it is much healthier in my opinion to have two or three large, healthy assemblies than to have eight or ten small, struggling assemblies. As long, that is, as a sense of Christian *community* can be maintained.

86. The name is fictitious. However, the statement came from an actual Brethren assembly. For a similar attempt to reassess and state Brethren distinctives as values, see Brian McLaren, "Rewriting Brethren Distinctives," *Christian Brethren Research Fellowship Journal* (NZ) 125 (August 1991): 39–42.

87. I suggest an overarching value system may be of some help as well, in order to capture some of the broader strokes. Brethren might, for e.g., address their historic distinctives in terms of catholicity (capturing the original spirit exemplified by Groves), non-clericalism, and the centrality of communion. The distinctives discussed in this chapter might well fit within the rubric, and the addition of catholicity retains the historic spirit in which the others may effectively operate today. See another specific example in appendix E.

CHAPTER 9: DEVELOPING A PERSONAL CATHOLICITY TODAY

1. He states further, "As pre-Orthodox Christians we had the right Savior, though we've come to know Him better, together with God the Father and God the Holy Spirit. We had the right Bible and have come to know it better. But we had overlooked that enormous missing factor—the right Church" (Gillquist, *Becoming Orthodox*, 182–83).

2. As noted earlier, in traditional (pre-Vatican II, at least) Roman Catholic thinking, the "Catholic Church" is the same as the visible Roman Catholic church, and a surrounding sphere outside of it would be the Orthodox, since they are out of communion with the Bishop (pope) of Rome. In Orthodox thinking, the opposite would be true. The Orthodox Church would be the "Catholic Church" while the Roman Church would be outside. Anglicanism has

tended to be more tolerant of the other episcopal models (such as Rome and Orthodoxy), but less tolerant toward non-episcopal models as representing any part of the "Catholic Church."

3. Anglican writers Hanson and Hanson were certainly correct when they wrote, "Any doctrine of the church that includes the assumption that millions of Christians, either now or in the past, must be judged not to be real members of the church at all refutes itself" (Hanson and Hanson, *The Identity of the Church*, 2).

4. Hanson and Hanson, as episcopate-oriented churchmen, observe well, "The progress of biblical and historical criticism has put a question mark against some of the 'catholic' claims of the ancient churches. For example, when a 'catholic' of any complexion claims 'my church is the original body which goes back to the apostles,' he can no longer justify such a claim on strictly historical grounds, since the specific sign of apostolic authority which embold-ens him to make this claim, to wit Episcopal succession back to the apostles, cannot be maintained. *The only body that goes uninterruptedly back to the apostles is the whole body of Christians*" (Hanson and Hanson, *The Identity of the Church*, 111.

5. Webber, *Common Roots*, 63–64.

6. Some fundamentalists more so than others. Many fundamentalists would not claim that they and they alone represent the true, catholic church and that genuine faith is only found with them. There is a pattern, however, toward claiming that they are more consistent and uncompromising in their faith than other Christians, a posture that does not bode well for relational unity.

7. The thinner line surrounding the separatist churches, as well as the thicker line around the individual churches indicates the strong autonomy model found here, as well as the tenuous links between such separatistic congregations.

8. Bloesch, *The Future of Evangelical Christianity*, 93.

9. Unless others separate from the denominations and gather only to Christ as we do, they are without an important dimension of the truth.

10. Wolfhart Pannenberg, *The Church*, trans. Keith Crim (Philadelphia: Westminster, 1983), 82.

11. Craik, *New Testament Church Order*, 30.

12. Again, Hanson and Hanson are right on the mark, "Is it not insulting to God thus to monopolize him for one denomination? If God wished it to be known that there is only one true church which can be wholly identified with one denomination, why has he so manifestly blessed the missionary activities (for instance) of a wide variety of denominations? . . . We conclude therefore that the church of Christ as given to us by God is one, but that we cannot identify this church exclusively with any existing denomination. Indeed we must resist doing so, recognizing this tendency as a temptation similar to the tempta-tion which Jesus met in the wilderness" (Hanson and Hanson, *The Identity of the Church*, 57).

13. I have derived the term for the "pistic" model from the Greek term for "faith." The idea of this chart is adapted from the excellent chart found in Jerry White, *Church and Parachurch: An Uneasy Marriage* (Portland, Ore.: Multno-mah, 1983), 68.

14. One of the most moving experiences of my recent Christian life was during a citywide worship time here in my home of Portland, Oregon, where over 13,500 Christians from hundreds of denominations gathered in anticipation of an upcoming evangelistic crusade. At a point late in the service, the moderator asked for all the pastors to come down front for prayer. As hundreds and hundreds of Christian leaders came forward, many of them looking most weary and stressed, the building erupted in spontaneous, sustained applause for these warriors for the kingdom. They recognized that this was the leadership God had given the church in Portland, and they needed support and encouragement in their task.

15. H.L. Ellison, *The Household Church*, 2nd ed. (Exeter: England: Paternoster, 1979).

16. Ibid., 26.

17. See Joe Aldrich, *Prayer Summits: Seeking God's Agenda for Your Community* (Portland, Ore.: Multnomah, 1992).

18. *NRM Newsline* (November 1991), 1.

19. Recorded in Aldrich, *Prayer Summits*, 15–18.

20. Ibid., 209–13.

21. *Crusade Update* 1.1, 4. in *Mission Portland Update* 2.1.

22. For a brief description of the impact of this Graham Portland Crusade, see "Portland Teeters on Revival's Edge; Graham Gives a Push," *Christianity Today* 9 November 1992, 60, 71.

23. For the terrible impact on genuine believers in the Soviet church that the WCC had because of its politicization, see Kent R. Hill, *The Puzzle of the Soviet Church: An Inside Look at Christianity & Glasnost* (Portland, Ore.: Multnomah, 1989), especially chapter 9, "Playing By Someone Else's Rules: Ecumenical Church Bodies and Christians in the USSR."

24. See especially Frame, *Evangelical Reunion*.

25. As noted, theological liberalism spawned the fundamentalist reaction. And the kind of liberalism that shaped it was a liberalism that rejected a number of the core orthodox doctrines of the faith. They rejected apostolic Christianity in favor of what was in vogue at the time: modernity and relevance. But classical liberalism is not much represented today, and some forms of neo-liberalism have returned to a recognition of the sinfulness of humankind and the need for redemption in Christ. See David L. Smith, *A Handbook of Contemporary Theology* (Wheaton, Ill.: BridgePoint/Victor, 1992), 72–86.

Theological liberalism is no longer all the same, with the passage of almost a century since the fundamentalist controversy. If you read fundamentalist literature the term is liberalism all the same, with no differentiation at all. Does that mean that one must define all who express problems with an inerrant Bible as liberal when they otherwise affirm the Trinity, the deity of Christ, and justification by faith? Certainly this rejection of the full authority base of Scripture cannot long be sustained and still maintain a healthy evangelical faith. But one suspects that there are radical liberals and moderate liberals just as there are radical fundamentalists and moderate fundamentalists. And catholicity of faith may well include some moderate liberals as well while it rejects some radical fundamentalists who have gone off into sectarianism. Some issues have not changed (such as the magisterial use of reason by liberals), but others have. Dialogue and understanding must precede critique. For an excellent example of dialogue with critique, see David L. Edwards and John Stott, *Evangelical Essentials: A Liberal-Evangelical Dialogue* (Downers Grove, Ill.: InterVarsity, 1988).

26. A robust evangelical faith is clearly present in some of the mainline liberal denominations, as is evident, e.g., in the Good News movement among the highly liberal United Methodist Church. See the insightful evangelical thinking in Jerry L. Walls, *The Problem of Pluralism: Recovering United Methodist Identity,* rev. ed. (Wilmore, Ky: Bristol, 1988). For a description of some 200,000 conservative United Methodists who signed a Memphis Declaration calling upon the liberal ruling element to return to the witness of Scripture and historic Christian faith, see Randy Frame, "United Methodists: Conservatives Force Global Ministries Move," *Christianity Today,* 22 June 1992, 56–58.

27. To me, the most viable approach to ecumenicity is that which allows the individual denominations' integrity and unique traditions to enrich the entire church, such as a form of "federal relationship" which accepts and encourages the diversity extant within the church. For an excellent discussion of the model, see Oscar Cullman, *Unity through Diversity,* trans. M. Eugene Boring (Philadelphia: Fortress, 1988).

28. *National Association of Evangelicals,* P.O. Box 28, Wheaton, IL 60189.

29. *Leadership Through Cooperation* (Wheaton, Ill.: NAE, 1991), 2.

30. Ibid.

31. *NAE Resolutions: Selected Resolutions Adopted by the National Association of Evangelicals During the Past Four Decades* (Wheaton, Ill.: NAE, 1988).

32. Ibid., 12–13.

33. The *National Council of Churches* is far broader than evangelical in scope and has significant liberal influences. It is a shame, however, that evangelicals have abandoned this group as much as they have, rather than attempting to serve as an influencing factor. The Eastern Orthodox, who serve as an affiliate rather than a full member, threatened to walk from this organization in 1992 due to serious liberal trends. The threat caused change, and the Orthodox stayed on board. An evangelical block could do much the same it seems. However, a united evangelicalism may be much more effective in joining and influencing this organization than would a piecemeal joining.

34. *World Evangelical Fellowship* 1 Sophia Rd., 07-09 Peace Centre, Singapore 0922. Their North American address is: P.O. Box WEF, Wheaton, IL 60189. For the story of the WEF, see David M. Howard, *The Dream That Would Not Die: The Birth and Growth of the World Evangelical Fellowship 1846-1986* (Exeter, Great Britain: Paternoster, 1986).

35. See their Statement of Faith in appendix D.

36. *Rallying Believers in a Chaotic World: WEF 1990 Progress Report.* WEF publication.

GLOSSARY

Assembly: a Christian Brethren preferred term for a local church.

Autonomy: a congregational model of church polity which affirms that there is no higher ecclesiastical authority than Christ within the local church.

Catholic: as an adjective, it means broad, general, with a unity around diversity.

Catholicity: the attitude of recognizing the universality of the body of Christ, the church, beyond one's own circles of fellowship, and around a core of Gospel orthodoxy.

Church, house: the common and normal gathering place of Christians in the first century. Not exactly the same as the "local" or "city-" church, (such as the church at Corinth), which met less frequently.

Church, local: the church of a geographical locality in which all the believers could know and gather with one another if a suitable meeting place was available—such as in a city. The "church at Corinth" would be an example.

Church, universal: the entire body of believers everywhere, who never are able to gather to meet in this life; the body of Christ; the church catholic.

Clericalism: the attitude of superiority or special privilege conveyed by formal or gifted leadership to those within the Christian community. It often unnecessarily restricts certain functions of the church to that class of persons.

Conciliarism: a movement in the Middle Ages which sought to limit papal power by a broader-based ecumenical council emphasis.

Creed: a formal statement of doctrinal formulation requiring assent by those churches which comprise a denominational grouping. Often used as a synonym for a confession or doctrinal statement.

Cult (Christian): a group which maintains Christian terminology but which has shifted from the core of Christian orthodoxy.

Denomination: a formal or informal association of churches sharing a common heritage and set of doctrinal distinctives.

Denominationalism: a catholic theory of the church which maintains that each denominational grouping is only one facet of the entire church.

Dispensationalism: an approach to interpreting the Scriptures which sees strong discontinuities between the testaments. The church is especially viewed as distinct from Israel, whose divinely given promises remain to be fulfilled in the millennium.

Ecumenical movement: the movement promoting interdenominational Christian unity that often sees denominationalism as the chief inhibition to Christian unity. The unity sought is often structural or organizational.

Eisegesis: imposing meaning onto the text of Scripture that was not intended by the original author.

Exegesis: drawing meaning out of the text of Scripture that was intended by the original author.

Extra ecclesiam nulla salus: A Latin phrase derived from Cyprian, which means "outside the church there is no salvation."

Fundamentalism: separatistic evangelical groups and denominations.

Hermeneutics: the principles used in interpreting and applying the Scriptures.

Liberalism: a system of belief which, while neglecting the divine authority of the Bible, seeks to adapt religious ideas to modern culture and philosophy.

Negative hermeneutic: the application of the argument from silence to interpretation of Scripture — because a thing is not found in the Bible it is wrong or prohibited.

Norma normans: Latin for "the rule that rules," referring to Scripture.

Norma normata: Latin for "the rule that is ruled" (by Scripture). Refers to tradition.

Perspicuity: the "clarity" of the Scriptures. This is an aspect of the Protestant principle of priesthood of all believers, in which an intermediating agency is unneeded in finding out the main message of the Bible.

Pluralism, doctrinal: the belief that there can be great diversity on what has historically been considered the core of orthodoxy.

Pluralism, theological: the belief that there can be great diversity on the expression and cultural application of the core of orthodoxy (which is itself not subject to modification).

Right of private judgment: the right (and responsibility) of assessing the interpretation of the Bible for oneself, without the necessity of a priestly mediator.

Sectarianism: the posture of believing that one particular group has a superior or unique claim on representing the body of Christ, to the exclusion or minimization of other genuinely Christian groups. In practical terms, it restricts fellowship and cooperation to those of my own particular group.

Sola Scriptura: Latin for "Scripture alone." A key phrase of the Reformers, meaning that when Scripture and tradition conflicted, Scripture was the final authority in the church.

Territorialism: A Reformational model of the church in which each territorial governor established a "state church" into which all children born into that country were automatically members.

Tradition, macro: Christian doctrine or practice held broadly by the church catholic.

Tradition, micro: Christian doctrine or practice held narrowly by a denomination or smaller group of Christians.

Tradition: matters of expressing Christian doctrine or practice that is passed on from generation to generation and is distinct from the Bible.

Subject and Person Index

(Index edited by Don Sheets)

A

American Council of Christian Churches (ACCC)   **80–81**
Anglican, Anglicanism   **23, 65, 67, 71, 99, 177, 183, 188–89, 192, 194,
    203–4, 206, 216–19, 238, 263**
Antioch   **40**
Apostle's Creed   **44, 202, 289**
Apostolic, apostolicity   **24, 32–33, 37, 42, 44, 48, 52–53, 55–56, 59, 65, 72,
    78, 84, 92–93, 109, 114, 127, 132, 144, 147, 156, 191, 194–95, 199–202,
    205–10, 253, 261**
Asbury, Francis   **173**
Athanasian Creed   **202, 291**
Augsburg Confession   **63, 67, 143, 186, 205**
Autonomy (of the church)   **89, 99, 115–16, 132, 222, 226, 251–53**
Avis, Paul   **65, 193**

B

Barrett, C.K.   **34**
Belgic Confession   **63, 206**
Bellett, J.G.   **217–19, 248**
Bernard, J.H.   **33**
Bethesda Chapel   **222, 248, 256**
Bible Truth Publishers   **226**
Bloesch, Donald   **65, 133, 267**
Boniface   **60**
Brethren, Christian (or Plymouth Brethren)   **45, 88, 96, 99, chapters 7–8**
Brethren, Closed (Tights, or Closed-Open)   **224, 226**
Brethren, Exclusive   **217, 222–23, 225–26, 266**
Brethren, Open   **217, 222–27, 255–56**
Brown, Robert McAfee   **136, 177**
Bruce, F.F.   **134, 214, 229**
Burroughes, Jeremiah   **98–101**
Burton, Henry   **100**

C

Caldecott (friend of A.N. Groves) **218–19**
Calvin, John **67, 134, 173, 183, 192, 205**
Campbell, Thomas and Alexander **96, 134**
Campus Crusade for Christ **113, 210, 277**
Carey, William **264**
Catholic, catholicity **24, 42–49, 51–54, 56–65, 67–68, 71–77, 79–85, 87–91, 95, 97–98, 100–111, 113, 115–18, 120, 122–23, 139, 151, 154, 156–57, 179, 181–82, 188, 190–91, 194, 196–97, 207, 210, 213–23, 227, 230, 260–76, 278–87**
Chalcedonian Definition **202, 290–91**
Chicago Call **79, 84, 292–95**
Chillingworth, William **183–84**
Christian Missions in Many Lands (CMML) **225, 254**
Circumcision **41**
City-church **29, 244, 256, 275, 277, 279–83**
Clericalism **238–39**
Clinton, Stephen M. **194**
Community exegesis **172**
Conscience **37**
Constantine **57–59**
Consultation on Church Union (COCU) **80**
Crabb, Larry **214**
Craik, Henry **132, 173, 222–23, 248, 256, 269**
Cronin, Edward **216**
Cullmann, Oscar **93**
Cyprian **55–56**
Cyril of Jerusalem **58**

D

Darby, John Nelson **134, 173, 216, 219–23, 226–27, 248, 251, 255–56**
Davis, John Jefferson **138**
Deacons **26**
Decian **56**
Denomination(s), denominational, denominationalism **23–25, 45–47, 68–69, 71–85, 87–100, 102–25, 133, 135–37, 139, 143, 148, 151–57, 162, 167, 170, 171–79, 182, 196, 210, 213–17, 220, 225, 227–31, 241, 245–46, 252–53, 257, 259–60, 262–63, 265–70, 274–84, 287**
"Distanciation" **165**
Distinctives (denominational) **24, 88–89, 94, 99, 103, 105–7, 118, 121, 123, 133, 135, 137–39, 143, 145, 148, 152, 155–56, 162, 173–74, 179, 215, 226–33, 243–44, 251, 257–60, 262–63, 267–68, 275, 287**

Donatists, Donatism   56–59, 61, 83, 190, 266
Dulles, Avery   43, 230
Dunning, H. Ray   106

E

Ecumenical, ecumenism, ecumenicalism   61, 79–82, 84–85, 91, 94, 110,
    137, 177, 182, 188–89, 192, 203, 277, 283–85
Edict of Milan   57, 59
Elliot, Jim   214
Ellison, H.L.   276
Emmaus Bible College   225
Episcopal, episcopate   23–24, 55–56, 263–64
Evangelical Theological Society (ETS)   178, 184–85
Evangelical(s), evangelicalism   23, 75–76, 78–82, 84–85, 91, 110–112,
    114, 123–25, 128, 130–33, 135–39, 145, 147–48, 152, 162, 169, 184,
    187–88, 193–94, 195–96, 200–202, 208–9, 216, 224, 256, 264–65, 274,
    281, 283–87
Ex opere operato (understanding of the sacraments)   200

F

Fee, Gordon   230
Finger, Thomas   106
Finney, Charles   119
Flew, R. Newton and Rupert E. Davies   47
Formula of Concord   206
Frame, John   91, 194
Free-church tradition   23, 79, 196
Fundamentals, The   187, 296–97
Fundamentalists   78–81, 84, 109, 120, 162, 187–88, 266, 274

G

Gasque, W. Ward   214
Genre, biblical   168
Getz, Gene   245
Gillquist, Peter   264
Gnostics   44
Goen, Clarence   89, 98
Gospel   22, 29, 34, 40–42, 47–48, 52–54, 56, 63–66, 74, 78–79, 81, 83, 95,
    110–11, 134, 141–43, 168, 182, 189–90, 193–211, 215, 224, 261–62, 265,
    269–71, 273, 276–77, 282, 284–87
Graham, Billy   79, 113, 119, 282

Orthodoxy, core   **44, 181, 185, 189**
Orthodoxy, Eastern   **23, 47, 60–61, 63, 83, 99, 127–28, 138, 144, 147, 177, 188–90, 208, 263–65, 274**
Orthodoxy, saving (level I orthodoxy)   **197, 201–2, 207–8, 210**
Orthodoxy, sustaining (level II orthodoxy)   **197, 201–3, 205, 207–10**

P

Palau, Luis   **113, 214, 282**
Pannenberg, Wolfhart   **69, 104, 121, 269**
Parachurch ministries   **96, 108, 112–13, 152, 209, 277–79**
Patternism   **169–70**
Paul, the Apostle   **25, 27, 30–32, 35–41, 46, 53, 63, 91–93, 141–43, 161, 164–67, 170–71, 196, 198, 206, 229, 233–34, 237–38, 241–42, 247, 251–52, 268**
Peter, the Apostle   **25, 29, 39–41, 164, 188, 268**
Pinnock, Clark   **107, 136, 151**
Plantinga, Cornelius, Jr.   **193**
Polycarp   **43, 55**
Private Judgment   **153–56, 184**
Protestant, Protestantism   **23–24, 43, 53, 55, 60–61, 65–68, 71–77, 83, 91, 103, 106, 110, 123–25, 127–28, 130–39, 143–48, 153–56, 173–74, 177, 183–84, 187–89, 191, 201, 206, 209, 214, 217, 226, 264, 274, 283**

R

Reformation   **23, 53, 61, 63, 65–68, 70–71, 74, 77, 83, 93, 123, 127–28, 130–31, 143, 153–54, 173, 183, 189, 193–95, 203–4, 207–10, 262**
Reformers   **63, 65, 67, 70–71, 83, 127, 130–31, 143–44, 156, 161, 186, 189, 192–94, 203, 205, 207–9, 267**
Relational unity   **33, 35–36, 56, 59, 92, 271, 284**
Restorationist Movements   **95**
Roman Catholic, Roman Catholicism   **23, 47, 52, 60–61, 63, 80, 91, 99, 127–28, 131, 134, 137–38, 144, 147, 200, 203, 263–65, 274**
Ryan, Thomas   **182**

S

Sasse, Hermann   **190**
Scholes, Alan K.   **194**
Sectarian, sectarianism   **24, 44–47, 59, 73–76, 79–80, 83–84, 87, 95–97, 100, 102–3, 105, 107–8, 116, 120–23, 133, 138–39, 145, 149, 152, 177, 179, 182–83, 214–16, 218, 221, 223, 227, 249, 260–64, 266–68, 271–72, 274–75, 287**
Shelley, Bruce   **136**

V

W

Y

Scripture Index

(Index edited by Don Sheets)